Clean Air Handbook

4th Edition

D1569923

Hunton & Williams

Washington, DC

PORTER COUNTY PUBLIC LIBRARY

Principal Author and Editor

F. William Brownell

Valparaiso Public Library
103 Jefferson Street
Valparaiso, IN 46383

Radoslawa Boczkaj-Gonzalez   Elizabeth L. Horner
Sherry L. Fisher   Andrew D. Knudsen
Aaron M. Flynn   Lucinda Minton Langworthy
Lauren E. Freeman   Tauna M. Szymanski
David
Craig

vabnf   VAL   CARD
344.7304 CLEAN   County
System

Clean air handbook
33410013214897   02/23/15

⊻ Bernan Press

Lanham • Boulder • New York • London

Published by Bernan Press
An imprint of The Rowman & Littlefield Publishing Group, Inc.
4501 Forbes Boulevard, Suite 200, Lanham, Maryland 20706
www.rowman.com
800-865-3457; info@bernan.com

Unit A, Whitacre Mews, 26-34 Stannary Street, London SE11 4AB

Copyright © 2015 by Bernan Press

All rights reserved. No part of this book may be reproduced in any form or by any
electronic or mechanical means, including information storage and retrieval systems,
without written permission from the publisher, except by a reviewer who may quote
passages in a review. Bernan Press does not claim copyright in U.S. government
information.

British Library Cataloguing in Publication Information Available

Library of Congress Cataloging-in-Publication Data
Clean air handbook / Hunton & Williams ; F. William Brownell [and others]. — Fourth
Edition.
    pages cm
  Includes bibliographical references.
    ISBN 978-1-59888-647-4 (pbk. : alk. paper) — ISBN 978-1-59888-648-1 (electronic)
  1. Air—Pollution—Law and legislation—United States. I. Brownell, F. William,
author. II. Hunton & Williams, sponsoring body.
  KF3812.B769 2015
  344.7304'6342—dc23

                                                                    2014044150

∞™ The paper used in this publication meets the minimum requirements of American
National Standard for Information Sciences—Permanence of Paper for Printed Library
Materials, ANSI/NISO Z39.48-1992.

Printed in the United States of America

SUMMARY CONTENTS

CONTENTS

PREFACE

The Clean Air Act is the most complex piece of environmental legislation ever enacted. From modest beginnings in 1967, the Act has grown in length to hundreds of pages and is implemented through thousands of pages of regulations.

The Clean Air Act requires the expenditure of billions of dollars on pollution control programs. It governs what industrial growth may take place in communities that have been unable to attain clean air goals. It dictates basic changes in lifestyle where necessary to achieve air quality standards. It allocates among regions of the country marketable rights to emit pollution. And it defines the levels of public health risks that are acceptable as a result of exposure to air pollution. For these reasons, the Clean Air Act has generated intense political debate over the past four decades.

This fourth edition of the Clean Air Handbook provides a starting point for understanding the complex regulatory requirements of the Act. Beyond offering an introduction to the history and structure of the Act, the handbook discusses the efforts of the U.S. Environmental Protection Agency (EPA) to implement the Act. For example, the handbook discusses EPA initiatives to impose more stringent emission reduction requirements through a plethora of more stringent air quality standards promulgated in the new millennium; it addresses EPA rules and guidance implementing the Title I nonattainment program and ongoing federal efforts to address interstate pollution issues; it summarizes EPA's rules for state-administered Title V operating permit programs and discusses issues applicable to Title V permit applications; it reports on EPA's implementation of the air toxics program under Title III of the 1990 Amendments to the Act; and it reviews the key rules promulgated by EPA to implement the Title IV acid rain program. This edition of the Clean Air Handbook also addresses developments under the stratospheric ozone protection program (Title VI of the 1990 Amendments), EPA's actions to resolve controversies concerning the applicability of new source review requirements, and EPA's implementation of key Title II programs regarding motor vehicles and fuels and fuel additives. The handbook also reviews recent developments in civil and criminal enforcement under the Act, including EPA's enforcement effort under the new source review program. Finally, this edition of the Clean Air Handbook has new chapters to address EPA's recent efforts to address visibility and to regulate greenhouse gas emissions under the Act to address climate change.

The Clean Air Act is constantly evolving. Because of the recent gridlock in Congress, more than 20 years have passed since the Act last underwent a major amendment. This has resulted in EPA attempting to accomplish new objectives under an old framework that in many cases is poorly suited to its objectives. This has resulted in several EPA programs being overturned and in regulatory uncertainty for the regulated community. The challenge for industry over the next several years will be not only to determine how to comply with the requirements resulting from these numerous regulatory proceedings, but to determine how best to participate in these and future proceedings to ensure the development of sound rules.

Besides developing new rules, EPA continues to supplement its existing rules with guidance documents and policy statements. These materials are often critical to evaluating one's compliance obligations. As a result, it is important to consult the materials referenced in this handbook, responsible regulatory personnel, and environmental counsel when confronted with specific regulatory compliance issues. With this caveat in mind, we hope that this handbook provides a useful starting point for understanding the Clean Air Act.

F. William Brownell
Washington, D.C.

Chapter 1

FEDERAL-STATE PARTNERSHIP:
AN OVERVIEW OF THE CLEAN AIR ACT

The Clean Air Act has been with us for almost fifty years. During that time, the Act has evolved from a set of principles to guide states in controlling sources of air pollution (the Air Quality Act of 1967) to an extensive series of standards prescribed initially by the federal government and administered in coordination with the states.

The evolution of air quality regulation has tracked advances in our understanding of the environment. As our knowledge of the environment has improved, new concerns have emerged and shortcomings have been identified in methods provided by the Act for regulating air pollution. A brief review of the experience with the Clean Air Act beginning in the 1960s is helpful context for understanding the multiple layers of regulatory requirements that exist today.

The Air Quality Act of 1967

In response to concerns with deteriorating urban air quality, Congress in 1967 enacted the Air Quality Act.[1] The purposes of the 1967 Act were:
(1) To protect and to enhance the quality of the Nation's air resources so as to promote the public health and welfare and the productive capacity of its population;
(2) To initiate and to accelerate a national research and development program to achieve the prevention and control of air pollution;
(3) To provide technical and financial assistance to State and local governments in connection with the development and execution of their air pollution prevention and control programs; and
(4) To encourage and to assist the development and operation of regional air pollution control programs.[2]

The 1967 Act focused on regulation of ambient air quality to protect public health and welfare. The centerpiece of this regulatory program was the development of air quality "criteria" by the Department of Health, Education, and

Welfare's ("HEW") Air Quality Advisory Board, for widespread and pervasive air pollutants.[3] The "criteria" were to "accurately reflect the latest scientific knowledge" on the health and welfare effects of individual pollutants, such as sulfur dioxide ("SO_2"), nitrogen oxides ("NOx"), and particulate matter ("PM").[4] Although Congress gave the federal government, through HEW, the responsibility for developing air quality criteria, air quality problems were viewed principally as state and local concerns. Congress therefore left to the states the responsibility for developing, administering, and enforcing specific standards based on the federal criteria.[5]

By contrast, Congress viewed mobile source regulation as a federal concern. The Act therefore directed the Secretary of HEW to establish nationally applicable emissions standards and a fuel and fuel additive registration program.[6] The Act required that these standards take into account economic and technological feasibility.[7] These first efforts at air quality control were hampered by scientific uncertainties and technical difficulties that continued to challenge regulatory agencies over the subsequent decades. For example, the criteria document development process proved long and cumbersome. States had difficulty translating the information made available by HEW into source-specific standards. Techniques for relating source-specific emissions to air quality impacts (*e.g.*, atmospheric dispersion models) were not well-developed. And the focus on improving ambient air quality through state and local action proved unduly narrow. Because air quality is influenced by regional as well as local factors, more broadly based regulatory programs and control methods were needed.

The 1970 Clean Air Act

This early experience with air quality regulation provided a starting point for comprehensive amendments to the Clean Air Act in 1970.[8] The 1970 Amendments remain the centerpiece of the current Clean Air Act.

To overcome the inertia experienced in implementing the 1967 Air Quality Act, Congress in 1970 gave the federal government a more prominent role in regulating air quality. Now, not only was the federal government required to develop air quality criteria describing levels of air quality associated with specific public health and welfare concerns, but the federal government, through the newly created Environmental Protection Agency ("EPA"), was required to establish national ambient air quality standards ("NAAQS") that define specific levels of air quality that must be achieved to protect public health and welfare.[9] The NAAQS, in turn, were to be used as the basis for individual source emission limitations to be established by the states in "state implementation plans" ("SIPs").[10]

Congress also directed EPA to develop regulatory guidance to be used by states in implementing the NAAQS for individual sources through the SIPs, and to use this guidance in reviewing the adequacy of these SIPs. Congress gave EPA a continuing oversight role to ensure that states continued to implement and enforce the requirements of the SIP.[11] If a state did not develop an adequate SIP, did not act in a timely fashion to adopt a SIP, or did not respond promptly to a notice from EPA that its SIP failed to meet the requirements of the Act, EPA would step in to implement the Act for the state through what became known as a federal implementation plan ("FIP") in later amendments to the Act.[12] This basic federal-state partnership – sometimes referred to as "cooperative federalism" – remains a hallmark of Clean Air Act regulation today.

In an attempt to make this system of air quality regulation work in a more timely fashion, Congress used regulatory deadlines to spur administrative decisionmaking. For example, in response to delays experienced in criteria document development and implementation of associated air pollution control measures, Congress set deadlines for developing criteria documents, for developing NAAQS based on those documents, and for state development and EPA review of SIPs.[13]

Besides creating a more detailed regime for the protection of public health and welfare through ambient air quality regulation, Congress in 1970 adopted stringent control technology requirements for new sources, called the new source performance standards ("NSPS") program of section 111 of the Act. Congress also enacted a preconstruction review program to ensure that emissions from new facilities that had not yet been reviewed under the SIP program were reviewed for compliance with the NAAQS prior to construction.[14] Congress also made clear in the Act's general purposes clause that a key objective guiding implementation of the Act was the prevention of significant deterioration ("PSD") of air quality in clean air areas.[15]

Congress in 1970 also recognized and began to address pollution problems other than those associated with the "criteria" pollutants regulated under the NAAQS. For example, Congress in 1970 enacted the first program to regulate "hazardous air pollutants" ("HAPs"), or air toxics, under section 112 of the Act.

Finally, Congress continued to refine regulation of mobile sources in Title II of the Act. Recognizing the political and technical difficulties associated with control of vehicle tailpipe emissions, Congress balanced environmental and economic concerns and set specific, technology-forcing emissions standards and deadlines for attainment.[16]

The 1977 Clean Air Act Amendments

In the early 1970s, EPA and the states began to implement the basic regulatory programs of the 1970 Amendments, including the NAAQS, the NSPS, the PSD program, and the HAPs program. These activities produced controversies that gave rise to the first wave of litigation under the Clean Air Act and ultimately led to comprehensive amendments to the Act in 1977.

The 1977 Clean Air Act Amendments[17] refined the basic programs of the 1970 Act. For example, Congress adjusted the dates for attainment of the NAAQS[18] and provided additional guidance for development by the states of programs for areas that remained out of compliance with the NAAQS (i.e., the "nonattainment" SIP requirements).[19] With respect to the hazardous air pollutants program, Congress directed EPA to consider regulation of several specific substances (radioactive pollutants, cadmium, arsenic, and polycyclic organic matter) and required EPA to make regulatory decisions regarding these and other pollutants according to specific deadlines.[20]

Congress in the 1977 Amendments also codified the PSD program,[21] and adopted requirements aimed at improving visibility in national parks.[22] In an early attempt to deal with regional transport of pollution, Congress adopted limitations on the degree to which a source could rely on atmospheric dispersion of its emissions (e.g., through "tall stacks") to achieve the NAAQS.[23] These broader concerns about air pollution's effects on aesthetics and interstate pollution transport foreshadowed a lengthy debate that continues today regarding the need for more prescriptive regulatory programs for regional transport of criteria pollutants, visibility, and greenhouse gases.

Finally, as the scope of the Act expanded, Congress became more sensitive to the impact of the Act on significant sectors of the national economy. With respect to the NSPS program, for example, Congress acted to protect the nation's reserves of high sulfur coal and the jobs of high sulfur coal miners by requiring that large, new fossil fuel-fired boilers install "flue gas desulfurization" systems, or SO_2 scrubbers.[24] Congress also enacted measures that could be used to prevent economic disruption or unemployment associated with standards that disrupted the use of locally or regionally available coal.[25]

Efforts to Implement The Clean Air Act Through The 1980s

The 1977 Clean Air Act Amendments can be summarized in terms of three program categories. The first addresses air quality regulation. In this category fall the NAAQS and SIP programs,[26] which are designed to regulate widespread and pervasive pollution problems. The substances addressed by the NAAQS are referred to as "criteria pollutants," and include SO_2, NOx, PM, carbon monoxide ("CO"), lead, and ozone. All sources of air pollution are subject to the NAAQS and are regulated as necessary through emission limitations set by states in SIPs (although the states are limited in their regulation of mobile sources). A stationary source must either take steps necessary to meet the NAAQS or shut down.[27] In this sense, the NAAQS program is the most important technology-forcing program of the Act.

The SIPs are the principal Clean Air Act tool for control of emissions from existing stationary sources of air pollution. In areas with clean air, emission limitations in SIPs must be set at a level that ensures that compliance with the NAAQS is maintained. In areas that do *not* attain the NAAQS (*i.e.*, in "nonattainment areas"), sources are subject to more stringent controls designed to bring those areas into attainment with the NAAQS. For example, states with nonattainment areas must develop requirements that ensure "reasonable further progress" toward attainment, and large existing stationary sources of nonattainment pollutants must install "reasonably available control technology" ("RACT").[28]

The second type of program contained in the 1977 Amendments involves regulation of new and modified stationary sources of air pollution.[29] Categories of stationary sources that cause or contribute significantly to air pollution may be listed for regulation subject to the section 111 NSPS program, pursuant to which emission limitations are set to reflect best adequately demonstrated control technology. New sources in areas that attain the NAAQS are also subject to the PSD preconstruction permitting program, which requires compliance with (1) "air quality increments" that represent levels of ambient air quality more stringent than the NAAQS,[30] and (2) control technology requirements that must be at least as stringent as NSPS (*i.e.*, that must reflect "best available control technology," or "BACT," for that individual source).[31] New and modified sources in areas that do not attain the NAAQS are subject to a different preconstruction permitting program, called nonattainment new source review ("NNSR"), which requires that major stationary sources (1) offset projected emission increases of nonattainment pollutants with emission reductions of those pollutants at existing facilities, and (2) install control technology to achieve the "lowest achievable emission rate" ("LAER") for that pollutant for that source category.[32]

The third category of programs under the 1977 Amendments concerned special pollution problems that Congress felt needed attention beyond the air quality and control technology programs discussed above. The most important of these address national emission standards for hazardous air pollutants ("NESHAPs"),[33] and the protection of visibility in national parks.[34]

The NAAQS/SIP Program

EPA originally promulgated the NAAQS for criteria pollutants in the early 1970s in response to the 1970 Amendments. As amended in 1977, the Act called on EPA to review these standards at five-year intervals to determine whether different or stricter standards are necessary to protect public health and welfare.

Pursuant to this mandate, EPA after 1977 periodically reviewed both the "primary" (*i.e.*, health-based) and "secondary" (*i.e.*, welfare-based) NAAQS for each criteria pollutant. This review produced new standards for small particles, minor adjustments to the CO standards, and a host of administrative proceedings and litigation regarding the need to revise the NAAQS for other criteria pollutants.

For example, in 1987 EPA revised the PM NAAQS, changing the basis for the standard from total particulate matter to "PM_{10}," or particles with an aerodynamic diameter of a ten micrometers or less.[35] In 1997, EPA revised the PM NAAQS, adding standards for "$PM_{2.5}$," or particles with an aerodynamic diameter of two and a half micrometers or less.[36] In 2013, EPA revised and tightened the $PM_{2.5}$ standard.[37]

EPA also considered during the 1980s whether to adopt a stringent, short-term average (*i.e.*, five-minute to one-hour) NAAQS for SO_2 to address "peak" emission episodes to protect asthmatics. In 1989, EPA was ordered by a federal court to complete its review of the primary SO_2 NAAQS.[38] EPA ultimately decided not to revise the NAAQS.[39] In 2007, however EPA began another review of the SO_2 NAAQS, again in response to a court order.[40] This further review produced a revised, more stringent SO_2 NAAQS in 2010.[41]

With respect to the NAAQS for ozone, EPA began a review proceeding after the 1977 Amendments which resulted, in 1979, in a relaxation of the ozone NAAQS that EPA had established in 1971.[42] After further extensive review, the Agency concluded in 1993 that the existing data did not support further revision of that NAAQS.[43] The Agency nevertheless began another review of the ozone standard after issuance of the 1993 notice, and in 1997 tightened that standard significantly.[44] In 2008, EPA revised that standard yet again to make it more stringent,[45] and has said it will complete another review of the ozone NAAQS by 2014.[46]

Since many areas of the country were unable to meet even the existing NAAQS for ozone by the 1987 attainment date set by the 1977 Amendments, EPA in 1987 proposed a policy for bringing such areas into attainment with the NAAQS.[47] Under EPA's policy, sanctions for failure to meet the Act's attainment deadlines (*e.g.*, a moratorium on new construction) would not apply as long as the SIP for the area was revised to provide for reasonable further progress toward attainment, with a demonstration of attainment within a set period of time. This policy prompted litigation that cast doubt on EPA's authority to provide flexibility for states to meet attainment deadlines,[48] and ultimately led Congress to amend the Act in 1990 to adopt new deadlines for attainment and more prescriptive nonattainment programs.

New Source Control Programs

The control technology programs for new and modified sources of air pollution (*i.e.*, the NSPS and PSD/NNSR program) have proved to be among the more successful Clean Air Act programs. By the end of the 1980s, EPA had developed NSPS for over 60 source categories. Moreover, given the difficulty that EPA experienced with hazardous air pollution regulation during the 1980s, EPA began in the late 1980s to explore how the NSPS program might be used to regulate HAPs.

Rulemaking proceedings to establish and revise NSPS, however, have proved increasingly costly and time-consuming. Starting in the late 1980s, this led to an increased focus on the use of policy statements and guidance to refine, and even to revise, the new source programs. Two issues exemplify EPA's efforts since the 1980s to find a means other than legislative rulemaking to implement these programs.

First, EPA undertook through guidance and enforcement actions to expand the reach of the new source programs. Under the so-called *WEPCo* policy,[49] EPA stated that work undertaken to repair deteriorated equipment to allow a facility to operate up to its prior capacity could result in application of more stringent new source standards. The Seventh Circuit set aside EPA's decision with respect to the PSD preconstruction permitting program[50] and, in response to that decision, EPA issued guidance and rule changes in 1992 addressing when existing sources that undertake repair or replacement projects would become subject to new source controls under the NSPS, PSD, and NNSR programs.[51] These administrative determinations and guidance continue to be controversial in enforcement actions brought by EPA.

Second, EPA attempted to limit state discretion to determine BACT for new or modified sources through the PSD permitting process. Under the so-called "top-down" BACT policy announced in 1987, EPA said that new sources would have to apply the most stringent control technology available unless use of that technology could be shown to be infeasible at a given source. Litigation regarding the guidance memoranda that embody the top-down BACT policy resulted in a settlement, pursuant to which EPA made clear that states could elect to use, or not to use, the "top-down" policy.[52]

Both the "*WEPCo*" guidance and the top-down BACT policy reflect an effort to find less burdensome means of implementing the Act, by avoiding lengthy and contentious notice-and-comment public rulemaking proceedings. As discussed below, the search for new approaches to implement the Act intensified in the wake of the 1990 Amendments and has influenced Clean Air Act litigation since that time.

Specific Pollution Concerns

Besides the NAAQS and new source control programs, several specific pollution concerns were addressed by the 1977 Act. EPA's efforts to implement these programs were no less controversial than its efforts to implement the NAAQS and new source programs, and those controversies helped shape the 1990 Amendments to the Act.

Hazardous Air Pollutants

In 1970, the section 112 HAPs program targeted a limited number of especially hazardous substances.[53] Under the 1977 Amendments, by contrast, section 112 directed EPA to list and regulate as a hazardous air pollutant any substance that can cause serious health problems when emitted to the ambient air. Once listed, EPA was required to regulate the substance at a level that would protect public health with an ample margin of safety.

By 1977, EPA had implemented this program for only a few substances. Congress in the 1977 Amendments therefore directed EPA to determine whether to regulate four other specific pollutants under section 112.[54]

Virtually every aspect of this 1977 statutory directive resulted in litigation. For example, environmental groups argued that EPA had an obligation to list for regulation under this provision every known or probable carcinogen. They also argued that, once listed, EPA was obligated to regulate every source category of the substance, regardless of the magnitude of risk associated with emissions from the source category. According to these groups, EPA in setting emission standards was also required to eliminate all risk of adverse health effects.[55] In response to these controversies, Congress stepped in to revamp the hazardous air pollutant program in 1990 to provide a new, control technology-based approach for regulating hazardous air pollutant emissions that, Congress hoped, would eliminate much of this controversy.

Visibility Protection

In response to the 1977 Act, EPA in 1980 adopted the so-called "Phase I" visibility program addressing visible emission plumes from smokestacks or other emission points that impact the viewsheds of national parks and wilderness areas.[56] EPA did not promulgate rules to address the more widespread problem of "regional haze" – visibility impairment that is not clearly attributable to a single, identifiable source of pollution or a discrete group of sources. Rather, given the lack of techniques for attributing regional haze to individual sources, EPA left this concern for a future, "Phase II" visibility program. The limited scope of the initial visibility program gave rise during the 1980s to litigation, including an attempt to force EPA to set a secondary, visibility-based NAAQS for fine particles.[57]

While resisting development of a Phase II regulatory program in light of scientific uncertainties, EPA did take a step in that direction in the late 1980s in the case of one individual source. Based on the alleged contribution of the Salt River Project's Navajo Generation Station to regional haze in Grand Canyon National Park,[58] EPA imposed on this source a "best available retrofit technology" ("BART") requirement under the Phase I visibility program, which resulted in control expenditures in excess of $1 billion for the facility.[59] This decision foreshadowed lengthy rulemaking and litigation following the 1990 Amendments regarding requirements for sources that allegedly contribute to haze in national parks.[60]

Regional and International Air Pollution

During the 1980s, EPA was also the target of persistent litigation to force it to regulate acid rain and other forms of acidic deposition under section 115 of the 1977 Act, which addresses international air pollution concerns. Ultimately, the courts refused to grant relief to environmental groups and Northeastern states (which claimed that pollution from Midwestern sources was causing acid deposition in the Northeast United States as well as in Canada), leaving the litigants to seek relief by filing administrative petitions with the Agency under section 115. At the same time, the Executive Branch undertook an effort to negotiate an agreement with Canada addressing transboundary pollution. Most activity in this area was, once again, overtaken by the 1990 Amendments to the Act, in which Congress enacted a comprehensive program targeting utility emissions that contribute to acid rain.

The 1980s also saw the first attempts by states to force pollution reduction in other states through a petition process created in section 126 of the Act. These interstate petitions were ultimately unsuccessful, but laid the groundwork for more aggressive efforts to address interstate pollution transport beginning in the 1990s.

The 1990 Clean Air Act Amendments

Substantial administrative resources were devoted to implementation of the Clean Air Act through the 1970s and 1980s. In 1990, Congress acted to guide and to expedite regulation of air pollution through yet another set of major amendments to the Clean Air Act.[61] Congress has not undertaken substantial amendments to the Act since 1990. The 1990 Amendments were more lengthy and complex than any previous environmental legislation. They were also far different in form and content than the changes sought by either industry and environmental groups in the early 1980s.

The 1990 amendments, while confirming much of the structure that Congress had created in 1970 and 1977, also added to that structure. For example, while Congress enacted a comprehensive operating permit program in 1990 to group together all source-specific requirements in one document for each major emitting facility in the country, the 1990 amendments retained the SIP program. And while Congress created a comprehensive regulatory program addressing acid rain, it did not jettison earlier provisions that also could be used to reduce acid deposition, including the 1977 Amendments' international pollution provisions and dispersion requirements. Moreover, even though EPA had failed to meet the rulemaking deadlines in the 1977 Amendments, Congress set even more deadlines for Agency action in the 1990 Amendments.

As a result, the 1990 Amendments created substantial new regulatory responsibilities while leaving in place most of the pre-existing system of air pollution control. Briefly, Congress made the following major changes to the Clean Air Act in 1990:

First, Congress addressed in 1990 the continuing difficulty experienced in many areas of the country in attaining the ozone and other NAAQS by establishing new attainment deadlines and more prescriptive regulatory requirements keyed to the seriousness of the nonattainment problem. These requirements are discussed in detail in Chapter 2.

Second, to increase transparency of environmental requirements and to facilitate enforcement, Congress enacted an operating permit program as a new Title V to the Act. The purpose of these permits is to assemble in one place all Clean Air Act requirements applicable to an individual source. The Title V permitting program is discussed further in Chapter 4.

Third, Congress completely revamped the system for regulation of HAPs. Under the new regulatory approach, 189 substances were listed for regulation as HAPs,[62] with directions for EPA to list source categories and to establish control technology-based standards by specific deadlines. EPA's regulation of HAPs is addressed in Chapter 5.

Fourth, Congress substantially tightened mobile source emission standards in 1990, requiring significant reductions in tailpipe emissions from motor vehicles. Congress also established two new fuels-related programs designed to achieve emission reductions: the reformulated fuels program and the clean fuel vehicle program. Regulation of mobile sources is addressed in Chapter 8.

Fifth, although Congress debated extending new source control technology requirements to existing facilities, by requiring existing utility boilers either to retrofit new source control technologies or to shut down at age 30, Congress rejected expansion of these command-and-control new source programs. Instead, Congress adopted the Title IV acid rain program for utility boilers. This "cap-and-trade" program has become an important and highly successful example of how market-based principles can be used to control air pollution and is discussed further in Chapter 9.

Finally, although ozone in the lower atmosphere can have adverse effects on public health, ozone in the upper atmosphere – or stratosphere – is desirable because it helps shield the earth's surface from harmful radiation. Congress added Title VI to the Act in 1990 to address stratospheric ozone protection, and this program is addressed in Chapter 10.

New Directions In Air Pollution Regulation

The extensive regulatory programs of the 1970, 1977 and 1990 Clean Air Act Amendments have spawned complex rulemaking and litigation addressing both the Agency's substantive obligations and schedules for action. The experience with air pollution regulation in the two decades since the 1990 Amendments suggests a number of themes that have continued to shape air quality regulation in the new century.

First, air pollution is not merely a local concern but must be addressed in a broader geographic context. This has led to efforts by EPA to redefine the federal-state relationship in ways that strengthen the federal partner. EPA's continuing challenge remains finding the proper balance of federal compulsion and state discretion to reconcile national, regional, and local interests.

Second, to ensure that EPA acts, Congress increasingly has relied on statutory deadlines for regulatory action. Merely telling the Agency to act by a date certain does not guarantee timely action, however, and acting without sufficient deliberation does not produce sound regulation. EPA will continue to struggle with meeting deadlines that environmental groups and states have found can readily be enforced by citizen suit.

Third, as deadlines have proliferated and statutory mandates have become more complex, EPA has looked for alternatives to rulemaking for meeting its obligations under the Act. This trend was evident during the 1990s, as the Agency moved away from legislative rulemaking in several areas to explore strategies that require less public involvement and therefore – supposedly – less controversy and delay. Policy statements, adjudications, and enforcement guidance have all played, and will continue to play, an important role in Clear Air Act implementation.

Fourth, Congress' attention to aesthetic and welfare-based concerns has resulted in an escalation in the costs of regulation, which in turn has provided a strong incentive for market-oriented solutions to air quality problems. Congress specifically adopted a market-based approach to regulation of acid rain in the 1990 Amendments, and EPA has encouraged the states to employ market mechanisms in other areas of air quality regulation. The success of the Clean Air Act over the coming years will be influenced by the degree to which market-based alternatives can be used in place of the traditional command-and-control approach to regulation.

Fifth, with the maturation of many Clean Air Act programs, enforcement has assumed an increasingly important role. EPA's enforcement office is playing an active role in Clean Air Act implementation as well as enforcement, and that role includes shaping the interpretation of important Clean Air Act programs. Enforcement is discussed in more detail in Chapter 11.

Finally, each decade has presented a key air quality issue for national debate – from criteria pollutants in the 1970s, to air toxics in the 1980s, to acid rain in the 1990s, to visibility protection in the 2000s. The issue for the next decade is climate change. Because Congress has been unsuccessful in legislating a regulatory program for greenhouse gas emissions, advocacy groups are promoting regulatory programs for climate change under the Clean Air Act. These efforts, which are discussed in Chapter 7, will test the limits of the federal-state partnership in clean air regulation.

Each of these themes is reflected in ongoing controversies over implementation and enforcement of the Clean Air Act, the most lengthy and complex piece of environmental legislation ever enacted by Congress. Each aspect of the current Clean Air Act programs is discussed in more detail in the following chapters.

Notes

1. *See* Air Quality Act of 1967, Pub. L. No. 90-148, 81 Stat. 485 (codified as amended at 42 U.S.C. §§ 1857-1857*l* (1967)) (hereinafter "AQA").

2. AQA § 101(b).

3. *Id.* §§ 107(b)(1), 110.

4. *Id.* § 107(b)(2).

5. *Id.* § 108.

6. *Id.* §§ 202, 210.

7. *Id.* § 202.

8. *See* Clean Air Act Amendments of 1970, Pub. L. No. 91-604, 84 Stat. 1676 (codified as amended at 42 U.S.C. §§ 1857, *et seq.* (1970)).

9. Clean Air Act ("CAA") §§ 108, 109, 42 U.S.C. §§ 1857c-3, 1857c-4 (1976).

10. *Id.* § 110, 42 U.S.C. § 1857c-5 (1976).

11. *Id.* § 110(a), 42 U.S.C. § 1857c-5(a) (1976).

12. *Id.* § 110(c), 42 U.S.C. § 1857c-5(c) (1976).

13. *Id.* §§ 108(a), 109(a)(1), 110(a), 42 U.S.C. §§ 1857c-3(a), 1857c-4(a)(1), 1857c-5(a) (1976).

14. *Id.* § 110(a)(2)(D), (a)(4), 42 U.S.C. § 1857c-5(a)(2)(D), (a)(4) (1976).

15. *See Sierra Club v. Ruckelshaus*, 344 F. Supp. 253 (D.D.C.), *aff'd per curiam*, 4 Env't. Rep. Cas. (BNA) 1815 (D.C. Cir. 1972), *aff'd by an equally divided Court sub nom. Fri v. Sierra Club*, 412 U.S. 541 (1973).

16. CAA § 202, 42 U.S.C. § 1857f-1 (1976).

17. Clean Air Act Amendments of 1977, Pub. L. No. 95-95, 91 Stat. 685 (1977).

18. CAA § 171(a), (b), 42 U.S.C. § 7501(a), (b) (1982).

19. CAA Title I, Part D (1982).

20. CAA §§ 112, 122, 42 U.S.C. §§ 7412, 7422 (1982).

21. *Id.* §§ 160-169, 42 U.S.C. §§ 7470-7479 (1982); *see Ala. Power Co. v. Costle*, 636 F.2d 323 (D.C. Cir. 1980).

22. CAA § 169A, 42 U.S.C. § 7491 (1982).

23. *Id.* § 123(a), 42 U.S.C. § 7423 (1982); *see Natural Res. Def. Council v. Thomas*, 838 F.2d 1224, 1232-33, 1237-38 (D.C. Cir. 1988); *Sierra Club v. EPA*, 719 F.2d 436, 439, 440-42 (D.C. Cir. 1983).

24. *See* Bruce A. Ackerman & W.T. Hassler, *Clean Coal/Dirty Air* 32-33, 98-99 (Yale University Press 1981).

25. CAA § 125, 42 U.S.C. § 7425 (1982).

26. *Id.* §§ 109, 110, 42 U.S.C. §§ 7409, 7410 (1982).

27. *Union Electric Co. v. EPA*, 427 U.S. 246, 266 (1976).

28. CAA § 172(b)(3), 42 U.S.C. § 7502(b)(3) (1982).

29. *See id.* §§ 111, 165, 173, 42 U.S.C. §§ 7411, 7475, 7503 (1982).

30. *Id.* § 163, 42 U.S.C. § 7473 (1982).

31. *Id.* § 165(a), 42 U.S.C. § 7475(a) (1982).

32. *Id.* § 173, 42 U.S.C. § 7503 (1982).

33. *Id.* § 112, 42 U.S.C. § 7412 (1982).

34. *Id.* § 169A, 42 U.S.C. § 7491 (1982).

35. EPA, Revisions to the National Ambient Air Quality Standards for Particulate Matter: Final Rule, 52 Fed. Reg. 24,634 (July 1, 1987).

36. EPA, National Ambient Air Quality Standards for Particulate Matter: Final Rule, 62 Fed. Reg. 38,652 (July 18, 1997).

37. EPA, National Ambient Air Quality Standards for Particulate Matter: Final Rule, 78 Fed. Reg. 3,086 (Jan. 15, 2013).

38. *See Envtl. Defense Fund v. Thomas*, 870 F.2d 892, 894 (2d Cir. 1989).

39. EPA, National Ambient Air Quality Standards for Sulfur Oxides (Sulfur Dioxide) – Final Decision, 61 Fed. Reg. 25,566 (May 22, 1996).

40. *See* Consent Decree, *Ctr. for Biological Diversity v. Johnson*, Civ. No. 1:05-cv-01814-LFO (D.D.C. Nov. 19, 2007), ECF No. 41; *see also* Stipulation to Amend Consent Decree, *Ctr. For Biological Diversity v. Johnson*, Civ. No. 1:05-cv-01814-LFO (D.D.C. Dec. 4, 2008), ECF No. 48.

41. EPA, Primary National Ambient Air Quality Standard for Sulfur Dioxide: Final Rule, 75 Fed. Reg. 35,520 (June 22, 2010).

42. EPA, Revisions to the National Ambient Air Quality Standards for Photochemical Oxidants: Final Rulemaking, 44 Fed. Reg. 8,202 (Feb. 8, 1979).

43. EPA, National Ambient Air Quality Standards for Ozone – Final Decision, 58 Fed. Reg. 13,008, 13,011-12, 13,013-16 (Mar. 9, 1993).

44. EPA, National Ambient Air Quality Standards for Ozone: Final Rule, 62 Fed. Reg. 38,856 (July 18, 1997).

45. EPA, National Ambient Air Quality Standards for Ozone: Final Rule, 73 Fed. Reg. 16,436 (Mar. 27, 2008).

46. *See, e.g.,* E-mail from Rosalina Rodriguez, EPA, to Tricia Crabtree, EPA (Aug. 5, 2010), Doc. ID No. EPA-HQ-OAR-2005-0172-12954 (providing summary of August 2, 2010 meeting between American Petroleum Institute and U.S. EPA regarding 2013 ozone NAAQS review schedule calling for proposal in May 2013 and final rule in February 2014); *see also* Clean Air Scientific Advisory Committee, EPA, Comments on Recent Advancements in Modeling of Policy Relevant Background Ozone, Slide 6 (Feb. 18, 2011), Doc. ID No. EPA-HQ-OAR-2005-0172-13025.

47. EPA, State Implementation Plans; Approval of Post-1987 Ozone and Carbon Monoxide Plan Revisions for Areas Not Attaining the National Ambient Air Quality Standards; Notice; Proposed Policy, 52 Fed. Reg. 45,044 (Nov. 24, 1987).

48. *See Abramowitz v. EPA*, 832 F.2d 1071, 1072-73, 1079 (9th Cir. 1987).

49. *See* Letter from Don R. Clay, Acting Assistant Adm'r for Air & Radiation, EPA, to John W. Boston, Vice President, Wisconsin Electric Power Company (Feb. 15, 1989), *available at* www.epa.gov/NSR/ttnnsr01/psd2/pdf/ p2_35b.pdf; Letter from Lee M. Thomas, Adm'r, EPA, to John W. Boston, Vice President, Wisconsin Electric Power Company (Oct. 14, 1988), *available at* www.epa.gov/region07/air/nsr/nsrmemos/fnaldtrm.pdf; Memorandum from Don R. Clay, Acting Assistant Adm'r for Air & Radiation, EPA, to David A. Kee, Dir., Air & Radiation Division, EPA Region V (Sept. 9, 1988), *available at* www.dec.ny.gov/docs/air_pdf/part231rmrrfact.pdf.

50. *Wis. Electric Power Co. v. Reilly*, 893 F.2d 901, 918 (7th Cir. 1990) (*"WEP-Co"*).

51. *See* EPA, Requirements for Preparation, Adoption and Submittal of Implementation Plans; Approval and Promulgation of Implementation Plans; Standards of Performance for New Stationary Sources; Final Rule, 57 Fed. Reg. 32,314 (July 21, 1992).

52. *See* EPA, Prevention of Significant Deterioration (PSD) and Nonattainment New Source Review (NSR): Notice of Proposed Rulemaking, 62 Fed. Reg. 38,250, 38,282 (July 23, 1996) (addressing EPA's obligation under then-pending settlement agreement); *see also Alaska Dept. of Envtl. Conservation v. EPA*, 540 U.S. 461, 476 n.7 (2004) ("Nothing in the Act or its implementing regulations mandates top-down analysis.").

53. *See* S. Rep. No. 91-1196 at 415, 490-91 (1970), *reprinted in* 1 COMM. ON PUBLIC WORKS, A LEGISLATIVE HISTORY OF THE CLEAN AIR AMENDMENTS OF 1970 (1974).

54. CAA § 122, 42 U.S.C. § 7422 (1982).

55. *See Natural Res. Def. Council v. Thomas*, 885 F.2d 1067, 1072-75 (2d Cir. 1989); *Natural Res. Def. Council v. EPA*, 824 F.2d 1146, 1147-48 (D.C. Cir. 1987).

56. EPA, Visibility Protection for Federal Class I Areas: Proposed Rulemaking, 45 Fed. Reg. 34,762, 34,763 (May 22, 1980).

57. *See, e.g., Natural Res. Def. Council v. EPA*, 902 F.2d 962, 965 (D.C. Cir. 1990).

58. EPA, Assessment of Visibility Impairment; Proposed Rule, 54 Fed. Reg. 36,948, 36,949 (Sept. 5, 1989).

59. *See Cent. Ariz. Water Conservation Dist. v. EPA*, 990 F.2d 1531, 1533-34, 1537, 1542 (9th Cir. 1993).

60. *See, e.g., Am. Corn Growers Ass'n v. EPA*, 291 F.3d 1, 3-5 (D.C. Cir. 2002).

61. Clean Air Act Amendments of 1990, Pub. L. No. 101-549, 104 Stat. 2399 (1990).

62. CAA § 112(b), 42 U.S.C. § 7412(b).

Chapter 2

NATIONAL AMBIENT AIR QUALITY STANDARDS

The centerpiece of the Clean Air Act is a system for achieving healthful "ambient," or outdoor,[1] air through national air quality standards ("NAAQS") promulgated by EPA and implemented primarily by the states. The core provisions of the Act regarding NAAQS are sections 108, 109, and 110.

National Ambient Air Quality Standards

Section 108 of the Act requires EPA to list air pollutants that, in the judgment of the Administrator, "cause or contribute to air pollution which may reasonably be anticipated to endanger public health or welfare" and "the presence of which in the ambient air results from numerous or diverse mobile or stationary sources . . ."[2] These listed pollutants are known as the "criteria" pollutants under the Act, so called because EPA must issue "air quality criteria" for each listed pollutant, which is information that "reflect[s] the latest scientific knowledge useful in indicating the kind and extent of all identifiable effects on public health or welfare which may be expected from the presence of such pollutant in the ambient air, in varying quantities."[3] The criteria pollutants are sulfur oxides ("SOx"), particulate matter ("PM") (both coarse particulate matter ("PM_{10}") and fine particulate matter ("$PM_{2.5}$")),[4] carbon monoxide ("CO"), ozone, oxides of nitrogen ("NOx"), and lead.

Section 109 directs EPA to promulgate, through public notice-and-comment rulemaking, NAAQS for each of the criteria pollutants.[5] The NAAQS apply uniformly throughout the country. For each pollutant, EPA must establish "primary" NAAQS at a level that, in EPA's judgment, is "requisite to protect the public health" with "an adequate margin of safety," and must establish "secondary" NAAQS at a level that is "requisite to protect the public welfare from any known or anticipated adverse effects associated with the presence of such air pollutant in the ambient air."[6] The Act defines "effects on [public] welfare" broadly to include effects on soils, water, crops, vegetation, manmade materials, animals, wildlife, weather, visibility, climate, property damage, transportation

16

hazards, economic values, and personal comfort and well-being.[7] The current NAAQS are summarized in the following table:

POLLUTANT	TYPE OF NAAQS	LEVEL	FORM	CITATION
SOx (measured as sulfur dioxide ("SO_2")	Primary	0.030 parts per million ("ppm")	Annual arithmetic mean	40 C.F.R. § 50.4
		0.14 ppm	24-hour average, not to be exceeded more than once per calendar year	40 C.F.R. § 50.4
		75 parts per billion ("ppb")	99th percentile of daily maximum 1-hour values averaged over 3 years	40 C.F.R. § 50.17[8]
	Secondary	0.5 ppm	3-hour average, not to be exceeded more than once per calendar year	40 C.F.R. § 50.5
PM_{10}	Primary & Secondary	150 micrograms per cubic meter ("$\mu g/m^3$")	24-hour average, not expected to be exceeded more than once per calendar year	40 C.F.R. § 50.6
$PM_{2.5}$	Primary	15.0 $\mu g/m^3$	Annual arithmetic mean, based on 3 years of data	40 C.F.R. §§ 50.7, 50.13
		65 $\mu g/m^3$	98th percentile 24-hour concentration, based on 3 years of data	40 C.F.R. § 50.7
		35 $\mu g/m^3$	98th percentile 24-hour concentration,	40 C.F.R. § 50.13; 78 Fed. Reg.

POLLUTANT	TYPE OF NAAQS	LEVEL	FORM	CITATION
			based on 3 years of data	3,086 (Jan. 15, 2013) (to be codified at 40 C.F.R. § 50.18)[9]
		12.0 µg/m^3	Average annual arithmetic mean based on 3 years of data	78 Fed. Reg. 3,086 (Jan. 15, 2013) (to be codified at 40 C.F.R. § 50.18)[10]
	Secondary	15.0 µg/m^3 65 µg/m^3 35 µg/m^3	Annual average, based on 3 years of data 98th percentile 24-hour concentration, based on 3 years of data 98th percentile 24-hour concentration, based on 3 years of data	40 C.F.R. §§ 50.7, 50.13 40 C.F.R. § 50.7 40 C.F.R. § 50.13
CO	Primary	9 ppm	8-hour average, not to be exceeded more than once per year	40 C.F.R. § 50.8
		35 ppm	1-hour average, not to be exceeded more than once per year	40 C.F.R. § 50.8
Ozone	Primary & Secondary	0.12 ppm	1-hour average, not expected to be exceeded more than once per calendar year	40 C.F.R. § 50.9
		0.08 ppm	Average annual	40 C.F.R.

POLLUTANT	TYPE OF NAAQS	LEVEL	FORM	CITATION
			fourth-highest daily maximum 8-hour average, based on 3 years of data	§ 50.10[11]
		0.075 ppm	Average annual fourth highest daily maximum 8-hour average, based on 3 years of data	40 C.F.R. § 50.15[12]
NOx (with nitrogen dioxide ("NO$_2$") as the indicator)	Primary	53 ppb 100 ppb	Annual average 3-year average of the annual 98th percentile of daily maximum 1-hour values	40 C.F.R. § 50.11(a) 40 C.F.R. § 50.11(b) & (f)
	Secondary	0.053 ppm	Annual arithmetic mean	40 C.F.R. § 50.11(c)
Lead	Primary & Secondary	1.5 μg/m^3 0.15 μg/m^3	Maximum arithmetic mean, averaged over a calendar quarter Arithmetic mean concentration over a 3-month period	40 C.F.R. § 50.12 40 C.F.R. § 50.16[13]

At least every five years, EPA must review the air quality criteria and the NAAQS with advice from EPA's Clean Air Scientific Advisory Committee ("CASAC"), a standing committee of EPA's Science Advisory Board. After considering CASAC's recommendations, the EPA Administrator may revise the criteria and NAAQS and promulgate new NAAQS if he or she determines such actions are "appropriate" in accordance with the statute.[14]

Once EPA sets or revises NAAQS, states have the primary responsibility for implementing them.[15] The first step in the implementation process is "designation" of areas for the new NAAQS according to their air quality. Under section 107 of the Act, within one year after promulgation of a NAAQS (or such earlier date that EPA may reasonably require, but not earlier than 120 days after promulgation of the NAAQS),[16] each state is to submit to EPA a list of all areas in the state, designating—for that pollutant—each area as (1) nonattainment, if it does not meet (or if it "contributes to ambient air quality in a nearby area that does not meet") the NAAQS for that pollutant; (2) attainment, if it meets the NAAQS for the pollutant (and is not included in a nonattainment area under the "nearby area" clause); or (3) unclassifiable, if it cannot be classified as attainment or nonattainment "on the basis of available information" (generally, information from ambient air quality monitoring devices).[17] EPA must review the states' lists and, within two years after NAAQS promulgation (a period that EPA may extend by up to one year if it has "insufficient information"), EPA is to promulgate designations, modified from the states' lists as necessary in EPA's judgment.[18] Section 107 also contains provisions governing state- and EPA-initiated redesignations of areas, e.g., from nonattainment to attainment, attainment to nonattainment, and unclassifiable to attainment or nonattainment.[19]

States are also responsible for a plan, known as a "state implementation plan" or "SIP," that ensures the NAAQS are attained and maintained. Within three years after the promulgation of a new or revised NAAQS (or a shorter period if the Administrator so specifies), states must submit a SIP to EPA that provides for implementation, maintenance, and enforcement of the NAAQS in each air quality control region within the state.[20] Among other requirements, these SIPs must: (1) "include enforceable emission limitations and other control measures, . . . as well as schedules and timetables for compliance" with such limitations, that are needed to meet applicable requirements of the Act; (2) "provide for establishment and operation of appropriate devices, methods, systems, and procedures" to monitor and analyze ambient air quality and such other measures as may be necessary to ensure attainment and maintenance of the NAAQS; (3) include a permit program for modification or construction of stationary sources to assure the NAAQS are achieved and to prevent significant deterioration of air quality in the state; (4) provide for the installation, maintenance, and replacement of equipment to monitor emissions from major sources as required by the EPA Administrator; and (5) provide for air quality modeling as prescribed by the Administrator.[21]

States in which nonattainment areas are located must also address additional statutory requirements in their SIPs after nonattainment designations are finalized. These requirements are intended to bring nonattainment areas into attainment as expeditiously as practicable. The 1970 Clean Air Act set tight deadlines for states to achieve attainment. After widespread failure to meet these deadlines, Congress established new requirements for existing and new sources in nonattainment areas in the 1977 Amendments to the Act. Numerous areas of the country, however, still failed to attain the ozone and carbon monoxide NAAQS by the revised deadlines imposed by the 1977 Amendments. Moreover, EPA's efforts to address these nonattainment problems administratively were restricted by judicial decisions limiting EPA's discretion to create interim administrative solutions that balanced environmental and economic considerations.[22] In part because of the controversy over EPA's authority to make administrative adjustments to the nonattainment program, Congress, in enacting Title I of the 1990 Amendments to the Act, adopted further extensive revisions, focusing primarily on individual criteria pollutants.

Although states take the lead in NAAQS implementation, EPA has ongoing authority to review SIPs and to require states to revise their SIPs as necessary. If a state does not act promptly to revise its SIP in response to a new or revised NAAQS or to an EPA finding of SIP inadequacy, EPA has the authority to step in and to set emission limitations for sources within that state; when EPA takes that step, it promulgates these limitations in the form of a "federal implementation plan," or "FIP."[23]

The SIP program and the Act's nonattainment requirements are discussed below.

Overview of the General State Implementation Plan Program

As noted above, sections 107 and 110 of the Clean Air Act give each state primary responsibility for protecting air quality within its borders. This is achieved through the development of SIP requirements specifying how the primary and secondary NAAQS will be achieved. To ensure that SIP requirements are adequate to attain and maintain the NAAQS, all SIPs submitted by the states to EPA must meet certain minimum requirements specified in section 110 of the Act. The following discussion reviews the substantive and procedural requirements of the Act pertaining to SIP development and approval.

Minimum Substantive Requirements for All SIPs

Section 110(a)(2) of the Clean Air Act requires that all SIPs be adopted after reasonable notice and public hearing. Section 110(a)(1) requires that a SIP to implement a NAAQS, which EPA refers to as an "infrastructure SIP,"[24] be submitted to EPA not later than three years after promulgation of that NAAQS, although a shorter submission deadline may be set by EPA. (As described below, a later submission deadline applies to nonattainment SIP provisions.)

The general provisions that must be included in a SIP are:

Enforceable Emission Limitations. A SIP must include enforceable emission limitations and other control measures, including economic incentives and timetables, as well as schedules and compliance timetables.[25]

Air Quality Data. A SIP must include provisions for monitoring, compiling, and analyzing data on ambient air quality that must be made available to EPA.[26]

Enforcement Authority. A SIP must establish an enforcement program and include provisions regulating modification and construction of stationary sources, including permit programs for prevention of significant deterioration ("PSD") in attainment areas and for sources in nonattainment areas as required by Parts C and D of Title I of the Act.[27] The operation of existing stationary sources, however, is also subject to regulation and enforcement under the federal operating permit program established by Title V of the Act. The preconstruction and operating permit programs are discussed further in Chapter 4.

Means To Address Interstate Air Pollution. A SIP must prohibit, "consistent with the provisions" of Title I, emissions activities within the state from (1) "contribut[ing] significantly to nonattainment in, or interfer[ing] with maintenance [of the NAAQS] by, any other State," or (2) interfering with measures required to be included in another state's SIP under the PSD or visibility protection provisions of Title I Part C. A SIP also must include provisions ensuring compliance with applicable requirements in sections 126 and 115, which authorize certain actions by EPA to address interstate and international pollution, respectively.[28]

Adequate Personnel, Funding, and Authority. A SIP must provide assurances that the state (or state-designated local regulatory authority) has adequate resources and power to carry out the SIP under state or local laws. A SIP must also provide assurances that the state has retained ultimate responsibility for implementation despite any delegation of authority to local governments.[29]

Monitoring and Emission Data. A SIP must require monitoring and periodic reporting of emissions by stationary sources. A SIP also must require that the state correlate those emission reports with relevant emission limitations and make the reports available for public inspection.[30]

Contingency Plans. A SIP must provide authority for certain emergency powers and for adequate contingency plans to restrict emissions of pollutants that present an imminent and substantial danger.[31]

Revision Authority. A SIP must provide for revision of the plan as necessary to take into account any revisions to the NAAQS, improved methods of attainment, or any finding by EPA that the SIP is "substantially inadequate" to attain the NAAQS or to meet other Clean Air Act requirements.[32]

Part D Requirements for Nonattainment Areas. For states that have a nonattainment area, a SIP must meet the requirements of Part D of Title I of the Act relating to special, more stringent provisions for those areas.[33] These requirements are discussed in more detail in Section B below.

Air Quality Modeling. A SIP must provide for air quality modeling and submission of related data as prescribed by the Administrator. Air quality modeling is used to predict the effect of the emissions of any criteria pollutant on ambient air quality.[34]

Permit Fees. A SIP must include provisions requiring the owner or operator of each major stationary source to pay, as a condition of any Clean Air Act-required permit, a fee sufficient to cover the reasonable costs of reviewing and acting on permit applications and implementing and enforcing permits (not including costs for court actions or other enforcement actions) until superseded by a fee program under the state's Title V operating permit program.[35] As states have received EPA approval of their Title V programs, including Title V permit fee provisions, section 110(a)(2)(L) has become largely moot. The Title V permitting program is discussed in Chapter 4.

Local Consultation. A SIP must provide for consultation and participation by local political subdivisions affected by the plan.[36]

Conformity Requirements. Section 176(c), which was amended by the 1990 Amendments, prohibits the federal government from engaging in, supporting, licensing, or approving any activity that does not conform to an approved SIP, Transportation Improvement Plan, or FIP. EPA's rules address two types of conformity: transportation conformity and general conformity. EPA's transportation conformity rule, which was developed in coordination with the Department of Transportation, was originally published on November 24, 1993,[37] and has been amended several times. The most recent rule was published March 2012.[38] EPA's rule on general conformity was promulgated in November 1993.[39] Updates to that rule were promulgated in 2010.[40]

Technical Assistance for Small Business Sources. Under section 507 of the Act, added by the 1990 Amendments, each state must establish a "small business stationary source technical and environmental compliance assistance program." These programs must meet certain minimum requirements, including mechanisms for the development and collection of information concerning compliance technologies, assistance with pollution prevention, designation of a state agency to serve as ombudsman, assistance with permit applications and compliance auditing, and procedures for modifying compliance methods and milestones.[41]

EPA must establish guidelines to help states develop these programs and must develop a program in the event that a state fails to submit one.[42] EPA released guidance in January 1992, outlining alternative control technologies and pollution prevention methods for small business stationary sources.[43] In addition, states and EPA must consider factors such as the financial resources and technical capabilities of small business stationary sources when imposing permit or other fees, when applying continuous emission monitoring requirements, and when issuing control technique guidelines ("CTGs") under the Act.[44]

Other Requirements. A SIP must meet the requirements of Part C of Title I of the Act (relating to PSD and visibility protection[45]), section 121 (relating to consultation with local governments and federal land managers with authority over federal lands to which the SIP would apply), and section 127 (relating to public notification of instances in which NAAQS are exceeded).[46]

Additional Requirements for Nonattainment Area SIPs

In addition to including the general requirements described above, SIPs for states that contain nonattainment areas also must provide a mechanism for achieving (and maintaining) attainment of the relevant NAAQS, as specified in Subpart 1 of Title I Part D of the CAA (§§ 171-179B). First, the SIP must include provisions designed to achieve attainment by the "attainment date" specified by EPA. The general rule is that, for a particular nonattainment area, the attainment date is to be "the date by which attainment can be achieved as expeditiously as practicable . . . ."[47] For primary NAAQS, attainment is required "no later than 5 years from the date such area was designated nonattainment," except that EPA may extend that date to as long as 10 years from the date of designation "considering the severity of nonattainment and the availability and feasibility of pollution control measures."[48] EPA may classify nonattainment areas for purposes of applying an attainment date (and unspecified other purposes) according to the severity of nonattainment and the availability and feasibility of emission control measures for achieving attainment.[49] In addition, EPA may provide up to 2 additional 1-year extensions of the attainment date under certain circumstances.[50] These general provisions for Subpart 1 of Title I Part D of the Act concerning nonattainment area SIPs were supplemented by Congress in 1990 with the addition of Subparts 2, 3, 4, and 5 of Title I Part D, which contains specific provisions addressing ozone (CAA §§ 181-185B) (Subpart 2); carbon monoxide (CAA §§ 186-187) (Subpart 3); particulate matter (CAA §§ 188-190) (Subpart 4); and SOx, NO_2, and lead (CAA §§ 191-192) (Subpart 5).[51]

General Requirements for Nonattainment Area SIPs

Subpart 1 of Title I Part D of the Act specifies additional requirements for nonattainment area SIPs, for the purpose of "provid[ing] for attainment of the national primary ambient air quality standards."[52] These requirements include:

Reasonably Available Control Technology

SIPs must require all reasonably available control measures ("RACM") as expeditiously as practicable and must, at a minimum, require reasonably available control technology ("RACT") for existing sources of nonattainment pollutants.[53] Only technology that will accelerate attainment is considered RACT.[54]

Reasonable Further Progress

SIPs must provide for such "annual incremental reductions" in emissions of relevant air pollutants as are "reasonably" required by EPA in order to ensure attainment of the NAAQS by the applicable attainment date.[55] In some cases, measures that are otherwise required in nonattainment area SIPs may satisfy the requirement for reasonable further progress ("RFP").[56]

Inventory of Current Emissions

SIPs must include "a comprehensive, accurate, current inventory of actual emissions from all sources of the relevant pollutant or pollutants in [the nonattainment] area." EPA may require periodic revisions to the inventory.[57]

Permits for New and Modified Major Stationary Sources

SIPs must require permits for the construction and operation of new or modified "major stationary sources" anywhere in the nonattainment area.[58] Plans must meet the requirements of the nonattainment-area new source review program, which are discussed in Chapters 3 and 4 of this Handbook.

Quantify New Emissions To Be Allowed

SIPs must identify and quantify emissions that will be allowed from certain new or modified major stationary sources and demonstrate that those emissions will be consistent with the achievement of RFP toward attainment.[59]

Contingency Measures

SIPs must provide specific measures that will automatically be implemented if the area either fails to make RFP toward attainment or fails to attain the primary NAAQS by the applicable attainment date.[60]

Equivalent Techniques

EPA may allow, upon application by the state, the use of equivalent modeling, emission inventory, and planning techniques provided that they are not, in the aggregate, less effective than the methods specified by EPA.[61]

Other Measures

Section 172(c)(6) of the Act contains a catch-all requirement that the SIP include, in addition to the specific provisions discussed above, "enforceable emission limitations, and such other control measures, means or techniques (including economic incentives such as fees, marketable permits, and auctions of emission rights), as well as schedules and timetables for compliance, as may be necessary or appropriate to provide for attainment of such standard in such area by the applicable attainment date . . . ."

The Use of Air Quality Models in SIP Development

Air quality models are the key technique used to demonstrate that source-specific SIP requirements will assure attainment and maintenance of the NAAQS.[62] The Act requires EPA to "specify with reasonable particularity each air quality model or models to be used under specified sets of conditions" in performing ambient air quality analyses with respect to new sources under the PSD program.[63] Congress also required EPA to conduct a conference on air quality modeling at least every three years, with special attention to be given to PSD new source modeling.[64] Information on EPA's modeling conferences can be found on its website.[65]

EPA's Guideline on Air Quality Models identifies the models that EPA recommends be used for a wide variety of applications, discusses the data required for their use, and specifies the procedures that are to be followed if the Agency has not recommended a model for a particular situation or if approval is sought for the use of a model other than the one recommended by EPA.[66] The models that EPA recommends are intended to be conservative. Although entitled a "guideline," the Guideline on Air Quality Models is actually a rule.[67] It was promulgated and can be revised only through rulemaking. Nevertheless, EPA frequently issues generic interpretations of the Guideline in the form of decisions of the Agency's Model Clearinghouse or letters to its Regional Meteorologists. These interpretations can substantially affect obligations under the Guideline. Thus, it is often difficult to determine current Agency modeling requirements without contacting the Agency directly. The Guideline affirmatively encourages such contact.

SIP Requirements for Ozone Nonattainment Areas (Subpart 2 of Part D)

The 1990 Amendments to the Clean Air Act made major changes to the program for addressing areas that failed to attain the ozone NAAQS, which at that time was a 1-hour standard of 0.12 ppm, not to be exceeded more than once in a calendar year.[68] These changes, as summarized below, involved classification of ozone areas as a matter of law, specification of new requirements for SIPs based on those classifications, imposition of new federal measures, and provision for multi-state ozone transport regions.

Since the 1990 Amendments, EPA has replaced the 1-hour ozone NAAQS with more stringent NAAQS with an 8-hour averaging time. The Supreme Court has determined that the requirements of Subpart 2 also largely apply to SIPs for nonattainment areas for the 8-hour NAAQS.[69] EPA has had to translate some of the requirements in Subpart 2 for application to the revised 8-hour standards.

Classifications and Attainment Deadlines

Section 181(a)(1) of the Act, enacted as part of the 1990 Amendments, classified ozone nonattainment areas based on the area's ozone "design value" (a measure of a one-hour average ozone concentration in the air). The areas were given the following attainment dates:

Classification	Design Value (ppm)	Attainment Deadline
Marginal	0.121 to 0.138	November 15, 1993
Moderate	0.138 to 0.160	November 15, 1996
Serious	0.160 to 0.180	November 15, 1999
Severe	0.180 to 0.280	November 15, 2005[70]
Extreme	0.280 and above	November 15, 2010

Section 181(a)(5) authorizes EPA to adjust these classifications for areas that were on the margin between classifications and to grant up to two one-year extensions of the attainment deadline under specified circumstances.[71] Newly designated ozone nonattainment areas are to be classified at the time of their nonattainment designation and are provided with time for attainment equivalent to areas that were classified upon enactment of the 1990 Amendments.[72]

In certain cases, areas may be reclassified to a higher classification or "bumped up." Such areas would receive a later attainment date, but also would face the additional requirements associated with the higher classification. If EPA finds that an area classified as marginal, moderate, or serious has failed to attain the NAAQS by its attainment date (including any extensions of that date), that area will be reclassified by operation of law to the higher of either (1) the next higher classification or (2) the classification associated with its design value when EPA found it had not attained, but not as high as extreme nonattainment.[73] A state may also request a voluntary bump-up (including to extreme nonattainment), which EPA must grant.[74]

When it adopted an ozone NAAQS of 0.08 ppm with an 8-hour averaging time in 1997 to replace the 1-hour ozone NAAQS,[75] EPA determined that the Subpart 2 requirements would apply only to nonattainment areas for the 8-hour NAAQS that had also exceeded the 1-hour NAAQS. To classify those areas that were to be subject to Subpart 2 requirements, EPA adjusted the categories and associated attainment deadlines that Congress had codified in section 181(a)(1) of the Act as follows:[76]

Classification	Design Value (ppm)	Attainment Deadline (years)
Marginal	0.085 to 0.092	3

Moderate	0.092 to 0.107	6
Serious	0.107 to 0.120	9
Severe-15	0.120 to 0.127	15
Severe-17	0.127 to 0.187	17
Extreme	0.187 and above	20

The Supreme Court, however, disagreed with EPA's assessment of the role of Subpart 2 in implementation of the 8-hour ozone NAAQS. In *Whitman v. Am. Trucking Ass'ns,* the Court stated:

> To use a few apparent gaps in Subpart 2 to render its textually explicit applica-
> bility to nonattainment areas under the new standard utterly inoperative is to go
> over the edge of reasonable interpretation. The EPA may not construe the stat-
> ute in a way that completely nullifies textually applicable provisions meant to
> limit its discretion.[77]

In 2012, EPA determined that any areas that remained in nonattainment for the 8-hour standard would be implemented under Subpart 2 and classified according to the table above.[78] EPA also determined that the revised 8-hour NAAQS of 0.075 ppm that it adopted in 2008 would be implemented under Subpart 2 and that nonattainment areas would again be classified under a modification of the classifications in section 181(a)(1) of the Act,[79] as follows:

Classification	Design Value (ppm)	Attainment Deadline (years)
Marginal	0.076 to 0.086	3
Moderate	0.086 to 0.100	6
Serious	0.100 to 0.113	9
Severe-15	0.113 to 0.119	15
Severe-17	0.119 to 0.175	17
Extreme	0.175 and above	20

b. Required SIP Revisions

States with ozone nonattainment areas are required by Subpart 2 of Part D to make the following revisions to their SIPs. While some of these requirements apply regardless of classification, for others, the requirements become increasingly onerous for higher classifications.

State Planning and Demonstration Requirements

Emission Inventories. States were required to submit by November 15, 1992, a "comprehensive, accurate, current inventory" of actual emissions of volatile organic compounds ("VOCs") and NOx in all ozone nonattainment areas.[80] These inventories are used by states in air quality modeling and to assess compliance with percent emission reduction requirements. States must update their emission inventories every three years until attainment is achieved.[81]

Percent Reductions for Reasonable Further Progress (RFP). Each state with an ozone nonattainment area classified as *moderate or above* for ozone was required to submit a SIP revision by November 15, 1993, providing for annual reductions in VOC emissions in such areas of at least 15 percent over the period from November 15, 1990, to November 15, 1996, in order to show "reasonable further progress" toward attainment.[82] The 15 percent reduction in VOCs is to be measured from the 1990 baseline of actual emissions (adjusted to account for net growth in emissions).[83] For any area other than an *extreme* area, however, a percentage of less than 15 percent for VOC reductions may be used if specific additional requirements are imposed.[84]

To be creditable, emission reductions must be "real, permanent, and enforceable" and must be the result of emission reduction strategies implemented "in the designated nonattainment area."[85] Some sources of creditable reductions are: (1) RACT or motor vehicle inspection and maintenance ("I/M") reductions not associated with required SIP corrections (*i.e.*, reductions from lower emission rates or applicability thresholds); (2) application of regulations to areas not previously subject to them; (3) adoption of transportation control measures ("TCMs") not previously included in the SIP; and (4) improvements in "rule effectiveness."[86]

Emission reductions may not be "double-counted" (*e.g.*, counted for both a new source offset and for RFP).[87] In addition, emissions eliminated by regulations governing motor vehicle exhaust or evaporative emissions promulgated by January 1, 1990, Reid Vapor Pressure, RACT "fix-up," corrections to existing I/M programs, and pre-enactment banked emission reduction credits are not creditable toward the 15 percent reduction.[88] All other reductions from the implementation of control measures under the SIP, from EPA-adopted federal control measures, or from the state's operating permit program are creditable.[89]

Each state containing an ozone nonattainment area classified as *serious or above* for ozone was also required to submit by November 15, 1994, a SIP revision for the area providing for reductions in VOC emissions of at least 3 percent per year averaged over each subsequent three-year period (*i.e.*, 9 percent over each three-year period) from November 1996 until attainment. A reduction of less than 3 percent may be allowed for any area other than an *extreme* area upon a demonstration that the plan includes all measures that can "feasibly" be implemented in light of "technological achievability."[90] In lieu of the post-1996 reductions in VOCs, states may provide instead for a combination of NOx and VOC emission reductions if those reductions would result in a reduction in ozone concentrations equivalent to the reduction that would result from VOC emission reductions alone.[91]

Attainment Demonstrations. Each state with an ozone nonattainment area classified as *moderate* was required to submit a SIP revision by November 15, 1993, providing for "such specific annual reductions" in emissions of VOCs and

NOx in the area "as necessary to attain" the ozone NAAQS by the applicable deadline.[92] States were required to demonstrate through application of EPA-approved computer air quality modeling techniques described in EPA's "Guidelines on Air Quality Models," 40 C.F.R. part 51, Appendix W, that the specified reductions and other control strategy measures were sufficient to achieve attainment. State attainment and progress demonstrations for ozone nonattainment areas classified as *serious or above* required "photochemical grid modeling or any other analytical method determined by the Administrator" to be "at least as effective," and were due by November 15, 1994.[93]

The states generally failed to submit these demonstrations—and failed to submit SIP provisions implementing the post-1996 RFP reductions—by this deadline. Finding that the states' failure to make their required SIP submittals was due in part to interstate transport of ozone and its precursors in the Eastern United States, EPA promulgated a SIP call in October 1998, which is commonly known as the "NOx SIP Call." The NOx SIP Call is discussed in Section III below, addressing interstate transport of air pollution.

Milestone Demonstrations. Starting in 1996 and every three years thereafter, states with ozone nonattainment areas classified as *serious or above* must demonstrate compliance with any required milestones (including the 15 percent and 3 percent reduction requirements under section 182(b)(1) and (c)(2)).[94] Within 90 days after each milestone, the state must submit to EPA a demonstration that the reduction has been met. The Administrator has 90 days to determine whether the demonstration is adequate.[95]

In addition, starting in 1996 and every three years thereafter, states must submit for each ozone nonattainment area classified as *serious or above* a demonstration that certain relevant transportation parameters (including aggregate vehicle mileage, aggregate vehicle emissions, and congestion levels) are consistent with projections made in the area's attainment demonstration. If the parameters exceed those projected, the state has 18 months to submit a SIP revision with TCMs, including TCMs listed in section 108(f) of the Act, that are capable of bringing emissions within the projected levels. The revisions must be consistent with EPA guidelines.[96] TCMs listed in section 108(f) include requirements for employer-based transportation management plans and employer-sponsored flexible work schedules.

Contingency Measures. States with moderate or above ozone nonattainment areas were required to comply with a section 172(c)(9) requirement to provide for contingency measures that are to be undertaken if an area fails to make reasonable further progress or to achieve attainment by the deadline.[97] Measures must take effect "without further action" by EPA or the state.

Enhanced Ozone Monitoring Programs. Under section 182(c)(1), EPA was required to promulgate rules for enhanced ambient monitoring of ozone, NOx, and VOCs and for enhanced emissions monitoring of NOx and VOCs. Final rules for ambient monitoring were published on February 12, 1993.[98] States with *serious and above* ozone nonattainment areas were required to immediately adopt and implement a monitoring program based on those rules.

Required Revisions Affecting Stationary Sources. States are required to submit SIP revisions providing for the following requirements and control measures for stationary sources.

Annual Emission Statements for Stationary Sources. All states with ozone nonattainment areas were required to submit a SIP revision requiring stationary sources of NOx and VOCs to submit annual emission statements beginning November 15, 1993, showing actual emissions.[99] States may waive the requirement, however, for any class of sources emitting less that 25 tons per year of the relevant pollutant if the state includes those sources' emissions in its periodic inventories.[100]

New Requirements for Permit Programs. All states with ozone nonattainment areas were required to submit SIP revisions requiring permits for the construction or modification of major new or modified stationary sources in the nonattainment area.[101] This new source review requirement applies to "major stationary sources" of VOCs and NOx.[102] The required revisions must apply the following definitions of "major stationary source" (based on potential to emit) and emission offset ratios:[103]

Classification	"Major Source"	NSR Offset Ratio
Marginal	100 tons per year	1.1 to 1
Moderate	100 tons per year	1.15 to 1
Serious	50 tons per year	1.2 to 1
Severe	25 tons per year	1.3 to 1
Extreme	10 tons per year	1.5 to 1

For *severe* and *extreme* areas, a ratio of 1.2 to 1 may be used if all existing major sources use "best available control technology."[104]

Special provisions apply in *serious*, *severe*, and *extreme* ozone nonattainment areas to evaluate proposed "modifications" to determine whether new source review will apply.[105]

RACT Fix-up. For areas classified as *marginal or above* for ozone nonattainment, states were required to submit to EPA, within six months after classification of the area (*i.e.*, by May 15, 1991, for those areas classified upon enactment), all rules and corrections to existing rules for application of RACT at existing sources of VOCs, as previously required by EPA guidance under section 172(b) of the pre-1990 Act.[106]

RACT Catch-up. States also were required to impose RACT in areas classified as *moderate or above* that were previously exempt from RACT. Specifically, states were required to submit SIP revisions for all *moderate or above* ozone nonattainment areas requiring RACT at all existing stationary sources of VOCs for which EPA had issued a CTG specifying RACT for a source category before enactment of the Amendments in November 1990. By the time of enactment, EPA had issued CTGs for at least 28 VOC source categories. In addition, states were to require RACT at all existing "major stationary sources" of VOCs in the area not covered by a CTG.[107]

Clean Fuel for Boilers. New, modified, and existing electric utility and industrial and commercial boilers emitting more than 25 tons per year of NOx that are located in an *extreme* ozone nonattainment area are required to either burn "clean fuel" (generally, natural gas, methanol, or ethanol) at least 90 percent of the time or use "advanced control technology" (*e.g.*, catalytic control technology) for NOx emissions. As the only state to contain an extreme ozone nonattainment area, California was required to submit a SIP revision by November 15, 1993, requiring implementation of the provision by November 15, 1998.[108] This requirement applies only to boilers that actually emit more than 25 tons per year.

Required Revisions Related to Mobile Sources. States with ozone nonattainment areas are required to submit the following SIP revisions for control of emissions from mobile sources.

Motor Vehicle I/M Programs. Three separate levels of motor vehicle I/M programs apply in ozone nonattainment areas depending upon the area's classification.[109] States with ozone nonattainment areas classified as *marginal or above* were required, immediately following enactment of the Amendments on November 15, 1990, to make corrections to any I/M program that were in place in the area (or was previously required by section 172(b)(11)(B) of the pre-1990 Act) to ensure compliance with existing EPA guidelines.[110] States with ozone nonattainment areas classified as *moderate or above* were required to submit a SIP revision establishing a "basic" I/M program in the area as required for *marginal* areas under section 182(a)(2)(B), regardless of whether or not such a program was previously required for the area.[111] Each state containing an ozone nonattainment area classified as *serious or above* was to provide for and begin implementation of an enhanced I/M program by November 15, 1992, in urban nonattainment areas with a 1980 population of 200,000 or more.[112] I/M programs are aimed at reducing hydrocarbons and NOx in ozone nonattainment areas. The program must meet the requirements set out in section 182(c) (including the use of computerized emission analyzers and on-road testing devices), as well as all published guidelines.[113] Requirements for I/M programs are codified in Subpart S of 40 C.F.R. part 51.

Stage II Vapor Recovery. By November 15, 1992, each state with a *moderate or above* ozone nonattainment area was required to submit a SIP revision mandating that all owners or operators of gasoline dispensing facilities (including private and governmental facilities) in such areas install and operate a system to recover vapor emissions from the fueling of motor vehicles. Under section 202(a)(6) of the Act, however, areas classified as *moderate* were exempted from the requirement for such Stage II vapor recovery systems after EPA's April

1994 promulgation of "onboard" vapor recovery systems for motor vehicles,[114] although states may retain a requirement for Stage II vapor recovery systems to satisfy other air quality requirements. Areas classified as *serious or above* could also be exempted from Stage II requirements where the Administrator makes a finding that use of "onboard" vapor recovery systems is widespread,[115] but, again, states may chose not to do so. In 2012, EPA concluded that Stage II vapor recovery systems were no longer required.[116]

Clean-Fuel Vehicle Programs in Some Areas. States with certain highly populated *serious or above* ozone nonattainment areas were required to submit a SIP revision providing for a specific percentage of clean-fuel vehicles in centrally fueled fleets for each area covered by the clean-fuel vehicle program of Title II.[117] A centrally fueled fleet is 10 or more vehicles that are owned or operated by a single person and that are, or are capable of being, centrally fueled. Alternatively, states could submit a SIP revision consisting of fully adopted control measures resulting in reductions equal to those that would be achieved with a clean-fuel vehicle program.

Transportation Control Measures. For areas classified as *severe or above*, states were required to adopt specific, enforceable TCMs sufficient to offset any growth in emissions of VOCs from an increase in vehicle miles traveled ("VMT") in the area and to help attain the required periodic emissions reductions for reasonable further progress.[118] SIP revisions were due by November 15, 1992. States were to consider for implementation the TCMs listed in section 108(f), which include employer-based transportation management plans and employer-sponsored flexible work schedules. In addition, beginning November 15, 1996, and every three years thereafter, each state with a *serious or above* ozone nonattainment area must submit a demonstration that aggregate vehicle mileage, aggregate vehicle emissions, and congestion levels (as well as other relevant parameters) in the area are consistent with projections made in the area's attainment demonstration. If the parameters exceed the projections, the state has 18 months to submit a SIP revision with TCMs for the area (including, but not limited to, those listed under section 108(f)) capable of bringing emissions within the projected levels.[119]

Although EPA took the position that TCMs were required only to offset growth in motor vehicle emissions in the aggregate, the U.S. Court of Appeals for the Ninth Circuit ruled in 2011 that TCMs were mandatory if emissions increased due to increased VMT, even if there was no overall increase in motor vehicle emissions (*i.e.*, emissions due to increased VMT were offset by emissions decreases for other reasons such as fleet turnover).[120] As a result, in 2012, EPA issued guidance to facilitate state determination of situations in which additional TCMs would not be required.[121]

Reformulated Fuels. The Act prohibits the sale of non-reformulated gasoline in certain ozone nonattainment areas to reduce VOC emissions.[122] The prohibition, which took effect on January 1, 1995, applied to nine highly polluted ozone nonattainment areas as specified under section 211(k)(10)(D) (Baltimore, Chicago, Hartford, Houston, Los Angeles, Milwaukee, New York, Philadelphia, and San Diego), but could also apply in other areas.[123] The prohibition may be applied to other ozone nonattainment areas at the request of the governor of the relevant state.[124] EPA's regulations on reformulated gasoline are found in Subpart D of 40 C.F.R. Part 80.

Sale of Low Emission Vehicles ("LEV"). Section 209 of the Act preempts the states from establishing their own standards directly regulating emissions from motor vehicles. California is entitled under the statute to a waiver from this preemption. In the 1977 Amendments to the Act, Congress enacted section 177 of the Act, which allows a state to adopt vehicle emission standards different from the federal standards if those standards (1) are "identical to the California standards for which a waiver has been granted" and (2) are adopted at least two years before commencement of the model year of the vehicles to which they will apply. The 1990 Amendments added another restriction to this authority: states cannot adopt standards so different from the federal or the California standards that they effectively call for a "third vehicle."[125]

California has taken advantage of its exemption under section 209 to establish the Low Emission Vehicle/Clean Fuels ("LEV/CF") program. EPA awarded the California standards a section 209 waiver in 1993. The California LEV/CF program includes both a vehicle component and a fuels component. Included in the vehicle component of the program is a requirement that, beginning in a future year, a specified percentage of vehicles manufactured by large-volume automobile manufacturers must be "Zero-Emission Vehicles" ("ZEV"), *e.g.*, electric vehicles.

Following the development of California's program, New York and Massachusetts sought EPA waivers under section 177 to permit those states to adopt and implement California-style standards. Automobile manufacturers challenged these Northeastern states' programs in a series of complex lawsuits, asserting that they violated the "identicality" requirement, the two-year lead-time requirement, and the prohibition against a "third vehicle." On many but not all issues, the two states prevailed in this protracted litigation.[126]

In 1995, EPA published a rule requiring adoption of the California LEV program (without the ZEV production mandate) in all of the Northeastern Ozone Transport Region states.[127] Virginia, one of the Ozone Transport Region states, challenged the rule in the U.S. Court of Appeals for the District of Columbia Circuit. The court held that EPA had exceeded its authority by *mandating* state adoption of the program.[128]

Subsequently, EPA completed rulemaking to establish a framework for a voluntary "National LEV" program. A final National LEV rule was signed by the Administrator in December 1997.[129] The program took effect when EPA found in March 1998 that nine Northeastern states and 23 automobile manufacturers committed to it.[130] The resulting tailpipe standards are enforceable in the same manner as any other federal new motor vehicle program.

Requirements for Ozone Transport Regions/Northeast Ozone Transport Region. Under the general SIP requirement of section 110(a)(2)(D), all SIPs must, consistent with the provisions of Title I of the Act, prohibit emissions that interfere with certain Clean Air Act requirements in other states. To ensure that this requirement is being met, the 1990 Amendments established a new provision to address the interstate transport of air pollutants. Whenever the Administrator determines (on the Administrator's own motion or upon petition from a state) that the interstate transport of pollutants from one or more states is contributing significantly to a violation of a NAAQS in another state or states, the Administrator may establish a "transport region" including those states (both the "contributing" and the "receiving" states). After designating a transport region, EPA must establish a transport commission, made up of representatives of the states, in accordance with section 176A.

While section 176A addresses transport generally, section 184 of the Act addresses *ozone* transport specifically. Section 184(a) of the Act specifically created an ozone transport region (the only transport region established under Part D thus far) consisting of the states of Connecticut, Delaware, Maine, Maryland, Massachusetts, New Hampshire, New Jersey, New York, Pennsylvania, Rhode Island, Vermont, and the Consolidated Metropolitan Statistical Area that includes the District of Columbia (which includes part of Virginia). This region is called the "Northeast Ozone Transport Region." Under section 184(b), all states within an ozone transport region are required to revise their SIPs to include: (1) enhanced I/M for motor vehicles in all Metropolitan Statistical Areas with a population of 100,000 or more; (2) RACT for all "major stationary sources" of VOCs and for VOC sources for which EPA issues or had issued a CTG; and (3) new source review for "major stationary sources" of VOCs. For ozone transport regions, the term "major stationary source" is defined as all sources with the potential to emit 50 tons or more per year of VOCs. "Major stationary sources" of NOx in ozone transport regions could also be required to comply with RACT and new source review under section 182(f). These requirements must be met in all areas in an ozone transport region regardless of their attainment status.

National Measures for Consumer or Commercial Products. EPA was required under section 183(e) to issue regulations for control of consumer and commercial products at the national level. On September 11, 1998, EPA adopted VOC emission standards for: (1) 24 categories of household consumer products ranging from bathroom and tile cleaners to hair mousse;[131] (2) automobile refinish coatings;[132] and (3) a variety of architectural coatings.[133] EPA was permitted to issue CTGs for consumer or commercial products in lieu of regulations if it determined they would be substantially as effective as regulations at reducing VOC emissions.[134] EPA has made this determination and issued CTGs for a variety of products.[135]

Consequences of the Failure by a Serious, Severe, or Extreme Area To Meet a Milestone or an Attainment Deadline. While marginal, moderate, and serious areas that fail to attain the ozone NAAQS will, as discussed above be "bumped up" to a higher classification, other remedies may be applied in severe and extreme ozone nonattainment areas. If they fail to attain by their attainment date, these areas must implement a fee program under section 185.[136] Until the NAAQS is attained, each major stationary source of VOCs in the area must pay an annual fee of $5,000 (adjusted upward for inflation) for each ton of VOC emitted by the source during the year in excess of 80 percent of a "baseline" amount of the lower of actual or allowable VOC emissions.[137] The fee provisions also may apply to major stationary sources of NOx under section 182(f).[138]

These areas—as well as areas classified as *serious*—also face sanctions if they fail to meet a milestone, as discussed above. For *serious and severe* areas, the state may elect to have the area "bumped up," to implement contingency measures adequate to meet the next milestone, or to adopt an economic incentive program.[139]

An *extreme* ozone nonattainment area that fails to meet a milestone is required to adopt such a program.[140]

SIP Revisions for CO Nonattainment Areas (Subpart 3 of Part D)

Classifications and Attainment Deadlines

CO nonattainment areas were classified according to statutory criteria upon enactment of the 1990 Amendments.[141] An area's classification and design value determine what requirements and control measures apply. *Serious* CO nonattainment areas must comply with the requirements for *moderate* areas as well as their own.

The attainment deadline for CO NAAQS is "as expeditiously as practicable," but no later than the following, for areas designated nonattainment at the time of enactment of the 1990 Amendments:[142]

Classification	Design Value (ppm)	Attainment Date
Moderate	9.1 to 16.4	December 31, 1995
Serious	16.5 and above	December 31, 2000

Up to two one-year deadline extensions are also available for CO nonattainment areas if all applicable requirements have been met and no more than one exceedance has occurred at any monitor in the year in which the area was to have attained.[143]

Required SIP Revisions

The following paragraphs outline the major SIP revisions required in CO nonattainment areas.

State Planning and Demonstration Requirements. States were required to submit a "comprehensive, accurate, current inventory" of actual emissions of CO in all CO nonattainment areas,[144] and to update the inventory every three years thereafter "until the area is redesignated to attainment . . . ."[145]

States with areas having a design value greater than 12.7 ppm were required to revise their SIP to provide for attainment of the CO NAAQS by the applicable attainment date and to specify annual emission reductions necessary to attain by that date, to require a forecast of VMT in the area for each year before the projected year of attainment, to require annual updates of that forecast, and to specify contingency measures that would take effect without further action by EPA or the state if actual VMT exceed the forecast or if the CO attainment date is not met.[146]

States with *serious* areas were required to demonstrate that they had achieved the specific emissions reductions required by a December 31, 1995 milestone and to implement an economic incentive or transportation control plan if they had not.[147] If stationary sources contributed significantly to CO levels in the area, states were also required to modify their definition of a "major source" to include any source with the potential to emit 50 tons or more per year of CO.[148]

Revisions Related to Mobile Sources

Motor Vehicle I/M Programs. States were required to make corrections to any previously required I/M program to assure compliance with existing EPA guidelines.[149] For areas with design values greater than 12.7 ppm, states were required to implement an "enhanced I/M" program that complies with the I/M requirements for *serious* ozone nonattainment areas but is aimed at reducing CO rather than hydrocarbon emissions.[150]

Clean-Fuel Vehicle Programs in Some Areas. States with certain highly populated CO nonattainment areas and design values of at least 16 ppm in 1988-1989 and in which mobile sources contribute significantly to CO nonattainment were to submit a SIP revision providing for a specific percentage of clean-fuel vehicles in centrally fueled fleets for each area covered by the clean-fuel vehicle program of Title II.[151] A centrally fueled fleet consists of 10 or more vehicles that are owned or operated by a single person and that are, or are capable of being, centrally fueled. Areas in which mobile sources do not contribute significantly to CO nonattainment were exempted.

Transportation Control Measures. States must submit provisions for each CO area classified as *serious* to comply with the TCMs required for *severe* ozone nonattainment areas, including the requirement for enforceable TCMs to offset growth in emissions and the employee trip reduction requirements, except that such provisions should be for the purpose of reducing CO emissions rather than VOC emissions.[152] Nonattainment areas that are also covered by the clean-fuel vehicle requirements of section 246 were required to implement all measures under section 108(f) (or achieve equivalent reductions) or explain why the reductions were not necessary for attainment.[153]

Oxygenated Gasoline. Sections 187(b)(3) and 211(m) of the Act require the use of oxygenated gasoline in certain CO nonattainment areas. Higher oxygen levels in gasoline promote more efficient combustion, thus reducing CO emissions. SIP revisions requiring oxygenated fuel were due by November 15, 1992.

Consequences of Failure To Meet a Milestone or an Attainment Deadline. Moderate CO nonattainment areas that fail to attain the standard by the relevant deadline are reclassified to serious as a matter of law.[154] Serious areas that failed to attain by the relevant deadline were required to adopt an economic incentive program sufficient, in combination with other elements of the plan, to reduce the total tonnage of CO emissions in the area by at least 5 percent per year in each year after approval of the revision, until attainment is reached.[155]

SIP Revisions for Particulate Matter Nonattainment Areas (Subpart 4 of Part D)

Classification and Attainment Deadlines

Prior to the 1990 Amendments, nonattainment designations had not been made with respect to the then current NAAQS for particulate matter, all of which used a PM_{10} indicator. Section 107(d)(4)(B) designated certain areas nonattainment for PM_{10} by operation of law. All of these areas were initially classified as *moderate*[156] and had an attainment deadline of December 31, 1994.[157] The Administrator was authorized to reclassify as *serious* any of these areas that EPA determined "cannot practicably attain" the PM_{10} NAAQS by that date.[158] These were given a new attainment date of December 31, 2001.[159] Areas subsequently designated as nonattainment were required to attain within six years, if classified as *moderate*, or within ten years, if classified as *serious*.[160]

Extensions of the attainment deadlines for *moderate* and *serious* areas are available, provided certain conditions are met.[161] In addition, the Administrator was permitted to waive a specific attainment date upon determining that non-manmade sources of PM_{10} "contribute significantly" to violation of the PM_{10} NAAQS in the area.[162]

Since the 1990 Amendments, EPA has added NAAQS using $PM_{2.5}$ as the indicator. EPA took the position that Subpart 4 did not apply to nonattainment areas for the $PM_{2.5}$ NAAQS. In January 2013, the D.C. Circuit held that the requirements of Subpart 4 apply to nonattainment areas for the NAAQS set in 1997 using a $PM_{2.5}$ indicator.[163] This decision likely means that the $PM_{2.5}$

NAAQS promulgated in 2006 and 2013 will also be implemented through Subpart 4.

Required SIP Revisions

States were required by November 15, 1991, to submit a SIP for each initial *moderate* PM_{10} nonattainment area that would provide for attainment by the applicable deadline,[164] or to demonstrate that attainment by such a deadline is "impracticable," thereby qualifying them for reclassification as *serious*.[165] The SIP was also required to include a new source permitting program for major stationary sources of PM_{10}[166] and to assure implementation of RACM for PM_{10} by December 10, 1993.[167] Finally, the SIP was required to contain quantitative milestones to be achieved every three years until the area was redesignated to attainment and to provide for demonstrations that those milestones were met.[168] Control requirements applicable to major stationary sources of PM_{10} were also to be applied to major stationary sources of PM_{10} precursors unless the Administrator determined that such sources did not contribute significantly to PM_{10} levels that exceeded the NAAQS.[169]

Areas reclassified as *serious* following their failure to attain were required to submit revised SIPs addressing additional requirements applicable to serious nonattainment areas within eighteen months of that reclassification.[170] Other areas receiving the *serious* classification had four years after their nonattainment designation to submit SIPs addressing the requirements.[171] In either case, these SIPs had to assure implementation of the *best* available control measures ("BACM") within four years of the *serious* classification.[172] Furthermore, the SIP was to define any stationary source or group of stationary sources located within a contiguous area as a "major source" or "major stationary source" if it had the potential to emit 70 tons per year of PM_{10}. The SIP was to include a modeled demonstration that it would provide for attainment by the applicable attainment date or, if attaining by that date would be "impracticable," provide for attainment "by the most expeditious alternative date practicable."[173]

Consequences of Failure To Meet a Milestone or an Attainment Deadline

States are required to submit a demonstration that a milestone specified in the SIP has been met within ninety days of the date of the milestone.[174] The Administrator must determine the adequacy of that demonstration within ninety days of its submission and if the milestone is not met, must require revision of the SIP within nine months to assure that the next milestone will be met or the NAAQS will be attained.[175]

Moderate PM_{10} nonattainment areas that fail to attain the standard by the relevant deadline are automatically reclassified to *serious*.[176] As noted above, they must submit a revised SIP addressing the requirements for serious nonattainment areas within eighteen months.[177]

The state in which a *serious* area fails to reach attainment by the applicable deadline must submit a revised SIP within twelve months of that failure.[178] This plan must provide for attainment of the PM_{10} NAAQS and for annual reductions in PM_{10} or PM_{10} precursor emissions within the area of not less than five percent until the NAAQS is attained.[179] An area that failed to demonstrate attainment of a milestone was required to submit a SIP revision that assured that the next milestone date would be attained of that attainment would be achieved if the attainment date was less than three years in the future.[180]

SIP Revisions for SO_2, NO_2, and Lead Nonattainment Areas (Subpart 5 of Part D)

The 1990 Amendments made few changes in SIP requirements for SO_2, NO_2, and lead. The amendments did specify, however, schedules for submission of SIPs under various circumstances. For example, the Amendments required that any state containing an area designated nonattainment for SO_2 or NO_2 that had a SIP that had not been fully approved was to submit to EPA by May 15, 1992, a plan meeting the requirements of Subpart 1 of Part D.[181] If a plan for SO_2 or NO_2 had been approved by EPA before enactment of the Amendments, but was subsequently determined by EPA to be inadequate, the state was required to submit a revised plan that provided for attainment within five years of EPA's determination of inadequacy.[182]

Given recent revisions of the SO_2, NO_2, and lead NAAQS, however, the implications of Subpart 5 have become more significant. Subpart 5 allows less time for the submission of SIPs for newly designated nonattainment areas than does Subpart 1 (which concerns nonattainment plans in general)—eighteen months compared to three years.[183] And, whereas other subparts of Part D specifically provide for attainment date extensions, Subpart 5 does not. It requires attainment "as expeditiously as practicable, but no later than 5 years from the date of the nonattainment designation."[184]

Procedural Requirements for SIPs

EPA Action on New or Revised SIPs

The 1990 Amendments enacted a new section 110(k), which sets out the requirements for EPA action on SIPs and revisions to SIPs that the states submit for approval. Section 110(k) required EPA to promulgate minimum criteria that a SIP or SIP revision submittal must meet to be deemed "complete."[185] Those criteria were promulgated in August 1991.[186] According to the Report of the House Committee on Energy and Commerce, the criteria are to apprise states of

EPA's concerns in objective terms at an early stage in the process, thereby avoiding delays in SIP approval.

Within 60 days of receiving a SIP or SIP revision, EPA is to determine whether the completeness criteria have been met. If, after six months, EPA has not determined whether the criteria have been met, the plan or revision is deemed complete.[187] If EPA determines during the six-month period that the plan or any part of the plan does not meet the completeness criteria, the state is treated as not having made the submission.[188]

Once a plan submission is deemed complete under the criteria, EPA must approve or disapprove the plan within 12 months.[189] A plan that meets all of the requirements of the Act will be approved in whole. If part of the plan does not meet the requirements, EPA may approve it in part and disapprove it in part. In addition, EPA may give conditional approval, contingent on the state adopting specific enforceable measures by a date certain no later than one year after the conditional approval.[190] If a state fails to make a required submission or makes a submission that EPA determines is incomplete, or if the Administrator disapproves a SIP submission in whole or in part, EPA must promulgate a FIP within two years. A FIP is not required if the state corrects the deficiency and obtains EPA approval of the SIP or SIP revision before EPA promulgates the FIP.[191]

Whenever EPA finds that a SIP is "substantially inadequate" to (1) attain or maintain a NAAQS, (2) mitigate interstate pollutant transport as described in the Act's interstate transport provisions (CAA §§ 176A and 184), or (3) comply with any other requirement of the Act, EPA is to issue a "SIP call." In a SIP call, EPA provides formal public notification to the state of the SIP deficiency and establishes a reasonable deadline for submission of SIP revisions. That deadline may not be later than 18 months after the notification to the state. EPA may adjust applicable deadlines as appropriate, except that attainment dates prescribed by the Act may not be adjusted unless the deadline has already passed.[192]

SIP revisions required for nonattainment areas in response to a finding by EPA of SIP inadequacy must correct the deficiency and satisfy all other applicable requirements of section 110 and Part D of Title I. To facilitate submittal of adequate and approvable plans, EPA is to issue, as appropriate, guidelines, interpretations, and information to the states and the public.[193]

A SIP revision must be approved by EPA unless the Agency determines that it would interfere with requirements for attainment, reasonable further progress toward attainment, or any other requirements of the Act.[194] EPA may make corrections to an approval, disapproval, or promulgation of a plan, or to an area designation or classification, without further submissions from the state. Corrections, along with their basis, must be provided to the state and announced to the public.[195]

If EPA revises a primary NAAQS in a way that makes the NAAQS less stringent, EPA must, within 12 months, promulgate emission control requirements for all areas that are nonattainment for that NAAQS. Notwithstanding the NAAQS relaxation, the new emission control requirements may not be less stringent than those in effect before the relaxation.[196]

Sanctions for Inadequate SIP Submittals or Implementation

If EPA finds that a state either has failed to submit an approvable SIP or SIP revision as required by the Act, or has failed to implement any requirement of an approved plan, EPA must impose certain sanctions on the state. Under section 179 of the Act, EPA may use two kinds of sanctions against states: (1) EPA may require the state to increase the emission offset ratio for new or modified major stationary sources to at least a 2-to-1 ratio[197]; and (2) EPA may cut off the state's federal highway funds (except for certain safety projects and certain other specific projects).[198] (EPA also may withhold federal grants for air pollution planning and control programs.[199]) In 1994, EPA published a rule on the timing and sequence of the sanctions.[200] Under the rule, once 18 months have passed since the state failure, the offset requirement is imposed. If the deficiency is not corrected after another 6 months, a highway-funds cut-off is imposed in addition to the offset provision. Sanctions are triggered in this sequence unless EPA decides in a case-specific rulemaking to alter it.[201] In addition, as discussed above, EPA must promulgate a FIP within two years of a state default pursuant to section 110(c)(1) of the Act.

EPA also is required by the Act to promulgate a rule to ensure that sanctions are not applied on a statewide basis if only one or more political subdivisions within the state are "principally responsible" for the deficiency.[202] In 1994, EPA published a final rule addressing this issue.[203]

Finally, if a state fails to comply with any requirement regarding new source review in a nonattainment area (including failure to submit an approvable program), EPA may ban construction or modification of any major stationary source in the area.[204]

Consequences of Failure To Meet Attainment Deadlines

EPA must determine whether an area has attained the NAAQS and publish the determination in the *Federal Register* as expeditiously as practicable, but not later than six months after the applicable attainment date. The determination is to be made based on the area's air quality as of the attainment date.[205] If the area has not achieved attainment, the state must submit a SIP revision within one year after EPA's publication of notice of its determination that includes all measures that EPA "may reasonably prescribe" and that "can be feasibly implemented in the [nonattainment] area in light of technological achievability, costs, and any nonair quality and other air quality-related health and environmental impacts."[206] The attainment deadline for such a revised SIP is as prescribed in section 172(a)(2) of the Act—*i.e.*, within 5 or 10 years (as determined by EPA), with 2 possible 1-year extensions—except that the attainment period is to be measured from the date of EPA's notice of failure to attain rather than from the nonattainment-area designation date.[207]

EPA Rules Addressing Interstate Transport

Since the mid-1990s, EPA has recognized that the interstate transport of pollutants is a significant factor in nonattainment in the Eastern United States. EPA promulgated a SIP call in October 1998 to address the contribution of interstate transport of ozone and ozone precursors to ozone nonattainment (the "NOx SIP Call"). This SIP call required 22 states and the District of Columbia to submit SIP revisions that would reduce emissions of NOx within their boundaries between May 1 and September 30 of each year (the "ozone season") to meet specific statewide NOx emissions budgets.[208] The NOx SIP Call permitted interstate trading as a way of meeting these budgets. The rule was largely upheld after a judicial challenge,[209] although the court extended the date for full implementation of control measures from May 1, 2003, to May 31, 2004.[210]

After adopting strict new NAAQS for ozone and $PM_{2.5}$ in 1997, EPA proposed to find that 29 states and the District of Columbia contributed significantly to nonattainment of either the 1997 ozone NAAQS or the 1997 $PM_{2.5}$ NAAQS, or both, in other states in the Eastern U.S. Based on this finding, EPA proposed to require that those states revise their SIPs to reduce such significant contributions, under a regional cap-and-trade program.[211] In 2005, EPA adopted the Clean Air Interstate Rule ("CAIR").[212]

CAIR, which was modeled on the NOx SIP Call, required reductions of SO_2 and NOx in 28 states and the District of Columbia.[213] The required reductions were to take pace in two phases, with the first phase requiring NOx emission reductions beginning in 2009 and SO_2 emission reductions beginning in 2010, and the second phase requiring additional reductions in both NOx and SO_2 reductions beginning in 2015. Most of the emissions reductions were expected to come from electric generating units. The rule includes an interstate trading program and allows banking of reductions that occur before the applicable deadlines. According to EPA, implementation of CAIR was expected, in and of itself, to bring several areas in attainment of the 1997 ozone and $PM_{2.5}$ NAAQS, and would make attaining those standards less expensive in the remaining nonattainment areas. Thus, EPA encouraged states to take credit for emission reductions related to CAIR in preparing their SIPs. When it adopted CAIR, EPA decided that the requirements of the NOx SIP Call would no longer apply after 2008.

CAIR was challenged by a number of parties, including the state of North Carolina. Although none of the petitioners advocated vacatur of the rule, on

July 11, 2008, the D.C. Circuit issued an opinion finding many problems with CAIR and vacating it.[214] Recognizing the disruptive effect of vacatur on state efforts to implement the ozone and $PM_{2.5}$ NAAQS, EPA asked for rehearing or rehearing *en banc* on the decision and, in particular, on the remedy. The court granted EPA's motion to the extent of remanding CAIR to EPA without vacating the rule: "[A]llowing CAIR to remain in effect until it is replaced by a rule consistent with our opinion would at least temporarily preserve the environmental values covered by CAIR."[215]

In 2011, EPA adopted the Cross-State Air Pollution Rule ("CSAPR") as a replacement for CAIR.[216] CSAPR required emissions reductions in 28 states, beginning in 2012.[217] At the same time, EPA issued FIPs for the included states that adopted the emission reductions required by CSAPR. EPA indicated that CSAPR would provide a template for future interstate air pollution rules if needed for future, more stringent NAAQS.

As had been the case for CAIR, numerous parties sought judicial review of CSAPR. On December 30, 2011, the D.C. Circuit took the unusual action of staying the rule and instructed EPA to continue to implement CAIR while it reviewed CSAPR.[218] On August 21, 2012, the court vacated both CSAPR and the FIPs implementing it and remanded them to EPA.[219] The court directed EPA to continue to administer CAIR until it had promulgated a valid rule to replace it. EPA sought review of the D.C. Circuit's opinion by the U.S. Supreme Court, and the Supreme Court granted review on June 24, 2013.[220] The case was argued on December 10, 2013.

Notes

1. EPA defines ambient air as "that portion of the atmosphere, external to buildings, to which the general public has access." 40 C.F.R. § 50.1(e). The Clean Air Act does not authorize regulation of indoor air quality.

2. CAA § 108(a)(1), 42 U.S.C. § 7408(a)(1).

3. *Id.* § 108(a)(2), 42 U.S.C. § 7408(a)(2). EPA used to call the document containing this information a "Criteria Document," but now calls it an Integrated Science Assessment ("ISA").

4. "PM10" and "PM2.5" refer to particles with aerodynamic diameters less than or equal to 10 and 2.5 micrometers, respectively.

5. CAA § 109(a), 42 U.S.C. § 7409(a).

6. *Id.* § 109(b), 42 U.S.C. § 7409(b).

7. *Id.* § 302(h), 42 U.S.C. § 7602(h).

8. The annual and 24-hour primary NAAQS for SOx will cease to apply in most areas one year after the effective date of designation for this NAAQS except in areas that are currently nonattainment for them or that are not meeting the requirements of a SIP call with respect to those NAAQS. Those areas must receive approval of a plan for attaining

and maintaining the 1-hour NAAQS before the annual and 24-hour NAAQS will no longer apply. 40 C.F.R. § 50.4(e).

9. This represents a revision of the 65 μg/m3 24-hour PM2.5 NAAQS, but that NAAQS has not been revoked.

10. This represents a revision of the primary 15 μg/m3 annual NAAQS, but that NAAQS has not been revoked.

11. Although the 1-hour ozone NAAQS have not been revoked, they have ceased to apply because a year has passed since designations of areas for these 8-hour NAAQS.

12. This represents a revision of the 0.08 ppm 8-hour average NAAQS, but that NAAQS has not been revoked. That NAAQS ceased to apply, however, for transportation conformity purposes on July 20, 2013, which was a year after the effective date of designations for the 0.075 ppb 8-hour NAAQS. *See* EPA, Air Quality Designations for the 2008 Ozone National Ambient Air Quality Standards for Several Counties in Illinois, Indiana, and Wisconsin; Corrections to Inadvertent Errors in Prior Designations; Final Rule, 77 Fed. Reg. 34,221 (June 11, 2012); EPA, Air Quality Designations for the 2008 Ozone National Ambient Air Quality Standards; Final Rule, 77 Fed. Reg. 30,088 (May 21, 2012).

13. The 1.5 μg/m3 lead NAAQS will cease to apply in most areas one year after the effective date of designation for this NAAQS except in areas that are currently nonattainment for lead. Those areas must receive approval of a plan for attaining and maintaining this NAAQS before the 1.5 μg/m3 lead NAAQS no longer applies.

14. CAA § 109(d), 42 U.S.C. § 7409(d).

15. *Id.* § 107(a), 42 U.S.C. § 7407(a) ("Each State shall have the primary responsibility for assuring air quality within the entire geographic area comprising such State by submitting an implementation plan for such State which will specify the manner in which national primary and secondary ambient air quality standards will be achieved and maintained within each air quality control region in such State.").

16. EPA has recently taken the position that the date of public distribution combined with signature of a final rule—not the date on which it is published in the *Federal Register* or its effective date—is the date of promulgation for purposes of interpreting Clean Air Act deadlines tied to promulgation. EPA, Extension of Deadline for Promulgating Designations for the 2010 Primary Sulfur Dioxide National Ambient Air Quality Standard, 77 Fed. Reg. 46,295, 46,295 n.1 (Aug. 3, 2012).

17. CAA § 107(d)(1)(A), 42 U.S.C. § 7407(d)(1)(A).

18. *Id.* § 107(d)(1)(B), 42 U.S.C. § 7407(d)(1)(B).

19. *Id.* § 107(d)(3), 42 U.S.C. § 7407(d)(3).

20. *Id.* § 110(a)(1), 42 U.S.C. § 7410(a)(1).

21. *Id.* § 110(a)(2), 42 U.S.C. § 7410(a)(2).

22. *See, e.g., Delaney v. EPA*, 898 F.2d 687, 689-92 (9th Cir. 1990).

23. CAA § 110(c)(1), 42 U.S.C. § 7410(c)(1) (requiring EPA to promulgate a FIP within two years after the state fails to submit a complete SIP or within two years after EPA disapproves a SIP submission, unless the state corrects the deficiency (and EPA approves a new SIP) before EPA promulgates the FIP).

24. EPA, *Infrastructure SIP Element Reports*, http://www.epa.gov/air quality/urbanair/sipstatus/infrastructure.html.

25. CAA § 110(a)(2)(A), 42 U.S.C. § 7410(a)(2)(A).

26. *Id.* § 110(a)(2)(B), 42 U.S.C. § 7410(a)(2)(B).

27. *Id.* § 110(a)(2)(C), 42 U.S.C. § 7410(a)(2)(C).

28. *Id.* § 110(a)(2)(D), 42 U.S.C. § 7410(a)(2)(D). Section 110(a)(2)(D) is one of the provisions on which EPA has relied for a series of regulatory programs addressing interstate transport of air pollutants. Those rules are discussed in Section III of this Chapter.

29. *Id.* § 110(a)(2)(E), 42 U.S.C. § 7410(a)(2)(E).

30. *Id.* § 110(a)(2)(F), 42 U.S.C. § 7410(a)(2)(F).

31. *Id.* § 110(a)(2)(G), 42 U.S.C. § 7410(a)(2)(G); *see also id.* § 303, 42 U.S.C. § 7603 (federal emergency enforcement authority).

32. *Id.* § 110(a)(2)(H), 42 U.S.C. § 7410(a)(2)(H); *see also id.* § 110(k)(5), 42 U.S.C. § 7410(a)(k)(5) (providing EPA's "SIP call" authority, *i.e.*, EPA authority to call for, or require, revisions to SIPs that EPA determines are substantially inadequate).

33. *Id.* § 110(a)(2)(I), 42 U.S.C. § 7410(a)(2)(I).

34. *Id.* § 110(a)(2)(K), 42 U.S.C. § 7410(a)(2)(K).

35. *Id.* § 110(a)(2)(L), 42 U.S.C. § 7410(a)(2)(L).

36. *Id.* § 110(a)(2)(M), 42 U.S.C. § 7410(a)(2)(M); *see also id.* § 121, 42 U.S.C. § 7421.

37. EPA, Criteria and Procedures for Determining Conformity to State or Federal Implementation Plans of Transportation Plans, Programs, and Projects Funded or Approved Under Title 23 U.S.C. or the Federal Transit Act; Final Rule, 58 Fed. Reg. 62,188 (Nov. 24, 1993).

38. EPA, Transportation Conformity Rule Restructuring Amendments; Final Rule, 77 Fed. Reg. 14,979 (Mar. 14, 2012) (codified at 40 C.F.R. §§ 93.101-119).

39. EPA, Determining Conformity of General Federal Actions to State or Federal Implementation Plans; Final Rule, 58 Fed. Reg.63,214, 63,247, 63,253 (Nov. 30, 1993) (codified, as amended, at 40 C.F.R. pt. 51, Subpart W & pt. 93, Subpart B).

40. EPA, Revisions to the General Conformity Regulations; Final Rule, 75 Fed. Reg. 17,254 (Apr. 5, 2010).

41. CAA § 507(a), 42 U.S.C. § 7661f(a).

42. *Id.* § 507(b), 42 U.S.C. § 7661f(b).

43. EPA, Guidelines for Implementation of Section 507 of the 1990 Clean Air Act Amendments: Final Guidelines (Jan. 1992), *available at* http://www.epa.gov/ttn/caaa/t5/memoranda/smbus.pdf.

44. CAA § 507(f)-(h), 42 U.S.C. § 7661f(f)-(h).

45. The principal visibility protection regulations under Part C are codified at 40 C.F.R. § 51.300 *et seq.* & 40 C.F.R. pt. 51, App. Y. Visibility protection is discussed in more detail in Chapter 6.

46. CAA § 110(a)(2)(J), 42 U.S.C. § 7410(a)(2)(J).

47. *Id.* § 172(a)(2)(A), 42 U.S.C. § 7502(a)(2)(A).

48. *Id.*

49. *Id.* § 172(a)(1)(A), 42 U.S.C. § 7502(a)(1)(A).

50. *Id.* § 172(a)(2)(C), 42 U.S.C. § 7502(a)(2)(C).

51. EPA published a "general preamble" and several supplements to it explaining the Agency's interpretations of the 1990 Amendments to Title I of the Act. EPA, State Implementation Plans; General Preamble for the Implementation of Title I of the Clean Air Act Amendments of 1990; General Preamble for Future Rulemakings, 57 Fed. Reg. 13,498 (Apr. 16, 1992); EPA, State Implementation Plans; General Preamble for the Implementation of Title I of the Clean Air Act Amendments of 1990; Supplemental; Gen-

eral Preamble for Future Proposed Rulemakings; Appendices, 57 Fed. Reg. 18,070 (Apr. 28, 1992); EPA, State Implementation Plans; Nitrogen Oxides Supplement to the General Preamble for the Implementation of Title I of the Clean Air Act Amendments of 1990; Supplement to the General Preamble for Future Proposed Rulemakings, 57 Fed. Reg. 55,620 (Nov. 25, 1992); EPA, State Implementation Plans for Lead Nonattainment Areas; Addendum to the General Preamble for the Implementation of Title I of the Clean Air Act Amendments of 1990; Addendum to General Preamble for Future Proposed Rulemakings, 58 Fed. Reg. 67,748 (Dec. 22, 1993); EPA, State Implementation Plans for Serious PM-10 Nonattainment Areas, and Attainment Date Waivers for PM-10 Nonattainment Areas Generally; Addendum to the General Preamble for the Implementation of Title I of the Clean Air Act Amendments of 1990; Addendum to General Preamble for Future Proposed Rulemakings, 59 Fed. Reg. 41,998 (Aug. 16, 1994).

52. CAA § 172(c), 42 U.S.C. § 7502(c).

53. *Id.* § 172(c)(1), 42 U.S.C. § 7502(c)(1).

54. *See Natural Res. Def. Council v. EPA*, 571 F.3d 1245, 1253 (D.C. Cir. 2009).

55. CAA § 171(1), 42 U.S.C. § 7501(1).

56. *Id.* § 172(c)(2), 42 U.S.C. § 7502(c)(2).

57. *Id.* § 172(c)(3), 42 U.S.C. § 7502(c)(3).

58. *Id.* §§ 172(c)(5), 173, 42 U.S.C. §§ 7502(c)(5), 7503.

59. *Id.* § 172(c)(4), 42 U.S.C. § 7502(c)(4).

60. *Id.* § 172(c)(9), 42 U.S.C. § 7502(c)(9).

61. *Id.* § 172(c)(8), 42 U.S.C. § 7502(c)(8).

62. 40 C.F.R. §§ 51.112(a), 51.166(l).

63. CAA § 165(e)(3)(D), 42 U.S.C. § 7475(e)(3)(D).

64. *Id.* § 320(a), 42 U.S.C. § 7620(a).

65. *See* EPA, Technology Transfer Network, Support Center for Regulatory Atmospheric Modeling, http://www.epa/gov/scram001/conferenceindex.htm.

66. 40 C.F.R. pt. 51, App. W.

67. *Alabama Power Co. v. Costle*, 636 F.2d 323, 383 (D.C. Cir. 1979).

68. *See* 40 C.F.R. § 50.9.

69. *See Whitman v. Am. Trucking Ass'ns*, 531 U.S. 457, 476-86 (2001).

70. Severe areas with a design value between 0.190 and 0.280 ppm have an attainment deadline of November 15, 2007. CAA § 181(a)(2), 42 U.S.C. § 7511(a)(2).

71. *Id.* § 181(a)(5), 42 U.S.C. § 7511(a)(5); *see also id.* § 181(a)(4), 42 U.S.C. § 7511(a)(4).

72. *Id.* § 181(b), 42 U.S.C. § 7511(b).

73. *Id.* § 181(b)(2), 42 U.S.C. § 7511(b)(2).

74. *Id.* § 181(b)(3), 42 U.S.C. § 7511(b)(3).

75. EPA determined that the 1-hour NAAQS would no longer apply to any area one year after the effective date of designations for the 8-hour standard. Thus, the Agency reasoned, it would not make findings of failure to attain for the 1-hour NAAQS and would not "bump-up" to a higher nonattainment classification for the 1-hour NAAQS under Subpart 2 of the Act. Similarly, redesignation of such 1-hour nonattainment areas to attainment would not be necessary. EPA, Final Rule to Implement the 8-Hour Ozone National Ambient Air Quality Standard—Phase 1; Final Rule, 69 Fed. Reg. 23,951 (Apr. 30, 2004).

76. *Id.* at 23,954, 23,997 (codified as 40 C.F.R. §§ 51.902(a) & 51.903(a)), 23,998 Table 1 (Apr. 30, 2004).

77. *Whitman*, 531 U.S. at 485.

78. EPA, Final Rule to Implement the 1997 8-Hour Ozone National Ambient Air Quality Standard: Classification of Areas That Were Initially Classified Under Subpart 1; Revision of the Anti-Backsliding Provisions to Address 1-Hour Contingency Measure Requirements; Deletion of Obsolete 1-Hour Ozone Standard Provision, 77 Fed. Reg. 28,424, 28,426 (May 14, 2012).

79. EPA, Implementation of the 2008 National Ambient Air Quality Standards for Ozone: Nonattainment Area Classifications Approach, Attainment Deadlines and Revocation of the 1997 Ozone Standards for Transportation Conformity Purposes; Final Rule,77 Fed. Reg. 30,160, 30,163 (May 21, 2012).

80. CAA § 182(a)(1), 42 U.S.C. § 7511a(a)(1). Emissions inventories were required two years after nonattainment designations for the 1997 8-hour NAAQS. 40 C.F.R. § 51.915.

81. CAA § 182(a)(3)(A), 42 U.S.C. § 7511a(a)(3)(A).

82. *Id.* § 182(b)(1)(A), 42 U.S.C. § 7511a(b)(1)(A). Certain ozone nonattainment areas may be treated as marginal areas despite a higher design value. If the EPA Administrator determines that sources of VOCs and NOx emissions in an ozone nonattainment area do not contribute significantly to the area's failure to meet the ozone NAAQS, EPA may designate the zone a rural transport area ("RTA") subject only to the SIP requirements applicable to marginal areas, regardless of air quality. *Id.* § 182(h), 42 U.S.C. § 7511a(h). According to EPA, an RTA that fails to meet the marginal area attainment deadline will be "bumped up" to the appropriate classification (with the extended deadline) but will still only be subject to the SIP requirements for marginal areas as long as it meets the requirements of an RTA. 57 Fed. Reg. at 13,506.

83. CAA § 182(b)(1), 42 U.S.C. § 7511a(b)(1).

84. *Id.* § 182(b)(1)(A)(ii), 42 U.S.C. § 7511a(b)(1)(A)(ii). Areas are only subject to the 15 percent RFP requirement one time. Newly designated nonattainment areas for the 1997 8-hour NAAQS must meet the Subpart 2 RFP requirements. RFP plans for newly-designated nonattainment areas are due within three years of that designation. EPA, Final Rule to Implement the 8-Hour Ozone National Ambient Air Quality Standard—Phase 2; Final Rule to Implement Certain Aspects of the 1990 Amendments Relating to New Source Review and Prevention of Significant Deterioration as They Apply in Carbon Monoxide, Particulate Matter and Ozone NAAQS; Final Rule for Reformulated Gasoline, 70 Fed. Reg. 71,612, 71,615-16 (Nov. 29, 2005).

85. 57 Fed. Reg. at 13,507, 13,509.

86. *Id.* at 13,502, 13,503-04.

87. *Id.* at 13,509.

88. *See* CAA § 182(b)(1)(B), (D), 42 U.S.C. § 7511a(b)(1)(B), (D).

89. *Id.* § 182(b)(1)(C), 42 U.S.C. § 7511a(b)(1)(C).

90. *Id.* § 182(c)(2)(B)(ii), 42 U.S.C. § 7511a(c)(2)(B)(ii).

91. *Id.* § 182(c)(2)(C), 42 U.S.C. § 7511a(c)(2)(C).

92. *Id.* § 182(b)(1)(A)(i), 42 U.S.C. § 7511a(b)(1)(A)(i). Attainment demonstrations for the 2008 8-hour NAAQS were due three years after an area was designated nonattainment. 70 Fed. Reg. at 71,615.

93. CAA § 182(c)(2)(A), 42 U.S.C. § 7511a(c)(2)(A).

94. *Id.* § 182(g)(1), 42 U.S.C. § 7511a(g)(1). EPA initially established 2002 as the baseline year for milestones with regard to Subpart 2 nonattainment areas for the 1997 8-

hour ozone NAAQS, 70 Fed. Reg. at 71,638, meaning that the first milestone compliance date for nonattainment areas for the 1997 8-hour NAAQS was 2008. When EPA determined that additional areas were also subject to Subpart 2 implementation requirements, none of those areas were classified as serious or above, meaning that they were not required to demonstrate compliance with milestones.

95. CAA § 182(g)(2), 42 U.S.C. § 7511a(g)(2).

96. *Id.* § 182(c)(5), 42 U.S.C. § 7511a(g)(5).

97. *Id.* § 172(c)(9), 42 U.S.C. § 7502(c)(9).

98. EPA, Ambient Air Quality Surveillance; Final Rule, 58 Fed. Reg. 8452 (Feb. 12, 1993). These rules were substantially revised in 2006. EPA, Revisions to Ambient Air Monitoring Regulations; Final Rule, 71 Fed. Reg. 61,236 (Oct. 17, 2006).

99. CAA § 182(a)(3)(B)(i), 42 U.S.C. § 7511a(a)(3)(B)(i). For 1997 8-hour ozone nonattainment areas, these emission statements are to be submitted within two years of the nonattainment designation. 70 Fed. Reg. at 71,702 (as codified under 40 C.F.R. § 51.915).

100. CAA § 182(a)(3)(B)(ii), 42 U.S.C. § 7511a(a)(3)(B)(ii).

101. *Id.* § 182(a)(2)(C), 42 U.S.C. § 7511a(a)(2)(C).

102. Requirements under Subpart 2 of Part D for major stationary sources of VOCs are also generally applicable to major stationary sources of NOx. The Administrator, however, may, under specified conditions, determine that the requirement for control of NOx emissions should not apply to or should be limited in a given area. *Id.* § 182(f), 42 U.S.C. § 7511a(f).

103. *Id.* § 182, 42 U.S.C. § 7511a.

104. *Id.* § 182(d)(2), (e)(1), 42 U.S.C. § 7511a(d)(2), (e)(1).

105. *See id.* § 182(c)(6), (7), (8), (e)(2), 42 U.S.C. § 7511a(c)(6), (7), (8), (e)(2).

106. *Id.* § 182(a)(2)(A), 42 U.S.C. § 7511a(a)(2)(A).

107. *Id.* § 182(b)(2), 42 U.S.C. § 7511a(b)(2).

108. *Id.* § 182(e)(3), 42 U.S.C. § 7511a(e)(3).

109. These requirements also apply to Subpart 2 nonattainment areas. 70 Fed. Reg. at 71,619.

110. CAA §§ 182(a)(2)(B), 187(a)(4), 42 U.S.C. §§ 7511a(a)(2)(B), 7512a(a)(4). A similar requirement applied to CO nonattainment areas that were classified as *moderate or serious. Id.* § 187(a)(4), 42 U.S.C. § 7512a(a)(4).

111. *Id.* § 182(b)(4), 42 U.S.C. § 7511a(b)(4).

112. *Id.* § 182(c)(3)(A), 42 U.S.C. § 7511a(c)(3)(A).

113. *Id.* § 182(c)(3)(B)-(C), 42 U.S.C. § 7511a(c)(3)(B)-(C). This enhanced I/M requirement also applies in CO nonattainment areas *with design values greater than 12.7 ppm* (*i.e.*, all serious and some moderate CO nonattainment areas), although programs in those areas must be designed to reduce CO emissions. *Id.* § 187(a)(6), 42 U.S.C. § 7512a(a)(6).

114. EPA, Control of Air Pollution From New Motor Vehicles and New Motor Vehicle Engines; Refueling Emission Regulations for Light-Duty Vehicles and Light-Duty Trucks; Final Rule, 59 Fed. Reg. 16,262 (Apr. 6, 1994).

115. CAA § 202(a)(6), 42 U.S.C. § 7521(a)(6).

116. EPA, Air Quality: Widespread Use for Onboard Refueling Vapor Recovery and Stage II Waiver; Final Rule, 77 Fed. Reg. 28,772, 28,772 (May 16, 2012).

117. CAA §§ 182(c)(4)(A), 246(a)(2)(A) & (3), 42 U.S.C. §§ 7511a(c)(4)(A), 7586(a)(2)(A) & (3).

118. *Id.* § 182(d)(1)(A), 42 U.S.C. § 7511a(d)(1)(A).

119. *Id.* § 182(c)(5), 42 U.S.C. § 7511a(c)(5).

120. *Ass'n of Irritated Residents v. EPA*, 686 F.3d 668, 679-81 (9th Cir. 2011).

121. EPA, EPA-420-B-12-053, Implementing Clean Air Act Section 182(d)(1)(A): Transportation Control Measures and Transportation Control Strategies to Offset Growth in Emissions Due to Growth in Vehicle Miles Travelled (Aug. 2012), *available at* http://www.epa.gov/otaq/stateresources/ policy/general/420b12053.pdf.

122. CAA § 211(k)(5), 42 U.S.C. § 7545(k)(5).

123. Transportation & Air Quality – RFG Areas, EPA, http://www.epa.gov/otaq/fuels/gasolinefuels/rfg/areas.htm (listings of those areas requiring reformulated gasoline).

124. CAA § 211(k)(6), 42 U.S.C. § 7545(k)(6).

125. EPA, Final Rule on Ozone Transport Commission; Low Emission Vehicle Program for the Northeast Ozone Transport Region, 60 Fed. Reg. 4712, 4727 (Jan. 24, 1995).

126. *See, e.g., Motor Vehicle Mfrs. Ass'n v. New York State Dep't of Envtl. Conservation*, 79 F.3d 1298 (2d Cir. 1996); *Am. Auto. Mfrs. Ass'n v. Comm'r of Massachusetts Dep't of Envtl. Prot.*, 31 F.3d 18 (1st Cir. 1994); *Motor Vehicle Mfrs. Ass'n v. New York State Dep't of Envtl. Conservation*, 17 F.3d 521 (2d Cir. 1994).

127. 60 Fed. Reg. at 4712.

128. *Virginia v. EPA*, 108 F.3d 1397, 1415 (D.C. Cir.), *modified on other grounds,* 116 F.3d 499 (D.C. Cir. 1997).

129. EPA, Control of Air Pollution from New Motor Vehicles and New Motor Vehicle Engines: State Commitments to National Low Emission Vehicle Program; Final Rule, 63 Fed. Reg. 926 (Jan. 7, 1998).

130. EPA, Control of Air Pollution from New Motor Vehicles and New Motor Vehicle Engines: Finding of National Low Emission Vehicle Program in Effect, 63 Fed. Reg. 11,374 (Mar. 9, 1998).

131. EPA, National Volatile Organic Compound Emission Standards for Consumer Products; Final Rule, 63 Fed. Reg. 48,819 (Sept. 11, 1998) (codified at Subpart C of 40 C.F.R. pt. 59).

132. EPA, National Volatile Organic Compound Emission Standards for Automobile Refinish Coatings; Final Rule, 63 Fed. Reg. 48,806 (Sept. 11, 1998) (codified at Subpart B of 40 C.F.R. pt. 59).

133. EPA, National Volatile Organic Compound Emission Standards for Architectural Coatings; Final Rule, 63 Fed. Reg. 48,848 (Sept. 11, 1998) (codified at Subpart D of 40 C.F.R. pt. 59).

134. CAA § 183(e)(3)(C), 42 U.S.C. § 7511b(e)(3)(C).

135. EPA, Consumer and Commercial Products, Group IV: Control Techniques Guidelines in Lieu of Regulations for Miscellaneous Metal Products Coatings, Plastic Parts Coatings, Auto and Light-Duty Truck Assembly Coatings, Fiberglass Boat Manufacturing Materials, and Miscellaneous Industrial Adhesives; Final Rule; Notice of Final Determination and Availability of Final Control Techniques Guidelines, 73 Fed. Reg. 58,481 (Oct. 7, 2008); EPA, Consumer and Commercial Products: Control Techniques Guidelines in Lieu of Regulations for Paper, Film, and Foil Coatings; Metal Furniture Coatings; and Large Appliance Coatings; Final Rule; Notice of Final Determination and Availability of Final Control Techniques Guidelines, 72 Fed. Reg. 57,215 (Oct. 9, 2007);

EPA, Consumer and Commercial Products, Group II: Control Techniques Guidelines in Lieu of Regulations for Flexible Packaging Printing Materials, Lithographic Printing Materials, Letterpress Printing Materials, Industrial Cleaning Solvents, and Flat Wood Paneling Coatings; Notice of Final Determination and Availability of Final Control Techniques Guidelines, 71 Fed. Reg. 58,745 (Oct. 5, 2006).

136. CAA §§ 181(b)(4)(A), 185, 42 U.S.C. §§ 7511(b)(4)(A), 7511d.

137. *Id.* § 185(b), 42 U.S.C. § 7511d(b).

138. The Act provides an exemption for nonattainment areas with a population of less than 200,000 that demonstrate that attainment is prevented by transport of ozone or ozone precursors from other areas. *Id.* § 185(e), 42 U.S.C. § 7511d(e).

139. *Id.* § 182(g)(3), 42 U.S.C. § 7511a(g)(3). EPA's regulations concerning such Economic Incentive Programs are codified at 40 C.F.R. pt. 51, Subpart U.

140. *Id.* § 182(g)(5), 42 U.S.C. § 7511a(g)(5).

141. *Id.* § 186(a)(1), 42 U.S.C. § 7512(a)(1).

142. *Id.*

143. *Id.* § 186(a)(4), 42 U.S.C. § 7512(a)(4).

144. *Id.* § 187(a)(1), 42 U.S.C. § 7512a(a)(1).

145. *Id.* § 187(a)(5), 42 U.S.C. § 7512a(a)(5).

146. *Id.* § 187(a)(2)(A), (3), (7), 42 U.S.C. § 7512a(a)(2)(A), (3), (7).

147. *Id.* § 187(d), 42 U.S.C. § 7512a(d).

148. *Id.* § 187(c)(1), 42 U.S.C. § 7512a(c)(1).

149. *Id.* § 187(a)(4), 42 U.S.C. § 7512a(a)(4).

150. *Id.* § 187(a)(6), 42 U.S.C. § 7512a(a)(6).

151. *Id.* § 246, 42 U.S.C. § 7586.

152. *Id.* § 187(b)(2), 42 U.S.C. § 7512a(b)(2).

153. *Id.*

154. *Id.* § 186(b)(2)(A), 42 U.S.C. § 7512(b)(2)(A).

155. *Id.* § 187(g), 42 U.S.C. § 7512a(g).

156. *Id.* § 188(a), 42 U.S.C. § 7513(a).

157. *Id.* § 188(c)(1), 42 U.S.C. § 7513(c)(1).

158. *Id.* § 188(b), 42 U.S.C. § 7513(b).

159. *Id.* § 188(c)(2), 42 U.S.C. § 7513(c)(2).

160. *Id.* § 188(c), 42 U.S.C. § 7513(c).

161. *Id.* § 188(d), (e), 42 U.S.C. § 7513(d), (e).

162. *Id.* § 188(f), 42 U.S.C. § 7513(f).

163. *Natural Res. Def. Council v. EPA*, 706 F.3d 428, 433-37 (D.C. Cir. 2013).

164. CAA § 189(a)(2)(A), 42 U.S.C. § 7513a(a)(2)(A). SIPs are required for later-designated moderate nonattainment areas within eighteen months of that designation. *Id.* § 189(a)(2), 42 U.S.C. § 7513a(a)(2).

165. *Id.* §§ 188(b)(1), 189(a)(1)(B), 42 U.S.C. §§ 7513(b)(1), 7513a(a)(1)(B).

166. *Id.* § 189(a)(1)(A), 42 U.S.C. § 7513a(a)(1)(A).

167. *Id.* § 189(a)(1)(C), 42 U.S.C. § 7513a(a)(1)(C). Areas that were designated nonattainment for PM10 later had to implement RACM within four years after the nonattainment designation.

168. *Id.* § 189(c), 42 U.S.C. § 7513a(c).

169. *Id.* § 189(e), 42 U.S.C. § 7513a(e).

170. *Id.* § 189(b)(2), 42 U.S.C. § 7513a(b)(2).

171. *Id.*

172. *Id.* § 189(b)(1)(B), 42 U.S.C. § 7513a(b)(1)(B). EPA was required to issue technical guidance on RACM and BACM within eighteen months to three years after November 15, 1990, depending on category of the source of PM10. *Id.* § 190, 42 U.S.C. § 7513b.

173. *Id.* § 189(b)(1)(A), (3), 42 U.S.C. § 7513a(b)(1)(A), (3).

174. *Id.* § 189(c)(2), 42 U.S.C. § 7513a(c)(2).

175. *Id.* § 189(c)(2), (3), 42 U.S.C. § 7513a(c)(2), (3).

176. *Id.* § 188(b)(2), 42 U.S.C. § 7513(b)(2).

177. *Id.*

178. *Id.* § 189(d), 42 U.S.C. § 7513a(d).

179. *Id.*

180. *Id.* § 189(c)(3), 42 U.S.C. § 7513a(c)(3).

181. *Id.* § 191(b), 42 U.S.C. § 7514(b).

182. *Id.* § 192(c), 42 U.S.C. § 7514a(c).

183. *Compare id.* § 191(a), 42 U.S.C. § 7514(a), *with id.* § 172(b), 42 U.S.C. § 7502(b).

184. *Compare id.* § 192(a), 42 U.S.C. § 7514a(a), *with id.* §§ 172(a)(2), 42 U.S.C. § 7502(a)(2) (allowing an extension for a period no great than 10 years from the data of designation and for two possible extension years), 181(a)(5), 42 U.S.C. § 7511(a)(5) (providing for two possible one-year extensions).

185. *Id.* § 110(k)(1)(A), 42 U.S.C. § 7410(k)(1)(A).

186. EPA, State Implementation Plan Completeness Criteria; Final Rulemaking, 56 Fed. Reg. 42,216 (Aug. 26, 1991).

187. CAA § 110(k)(1)(B), 42 U.S.C. § 7410(k)(1)(B).

188. *Id.* § 110(k)(1)(C), 42 U.S.C. § 7410(k)(1)(C).

189. *Id.* § 110(k)(2), 42 U.S.C. § 7410(k)(2).

190. *Id.* § 110(k)(3), (4), 42 U.S.C. § 7410(k)(3), (4).

191. *Id.* § 110(c)(1), 42 U.S.C. § 7410(c)(1).

192. *Id.* §§ 110(k)(5), 172(d), 42 U.S.C. §§ 7410(k)(5), 7502(d).

193. *Id.* § 172(d), 42 U.S.C. § 7502(d).

194. *Id.* § 110(*l*), 42 U.S.C. § 7410(*l*).

195. *Id.* § 110(k)(6), 42 U.S.C. § 7410(k)(6).

196. *Id.* § 172(e), 42 U.S.C. § 7502(e).

197. *Id.* § 179(b)(2), 42 U.S.C. § 7509(b)(2).

198. *Id.* § 179(b)(1), 42 U.S.C. § 7509(b)(1).

199. *Id.* § 179(a), 42 U.S.C. § 7509(a).

200. EPA, Selection of Sequence of Mandatory Sanctions for Findings Made Pursuant to Section 179 of the Clean Air Act; Final Rule, 59 Fed. Reg. 39,832 (Aug. 4, 1994) (codified at 40 C.F.R. § 52.31).

201. If EPA finds that the state has not acted in good faith, EPA is to apply both the offset and highway funding sanctions at the 18-month point. CAA § 179(a), 42 U.S.C. § 7509(a).

202. *Id.* § 110(m), 42 U.S.C. § 7410(m).

203. EPA, EPA, Criteria for Exercising Discretionary Sanctions Under Title I of the Clean Air Act; Final Rule 59 Fed. Reg. 1476 (Jan. 11, 1994) (codified at 40 C.F.R. § 52.30).

204. CAA § 113(a)(5), 42 U.S.C. § 7413(a)(5).

205. *Id.* § 179(c), 42 U.S.C. § 7509(c).

206. *Id.* § 179(d)(2), 42 U.S.C. § 7509(d)(2).

207. *Id.* § 179(d)(3), 42 U.S.C. § 7509(d)(3).

208. EPA, Finding of Significant Contribution and Rulemaking for Certain States in the Ozone Transport Assessment Group Region for Purposes of Reducing Regional Transport of Ozone; Final Rule, 63 Fed. Reg. 57,356, 57,456 (Oct. 27, 1998). The jurisdictions for which NOx emissions budgets were established were Alabama, Connecticut, Delaware, the District of Columbia, Georgia, Illinois, Indiana, Kentucky, Massachusetts, Maryland, Michigan, Missouri, North Carolina, New Jersey, New York, Ohio, Pennsylvania, Rhode Island, South Carolina, Tennessee, Virginia, West Virginia, and Wisconsin.

209. *Michigan v. EPA*, 213 F.3d 663 (D.C. Cir. 2000). The rule was vacated and remanded, however, with regard to Wisconsin, Missouri, and Georgia.

210. *Michigan v. EPA*, No. 98-1497, 2000 WL 1341477, at *1 (D.C. Cir. Aug. 30, 2000).

211. EPA, Rule To Reduce Interstate Transport of Fine Particulate Matter and Ozone (Interstate Air Quality Rule); Proposed Rule, 69 Fed. Reg. 4566 (Jan. 30, 2004); EPA, Supplemental Proposal for the Rule to Reduce Interstate Transport of Fine Particulate Matter and Ozone (Clean Air Interstate Rule); Supplemental Notice of Proposed Rulemaking, 69 Fed. Reg. 32,684 (June 10, 2004).

212. EPA, Rule To Reduce Interstate Transport of Fine Particulate Matter and Ozone (Clean Air Interstate Rule); Revisions to Acid Rain Program; Revisions to the NOx SIP Call; Final Rule, 70 Fed. Reg. 25,162 (May 12, 2005).

213. The states are Alabama, Arkansas, Connecticut, Delaware, Florida, Georgia, Illinois, Indiana, Iowa, Kentucky, Louisiana, Maryland, Massachusetts, Michigan, Minnesota, Mississippi, Missouri, New Jersey, New York, North Carolina, Ohio, Pennsylvania, South Carolina, Tennessee, Texas, Virginia, West Virginia, and Wisconsin. Some of the states are covered only for emissions of either SO2 or NOx.

214. *North Carolina v. EPA*, 531 F.3d 896, 900, 929-30 (D.C. Cir. 2008).

215. *North Carolina v. EPA*, 550 F.3d 1176, 1178 (D.C. Cir. 2008).

216. EPA, Federal Implementation Plans: Interstate Transport of Fine Particulate Matter and Ozone and Correction of SIP Approvals; Final Rule, 76 Fed. Reg. 48,202 (Aug. 8, 2011).

217. The states subject to CSAPR are Alabama, Arkansas, Florida, Georgia, Illinois, Indiana, Iowa, Kansas, Kentucky, Louisiana, Maryland, Michigan, Minnesota, Mississippi, Missouri, Nebraska, New Jersey, New York, North Carolina, Ohio, Oklahoma, Pennsylvania, South Carolina, Tennessee, Texas, Virginia, West Virginia, and Wisconsin. Some of the states are included for only their NOx or SO2 emissions.

218. *EME Homer City Generation LP v. EPA*, No. 11-1302 (D.C. Cir. Dec. 30, 2011) (order granting motions for stay).

219. *EME Homer City Generation LP v. EPA*, 696 F.3d 7 (D.C. Cir. 2012), *cert. granted* 133 S. Ct. 2857 (2013).

220. *EPA v. EME Homer City Generation, L.P.*, 133 S. Ct. 2857 (2013).

Chapter 3

CONTROL TECHNOLOGY REGULATION

The Clean Air Act provides for two types of air pollution control measures: (1) ambient air quality-based emission standards designed to protect public health and welfare; and (2) control technology-based emission standards designed to preserve air quality and to ensure the use of advanced emission controls.

As discussed in Chapter 2, both existing and new sources of air pollution are subject to the ambient air quality-based program through the national ambient air quality standards ("NAAQS") established by EPA and the state implementation plan ("SIP") program.

By contrast, the Clean Air Act contains a general control technology program only for *new* sources of air pollution. The "new source performance standard" ("NSPS") program authorizes establishment of emission standards for categories or subcategories of major "new," "modified," or "reconstructed" sources, based upon the capabilities of "best adequately demonstrated control technology," taking into account economic, energy, and non-air quality environmental factors.

In addition to the NSPS program, the Act requires development of source-specific control technology standards for new and modified sources of air pollution through a preconstruction permit program. This new source permitting program imposes control technology requirements of varying stringency, depending upon whether the source is to be located in an area that attains or that does not attain the NAAQS (*i.e.*, in an "attainment" or a "nonattainment" area). In attainment areas, this control technology requirement is referred to as "best available control technology" ("BACT"). In nonattainment areas, it is referred to as "lowest achievable emission rate" ("LAER"), or the lowest rate achieved by any source in the same or a similar source category.

Although the Clean Air Act does not establish a national control technology program for existing sources, existing sources may nonetheless be subject to specific control technology provisions that address special pollution problems. In nonattainment areas, for example, existing sources of a nonattainment pollutant may be required to install "reasonably available control technology" ("RACT") to ensure progress toward attainment of the NAAQS. In areas close to larger national parks and wilderness areas (referred to as "mandatory Class I areas"), existing sources that contribute to visibility impairment may be required to install "best available retrofit technology" ("BART"), which is described in Chapter 6. Under section 111(d), EPA has claimed authority to establish guidelines for performance standards for existing sources of air pollutants subject to regulation under the NSPS program, but for which a NAAQS has not been set or where the source category is not already regulated under section 112. Finally, the 1990 Amendments created a control technology-based regulatory program for new and existing stationary sources of hazardous air pollutants, which is described in Chapter 5.

This chapter focuses first on the generally applicable new source control technology requirements of the Act – *i.e.*, the NSPS, BACT, and LAER requirements. It then discusses the circumstances under which existing sources of air pollution may become subject to these new source control technology requirements under the "reconstruction" and "modification" rules. Finally, this chapter summarizes other control technology requirements that may apply in specific cases to existing sources that contribute to specific pollution problems.

Control Technology Requirements for New Sources

New Source Performance Standards

In enacting the 1970 and 1977 Amendments to the Act, Congress expressed concern that retrofitting existing sources with state-of-the-art control technologies could be prohibitively expensive. Congress concluded that it would be far more cost-effective to require such technologies at new sources, which have more flexibility with respect to location and design than do existing sources.[1]

Under section 111 of the Act, Congress required the EPA Administrator to identify categories of new and modified sources that contribute significantly to air pollution that endangers public health or welfare. To date, EPA has identified about 80 such source categories, including most major industrial processes. A list of these source categories appears in Appendix 2 of this Handbook.

For these source categories, EPA has set emission standards that reflect the "degree of emission limitation achievable" through the best technology or system of emission reduction that the Agency determines has been "adequately demonstrated," taking into consideration "nonair quality health and environmental impact and energy requirements."[2] These standards appear at 40 C.F.R. Part 60. Where numerical emission limitations are not feasible, these NSPS may be promulgated as design, equipment, work practice, or operational standards.[3]

NSPS apply to facilities on which construction (or "reconstruction") is commenced after proposal of the emission standards, or which are "modified" after the date of proposal. The terms "modification" and "reconstruction" are by no means simple to apply, and are discussed at length in section II of this chapter. Once set, NSPS serve as the *minimum* level of control that can be required through the control technology requirements of the new source preconstruction permitting program.

NSPS must be reviewed at least every eight years and, if appropriate, revised through notice and comment rulemaking.[4] Although EPA has often failed to revise the NSPS as frequently as mandated by the Act, it nevertheless has done so often enough that technology requirements tend to become more stringent as new technologies are developed and existing technologies improved.

The 1990 Amendments mandated several revisions to specific NSPS. For example, section 403 of the 1990 Amendments repealed section 111(a)(1) of the Act, which included a percentage reduction requirement for sulfur dioxide ("SO_2") emissions from large fossil fuel-fired boilers, and instead required EPA to set specific emission limits. In 1998, EPA finalized rules to revise the NSPS only for NOx emissions from those sources.[5] In 2006 and again in 2012 the Agency revised the NSPS for NOx, set an emission limit for SO_2, and revised the NSPS for particulate matter.[6]

The 1990 Amendments imposed new regulatory schedules for source categories that were listed but not regulated under section 111 prior to enactment of the 1990 Amendments.[7] EPA's priority list of source categories for NSPS development appears at 40 C.F.R. § 60.16. This list includes a variety of chemical manufacturing, mineral processing, and other industrial source categories.

New Source Permits and Control Technology Review

As noted above, the NSPS program sets a minimum level of control for new and modified sources of air pollution. More stringent control may be required under either the prevention of significant deterioration ("PSD") or the nonattainment preconstruction permitting programs. These source-specific control technology requirements are discussed below.

The Best Available Control Technology Standard

Pursuant to the 1977 Amendments to the Clean Air Act,[8] an applicant for a PSD permit must show that the proposed source will employ BACT for each regulated pollutant that it emits in significant amounts. According to the Act and EPA's regulations, BACT limits are to be determined on a case-by-case basis after taking into account energy, environmental, and economic impacts and other costs.[9] As Congress has explained, "[t]he weight assigned to such factors is to be determined by the State. . . . Flexibility and State judgment are the foundations" of BACT determinations.[10] In making a BACT determination, therefore, the permitting authority should consider both environmental and economic factors, including "the size of the plant, the increment of air quality which will be absorbed by any particular major emitting facility, and such other considerations as anticipated and desired economic growth for the area."[11]

In a contemporaneous interpretation of the Act, EPA's 1978 Guidelines for Determining Best Available Control Technology state that the decision regarding how much weight should be assigned to energy, environmental, and economic factors should be made by the state. This will "allow[ ] some flexibility in emission control requirements depending on local energy, environmental and economic conditions and local preferences."[12]

Similarly, EPA's 1980 Prevention of Significant Deterioration Manual embraces a flexible balancing approach to making BACT determinations.[13] The manual makes clear that where the environmental benefits of additional controls are negligible but the economic or energy costs of additional controls are significantly greater, BACT does not require application of the most stringent level of control.[14]

Since 1987, EPA has sought to limit the discretion of state permitting agencies to balance the statutory criteria in making BACT determinations.[15] The result has been a fundamental change in the approach taken to specifying the control technologies that PSD permit applicants must consider for proposed sources. EPA developed a "top-down" approach to BACT such that if a specific level of control is *not* technically or economically infeasible, it is BACT. This approach, if rigidly applied, would equate the BACT determination with the more stringent LAER determinations, which, as discussed below, are required only for major new or modified sources in nonattainment areas.

In March 1990, EPA's Office of Air Quality Planning and Standards ("OAQPS") finished a draft of a Top-Down Best Available Control Technology Guidance Document ("Guidance Document") and sent this draft document to each of the EPA regional offices and states.[16] The draft Guidance Document addresses virtually every aspect of BACT review. For example, the draft guidance purports to: (1) establish procedures for determining the range of technologies that a PSD permit applicant (and permit-issuing agency) must consider in a BACT demonstration; (2) define a control technique to be "applicable" and worthy of BACT consideration if it has been used anywhere else, or even if someone has simply agreed to use it somewhere else; and (3) specify how to calculate the cost of various control technologies (*i.e.*, dollars per ton of pollutant removed) in a way that is designed to reduce control cost estimates in making a BACT decision.

Although the draft (and never finalized) Guidance Document states that it is not binding, many states have signed PSD delegation agreements that require them to follow the top-down approach. Even in states with approved PSD SIPs, EPA may take action to persuade states to implement Agency policies "voluntarily," *e.g.*, by conditioning federal grant money on state implementation of EPA policies. The result has been relatively widespread adherence to the top-down policy.

BACT determinations are subject to public comment. For most large proposed new sources, environmental advocacy groups often claim that the permit limits do not reflect BACT, and file appeals based on those comments. The state or local permit authorities are required to respond in detail. As a result, the permitting process can be extended by years – even for facilities whose developers have agreed to install state-of-the-art emission control technology.

In conducting a case-by-case BACT analysis, the permitting agency must consider site-specific and source-specific characteristics, such as the type of fuel that will be used (*e.g.*, eastern bituminous coal versus Powder River Basin coal), the type of source (*e.g.*, pulverized coal boiler versus natural gas-fired turbine), and geographic considerations (*e.g.*, water availability). Consequently, there is no such thing as presumptive BACT for a proposed source, and case-by-case BACT analyses do not necessarily yield a single, independently-correct BACT determination.[17] The permitting agency must exercise a high degree of technical judgment in any BACT analysis, particularly for coal-fired plants, which utilize a wide variety of coals, facilities, and other site-specific factors.

EPA's Environmental Appeals Board ("EAB") has found that BACT does not necessarily have to be the lowest limit reported, emphasizing the case-by-case nature of the determination:

> [The] Petition [contains] a compilation of one-page printouts from the RBL Clearinghouse showing the CO [carbon monoxide] limits for 14 facilities with CO limits ranging from 7.4 ppmvd to 25 ppmvd. We first note that the [Illinois Environmental Protection Agency's ("IEPA's")] determination falls within this range, albeit at the top-end of the range. . . . Although this emission limit may be somewhat lower than the limit set by IEPA in the present case, it does not show clear error in IEPA's decision . . . . [Thus, the] Petition actually demon-

strates that IEPA's CO limit in this case is consistent with other similar permitting decisions.[18]

The permitting agency determines what is achievable for a source, exercising its technical judgment on a case-by-case basis. "Achievable" means an emission limit that the source can meet on a continual basis over each averaging period for the lifetime of the facility. The penalties for noncompliance with a permitted BACT limit are severe. When establishing a BACT limit, the permitting agency should account for the permittee's obligation to meet the limit on a continual basis to avoid an enforcement action. BACT limits are therefore not established based on what a source can achieve on its best possible day. BACT limits should reflect what the source can achieve throughout its lifetime under all reasonably foreseeable conditions. It is appropriate to include "safety factors" or "cushions" (*e.g.*, emissions averaging times) to ensure that BACT limits are achievable at all times.

The EAB has repeatedly supported the use of a safety factor to allow the permittee to be able to achieve compliance consistently:

> When [EPA] prescribes an emissions limitation representing BACT, the limitation does not necessarily reflect the highest possible control efficiency achievable by the technology on which the emissions limitation is based. Rather, [EPA] has discretion to base the emissions limitation on a control efficiency that is somewhat lower than the optimal level. . . . To account for these possibilities, a permitting authority must be allowed a certain degree of discretion to set the emissions limitation at a level that does not necessarily reflect the highest possible control efficiency, but will allow the permittee to achieve compliance consistently.[19]

For emissions from operating facilities to be demonstrated as achievable and thus applicable to a new facility, there must be sufficient data to gauge whether those emissions rates are achievable over the long term. Limited stack test data are insufficient to form the basis of what is achievable for new facilities and to establish BACT.[20]

A control technology must be "available" to be considered in a BACT determination (*e.g.*, demonstrated in practice). This means that the technology has progressed beyond the conceptual stage and pilot testing phase and must have been demonstrated successfully on full-scale operations for a sufficient time. Theoretical, experimental, or developing technologies are not "available" under BACT. A control technology is neither demonstrated nor available if government subsidies are required to fund evaluations of the technology. In many cases, a technology that is "available" at one size of unit is not "available" at a larger unit. A control technology must also be "commercially available." This means that the technology must be offered for sale with commercial terms that allow the applicant to meet the limits in the permit.

The BACT analysis focuses on the determination of an emission limitation for the applicant's "proposed facility."[21] Consistent with this reading that BACT applies to the source as proposed, EPA has long observed that the BACT requirements are "not intended to redefine the source."[22] In 2005, EPA reconfirmed in the context of whether an applicant for a proposed pulverized coal facility needed to include an evaluation of an integrated gasification combined cycle ("IGCC") unit that it "does not consider the BACT requirement as a means to redefine the basic scope of the source or change the fundamental scope of the project when considering available control alternatives."[23] Accordingly, BACT does not require evaluation of different processes by which to generate electricity. For instance, BACT does not require a coal-fired facility to consider wind, gas, or hydroelectric processes to generate electricity. Likewise, BACT does not require a source to change the type of boiler or fuel proposed for the project.[24] In 2007, the Seventh Circuit Court of Appeals held that BACT at a proposed power plant in Illinois that was located adjacent to a high sulfur coal mine did not require the consideration of burning a low sulfur coal from a mine a thousand miles away.[25] While "clean fuels" is one of the control technologies that the Act requires EPA to consider, the Seventh Circuit rejected any requirement that the proposal evaluate the use of nuclear fuel, hydroelectric power, wind turbines or low sulfur coal because such fuels would constitute a redesign of the project.[26]

When establishing BACT for individual pollutants, the permitting agency must also consider possible interactions among the pollutants.[27] As emission limits are driven lower, reducing emissions of one pollutant may increase emissions of another pollutant. The relationship between emissions of NOx and CO is an example of this type of interaction.

Similarly, some techniques to lower emissions of one pollutant may create interactions that produce deleterious effects on downstream equipment. For example, increasing the injection of ammonia to reduce NOx emissions can produce unacceptable levels of sulfur trioxide and ammonium bisulfates if the source uses a high sulfur fuel. These substances can cause serious maintenance and reliability problems in downstream equipment.

Decisions concerning technical feasibility are the responsibility of the review authority. A control technology that is "demonstrated" for a given type or class of sources is assumed to be technically feasible unless source-specific factors exist and are documented to justify technical infeasibility. Specifically, EPA's Draft NSR Workshop Manual states: "Technologies which have not yet been applied to (or permitted for) full scale operations need not be considered available; an applicant should be able to purchase or construct a process or control device that has already been demonstrated in practice."[28]

The Lowest Achievable Emission Rate Requirement

To obtain a preconstruction permit in a nonattainment area, a new or modified major stationary source must demonstrate that it will install control technology that will comply with the LAER for that source category or similar source categories. The LAER requirement applies only for those pollutants for which an area is in nonattainment and which the source will emit in "major" amounts (defined generally as emissions of 100 tons per year ("tpy") or more, except in the case of serious and worse nonattainment areas). Alternatively, nonattainment review and LAER apply when a major source proposes to undertake a modification that will result in a "significant" increase in emissions of the nonattainment pollutant for which the source is major.

LAER is defined as "the most stringent emission limitation . . . contained in the implementation plan of any State" or "the most stringent emission limitation . . . achieved in practice [by the same or similar source category] . . . whichever is more stringent."[29] LAER must be at least as stringent as any NSPS that applies to the source category. The House Report accompanying the 1977 Amendments emphasizes that cost is less of a factor in LAER determinations than it is in setting NSPS, but notes that "if the cost of any given . . . means of compliance is so great that new . . . sources could not build and operate, then emission reductions which necessitate [its] use . . . would not be considered achievable . . . ."[30]

As a practical matter, the LAER requirement has been applied to require the most sophisticated control technologies that are available with respect to the nonattainment pollutant.[31] The most stringent technologies to be examined in LAER determinations are often found in Southern California, where nonattainment problems for several pollutants (including NOx, volatile organic compounds ("VOCs"), and CO) are particularly severe. The full range of technologies to be considered can typically be identified based on EPA's BACT/LAER Clearinghouse but may also require consideration of foreign experience. Once the most stringent technologies have been identified, the owner or operator of the proposed facility has the burden of demonstrating that the particular control technology is so expensive that it should not be considered "feasible" or "achievable" as applied in the specific circumstances of the proposed facility.

The nonattainment provisions of the 1990 Amendments contain a variety of special rules pertaining to LAER. For example, in serious and severe ozone nonattainment areas, source modifications with a potential to emit VOCs or

NOx of less than 100 tpy may apply BACT as opposed to LAER.[32] Larger projects may avoid LAER if they obtain an "internal emission offset" in a ratio of at least 1.3 to 1.[33]

Control Technology Regulation of Existing Sources Through the "Reconstruction" and "Modification" Rules

A critical issue for existing sources concerns when the new source requirements discussed above apply. New source requirements can be triggered by either the reconstruction rule (in the case of the NSPS program) or the modification rule (in the case of the NSPS, PSD, or nonattainment programs). The 1990 Amendments provided refinements to the reconstruction and modification principles in several specific contexts. Additionally, from 1992 through 2007, EPA promulgated and proposed a number of important revisions to the modification rule. Finally, the scope of the modification program has been shaped by a series of enforcement actions filed by EPA starting in 1999. These issues are discussed below.

The Reconstruction Rule

EPA promulgated the reconstruction rule in 1975 to address projects designed to extend the useful life of existing industrial facilities.[34] The rule defines when a project to rebuild an existing facility becomes so extensive that it is substantially equivalent to replacing the facility "at the end of its useful life."[35]

Work to rebuild or to replace parts of an existing facility requires notification under the reconstruction rule when the project involves expenditures that are more than 50 percent of what it would cost to construct a comparable entirely new facility.[36] Triggering the reconstruction rule does not automatically result in application of NSPS. Rather, recognizing that control technology standards developed for new facilities may not be appropriate for existing facilities, if the notification requirement is triggered, the Administrator must determine whether reconstruction has occurred by balancing costs, remaining useful life, potential emission reductions, and other considerations.[37] As a result, triggering the 50 percent threshold does not automatically result in application of NSPS.

When EPA promulgated the reconstruction rule, it stated that it did not anticipate that many facilities would trigger reconstruction review and that it would address more specific concerns with "life extension" of existing facilities in rulemakings establishing NSPS for specific source categories.[38] It is important, therefore, to examine the NSPS rules applicable to an individual source category for further guidance on when capital projects trigger reconstruction review.

For example, the NSPS for emissions of VOCs from synthetic organic chemical manufacturing industry distillation operations specifically lumps together all components that are replaced over any two-year period for purposes of determining whether the 50 percent "capital expenditure" rule has been triggered.[39] This provision ensures that no owner or operator could spread out the costs of a single project over two years as a means of avoiding review under the reconstruction rule.

An issue that commonly arises under the reconstruction rule concerns what parts of a facility must be taken into account in determining whether the 50 percent capital expenditure threshold will be triggered. The "affected facility" for purposes of the NSPS program is the piece of equipment that produces the regulated emissions (*e.g.*, the boiler at a power plant). The capital expenditure computation is made based on repair and replacement costs that pertain to this "affected facility."[40]

It should be noted that, in contrast to the modification rule, the reconstruction rule applies regardless of whether the work in question causes an increase in the emissions of a regulated pollutant. In addition, all work that forms part of the project – including routine repair and replacement – is considered under the capital expenditure test.[41]

The reconstruction rule was developed under the NSPS program. After enactment of the 1977 Amendments, EPA considered whether to apply the reconstruction rule to the PSD program as well. After notice and comment rulemaking, the Agency decided that "the general PSD objective of safeguarding existing air quality from significant degradation" would be adequately served by review of major new sources and major modifications, without the reconstruction rule.[42] Similarly, EPA has declined to adopt the reconstruction rule for the nonattainment permit program.

The Modification Rule

Unlike the reconstruction rule, the modification rule applies to the PSD and nonattainment programs as well as the NSPS program.[43] The modification rule has the same basic elements for each of these programs. That is, a modification occurs when there is a "physical change" or change in the "method of operation" at a source that "results in" an "increase in emissions" of a regulated pollutant from the source.[44] The modification rule also provides examples of specific activities (*e.g.*, routine repair, replacement, and maintenance) that are not considered a modification. Together, these elements of the modification rule define the construction activities that trigger application of the new source programs.

The scope and meaning of each of these elements of the modification rule are further defined in EPA guidance and applicability determinations. Unfortunately, there is no single document that compiles all of the relevant reference materials and, indeed, individual guidance memoranda may have taken contradictory positions. Understanding the modification rule is further complicated by court decisions issued in recent years.

Reflecting the confusion that has existed regarding when activity at an existing facility triggers modification review, different district courts have read the same statutory and regulatory language and arrived at diametrically opposed conclusions.[45] The U.S. Courts of Appeals also have expressed differing views as to the scope and applicability of the modification provision.[46] In April 2007, the U.S. Supreme Court addressed one aspect of this program in *Environmental Defense v. Duke Energy*.[47] Unfortunately, the Supreme Court's decision does little to resolve the nature of the activity that triggers the modification program.

To begin to understand the modification rule, one must review the Seventh Circuit's decision in *Wisconsin Electric Power Company v. Reilly*[48] ("*WEPCo*"), the EPA interpretations that gave rise to that decision,[49] subsequent applicability determinations, recent judicial decisions, and recent rule revisions. The following sections follow this trail of regulations, interpretations, and guidance.

The Modification Rule Before 1976

In the 1970 Clean Air Act, the term "modification" appeared in only one place – the NSPS provision – section 111 of the Clean Air Act[50] – but governed two new source programs. First, under the 1970 Act, modification of an existing facility triggered application of any NSPS that applied to the source category.[51] Second, modification of an existing facility also triggered preconstruction review of the modified facility to ensure compliance with the NAAQS.[52]

EPA originally promulgated a modification rule for the NSPS program in 1971.[53] In language that parallels the statutory definition, the rule defines a "modified" facility as one at which a "physical or operational change" occurs that "results in an increase in the emission rate of any pollutant to which a standard applies."[54] In a later clarification of this rule, EPA provided that an emission rate increase would be determined using the facility's emission rate measured in kilograms per hour ("kg/hr").[55] EPA explained that, under this test, increased hours of operation were irrelevant to whether a "modification" occurred within the meaning of the statute.[56]

To define further the scope of this provision, the NSPS modification rule provided examples of activity that does not constitute a "modification." Such activities include: (1) "[routine] maintenance, repair, and replacement"; (2) "[a]n increase in production rate . . . or hours of operation" that can be accomplished without a "capital expenditure"; and (3) fuel conversions where the facility was originally designed to accommodate the alternative fuel.[57] As EPA explained in the preamble to the rule, such activities do not trigger NSPS because they do not create "new" pollution.[58] In other words, these provisions anticipate that an existing facility can use its existing capacity.

As noted above, the 1970 Clean Air Act also required review of the location of new or modified sources to ensure that emissions from those facilities which were *not* reviewed by states in establishing SIP emission limits (*i.e.*, "new" pollution) were reviewed for compliance with the NAAQS.[59] Under the 1970 Act, this preconstruction review program applied to modified facilities as defined in section 111 of the Act.

In 1974, EPA adopted regulations defining "modification" for the preconstruction review program, generally conforming the definition of "modification" for the PSD regulatory program to the definition of that term under the NSPS program.[60] As EPA explained when it promulgated the PSD modification rule, it intended this rule to be consistent with the NSPS modification rule.[61]

The "Major Modification" Rule

Prior to 1976, the only definition of "modification" for the preconstruction review program was the NSPS/PSD regulatory definition. In 1976, EPA issued an interpretive rule on preconstruction review of new and modified facilities located in areas not attaining an applicable NAAQS (*i.e.*, in "nonattainment" areas). In that interpretive rule, EPA coined a new regulatory term – "major modification."[62] Under this interpretive rule, a "modification" in a nonattainment area (as defined under the NSPS/PSD regulatory definition of that term) would become subject to the more stringent nonattainment new source review requirements only when that modification was "major" – *i.e.*, when the modification caused an increase in emissions above a specified tonnage level.[63]

In 1977, Congress amended the Clean Air Act to adopt *statutory* preconstruction review programs for PSD and nonattainment areas. In these amendments, Congress chose as the trigger for these new source review ("NSR") programs the term "modification" (*not* "major modification"), and defined "modification" by reference to its meaning and use under the NSPS program.[64] Congress further restricted application of these preconstruction review programs to "major stationary sources"[65] but, other than providing that the 1976 interpretive rule would remain in effect until states adopted nonattainment SIPs,[66] did not address the term "major modification" created by EPA in 1976 for the non-attainment program.

Following the 1977 Amendments to the Clean Air Act, EPA left in place the definition of "modification" that it had promulgated in 1974 for the 1970 Clean Air Act preconstruction review program. Activity that constituted a "modification" consistent with the NSPS modification rule, therefore, had to be reviewed to ensure compliance with the NAAQS.[67]

Following the 1977 Clean Air Act Amendments, however, EPA also adopted rules making "major modification" the trigger for review under the new statutory PSD and nonattainment programs. Under these rules, "modification" of existing facilities that are "major" must meet the *additional* requirements of these new source programs (*e.g.*, the BACT and LAER control technology requirements discussed above), in addition to being reviewed to ensure compliance with the NAAQS and NSPS.

The 1980 PSD and nonattainment rules define a "major modification" as a physical or operational change that results in a "significant emissions increase . . . of a regulated NSR pollutant . . . and a significant net emissions increase of that pollutant from the major stationary source."[68] A "significant net emissions increase" in turn is defined in terms of annual emissions (*i.e.*, tpy), and allows a source to avoid NSR by offsetting increased emissions at the unit undergoing the modification with contemporaneous and enforceable emission reductions at other emitting units at the same stationary source.

The 1980 PSD rules address how a "significant net emissions increase" is calculated.[69] First, to determine whether a project is a "major modification," one must determine the amount of emissions, in tpy, from the emitting unit that would undergo the "change." The 1980 rules provide that where the unit has not begun normal operations, its emissions must be determined based on its potential to emit following construction or modification.[70] Thus, where a new emissions unit is added to a source or an existing facility is replaced by a new one, the emissions that must be offset in the "significant net emissions increase" calculation are based on the new emitting unit's "potential to emit," assuming operation of the new emitting unit at full capacity throughout the year (unless an enforceable restriction is imposed on the facility's operations, which restriction is then used to define the facility's potential to emit).[71]

Having defined the amount of the emissions increase (in tpy) that must be offset, the major modification rules then explain how one is to calculate offsetting emission reductions at other emitting units at the stationary source. In contrast to EPA's 1978 "major modification" rules, which would have allowed calculation of emission offsets based on the "potential-to-emit" of the other emitting units at the stationary source,[72] the 1980 rules required emission offsets to be calculated based on a unit's historical "actual emissions" during a representative baseline period.[73] That baseline was defined as the average emissions (in tpy) for a two-year period preceding the project that were "representative" of normal source operation.[74]

Although the 1980 NSR rules define how to calculate the emissions that must be offset for an emitting unit that has not begun normal operations, they do not define how one calculates the increased emissions that must be offset for existing units that are established operations (*i.e.*, that have begun normal operations).[75] This gap in the 1980 rules has been at the heart of the NSR enforcement controversy over the past two decades, and is discussed further below.

The WEPCo Decision

In 1988, the Wisconsin Electric Power Company sought to replace deteriorated equipment at its five-unit Port Washington station to address safety concerns. The deteriorated equipment had led to operation of four units at reduced capacity for an extended period and to the shutdown of the fifth unit. All of the repair work involved replacement of broken equipment with equipment of similar design.[76]

The changes planned at these units were extensive – in the range of $80 million in capital costs in 1988 dollars. These costs, however, were only about twenty percent of the cost of comparable new units. As a result, the project did not trigger the reconstruction rule. EPA nevertheless expressed concern that because the project would permit the plant to operate as it had under its original design, all five of the Port Washington units should be treated as new units under both the NSPS and NSR programs if the project went forward.[77]

In reaching this conclusion, EPA found first that this project involved a "physical change" to the facilities, even though it consisted only of "like-kind" replacement of equipment that would not change the size, design, or nature of the facility's operations. Although the Wisconsin Electric Power Company argued that the work was not a "physical change" because it constituted "routine" repair, replacement, and maintenance, EPA reasoned that whether replacement of broken equipment is routine must be evaluated on a case-by-case basis, based on consideration of the nature, purpose, cost and extent of the project. Applying these factors, EPA concluded that the projects were not routine because, among other things, EPA could find "no examples of steam drum replacement" (the key component replaced) "at aged electric generating facilities."[78] Furthermore, according to EPA, the power company's air heater replacement projects were "too dissimilar to [other industry projects] . . . to support the company's contention that the work in question was routine."[79] Because the projects at issue had been undertaken at units that "comprise only a small fraction of total operating utility units" in the industry, and because the work at issue "was rarely, if ever, performed" in the utility industry, EPA reasoned that it could not be "routine."[80]

Having concluded that the Port Washington project was a physical change because it did not fall within any of the regulatory exclusions, EPA examined the "emissions increase" issue. EPA found that only two of the five Port Washington units would undergo an NSPS "modification" (*i.e.*, would have an hourly emission rate increase caused by the project), but nevertheless found that all five of the units would undergo "major modifications" triggering NSR. EPA reached this conclusion by filling the gap in the 1980 rules noted above regarding projection of post-project emissions in a manner that would *always* result in an emissions increase finding. That is, EPA reasoned that a "major modification" that triggers NSR occurs when an existing unit's future *potential to emit* (measured in tpy) is greater than its past actual emissions. In reaching this conclusion, EPA specifically rejected the company's argument that it should be allowed under the 1980 rules to project its future actual emissions, as opposed to using its future potential to emit. According to EPA, the "[1980] PSD regulations provide no support for this view" that "'projected' actual emissions after the renovation" should be used to calculate post-project emissions for an existing emissions unit.[81]

Because no facility ever operates at full capacity twenty-four hours a day, every day of the year, this "actual-to-potential" approach to calculating post-project emissions would as a practical matter *always* result in a finding of an emissions increase whenever nonroutine work is proposed at an existing facility. According to EPA, one could avoid this result only by accepting a federally enforceable permit condition restricting operations of the existing facility to the level experienced during the two-year period used to establish the facility's emissions baseline.[82]

In the *WEPCo* decision, the Seventh Circuit rejected EPA's "actual-to-potential" approach to calculating a "significant net emissions increase" for units that had begun normal operations.[83] The court remanded the WEPCo PSD applicability determination to EPA to determine "whether the renovated plant would cause a significant net emissions increase if it were operated under present hours and conditions."[84]

As of 1990, therefore, there were potentially three ways of calculating post-project emissions under the 1980 "major modification" rules for emitting units that had begun normal operations. First, in its WEPCo determination, EPA advanced an interpretation under which future emissions would be based on the existing unit's "potential to emit." The Seventh Circuit, however, rejected this interpretation.[85] Second, in that same proceeding, WEPCo advanced an interpretation under which one would project the future actual emissions of an existing unit. EPA, in its 1988 WEPCo determination, however, rejected this interpretation as having no basis in its 1980 rules.[86] Third, as the Seventh Circuit directed, on remand a "significant net increase" could be calculated under "present [representative] hours and conditions" of operation[87] – a position consistent with earlier EPA applicability determinations.[88] Many read this direction to mean that, for a unit that had begun normal operations, an emissions increase at that unit would require an increase in the hourly emission rate as under the NSPS modification rule, because annual emissions had to be calculated based on the same "representative" hours and conditions of operation before and after a project.[89] In *Duke III*, however, the Supreme Court ruled that a "reading of the 1980 PSD regulations, intended to align them with NSPS, was inconsistent with their terms and [would] effectively invalidate[] them."[90] Against this background, it is not surprising that the 1980 NSR rules have been the source of so much controversy.

The WEPCo Rule

After the Seventh Circuit's *WEPCo* decision, EPA sought to address some of the confusion created by its WEPCo determination by conducting a rulemaking. This 1992 rule is often referred to as the "WEPCo rule." This section summarizes the following provisions of the 1992 WEPCo rule: (i) the Routine Maintenance, Repair, and Replacement ("RMRR") preamble guidance; (ii) the NSPS emissions test; (iii) the NSR "significant net emissions increase" test; (iv) the pollution control project exclusion; and (v) the demand growth/causation preamble discussion.

RMRR. In the WEPCo rule preamble, EPA addressed the "routine maintenance, repair and replacement" provision by promising to issue more formal "guidance on this subject as part of an NSR regulatory update package."[91] In the interim, EPA "clarif[ied] that the "determination of whether the repair or replacement of a particular item of equipment is 'routine' under the NSR regulations, while made on a case-by-case basis, must be based on the evaluation of whether that type of equipment has been repaired or replaced by sources *within the relevant industrial category*."[92]

NSPS emission rate increase. In the 1992 rule-making, EPA clarified the NSPS emissions increase test by adding a new paragraph (h) to 40 C.F.R. § 60.14, which states that:

> No physical change, or change in the method of operation, at an existing electric utility steam generating unit shall be treated as a modification for the purposes of this section provided that such change does not increase the maximum hourly emissions of any pollutant regulated under this section above the maximum hourly emissions achievable at that unit during the 5 years prior to the change.[93]

In the preamble, EPA explains that this provision "*retain[s] the key concept in the [original] regulations* that the baseline be determined *during a period that is roughly contemporaneous with the proposed change at the affected facility*," thereby "enabl[ing] units to establish a baseline that is *representative* of [their] physical and operational capacity *in recent years,* while still precluding the use of a baseline tied to original design capacity, which . . . may bear no relationship to the facility's capacity in recent years."[94] This provision ensures that the NSPS regulations will not "unduly burden utilities undertaking physical or operational changes in conjunction with the acid rain program," by confirming that a source can "demonstrate that an earlier, higher capacity was more representative of the unit's maximum hourly emissions rate."[95]

NSR "significant net emissions increase" test. The WEPCo rule adds to the "major modification" rule a "projected actual" test for calculating a "significant net emissions increase." As promulgated, this 1992 "projected actual" test applies *only* to electric utility generating units because, as EPA explained, it lacked the time and resources to develop such a test for other industries.[96] Under this rule, all utility units, other than new or replacement units, can compare past actual emissions to a projection of "future representative actual emissions," a defined regulatory term.[97] In this way, a utility that projects that it would utilize a modified unit *less* than during the baseline period could avoid NSR even if it undertook a project that caused an hourly emission rate increase. In order to take advantage of this method, however, the utility must provide annual emissions reports for 5 to 10 years after the project in question to confirm that utilization has decreased.[98]

As EPA explained, under the 1980 major modification rules, the "linchpin" for deciding whether to use "potential to emit" in calculating a significant net emissions increase is "whether the unit has '*begun normal operations.*'"[99] According to EPA, however, the *Puerto Rican Cement* and *WEPCo* cases "occasion[ed] a reexamination" both of EPA's interpretation of the phrase "begun normal operations" and the "usefulness of the regulatory language itself."[100]

The WEPCo rule, EPA explained, eliminates the "began normal operations" concept for use of the new "future actual representative emissions" test. Rather, *any* utility unit can use this test whether it has begun normal operations or not, *except* those that are an "addition of a new unit or constitute a replacement of an existing unit."[101] EPA implemented this test by adding a new clause (v) to 40 C.F.R. § 52.21(b)(21)), stating that:

> For an electric utility steam generating unit (other than a new unit or the replacement of an existing unit), actual emissions of the unit following the physical or operational change shall equal the representative actual annual emissions of the unit, *provided* the source owner or operator maintains and submits to the permitting authority, on an annual basis for a period of 5 years from the date

the unit resumes regular operation, information demonstrating that the physical or operational change did not result in an emissions increase. A longer period, not to exceed 10 years, may be required by the permitting authority if it determines such a period to be more representative of normal source post-change operations.[102]

EPA explained in the preamble that, under this "future actual representative emissions" approach for calculating a "significant net emissions increase," one begins as under the 1980 rules by calculating baseline emissions for the modified unit.[103] According to EPA, the source owner or operator may "presume that any 2 consecutive years within the 5 years *prior to* the proposed change is representative of normal source operations for a utility."[104] Source owners or operators "desiring to use other than a 2-year period or a baseline period prior to the last 5 years" may seek EPA's "specific determination that such period is more representative of normal operations."[105]

As for future emissions, EPA defined the term "representative actual annual emissions" in a new 40 C.F.R. § 52.21(b) as:

> [T]he average rate, in tons per year, at which the source is projected to emit a pollutant for the 2-year period after a physical change or change in the method of operation of a unit, (or a different consecutive 2-year period within 10 years after that change, where the Administrator determines that such period is more representative of normal source operations), considering the effect any such change will have on increasing or decreasing the hourly emissions rate and on projected capacity utilization.[106]

The "future actual projection," therefore, is the product of:

- The hourly emissions rate, which is based on the unit's physical and operational capabilities and federally enforceable operational restrictions that would affect the hourly emissions rate following the change; and
- Projected capacity utilization, which is based on consideration of available information regarding the unit's likely post-change capacity utilization.

As noted above, this "projected actual" approach for electric utilities may be employed *only* if the "source owner or operator maintains and submits to the permitting authority on an annual basis for a period of 5 years from the date the unit resumes regular operation, information demonstrating that the physical or operational change did not result in an emissions increase."[107] If a utility declines to submit such information for a particular unit, the pre-existing 1980 NSR rules would continue to apply.[108]

The Pollution Control Project Exclusion. In the preamble to the final WEPCo rule, EPA explained that "Congress did not intend that pollution control projects be considered the type of activity that should trigger NSR," in other words, new source review under the PSD and nonattainment permitting programs.[109] According to the Agency, "when Congress enacted the NSR provisions of the Clean Air Act, it provided that the term 'modification' in NSR shall have the same meaning as the term 'modification' under NSPS."[110] EPA described the NSR pollution control project exclusion under the NSR rules as "reflect[ing] the existing regulatory exclusion for pollution control activities under NSPS regulations, and several recent case-specific nonapplicability determinations under the NSR programs."[111]

The final rule added a new subclause (h) to 40 C.F.R. § 52.21(b)(2)(iii), providing that a "physical change or change in the method of operation" does not include the "addition, replacement or use of a pollution control project at an existing electric utility steam generating unit," with two qualifications. First, NSR may apply where the "Administrator determines that such addition, replacement, or use renders the unit less environmentally beneficial." Second, NSR may apply:

- "[W]hen the Administrator has reason to believe that the pollution control project would result in a significant net increase in representative actual annual emissions of any criteria pollutant over levels used for that source in the most recent air quality impact analysis in the area conducted for the purpose of title I, if any," and
- Where "the Administrator determines that the increase will cause or contribute to a violation of any national ambient air quality standard or PSD increment, or visibility limitation."[112]

Corresponding regulatory changes were made to 40 C.F.R. § 51.166, the equivalent provision in the Part 51 rules concerning the requirements for approvable NSR SIPs.

Under the WEPCo rule, a "pollution control project" was defined as "any activity or project at an existing electric utility steam generating unit for purposes of reducing emissions from such unit." Such activities or projects were limited to:

- The installation of conventional or innovative pollution control technology, including but not limited to advanced flue gas desulfurization, sorbent injection for sulfur dioxide and nitrogen oxides controls and electrostatic precipitators;
- An activity or project to accommodate switching to a fuel which is less polluting than the fuel in use prior to the activity or project, including, but not limited to natural gas or coal re-burning, or the co-firing of natural gas and other fuels for the purpose of controlling emissions.[113]

The "pollution control project" definition also included certain permanent clean coal technology ("CCT") demonstrations funded under the Further Continuing Appropriations Act of 1985 or by EPA, as well as permanent CCT demonstrations that constitute a repowering project.[114]

Following promulgation of the WEPCo rule, EPA in July 1994 issued a guidance memorandum discussing when pollution control projects at non-electric utility sources should be excluded from NSR. This memorandum provided interim guidance pending promulgation of a formal regulatory exclusion for such projects in a future rulemaking. This guidance confirmed that the major modification rule did not apply to pollution control projects undertaken by industrial facilities.[115]

EPA ultimately promulgated a pollution control project exclusion applicable to *all* industry in December 2002.[116] In response to a challenge by environmental groups, however, the pollution control project exclusions of the 2002 NSR rule, as well as the 1992 WEPCo rule, were vacated by the D.C. Circuit in June 2005.[117] This decision, however, did *not* address the NSPS pollution control exclusion, nor did it address the NSR pollution control project exclusions contained in many SIPs. Furthermore, whether the decision has any impact on pollution control projects undertaken under the 1992 WEPCo rule and 2002 NSR rule prior to the *New York I* decision is unclear.[118]

The Causation Requirement/Demand Growth Exclusion. In the preamble to the WEPCo rule, EPA recognized that the "NSR regulatory provisions require that the physical or operational change 'result in' an increase in actual emissions in order to consider that change to be a modification."[119] EPA explained that the modification rules are "in no way intend[ed] to discourage physical or operational changes that increase efficiency or reliability or lower operating costs, or improve other operational characteristics of the unit."[120] Further, EPA "recognize[d] that improvements such as these are desirable for economic reasons and to assure a reliable supply of electricity."[121]

To address these issues, the 1992 WEPCo rule contained a specific provision clarifying the "result in" requirement of the "modification" definition:

[I]n projecting future emissions the Administrator shall:

(i) consider all relevant information, including but not limited to, historical operational data, the company's own representations, filings with the State or Federal regulatory authorities, and compliance plans under title IV of the Clean Air Act; and

(ii) exclude, in calculating any increase in emissions that results from the particular physical change or change in the method of operation at an electric utility steam generating unit, that portion of the unit's emissions following the change *that could have been accommodated during the representative baseline period and is attributable to an increase in projected capacity utilization at the unit that is unrelated to the particular change, including any increased utilization due to the rate of electricity demand growth for the utility system as a whole.*[122]

Although EPA explained that the amended rules *"clarify* this provision in the context of modifications at electric utility steam generating units,"[123] EPA also made clear that this change "merely incorporates into the actual-to-future actual methodology a requirement of the *pre-existing* statutory and regulatory scheme."[124]

In the preamble to the WEPCo rule, EPA identifies "physical or operational change[s] that significantly alter[] the efficiency of [a] plant" as the types of projects that could lead to increased emissions under this rule. EPA explains, however, that it "declines to create a presumption that every emissions increase that follows a change in efficiency is inextricably linked to the efficiency change," and that it "in no way intends to discourage physical or operational changes that increase efficiency or reliability or lower operating costs, or improve other operational characteristics of the unit." The WEPCo rule accomplishes this, EPA says, by making clear that "operational levels that a unit could *not* have achieved during the representative baseline period *but for* the . . . change are considered to result from the change." By contrast, where increased post-project operational levels could have been accommodated during the baseline period and are due to growth in demand, those increased operations are not "caused" by the project. Only where "efficiency improvements are *the predominant cause* of the change in emissions and demand growth is not," EPA continues, does "the exclusion [for increased emissions due to demand growth] . . . not apply."[125]

The "causation" element of the modification rule was addressed by the U.S. Court of Appeals for the D.C. Circuit in *New York I.* First, the court recognized that "causation" is a statutory requirement, *i.e.*, that a project must "cause" the emissions increase for there to be a modification. Second, the court upheld the WEPCo rule causation provision as a reasonable implementation of the statute.[126]

Changes to the Reconstruction and Modification Rules Made by the 1990 Amendments

Even though Congress decided not to address the modification provision generally in 1990, but rather to leave any needed clarifications to EPA,[127] Congress did address the reconstruction and modification issues in the context of several specific regulatory programs added by the 1990 Amendments. These provisions are summarized briefly below.

The Clean Coal Technology Program

To encourage the demonstration of CCT and the repowering of sources with such technologies, Congress in the 1990 Amendments clarified the applicability of NSPS and new source review to sources that undertake clean coal repowering and demonstration projects.

With respect to repowering projects, the 1990 Amendments provide that NSPS will not apply unless there is an increase in the actual hourly emission rate of a regulated pollutant.[128] Qualifying repowering projects are also to be given expedited consideration for PSD and/or nonattainment permits.[129] Moreover, any emissions increase must actually *result* from the repowering project before PSD review would be required.[130]

Installation or cessation of temporary CCT demonstration projects (defined as projects operated for a period of five years or less) that comply with applicable SIP requirements will not trigger NSPS, PSD, or nonattainment review.[131] Moreover, EPA is required to promulgate regulations or interpretive rulings to revise the NSPS, PSD, and nonattainment modification requirements to facilitate CCT demonstration projects.[132] EPA did so as part of the WEPCo rule discussed above.[133]

The Nonattainment Program

To encourage progress toward attainment of the NAAQS, Congress changed the modification rules for certain nonattainment areas that make it more likely that a proposal to modify a source will trigger nonattainment review. For example, in ozone nonattainment areas, Congress changed the definition of "significant" emissions increase as follows: for serious and severe nonattainment areas, the threshold is 25 tpy (net increase over five years)[134]; for extreme nonattainment areas, it is any emissions increase.[135] When nonattainment review is triggered in serious and severe areas, however, major sources emitting less than 100 tpy need only implement BACT as opposed to LAER.[136]

The Air Toxics Program

With the expanded emphasis on air toxics in the 1990 Amendments, Congress specifically addressed the regulatory consequences of "modification" and "reconstruction" activity for air toxics emissions from existing sources. Under the Amendments, a "modification" is defined as a physical or operational change that results in a greater than de minimis increase in *actual* emissions of a hazardous air pollutant.[137] A modification finding can be avoided, however, if the increase is offset by an equal or greater reduction of another hazardous air pollutant that is deemed more hazardous. EPA issued rules implementing this definition in 1996,[138] as discussed in Chapter 5 of this Handbook.

Under the new air toxics program, a modification that takes place after the effective date of a state permit program must meet "maximum achievable emission limitations" for existing sources.[139] Reconstructed sources must meet maximum achievable emission limitations applicable to new sources.[140]

The Operating Permit Program

In Title V, Congress required the development of comprehensive state operating permit programs and specified the minimum elements that must be addressed in those programs. Among other things, permit programs must allow changes that do *not* constitute a modification without requiring a permit revision, provided that written notification of the change is given a minimum of seven days in advance.[141] In June 1992, the Agency issued rules addressing this and other issues pertaining to state operating permit programs. These rules and subsequent litigation and rule revisions are discussed in Chapter 4 of this Handbook.

The NSR Enforcement Initiative

EPA in the late 1990s began to file enforcement actions against industry, alleging that companies had been violating the NSR "major modification" rule for decades by repairing and replacing broken or deteriorating equipment. NSR enforcement actions were filed against refineries, paper companies, electric utilities, and others.[142]

The most controversial of these NSR enforcement efforts was directed against the electric utility industry. In November 1999, EPA instituted enforcement proceedings against seven utilities and the Tennessee Valley Authority ("TVA") alleging that these companies modified their facilities without necessary new source preconstruction permits. The most complete statement of the EPA Enforcement Office's approach to the NSR modification rule is contained in an order of the EAB issued on September 15, 2000,[143] finding that TVA modified nine of its generating units without obtaining new source permits.[144]

The EAB Order was challenged by TVA and others in the U.S. Court of Appeals for the Eleventh Circuit in November 2000.[145] On June 24, 2003, the Eleventh Circuit issued a decision finding that the Clean Air Act provision for administrative compliance orders, the authority under which the EAB had found TVA in violation of the Clean Air Act, was unconstitutional under due process and separation of powers principles.[146] The court also found that EPA's procedures for development and review of the EAB Order were inadequate and "ignor[ed] the concept of the rule of law."[147] The court therefore declared the TVA order "legally inconsequential" and directed that TVA was free to ignore it.[148] The Supreme Court then denied the Solicitor General's petition for *certiorari* to the Eleventh Circuit in May 2004.[149] Because the Eleventh Circuit declared the EAB decision legally inconsequential, courts have since refused to rely on that decision as having precedential value.[150]

Following the *TVA* decision, district courts that have addressed the substance of EPA's NSR enforcement arguments have reached conflicting conclusions. In *Ohio Edison*, for example, the court deferred to EPA's enforcement position, finding (i) that whether activity is "routine maintenance, repair or replacement" must be determined based on the frequency with which an activity is undertaken at an individual unit, and that whether a project is common in the industry is irrelevant; and (ii) that a "significant net emissions increase" that triggers NSR can occur when hours of operation increase after a non-routine project.[151] The court noted that EPA had not previously enforced the law in this manner, but attributed this to an "abysmal breakdown" in the implementation and enforcement of NSR.[152] Although the court said that it would take this "abysmal breakdown" into account in fashioning an appropriate remedy, in March 2005, Ohio Edison announced that it had settled the case.

By contrast, in *Duke I*, the district court refused to defer to EPA's enforcement arguments, finding them inconsistent with the statute, the regulations, and previous EPA positions.[153] According to the court, the Clean Air Act and EPA's regulations require (i) that "routine" be evaluated in light of industry practice in addition to whether an activity is frequent at a unit; and (ii) that a "significant net emissions increase" can occur only where activity causes an increase in the facility's annual emissions, holding hours and conditions of operation constant at pre-project "representative" operating levels.[154] The Fourth Circuit issued a decision in June 2005 affirming the district court decision, on the grounds that the Clean Air Act requires that the term "modification" be defined "congruently" for the NSPS and NSR programs.[155] In April 2007, however, the Supreme

Court vacated the Fourth Circuit's decision.[156] The case has now been returned to the district court for further proceedings.[157]

A number of other district courts have addressed, or are addressing, these NSR issues. For example, in *United States v. Alabama Power Company*, the Northern District of Alabama decided to follow the *Duke I* decision.[158] The Eastern District of Kentucky decided to follow the *Duke I* decision on RMRR.[159] By contrast, the Southern District of Indiana decided to follow the *Ohio Edison* decision in *United States. v. Cinergy Corp.*[160] A number of other NSR enforcement actions are pending, and a number of utilities have entered settlements with EPA in order to avoid litigation.[161] The most significant recent decision in these cases – the Supreme Court's decision in *Environmental Defense v. Duke Energy Corp.* (*Duke III*) – is discussed in the next section.

Environmental Defense v. Duke Energy Corp.

As noted above, the Fourth Circuit in *Duke II* upheld the decision of the U.S. District Court for the Middle District of North Carolina rejecting EPA's NSR enforcement action against Duke Energy, finding that the Clean Air Act required "modification" to be defined "congruently" for the NSPS and NSR programs, such that "modification" had to be defined in terms of an hourly rate increase (not annual emissions) for both programs.

The Supreme Court's April 2007 rejection of the Fourth Circuit's statutory analysis in *Duke III* found that the common definition of "modification" for the NSPS and NSR programs does *not* mandate a common definition of the term for those programs. According to the Court, "three points are relatively clear about the [Clean Air Act 'modification'] regime": (i) "[t]he Act defines modification . . . as a physical [or operational] change . . . that increases [emissions]"; (ii) "EPA's NSPS regulations require . . . [an emissions increase] measured in kilograms per hour"; and (iii) "EPA's 1980 PSD regulations require a permit for a modification . . . only when it is a major one and only when it would increase the actual emission of a pollutant above the actual average for the two prior years."[162] Otherwise, the Court observed that the 1980 rules are "no seamless narrative" and that the regulatory definition of "major modification" specifies "no rate at all" for emissions calculations.[163] Nevertheless, because the definitions of " significant" and "net emissions increase" refer to "annual" emissions, the Court observed that what the 1980 PSD rules seem to be "getting at is a measure of actual operations averaged over time, and the regulatory language simply cannot be squared with a regime under which 'hourly rate of emissions' . . . is dispositive."[164] Finally, the Court noted that it had no occasion to address the "charges" of Duke Energy and others in enforcement proceedings "that the agency has taken inconsistent positions and is now retroactively targeting twenty years of accepted practice."[165] These issues would be left, the Court said, for future proceedings.

As noted above, the 1980 major modification rule does not address how one computes increased emissions for emitting units that have begun normal operations. Three possible readings of the 1980 NSR rules in this regard have been offered over time: a "projected actual" reading; an "actual-to-potential" reading; and a "constant, representative hours" reading. The Seventh Circuit and EPA have said that calculating future emissions for such units based on "potential to emit" is "impermissible."[166] Moreover, the Supreme Court has now said that an interpretation of the 1980 rules to conform them to the NSPS "hourly rate" test would "effectively invalidate[]" them.[167] But the Supreme Court also said that what the major modification rule appears to be "getting at is a measure of actual operations averaged over time"[168] – *i.e.*, a projection of post-project actual emissions.

What type of activity at an existing, operational unit then is a "major modification" under the 1980 PSD rules? Because the 1980 rules were the governing rules in all jurisdictions until 1992, and continued to be the governing rules even after 1992 in many jurisdictions (which did not immediately revise their SIPs to adopt the 1992 rule) and for many projects this thorny issue will continue to be debated in numerous NSR enforcement cases across the country.

The 2002 NSR Reform *Rule and Related Litigation*

Following promulgation of the WEPCo rule in 1992, EPA formed a New Source Review Workshop to discuss further changes to the modification rule. As a result of the discussions of that group, EPA in July 1996 published in the *Federal Register* a proposal to revise and to clarify the modification rules.[169] Two years later, on July 24, 1998, EPA issued a supplemental notice in which it proposed to repeal principal portions of the WEPCo rule and the interpretations announced in the preamble to that rule.[170]

In 2002, EPA issued a final rule concluding the rulemaking begun in 1996 to reform the NSR program.[171] The NSR reform rule issued in December 2002 had four components. First, the rule confirmed that "environmentally beneficial" pollution control projects do not trigger new source review.[172] Listed pollution control projects could proceed once notice is provided to the permitting authority, while other pollution control projects must undergo review to ensure that they will not have adverse collateral impacts. The rule provided, however, that emission reductions achieved by a project that takes advantage of the pollution control project exclusion cannot be used in the future for netting or emission reduction credits.[173] Industry is directed to calculate an "emissions increase" using a "projected actual" test.[174]

Second, the rule provided a "clean unit" exclusion from NSR.[175] Under this provision, a unit that meets a BACT-equivalent level of emission control for an NSR pollutant could avoid triggering NSR for ten years, provided that it did not undertake an activity that causes an increase in the facility's allowable emissions rate.

Third, the rule provided criteria and procedures for the development of "plantwide applicability limits" ("PAL").[176] A PAL is essentially a source-wide bubble. Once a PAL is established for a source, emissions-increasing activities can be undertaken at an emitting unit at the source as long as the activity does not cause an exceedance of the PAL.

Fourth, in an attempt to provide clarity regarding the emissions increase criterion, industry was directed to calculate an "emissions increase" using a "projected actual" test. Under the rule, if a source owner concludes that there is no "reasonable possibility" of an emissions increase based on his projection, he can proceed with construction provided he complies with certain recordkeeping and reporting requirements.[177] EPA made clear that it was not imposing any requirement for applicability determinations or for enforceable permit conditions to limit emission to projected levels. Rather, EPA explained that existing recordkeeping and reporting requirements and certain new reporting requirements imposed by this rule would ensure either that emissions would not increase, or would allow the permitting authority to address any NSR consequences if they did.[178]

The December 2002 NSR reform rule was challenged by environmental groups and certain states in the D.C. Circuit. Other states and industry intervened in defense of the rules. In June 2005, the D.C. Circuit upheld most of the 2002 NSR Reform rule in *New York I*.[179] In particular, the court rejected challenges to EPA's "projected actual" emissions increase methodology, the PAL program, and the demand growth/causation requirement. The court, however, vacated the clean unit and pollution control project exclusions as unlawful and remanded certain recordkeeping requirements.[180] As a result, pollution control retrofits undertaken in the future may be required to undergo preconstruction review and permitting before those projects can take place.

Conclusion

The Clean Air Act modification provision was premised on a simple concept: If an existing industrial facility engages in activity that creates new pollution, that new pollution must be reviewed and regulated. Over the past fifteen years, there have been repeated efforts to transform this simple program into one that regulates most if not all existing sources of air pollution. At stake in this controversy is the balance that Congress struck in the Clean Air Act regarding regulation of new and existing sources. This controversy will continue over the coming years as district courts address the "modification" and "major modification" rules in the enforcement context, as EPA proceeds with additional NSR rulemaking, and as the courts of appeals and perhaps the Supreme Court once again address EPA's rules and the lower court decisions.

Control Technology Requirements for Existing Sources

As discussed above, existing stationary sources are exempt from stringent new source control technology requirements unless they undertake projects that constitute "modification" or "reconstruction" of the source. Existing sources can be subject to any one of several control technology requirements, however, that address special environmental problems. These existing source control technology requirements are discussed briefly below.

"Reasonably Available Control Technology" in Nonattainment Areas

Existing stationary sources located in nonattainment areas may be required to install RACT.[181] RACT is defined as "devices, systems, process modifications, or other apparatus or techniques that are reasonably available taking into account: (1) [t]he necessity of imposing such controls in order to attain and maintain [the NAAQS]; (2) [t]he social, environmental, and economic impact of such controls; and (3) [a]lternative means of providing for attainment and maintenance . . . ."[182] EPA established RACT guidelines for over 30 categories of major sources of nonattainment pollutants and has guidelines under development for other categories.[183] These "control technique guidelines" ("CTGs") are implemented by the states through their SIPs. The nonattainment provisions of the 1990 Amendments set new deadlines for issuance of additional CTGs and imposition of RACT requirements in the 1990s.

"Best Available Retrofit Technology" Near National Parks

Any stationary source that is found to cause or contribute to impairment of visibility in a mandatory Class I area (*i.e.*, larger national parks and wilderness areas) is subject to the BART requirement.[184] BART is defined as "an emission limitation based on the degree of reduction achievable through the application of the best system of continuous emission reduction for each pollutant which is emitted by an existing facility."[185] BART limits are determined on a case-by-case basis, taking into consideration costs of compliance, energy and non-air quality environmental aspects of compliance, existing pollution control technology, the remaining useful life of the source, and the degree of improvement that might be expected from the use of such technology.[186] For further information on the BART requirement, see Chapter 6 of this Handbook.

"Maximum Achievable Control Technology" for Air Toxics

Section 112(d) of the Act imposes maximum available control technology ("MACT") requirements for both existing and new sources of listed hazardous air pollutants. MACT must be equal to *at least* the level of control achieved by the best performing 12 percent of regulated sources within the same source category. Where a category has fewer than 30 sources, MACT is defined as at least the level of control activity achieved by the best five sources. New source standards may be more stringent than existing source standards, and existing sources are subject to statutory schedules for retrofitting necessary technology.

The 1990 Clean Air Act Amendments designate 189 chemicals to be regulated under section 112.[187] Regulations for all source categories of these chemicals were generally promulgated by the year 2000. The air toxics provisions of the Act are discussed in Chapter 5 of this Handbook.

Existing Source Performance Standards

Under the NSPS program, EPA claims authority: (1) to develop guidelines on control technology standards for existing sources of pollutants for which NSPS have been set but which are not subject to NAAQS, and where the source category is not regulated under section 112; and (2) to establish requirements for implementation and enforcement of such standards. States are then required to implement these guidelines through their SIPs. In implementing these standards, states may take into account, among other things, the remaining useful life of the existing source to which the standard applies. The Administrator is authorized to implement these standards for the state if the state fails to act.[188]

Notes

1. S. Rep. No. 91-1196,15-18 (1970), *reprinted in* 1 COMM. ON PUBLIC WORKS, A LEGISLATIVE HISTORY OF THE CLEAN AIR AMENDMENTS OF 1970, at 415-18 (1974).
2. Clean Air Act ("CAA") § 111(a)(1), 42 U.S.C. § 7411(a)(1).
3. *Id.* § 111(h)(1), 42 U.S.C. § 7411(h)(1).
4. *Id.* § 111(b)(1)(B), 42 U.S.C. § 7411(b)(1)(B).
5. EPA, Revision of Standards of Performance for Nitrogen Oxide Emissions From New Fossil-Fuel Fired Steam Generating Units; Revisions to Reporting Requirements for Standards of Performance for New Fossil-Fuel Fired Steam Generating Units: Final Rule, 63 Fed. Reg. 49,442 (Sept. 16, 1998).
6. EPA, Standards of Performance for Electric Utility Steam Generating Units for Which Construction Is Commenced After September 18, 1978; Standards of Performance for Industrial-Commercial-Institutional Steam Generating Units; and Standards of Performance for Small Industrial-Commercial-Institutional Steam Generating Units: Final Rule, Amendments, 71 Fed. Reg. 9,866 (Feb. 27, 2006); EPA, National Emission Standards for Hazardous Air Pollutants From Coal- and Oil-Fired Electric Utility Steam Generating Units and Standards of Performance for Fossil-Fuel-Fired Electric Utility, Industrial-Commercial-Institutional, and Small Industrial-Commercial-Institutional Steam Generating Units: Final Rule, 77 Fed. Reg. 9,304 (Feb. 16, 2012).
7. CAA § 111(f)(1), 42 U.S.C. § 7411(f)(1).
8. The 1977 provisions still apply; Congress did not amend this part of the Clean Air Act in 1990.
9. *Id.* § 169(3), 42 U.S.C. § 7479(3); 40 C.F.R. § 52.21(b)(12).
10. *See* S. Rep. No. 95-127, at 31 (1977), *reprinted in* 3 COMM. ON PUBLIC WORKS, A LEGISLATIVE HISTORY OF THE CLEAN AIR ACT AMENDMENTS OF 1977, at 1405 (1978).
11. *Id.*
12. EPA, Guidelines for Determining Best Available Control Technology (BACT) at 4 (Dec. 1978), *available at* www.epa.gov/region7/air/nsr/nsrmemos/ bactupsd.pdf.
13. *See, e.g.*, EPA, Prevention of Significant Deterioration, Workshop Manual at I-B-2 (Oct. 1980), *available at* www.epa.gov/region07/air/nsr/ nsrmemos/1980wman.pdf.
14. *Id.*
15. *See, e.g.*, Memorandum from J. Craig Potter, Acting Adm'r, EPA Office of Air & Radiation, to Regional Adm'r and Regions I-X, EPA, regarding Improving New Source Review (NSR) Implementation (Dec. 1, 1987), *available at* www.epa.gov/region07/air/nsr/nsrmemos/establsh.pdf.

16. EPA, Top Down Best Available Control Technology: Guidance Docu-ment (Mar. 15, 1990).

17. *Alaska Dep't of Envtl. Conservation v. EPA*, 540 U.S. 461, 488-89 (2004).

18. *In re Kendall New Century Dev.*, 11 E.A.D. 40, 52-53 (EAB 2003) (upholding state CO BACT determination).

19. *In re Masonite Corp.*, 5 E.A.D. 551, 560-61 (EAB 1994); *accord In re Knauf Fiber Glass, GmbH*, 9 E.A.D. 1, 15 (EAB 2000); *In re Three Mountain Power, LLC*, 10 E.A.D. 39, 53 (EAB 2001).

20. *See, e.g., In re Newmont Nevada Energy Investment, LLC*, 12 E.A.D. 429 (EAB 2005).

21. CAA § 165(a)(4), 42 U.S.C. § 7475(a)(4).

22. *In the Matter of Pennsauken County, Res. Recovery Facility*, PSD Appeal No. 88-8, at 11 (Adm'r, Apr. 20, 1989); *In re Spokane Regional Waste-to-Energy*, PSD Appeal No. 88-12, at 5 n.7 (Adm'r June 9, 1989).

23. Letter from Stephen D. Page, Dir., Office of Air Quality Planning & Standards, EPA, to Paul Plath, Senior Partner, E3 Consulting, LLC, regarding Best Available Control Technology Requirements for Proposed Coal-Fired Power Plant Projects (Dec. 13, 2005), *available at* http://www.epa.gov/region07/air/nsr/ nsrmemos/igccbact.pdf.

24. *Id.* (concluding IGCC should not be considered in the BACT analysis for a pulverized coal fired boiler).

25. *Sierra Club v. EPA*, 499 F.3d 653, 657 (7th Cir. 2007).

26. *Id.* at 655.

27. *Id.* at 657-58.

28. EPA, New Source Review Workshop Manual, Prevention of Significant Deterioration and Nonattainment Area Permitting, Draft, at B.11 (Oct. 1990).

29. CAA § 171(3), 42 U.S.C. § 7501(3).

30. H.R. Rep. No. 95-294, at 215 (1977), *reprinted in* 1977 U.S.C.C.A.N. 1077, 1294.

31. *See generally* EPA, New Source Review Prevention of Significant Deterioration and Nonattainment Area Guidance Notebook (Jan. 1988).

32. CAA § 182(c)(7), 42 U.S.C. § 7511a(c)(7).

33. *Id.* § 182(c)(8).

34. EPA, Part 60—Standards of Performance for New Stationary Sources; Modification, Notification, and Reconstruction, 40 Fed. Reg. 58,416, 58,420 (Dec. 16, 1975); 40 C.F.R. § 60.15.

35. 40 Fed. Reg. at 58,420.

36. 40 C.F.R. § 60.15(b)(1).

37. *Id.* § 60.15(b)(2), (f).

38. EPA, Standards of Performance for New Stationary Sources; Modification Notification, and Reconstruction, 39 Fed. Reg. 36,946 (Oct. 15, 1974).

39. EPA, Standards of Performance for New Stationary Sources; Volatile Organic Compound (VOC) Emissions From the Synthetic Organic Chemical Manufacturing Industry (SOCMI) Air Oxidation Processes: Final Rule, 55 Fed. Reg. 26,912 (June 29, 1990).

40. *See, e.g.*, Letter from Donald R. Clay, EPA, to John W. Boston, Wisconsin Electric Power Company, at 1-5 (Feb. 15, 1989) ("Clay Letter").

41. *Id.* at 2-3.

42. EPA, Requirements for Preparation, Adoption, and Submittal of Implementation Plans; Approval and Promulgation of Implementation Plans: Final Rules, 45 Fed. Reg. 52,676; 52,703 (Aug. 7, 1980).

43. *See* EPA, Requirements for Preparation, Adoption, and Submittal of Implementation Plans; Approval and Promulgation of Implementation Plans; Standards of Performance for New Stationary Sources: Final Rule, 57 Fed. Reg. 32,314, 32,316 (July 21, 1992).

44. 40 C.F.R. § 60.14(a).

45. *Compare United States v. Ohio Edison*, 276 F. Supp. 2d 829 (S.D. Ohio 2003), *with United States v. Duke Energy Corp.*, 278 F. Supp. 2d 619 (M.D.N.C. 2003) ("*Duke I*"), *aff'd*, 411 F.3d 539 (4th Cir. 2005) ("*Duke II*"), *rev'd and judgment vacated, Envtl. Def. v. Duke Energy Corp.*, 549 U.S. 561 (2007) ("*Duke III*").

46. *Compare Duke II*, 411 F.3d 539, *rev'd and judgment vacated, Duke III*, 549 U.S. 561, *with United States v. Cinergy Corp.*, 458 F.3d 705 (7th Cir. 2006), *cert. denied*, 127 S. Ct. 2034 (2007).

47. *Duke III*, 549 U.S. 561.

48. *Wis. Electric Power Co. v. Reilly*, 893 F.2d 901 (7th Cir. 1990).

49. *See, e.g.*, Letter from Lee M. Thomas, Adm'r, EPA, to John W. Boston, Wis. Electric Power Co. (Oct. 14, 1988) ("Thomas Letter"); Clay Letter.

50. CAA § 111, 42 U.S.C. § 1857c-6 (1970).

51. *Id.* § 111(a)(4), 42 U.S.C. § 1857c-6(a)(4) (1970).

52. *Id.* § 110(a)(2)(D), (4), 42 U.S.C. § 1857c-5(a)(2)(D), (4) (1970).

53. EPA, Part 60 Standards of Performance for New Stationary Sources: Final Rule, 36 Fed. Reg. 24,876 (Dec. 23, 1971).

54. 40 C.F.R. § 60.2.

55. *Id.* § 60.14(b); EPA, 40 CFR Part 60 Standards of Performance for New Stationary Sources, Modification, Notification and Reconstruction: Proposed Rules, 39 Fed. Reg. 36,946 (Oct. 15, 1974); EPA, Part 60—Standards of Performance for New Stationary Sources, Modification, Notification and Reconstruction: Final Rule, 40 Fed. Reg. 58,418 (Dec. 16, 1975).

56. 39 Fed. Reg. at 36,947 (A kg/hr test is "sensitive to increased production capacity . . . . [and] automatically allow[s] increases in operating hours.").

57. 40 C.F.R. § 60.14(e).

58. 39 Fed. Reg. at 36,946 ("[T]he intent of section 111 [is] controlling facilities only when they constitute a new source of emission.").

59. *See* CAA § 110(a)(2)(D), (4) (1970), 42 U.S.C. § 7410(a)(2)(D), (4) (1970).

60. EPA, Part 52—Approval and Promulgation of Implementation Plans, Prevention of Significant Air Quality Deterioration: Final Rule, 39 Fed. Reg. 42,510 (Dec. 5, 1974); *compare* 40 C.F.R. § 60.14 *with* 40 C.F.R. § 52.01(d).

61. 39 Fed. Reg. at 42,513.

62. EPA, Part 51—Requirements for Preparation, Adoption, and Submittal of Implementation Plans: Interpretative Ruling, 41 Fed. Reg. 55,524 (Dec. 21, 1976).

63. *See id.* at 55,528 ("[A] 'major modification' shall include a modification . . . which increases the allowable emission rate by the amounts set forth above.").

64. *See* CAA §§ 169(2)(c), 171(4), 42 U.S.C. §§ 7479(2)(c), 7501(4).

65. *Id.* §§ 165(a), 169(1), 42 U.S.C. §§ 7475(a), 7479(1).

66. Clean Air Act Amendments of 1977, Pub. L. No. 95-95, § 129(a)(1), 91 Stat. 685, 745 (1977).

67. 40 C.F.R. §§ 52.01(d), 52.10.

68. *Id.* § 52.21(b)(2).

69. *See id.* § 52.21(b)(3).

70. *Id.* § 52.21(b)(21)(iv).

71. *But see Puerto Rican Cement v. EPA,* 889 F.2d 292 (1st Cir. 1989). In *Puerto Rican Cement*, the company proposed building a new cement kiln to replace two older kilns. Then-Judge Breyer observed that it might be unreasonable in certain circumstances to assume operation at full capacity, even absent an enforceable restriction on operations. *Id.* at 297-98; *see also WEPCo,* 893 F.2d at 917.

72. EPA, 1977 Clean Air Act Amendments to Prevent Significant Deterioration: Final Rule, 43 Fed. Reg. 26,388 (June 19, 1978).

73. 40 C.F.R. § 52.21(b)(21)(ii). This change in the "netting" rules in 1980 was in response to the concern that allowing offsets based on an emitting unit's "potential to emit" would allow what EPA called "paper credits" (*i.e.*, offsets based on unutilized emitting capacity). *See* 45 Fed. Reg. at 52,717-19.

74. 40 C.F.R. § 52.21(b)(21)(ii).

75. As EPA explained in an early enforcement action, the plain language of the 1980 rules "obviously describes a method of quantifying *past* [*i.e.*, pre-project] emissions," but does not "define[] post-change emissions." Response of United States to Duke Energy Motion for Summary Judgment (Mar. 31, 2003).

76. *See* Memorandum from Don Clay, Acting Assistant Adm'r for Air & Radiation, EPA, to David A. Kee, Director, Air & Radiation Division, EPA Region V, at 4 (Sept. 9, 1988) ("1988 Clay Memo").

77. Thomas Letter at 1.

78. 1988 Clay Memo at 5-6.

79. Memorandum from Don Clay, Acting Assistant Adm'r, EPA, to John W. Boston, WEPCo, at 7 (Feb. 15, 1989) ("1989 Clay Memo").

80. 1988 Clay Memo at 5; 1989 Clay Memo at 7 n.6.

81. 1988 Clay Memo at 7 n.4.

82. *WEPCo,* 893 F.2d at 916.

83. *Id.*; *see also Puerto Rican Cement,* 889 F.2d at 297-98.

84. *WEPCo,* 893 F.2d at 918 n.14.

85. *Id.* at 917.

86. 1988 Clay Memo at 7 n.4.

87. *WEPCo*, 893 F.2d at 918 n.14. Of course, if a unit has begun normal operations, only one period of "representative" operations should be necessary to characterize its "representative" operations.

88. *See Duke I*, 278 F. Supp. 2d at 641-43.

89. *See id.* at 645-46. Indeed, if an existing emission unit had begun normal operations, only one "representative" period would be needed to characterize those "normal" operations. Otherwise, differences in emissions would be driven merely by variations in "representative" operations, not the project at issue.

90. *Duke III*, 549 U.S. at 566.

91. EPA, Requirements for Preparation, Adoption and Submittal of Implementation Plans; Approval and Promulgation of Implementation Plans; Standards of Performance for New Stationary Sources: Final Rule, 57 Fed. Reg. 32,314, 32,326 (July 21, 1992).

92. *Id.* (emphasis added).

93. 40 C.F.R. § 60.14(h).

94. 57 Fed. Reg. at 32,330 (emphases added).

95. *Id.* at 32,331.

96. *Id.* at 32,332-33.

97. 40 C.F.R. § 52.21(b)(33); 57 Fed. Reg. at 32,337.

98. 40 C.F.R. § 52.21(b)(21)(v); 57 Fed. Reg. at 32,336.

99. 57 Fed. Reg. at 32,317 (emphasis added).

100. *Id.*

101. *Id.*

102. 40 C.F.R. § 52.21(b)(21)(v) (emphasis added).

103. 57 Fed. Reg. at 32,323.

104. *Id.* (emphasis added).

105. *Id.* (emphasis added).

106. 40 C.F.R. § 52.21(b)(33).

107. *See id.* § 52.21(b)(21)(v).

108. *See Duke I*, 278 F. Supp. 2d at 647 n.25.

109. 57 Fed. Reg. at 32,321.

110. *Id.* at 32,319.

111. *Id.*

112. 40 C.F.R. § 52.21(b)(2)(iii)(h).

113. *Id.* § 52.21(b)(32).

114. *Id.* § 52.21(b)(32)(iii), (iv).

115. Memorandum from John S. Seitz, Dir., EPA, to Regional Dirs., EPA, regarding Pollution Control Projects and New Source Review (NSR) Applicability (July 1, 1994).

116. EPA, Prevention of Significant Deterioration (PSD) and Nonattainment New Source Review (NSR): Baseline Emissions Determination, Actual-to-Future-Actual Methodology, Plantwide Applicability Limitations, Clean Units, Pollution Control Projects: Final Rule, 67 Fed. Reg. 80,186, 80,232 (Dec. 31, 2002).

117. *New York v. EPA,* 413 F.3d 3, 40 (D.C. Cir. 2005) ("*New York I*").

118. The D.C. Circuit specifically declined to address this issue. Order on Petitions for Rehearing, *New York v. EPA*, No. 02-1387, (D.C. Cir., Dec. 9, 2005) ("Because no specific retroactive application . . . is before the court, it would be premature to rule on this request [for clarification].)."

119. 57 Fed. Reg. at 32,326.

120. *Id*. at 32,327.

121. *Id*. (emphasis added).

122. 40 C.F.R. § 52.21(b)(33) (emphasis added).

123. 57 Fed. Reg. at 32,326 (emphasis added).

124. *Id*. at 32,327 (emphasis added).

125. *Id*. (emphasis added).

126. *New York I*, 413 F.3d at 31-33.

127. *See, e.g.*, H.R. Rep. 101-952, at 344-45 (1990), *reprinted in* 1 COMM. ON PUBLIC WORKS, A LEGISLATIVE HISTORY OF THE CLEAN AIR ACT AMENDMENTS OF 1990, at 1794-95 (1993) (as addressed in Joint Explanatory Statement of Conference Committee).

128. CAA § 409(d), 42 U.S.C. § 7651h(d).

129. *Id*. § 409(e), 42 U.S.C. § 7651h(e).

130. *Id*. § 415(b)(3), 42 U.S.C. § 7651n(b)(3).

131. *Id*. § 415(b)(1), 42 U.S.C. § 7651n(b)(1).

132. *Id*. § 415(b)(3), 42 U.S.C. § 7651n(b)(3).

133. 57 Fed. Reg. at 32,329-30.

134. CAA § 182(c)(6), 42 U.S.C. § 7511a(c)(6).

135. *Id*. § 182(e)(2), 42 U.S.C. § 7511a(e)(2).

136. *Id*. § 182(c)(7), 42 U.S.C. § 7511a(c)(7).

137. *Id*. § 112(g)(1)(A), 42 U.S.C. § 7412(g)(1)(A).

138. EPA, Hazardous Air Pollutants: Regulations Governing Constructed or Reconstructed Major Sources: Final Rule, 61 Fed. Reg. 68,384 (Dec. 27, 1996).

139. CAA § 112(g)(2)(A), 42 U.S.C. § 7412(g)(2)(A).

140. *Id*. § 112(g)(2)(B), 42 U.S.C. § 7412(g)(2)(B).

141. *Id*. § 502(b)(10), 42 U.S.C. § 7661a(b)(10).

142. *See generally* EPA, Air Enforcement, http://www.epa.gov/enforcement/air/index.html; *see also* EPA, Civil Cases and Settlements, http://cfpub.epa.gov/enforcement/cases/index.cfm (listing cases from 1998 through 2013).

143. Final Order on Reconsideration, *In re Tenn. Valley Auth.*, CAA Docket No. 00-6, 9 E.A.D. 357 (EAB Sept. 15, 2000), *available at* http://www.epa.gov/eab/disk11/tva.pdf.

144. *Id*. at 418, 439, 481-98.

145. *See TVA v. Whitman*, No. 00-15936 (11th Cir. filed Nov. 13, 2000); *Ala. Power Co. v. Whitman*, No. 00-16234 (11th Cir. filed Nov. 28, 2000); *TVA v. Whitman*, No. 00-16235 (11th Cir. filed Nov. 28, 2000); *Duke Energy v. Whitman*, No. 00-16236 (11th Cir. filed Nov. 28, 2000).

146. *TVA v. Whitman*, 336 F.3d 1236, 1239-40, 1249, 1260 (11th Cir. 2003).

147. *Id*. at 1246.

148. *Id.* at 1239-40.

149. *Leavitt v. TVA*, 541 U.S. 1030 (2004).

150. *See, e.g., Duke I*, 278 F. Supp. 2d at 630 n.8.

151. *Ohio Edison*, 276 F. Supp. 2d at 855-56, 862-69.

152. *Id.* at 832-33.

153. *Duke I*, 278 F. Supp. 2d at 637, 647.

154. *Id.*

155. *Duke II*, 411 F.3d at 550.

156. *Duke III*, 549 U.S. at 582.

157. *United States v. Duke Energy Corp.*, No. 1:00CV1262, 2010 WL 3023517, at *8-9 (M.D.N.C. July 28, 2010) (Plaintiffs' Motion to Vacate was granted in part and denied in part, and Duke Energy's Motion for Summary Judgment was denied.).

158. *United States v. Alabama Power Co.*, 372 F. Supp. 2d 1283, 1292-99, 1305-06 (N.D. Ala. 2005).

159. *United States v. East Kentucky Power Coop.*, 498 F. Supp. 2d 970, 972 (E.D. Ky. 2007).

160. *United States v. Cinergy Corp.*, 384 F. Supp. 2d 1272, 1278 (S.D. Ind. 2005), *aff'd,* 458 F.3d 705, 710-11 (7th Cir. 2006).

161. The key aspects of these settlements involve (i) EPA's confirmation of the traditional understanding of the NSR emissions increase test (as described in *Duke I*), in return for (ii) companies agreeing to install controls over the next 10 years that they were generally planning to install under other Clean Air Act programs. Makram B. Jaber, *Utility Settlements in New Source Review Lawsuits*, 18 NAT. RESOURCES & ENV'T 22, 25-26 (2004).

162. *Duke III*, 549 U.S. at 569.

163. *Id.* at 577.

164. *Id.* at 577-78 (internal citation omitted).

165. *Id.* at 581-82 (internal citation omitted).

166. *WEPCo*, 893 F.2d at 917; 57 Fed. Reg. at 32,317 (For projects that "do[] not 'change or alter' the design or nature of the facility . . . 'normal operations' have begun and the actual-to-potential test is impermissible."); *see also Ohio Edison*, 276 F. Supp. 2d at 863 (The plant "was operational at the time the activities were proposed. Thus, any use of the actual to potential to emit test is not legally supportable.").

167. *Duke III*, 549 U.S. at 566.

168. *Id.* at 578.

169. EPA, Prevention of Significant Deterioration (PSD) and Nonattainment New Source Review (NSR); Notice of Proposed Rulemaking, 61 Fed. Reg. 38,250 (July 23, 1996).

170. EPA, Alternatives for New Source Review (NSR) Applicability for Major Modifications; Solicitation of Comment; Notice of Availability, 63 Fed. Reg. 39,857 (July 24, 1998).

171. EPA, Prevention of Significant Deterioration (PSD) and Nonattainment New Source Review (NSR): Baseline Emissions Determination, Actual-to-Future-Actual Methodology, Plantwide Applicability Limitations, Clean Units, Pollution Control Projects: Final Rule, 67 Fed. Reg. 80,186 (Dec. 31, 2002).

172. *Id.* at 80,234-36.

173. *Id.* at 80,232-39 (discussing pollution control project exclusion).

174. *See, e.g., id.* at 80,189, 80,191-92

175. *Id.* at 80,249-51.

176. *Id.* at 80,255-58.

177. EPA issued a rule in December 2007 further defining the "reasonable possibility" concept. EPA, Prevention of Significant Deterioration and Nonattainment New Source Review: Reasonable Possibility in Recordkeeping: Final Rule, 72 Fed. Reg. 72,607 (Dec. 21, 2007).

178. *Id.* at 72,610-13.

179. *New York I*, 413 F.3d at 3.

180. EPA responded to this remand with a final rule further defining the "reasonable possibility" standard for recordkeeping requirements in late 2007. *See* EPA, Prevention of Significant Deterioration and Nonattainment New Source Review: Reasonable Possibility in Recordkeeping: Final Rule, 72 Fed. Reg. 72,607 (Dec. 21, 2007).

181. CAA § 172(b)(1), 42 U.S.C. § 7502(b)(1).

182. 40 C.F.R. § 51.100(o).

183. *See, e.g.*, EPA Region VI, Air Pollution Control (Ozone), http://www.epa.gov/region6/6pd/air/pd-l/control.htm; EPA, Reports for NAAQS (Title I) - Control Techniques Guidelines, http://www.epa.gov/ttn/oarpg/t1ctg. html.

184. CAA § 169A(b)(2)(A), 42 U.S.C. § 7491(b)(2)(A).

185. 40 C.F.R. § 51.301(c).

186. CAA § 169A(g)(2), 42 U.S.C. § 7491(g)(2).

187. Clean Air Act Amendments of 1990, Pub. L. No. 101-549, § 112, 104 Stat. 2399, 2531-74 (1990); 40 CFR § 68.130.

188. CAA § 111(d), 42 U.S.C. § 7411(d).

Chapter 4

OPERATING AND PRECONSTRUCTION PERMITTING PROGRAMS

Before enactment of the 1990 Amendments, the Clean Air Act was implemented principally through state implementation plans ("SIPs"), which specify the emission limitations applicable to individual sources of air pollution. With respect to permits, the Act provided only for a *preconstruction* permitting program for major new sources of air pollution and for major modifications of those sources.[1]

Although many states during the 1970s and 1980s established their own permit programs under state law to govern the operation of air pollution sources, EPA maintained that it had no authority to require or enforce these state operating permits until the late 1980s. In 1989, the Agency issued guidance addressing when permits issued pursuant to a state operating permit program authorized by a federally approved SIP could be considered to embody "federally enforceable" emission limits and operating restrictions.[2] As a practical matter, however, from the standpoint of federal law, existing sources were regulated almost exclusively through the application of SIP provisions and the terms of preconstruction permits.

The 1990 Amendments changed this by establishing a new *federal* operating permit program, contained in Title V of the Act, that requires a comprehensive, source-specific permit for major sources. Additional aspects of the new operating permit program are addressed in Title IV of the Act (the acid rain program) and in Title III of the 1990 Amendments (the air toxics program). This federal operating permit program does not replace, but rather supplements, the preconstruction permitting requirements of the federal Clean Air Act and existing state permit programs.

This chapter discusses the key elements of both the operating and preconstruction permit programs. It begins with an overview of the operating permit program, including the basic program elements, the content of permit applications and the permits themselves (including the treatment of current state operating permit requirements), the protections afforded by a permit, the consequences of the failure to obtain or to comply with a permit, and the roles of EPA, the public, and contiguous states in the issuance and enforcement of operating permits. This chapter then reviews other aspects of the Title V operating permit program, including monitoring requirements required under the Compliance Assurance Monitoring ("CAM") program, and the requirements of the acid rain and air toxic permit programs. Finally, this chapter addresses the preconstruction permit program for proposed new sources and modified sources of air pollutants regulated under the Act.

The Operating Permit Program

Title V of the Clean Air Act requires each state to develop and implement a comprehensive operating permit program for most sources of air pollution. The purpose of this new permit program is to consolidate in a single document all of the federally enforceable regulations applicable to a source, in order to facilitate source compliance and enforcement. With few exceptions, Title V does not authorize the creation of new substantive federal requirements. Permit programs are administered by the states; however, EPA retains authority to review and approve not only the overall permit program, but also each individual permit issued by the state. Additionally, after a permit is issued, EPA may terminate, modify, or revoke the permit upon determining that cause exists to do so.

This permitting program covers all major stationary sources, and many other sources as well. Each covered source must apply for and operate in compliance with the terms of an operating permit that contains (1) enforceable emission limitations and operating conditions; (2) a schedule for complying with any statutory requirements not yet being met; (3) inspection, monitoring, and reporting requirements; and (4) other conditions and measures as necessary to "assure compliance" with Clean Air Act requirements.

In July 1992, EPA issued final regulations addressing the minimum requirements for state operating permit programs.[3] These regulations are codified at 40 C.F.R. part 70. Based on these minimum requirements, most states developed Title V operating permit programs and had those "Part 70" programs approved by EPA. If a state failed to develop an adequate program, or fails to administer an EPA-approved program adequately, EPA may issue permits for sources in that jurisdiction pursuant to a federal program developed by EPA and codified at 40 C.F.R. part 71.[4]

Immediately after promulgation of the Part 70 regulations, several industry groups, environmental organizations, and states challenged the rules in federal court.[5] The parties jointly requested a stay in briefing for most issues in order to encourage settlement.[6] A number of the issues raised in the litigation were the focus of rulemaking proposals that were issued by EPA on August 29, 1994,[7] and August 31, 1995.[8] These proposals would have amended several elements of the Part 70 regulations, including those pertaining to when sources must seek revisions to their operating permits and the procedures applicable to each type of revision. The proposals sparked considerable debate concerning the scope of, and procedures necessary for, the Title V program. EPA never finalized any of those proposed amendments.

The following discussion summarizes the general features of the current program.

Applicability

Pursuant to section 502(a) of the Clean Air Act, section 70.3(a) of the Title V regulations initially required state programs to provide for the permitting of at least the following sources:

1. Any major source, defined in section 70.2 of the rules as any stationary source belonging to a single major industrial grouping and that is:
    (a) a major source under section 112 of the Act;
    (b) a major source of air pollutants that directly emits or has the potential to emit 100 tons per year ("tpy") or more of any air pollutant (including any major source of fugitive emissions of any such pollutant); and
    (c) a major source as defined in Part D of Title I of the Act;
2. Any source subject to a standard, limitation, or other requirement under section 111 of the Act;
3. Any source subject to a standard or other requirement under section 112 of the Act (although a source is not required to obtain a permit solely because it is subject to regulation under section 112(r) dealing with accidental release prevention);
4. Any affected source under Title IV of the Act; and
5. Any source in a source category designated by EPA.

In 2010, EPA revised the major source definition to limit the 100 tpy threshold to emissions of those air pollutants that are "subject to regulation," as newly defined in the rule. EPA adopted the revised definition to phase in over time the number of sources of greenhouse gases required to obtain Title V permits.[9] In 2011, EPA further limited applicability of the rule by excluding biogenic carbon dioxide emissions from that threshold for a period of three years.[10] The D.C. Circuit, however, vacated the biogenic exemption rule in July 2013.[11]

Section 502(a) provides EPA discretion to exempt one or more source categories upon finding that compliance is "impracticable, infeasible, or unnecessarily burdensome." Under this authority, EPA has allowed states to defer regulation of nonmajor sources, excluding solid waste incinerators, until the Agency "determine[s] how the program should be structured for nonmajor sources."[12] For nonmajor sources subject to new source performance or air toxics standards after July 21, 1992, EPA has reviewed the source category and determined whether to grant exemption at the time the new standard for such a source category is promulgated.[13] Section 70.5(c) of the rules also allows the states to develop exemptions for insignificant activities because of size, emission levels, or production rate. The rules preclude establishment of exemptions, however, if they would interfere with the determination or imposition of any applicable requirement or the calculation of fees.[14]

Under Title V, a single permit may be issued for a facility with multiple emission units that constitute a "Part 70 source" (*i.e.*, a source to which the Title V program applies).[15] The process of combining facilities for purposes of the permit application may not result in any reduction in permit fees, however.

Title V also provides that a permitting authority may issue a single permit for similar operations at multiple temporary locations. Such a permit must, however, include conditions that will assure compliance with all Clean Air Act requirements at all locations.[16]

Finally, states may establish general permits "by rule" covering "numerous similar sources."[17] Under this provision, individual sources in the identified categories would merely have to apply to the permitting authority for use of the general permit. EPA has indicated that examples of sources for which the general permit provision would be appropriate include dry cleaners, degreasers, service stations, small boilers, and storage tanks.

Development of State Permit Programs

Virtually all states (as well as local agencies with permitting authority) submitted, and received EPA approval for, operating permit programs. The states have some flexibility to tailor their programs to their particular objectives, while providing for the minimum elements of a Title V program as set out in Part 70. Whereas many programs received full approval, some programs initially were granted only interim approval because although those programs were found to "substantially meet" the requirements of Part 70, they were not fully approvable.[18] States initially were given two years to correct the deficiencies identified by EPA and to resubmit those elements of the program. To provide states with the opportunity to correct these deficiencies and simultaneously to modify their programs in response to the Agency's anticipated revisions to Part 70, EPA in 1997 delayed the date by which states with interim approval would have to amend their programs.[19] The last extensions of the interim approval deadline ended in 2001 when as part of a litigation settlement with environmental groups, EPA removed language from the Part 70 rules authorizing multiple extensions.[20]

EPA periodically audits each state's permit program to determine whether the program is being administered in accordance with EPA regulations and the conditions approved by EPA. If the Agency determines that the state is not administering and enforcing its permit program adequately, EPA must notify the state of the inadequacies. During the next 18-month period, EPA also *may* impose sanctions under section 179(a) of the Clean Air Act (restriction of federal highway funds and the imposition of an emission offset reduction ratio of two-to-one for projects subject to new source review ("NSR")). If the state fails to correct the program within 18 months, EPA *must* apply the sanctions. If the state has not corrected the deficiencies within six months thereafter, EPA must implement the federal operating permit program under Part 71.[21]

Permit Applications

Sources subject to the Title V program must submit a complete permit application, including a compliance plan describing how the source plans to comply with all applicable requirements where there is noncompliance, to the state permitting authority. Initial applications were due within one year after the permit program became effective.[22] A permit program is effective upon approval by EPA, whether that approval is interim, partial, or full.

For new sources (or modified sources that previously were not subject to Title V), a Title V permit application must be filed within 12 months of commencing operation.[23] In cases where an existing Title V permit would prohibit construction or a certain operational change, however, the source would need to satisfy the permit revision requirements of section 70.7 of the Title V rules before commencing operation.[24]

After receipt of an application, the permitting authority must determine whether the application is complete within sixty days. Unless the permitting authority requests additional information or otherwise notifies the applicant of incompleteness within this time period, the application is deemed complete by operation of law.[25]

In general, if a source submits a timely and complete permit application, failure to have a final permit is not considered a violation of the requirement contained in section 502(a) of the Act to operate with a permit, at least until the permitting authority takes final action on the application.[26] This protection is called the "application shield." The application shield may cease to exist, however, if, prior to the issuance of a final permit, the source fails to submit any additional information that the permitting authority has determined to be necessary to process the application.

A permit application must contain all information listed in section 70.5(c) of the rules, including: (1) emissions of pollutants for which the source is major and emissions of "regulated air pollutants"; (2) identification of all points of emissions; (3) emission rates in tpy and in other terms necessary to establish compliance; (4) description of air pollution control equipment; (5) identification of all federal air pollution control requirements; (6) monitoring and measurement techniques used to demonstrate compliance with federal applicable requirements; and (7) a statement of current compliance status with respect to all federally applicable requirements, and a schedule for compliance in the event of noncompliance.

States have developed standard application forms for use in satisfying the Title V permit application requirement. A particularly critical step in preparing the Title V application is identifying those requirements that are federally enforceable, as distinct from those that are only enforceable by the state. It is the federally enforceable requirements that are the true subject of Title V permits – and those to which the enforcement mechanisms apply. States may independently require sources to identify – and include in their Title V permits – state-only requirements. To the extent such requirements are included, they should be identified as "state-only," or they become federally enforceable as well.[27]

A responsible corporate official must submit a compliance certification that the source is in compliance with all applicable requirements. If necessary, this submission must also include a compliance schedule with respect to those applicable requirements with which the source will not be in compliance at the time of permit issuance.[28] The responsible official also must certify the truth, accuracy, and completeness of the application.[29]

In an effort to promote ways to streamline the application and permitting burdens associated with Title V, EPA issued two principal guidance documents, or "White Papers."[30] Many states have issued guidance or rules of their own to implement the principles contained in these EPA papers.

Permit Issuance

The permitting authority must take final action within 18 months after receiving a complete application.[31] Anticipating the administrative burden of establishing the new permitting program, however, Congress in section 503(c) of the Act provided for a phased schedule over three years for acting on initial Title V permit applications. The permitting authority was required to act on one-third of the permit applications received in the first year of the program in each year over a three-year period following program approval by EPA. EPA made clear in the preamble to the Title V rules that "act on" means final action rather than initial review.[32] As a practical matter, states had difficulty acting on permit applications within these deadlines.

The permitting authority must issue permits for a fixed term of no more than five years. Each permit must include: (1) applicable emission limitations and standards; (2) monitoring and related recordkeeping and reporting requirements; (3) a permit condition prohibiting emissions of sulfur dioxide ("SO_2") exceeding any allowances held under Title IV of the Act (for affected sources); (4) a severability clause to ensure continued validity of remaining permit requirements if any provisions are challenged; (5) a statement that any permit noncompliance constitutes a violation of the Act, and that the permit may be modified, revoked, reopened, and reissued or terminated for cause; (6) a provision to ensure that a source pays fees consistent with an approved state permitting fee schedule; and (7) the terms and conditions for reasonably anticipated alternative operating scenarios.[33] The permit also must contain the compliance requirements listed in section 70.6(c) of the rules, including (1) compliance certification, testing, monitoring, reporting, and recordkeeping requirements to assure compliance with the permit; (2) inspection and entry requirements for permitting authority officials; and (3) a schedule of compliance and provisions for regular progress reports. Insignificant emission units must be covered by the permit to the extent they are subject to applicable requirements.[34] Monitoring required under the CAM rule, which was issued in late 1997, must also be included in Title V permits.[35]

From 1992 to 2004, EPA's interpretation of the requirement in section 70.6(c) of the rules that permits specify monitoring to assure compliance, as well as the requirement in section 70.6(a)(3)(B) for periodic testing or monitoring representative of compliance, changed several times. Each change prompted some judicial challenge. The issue was resolved in 2008 when the D.C. Circuit vacated a 2006 rule revision that explicitly prohibited permitting authorities from supplementing monitoring requirements where existing rules already provided for periodic monitoring. Specifically, the court found that because section 504(c) of the Act requires that Title V permits contain monitoring "to assure compliance," permitting authorities must have authority to supplement existing monitoring that is not adequate for that purpose.[36] The court did not decide, however, what would happen if EPA and a permitting authority could not agree on whether an existing monitoring requirement was adequate.

Finally, as discussed above, pursuant to section 70.6(b)(2) of the rules, the permit must "specifically designate as not being federally enforceable . . . any terms and conditions included in the permit that are not required under the Act or any of its applicable requirements" (*e.g.*, state-only requirements). Such terms and conditions are not subject to Title V requirements regarding permit issuance, permit modification, and EPA and affected state review. Any terms not otherwise designated but that appear in the permit, however, *become federally enforceable* by either EPA or citizens under the citizen suit provisions of the Act.

EPA, Public and Affected State Participation in the Permit Process

EPA Review

Even after the state Title V program is in place, the Act gives EPA a significant role in overseeing the permitting process. Section 505(a)(1) requires the permitting authority to provide to EPA a copy of each permit application, draft permit, and final permit issued under Part 70.[37] EPA may comment on a permit application or draft permit. For example, once it receives a draft permit, EPA has 45 days to object in writing to the issuance of the permit (or permit modification/revision).[38] EPA must object to issuance of any proposed permit deemed not to be in compliance with the requirements of the Act. If EPA objects to a proposed final permit within 45 days of receipt, the permitting authority may not issue the permit. If the state does not revise and resubmit the permit in accordance with EPA's objections within 90 days, EPA must either issue or deny the permit pursuant to the federal program contained in 40 C.F.R. part 71.[39]

Public Involvement

Interested members of the public can be involved in virtually all phases of the Title V permitting process. Prior to permit issuance, the permitting authority must provide procedures for public notice, a comment period of at least 30 days, and the opportunity to request a public hearing on the draft permit.[40] The materials in the record must be made available for public review.

In addition to giving the public the right to review and comment on each permit application, interested citizens may challenge the terms of any permit with which they disagree. Specifically, members of the public (including an affected state) may petition the Administrator to prevent issuance of a permit based on objections to the permit that were raised "with reasonable specificity" during the comment period (unless the petitioner demonstrates that it was impracticable to raise such objections within that period, or unless the grounds for the objection arose after the comment period).[41] Such a petition must be filed within 60 days of the expiration of the 45-day period within which EPA may object to a permit (as discussed above). EPA must then grant or deny the citizen petition within 60 days.[42] Although EPA is not required to publish objections, EPA Region VII operates a website that provides access to many of them, and EPA routinely publishes notice of its actions on such petitions in the *Federal Register*. If EPA denies the citizen petition, that denial is subject to judicial review.

After permit issuance, the public continues to have access to Title V materials, including compliance plans, emissions and compliance monitoring reports, and certifications. The public thus has access to information that could form the basis for enforcement actions brought under the Act.

Participation of Affected States

The permitting authority must also give notice of each draft permit to any affected state on or before the time public notice is provided.[43] An affected state is one whose air quality may be affected *and* that is contiguous to the state in which the source is located, or within 50 miles of the source. The affected state must be afforded the opportunity to submit written recommendations on the proposed permit. If the permitting state does not accept a recommendation from an affected state, it must provide both the affected state and EPA with its reasons for rejecting the recommendation.[44] Affected states may then avail themselves of the administrative petition process that is available to citizens, as described above.

Protections Afforded by an Operating Permit: The Permit Shield

Section 504(f) of the Act provides that compliance with the permit shall be deemed compliance with applicable provisions of the Act. This permit shield is optional with the states, however. Section 70.6(f) of EPA's Title V rules provides that the permitting authority may include in a permit an express statement that compliance with the conditions of the permit shall be deemed compliance with any applicable requirements *as of the date of issuance of the permit* if (1) the applicable requirements are specifically identified in the permit, or (2) the permitting authority determines in writing that other requirements specifically identified do not apply to the source and the permit includes that determination. If the permit does not expressly state that a permit shield applies, then no shield will be presumed. Consequently, a source must take care to identify not only applicable requirements, but also those Clean Air Act requirements that do *not* apply to the source. In addition, sources must continue to track newly promulgated requirements, because compliance with the terms of the Title V permit may not constitute full compliance with all Clean Air Act requirements.

Renewal, Reopening, and Revision of the Title V Operating Permit

Renewal

Operating permits are to be issued for a specific period, not to exceed five years. Permit expiration terminates a source's right to operate unless a timely and complete renewal application has been filed.[45] To be timely, a renewal application must be filed no later than six months before the permit expires. The state, however, may require a source to file a renewal application up to 18 months before the permit expires.[46]

Reopening

An operating permit may also be "reopened" before it expires for a number of reasons, including changes in regulatory requirements and changes in source operations. A source must reopen its permit if additional requirements under the Act become applicable to the source and the remaining permit term is three or more years. Reopening for this reason must be undertaken within 18 months after the promulgation of the additional applicable requirement.[47] Reopening also is necessary if additional requirements become applicable to affected sources under Title IV.[48] Moreover, the permitting authority or EPA may seek to reopen the permit if they determine that the permit contains a material mistake, that inaccurate statements were made in establishing the permit terms, or that the permit must be revised to assure compliance with applicable requirements.[49] Proceedings to reopen a permit are subject to the same procedures applicable to initial permit issuance, but affect only those parts of the permit in question.[50] Procedures applicable to EPA when it seeks to reopen a permit are outlined in 40 C.F.R. § 70.7(g).

Revision

The Title V rules establish several categories of permit revisions (or "modifications"). These requirements were the subject of intense debate throughout the rulemaking and the ensuing litigation, with industry and state agencies generally arguing for limited review of permit revisions during the five-year permit term and environmental groups arguing in favor of more extensive review. At the heart of this debate was the issue of how much flexibility a source should have to change its operations without having to undertake a full permit proceeding to accomplish that change.

As a result of the judicial challenges to the final rule, EPA proposed revisions to the flexibility provisions of 40 C.F.R. part 70 in August 1994[51] and then again in August 1995.[52] EPA's 1994 proposal provided for four revision tracks, rather than the three contained in the 1992 rules. The complexity of this proposal, however, raised questions as to whether this four-track approach actually would further limit flexibility to change operations in response to competition and other market conditions. Numerous parties, including states and regulated industries, criticized the proposal as too complex for both sources and permitting authorities.

In response to this criticism, EPA proposed a fundamental restructuring of the permit revision portions of the Title V rule in August 1995. Under the proposal, during the five-year permit term, a source would have been able to undertake many changes in operations that require a permit revision simply by notifying the permitting authority at the time of the change and submitting a statement describing the revised permit term or new applicable requirements. This statement would have been attached to the permit itself. For "environmentally significant" changes, this streamlined "notice-and-go" procedure would have been available for those changes for which (1) a public review process was afforded in conjunction with the development or implementation of the applicable requirement, and (2) that review process was equivalent to the Title V permit procedures. States would have had more discretion to establish the requisite procedures for less environmentally significant changes. Formal review under the Title V program would have occurred during the next permit renewal.

This second reproposal prompted continued debate about the scope and procedures of the permit revision provisions. EPA proposed additional revisions to the permit modification rules in 1997 but did not promulgate final rules.[53]

Below is a summary of the permit revision system as set out in the current Title V rule.

Scope. Under the current Title V rule, a source must seek a permit revision *only* if the contemplated change could not be operated without violating a term of the existing permit, or if the change would trigger an applicable requirement to which the source had not previously been subject.

Administrative permit amendments.[54] An administrative permit amendment is generally a simple revision that corrects typographical errors, identifies a change in name or similar information, requires more frequent monitoring, or incorporates requirements into the operating permit from a preconstruction review permit (if the state review for preconstruction permits also satisfies the procedural participation requirements of Title V). In light of the ministerial nature of the changes in this category, no public notice is required for administrative amendments. Administrative amendments may typically be implemented upon the filing of an application.

Minor permit revisions.[55] Minor permit revisions are subject to limited review requirements and streamlined procedures. The Title V rules do not require public review of such revisions, but do require that EPA and affected states be notified of the proposed change. To qualify for the minor permit revision procedure: (1) the source may not be in violation of the permit term it seeks to change; (2) the revision may not violate any requirement applicable to the source; (3) the revision may not involve significant changes to existing monitoring, reporting, or recordkeeping requirements; (4) the revision may not require or change a case-by-case determination of an emission limitation or other standard; and (5) the revision may not seek to change or establish a permit term or condition for which there is no corresponding underlying applicable requirement. The source may make the proposed change immediately but, once it makes the change, the source may be liable for violating its permit if the revision is ultimately denied (e.g., in response to EPA or affected state comments, or a citizen suit challenging the state's failure to object to the proposed change).

Significant permit revisions.[56] Significant permit revisions are those that would not qualify as administrative or minor revisions. They are subject to the procedural requirements applicable to permit issuance and renewal, including the requirements for public participation and review by affected states and EPA.

Achieving Operational Flexibility

In light of the constraints that a source may face if it wishes to revise its permit during the permit term, it is of critical importance to ensure maximum flexibility when drafting the final permit. The Clean Air Act mandates that the permit program offer operational flexibility. For example, pursuant to section 502(b)(10), as interpreted by EPA, states must allow sources to engage in trading under a federally enforceable cap established in the permit.[57]

By far the best way to ensure operational flexibility, however, is to write a permit that specifies operation under all of the reasonably anticipated operating scenarios of the facility ("alternative operating scenarios").[58] A source owner or operator is then obligated simply to record in a contemporaneous log which operating scenario is in effect. This approach becomes less effective to the extent that it is difficult or impossible for an industry to predict new products or new market demands over a five-year period.

In the preamble to the final Title V rules, EPA also recognized that an appropriate way to avoid the need for permit revisions is to base permit terms and conditions on reasonably conservative assumptions regarding source emissions and operations (*i.e.*, the "worst-case" scenario). In this manner, a range of operations may be accommodated under the permit without the need to specify alternative operating scenarios.

In 2007, EPA proposed additional revisions to Part 70 as part of its Flexible Air Permitting Rule.[59] EPA's goal was to clarify how additional operational flexibility can be achieved through advance approvals under the Act's NSR provisions and the use of alternative operating scenarios ("AOS"). EPA also proposed to add major NSR requirements for something it termed "Green Groups," which would allow future changes to occur within a group of emissions activities, provided that they were ducted to a common air pollution control device determined to meet "best available control technology" or "lowest achievable emission rate," as applicable, and provided they complied with all relevant ambient air quality requirements. As finalized in 2009, the revisions added definitions for AOS and something called an "approved replicable methodology," and codified some clarifications to existing provisions.[60] EPA withdrew its Green Groups proposal, however, and instead encouraged states and sources to take advantage of flexibilities already provided under the major NSR regulations.

Permit Fees

States must establish a fee schedule that results in collection of revenue sufficient to cover permit program costs.[61] The costs to be covered by the fee schedule are listed in section 70.9(b)(1). A state fee schedule may include emissions fees, application fees, service-based fees, or other types of fees.[62] EPA will assume that the fees are adequate to cover the costs of the state program if the fees are equal to $25 per year multiplied by the total tons of the *actual* emissions of each regulated pollutant emitted.[63] States are free to propose a different fee schedule so long as they demonstrate that the fees generated thereunder are adequate. The fee schedule ultimately adopted by the state must be increased annually by the percentage increase in the Consumer Price Index in order to ensure adequate funding of the state program.[64] Many states initially adopted fees in the $25 to $30 per ton range and established caps on the maximum fee that can be collected from a source.

The Title V Performance Task Force

In 2004, in an attempt to address some of the outstanding disagreements over Title V implementation without litigation and to determine if further rulemaking is warranted, EPA formed a task force under the Agency's Clean Air Act Advisory Committee ("CAAAC"). The mission of the "Title V Performance Task Force" was to seek input from stakeholders on the performance of the Title V program, including what is working well (or poorly) and what improvements might be made. The Task Force's Final Report identified and discussed issues, summarized testimony of stakeholders, and provided recommendations for further action (although few were unanimous).[65]

In April 2006, the CAAAC forwarded the Task Force's Final Report to EPA and directed the Agency to report back with a response and a plan for implementing the recommendations. In September 2006, EPA provided the CAAAC with a list of the recommendations it deemed to be of the highest priority along with a timeframe for Agency action. EPA estimated most of the recommendations would take between one and three years to implement.

Other Operating Permit Requirements

While Title V of the 1990 Amendments contains the basic federal operating permit program, other provisions of the 1990 Amendments address special operating permit requirements that apply under other Titles of the Act.

Compliance Assurance Monitoring

Under section 114(a)(3) of the Act, EPA was required to promulgate regulations that require "enhanced monitoring" and submission of compliance certifications for all major stationary sources.[66] EPA satisfied those requirements through promulgation of the Title V operating permit rules and the 1997 CAM rule. The CAM rule applies to significant emission units that use control devices to achieve compliance with emission limits and that are not already required to perform continuous compliance monitoring in the units of the applicable emission standard.[67]

Sources covered by the CAM rule must develop and implement "CAM plans" that document continued proper operation of control devices by monitoring control device parameters and keeping those parameters within a specified range of performance that provides a reasonable assurance of compliance with applicable emission limits.[68] To the extent that a source monitors excursions from the specified range, it must investigate and take corrective action as necessary to bring the control device parameters back to within the specified range.[69] If a source fails to adequately correct the performance of the control device, the source must develop and implement a quality improvement plan, which consists of additional investigation and corrective action phases.[70]

The CAM rule is implemented on a source-by-source basis through the Title V permitting program. To ensure enforceability, certain elements of required

CAM plans must be reflected in a source's Title V permit.[71] In the regulatory impact analysis accompanying the CAM rule, EPA estimated that the rule would affect approximately 27,000 emission units. To stagger implementation, the CAM rule delayed implementation for all but the largest emission units until the source renewed its initial Title V permit.[72]

Like most of EPA's Title V rules related to emissions monitoring, the CAM rule was challenged judicially as insufficient to satisfy the compliance assurance requirements of the Act. In 1999, the rule was upheld by the D.C. Circuit as sufficient to satisfy the Agency's obligation to require "enhanced monitoring," but was remanded to require that responsible officials signing compliance certifications specify whether compliance was "continuous" or "intermittent," as required under section 114(a)(3) of the Act.[73] EPA revised the compliance certification rules in 2003 to implement that requirement.[74]

Permit Requirements of the Acid Rain Program

Recognizing that many Title V permits would not be issued by 1995, Congress took steps to ensure that sources covered by the Title IV acid rain program would be issued operating permits in time to comply with the requirements of that program. The Title IV acid rain permitting program is described in Chapter 9 of this Handbook.

Permit Requirements of the Air Toxics Program

Source-Specific Emission Standards

The Title V operating permit program must also address existing section 112 standards for sources of hazardous air pollutants as well as future control technology standards.[75] Under section 112(j), if the Administrator fails to promulgate a section 112 standard for a category or subcategory of major sources within 18 months of the applicable date set forth by EPA pursuant to section 112, the owner of operator of a source in that source category will be required to file a permit application that contains emission limitations that are "equivalent" to the limitations that would have applied if the source category standard had been promulgated.[76] These "equivalent" emission limitations must be determined on a case-by-case basis to require the maximum degree of reduction in emissions of hazardous air pollutants (including a prohibition of such emissions, where achievable), taking into account cost, energy requirements, and non-air quality health and environmental impacts.[77]

The requirements of section 112(j) are discussed further in Chapter 5 of this Handbook.

Early Reductions

Under section 112(i)(5) of the Act, EPA, or a state acting under a Title V permit program, may allow an existing source to meet an alternative emission limitation if the source demonstrates that it has achieved reductions of 90 percent or more in emissions of non-particulate hazardous air pollutants, or reductions of 95 percent or more in hazardous pollutants emitted as particulates.[78] Sources that make these reductions before a standard is proposed will receive a six-year extension from the compliance date for meeting the otherwise applicable maximum achievable control technology ("MACT") standard.[79] Extensions and alternative emission limitations are to be reflected in Title V permits. The provisions of the section 112(i)(5)(B) early reductions program are discussed further in Chapter 5 of this Handbook.

State Programs and Delegation of EPA Authority

Under section 112(l), states may develop and submit to EPA for approval programs to implement and enforce the air toxics standards. Such state programs may provide for either full or partial delegation of EPA authority. The section 112(l) provisions are discussed further in Chapter 5.

State Operating Permit Programs

Even though not required prior to 1990, many states developed their own operating permit programs. Operating permits issued pursuant to these programs may have included limits and standards that are also contained in the SIP, but may include additional requirements that are based on state law. Existing state operating permit programs were generally folded into the Title V program.

The 1990 Amendments, however, provided that "[n]othing in . . . [T]itle[V] shall prevent a state, or interstate permitting authority, from establishing additional permitting requirements not inconsistent with this Act.[80] Elaborating on this provision, the House and Senate Conferees explained that "[c]onsistent with the general provisions of section 116 of the Clean Air Act, the conferees understand that a state may establish additional more stringent permitting requirements, but a state may not establish permit requirements that are inconsistent with the national permitting requirements of this Act, including this title."[81]

While more stringent substantive requirements of existing operating permit programs may generally be continued in new state programs, section 70.6(b) of the Part 70 rules explains that "[a]ll terms and conditions in a Part 70 permit" are federally enforceable by the Administrator and citizen groups (through the citizen suit provision of the Act), unless the state specifically designates a provision as a state, rather than a federal, requirement. As a result, it is important for individual sources to ensure that the states delineate carefully whether specific substantive requirements are based in federal or state law. If a state does not specifically identify more stringent state-law requirements, those requirements become enforceable by EPA and by private citizens under the CAA citizen suit provision.

Preconstruction Permits

Under the PSD and nonattainment NSR programs, major new sources of air pollution (and, under certain conditions, major modifications to large existing sources) are subject to preconstruction review and permitting. In other words, under these programs, one cannot begin construction of a major new facility, or a major modification of a major existing facility, without first obtaining a permit.[82]

These programs are not supplanted by the Title V operating permit program.[83] Nevertheless, because sources subject to the PSD and nonattainment permitting programs are also subject to the Title V operating permit program, they must pay attention to how those programs are coordinated. The following discussion provides an overview of the preconstruction permit program, including certain changes made by the 1990 Amendments, and then discusses several issues related to coordination of the Title V and preconstruction permit programs.

The PSD Program

Under the Clean Air Act, before one can construct a "major" new source or undertake a "major modification" of a major existing source in an area that attains the national ambient air quality standard ("NAAQS"), one must obtain a permit under the PSD program.[84] In order to receive a PSD permit, the owner or operator of a proposed facility must demonstrate that the proposed source will (1) comply with the NAAQS and the PSD "increments"; (2) employ "best available control technology" ("BACT") for regulated pollutants emitted in significant amounts; and (3) have no adverse impact on other air quality-related values ("AQRVs"). The following discussion summarizes these requirements.

The Applicability Determination

Major Source

A PSD permit must be obtained before one can begin construction or modification of a major source of a regulated air pollutant for which an area is classified as "attainment" (or is not classifiable). A "major source" for purposes of the PSD program is defined as either (1) a source that belongs to one of 28 listed source categories that has a "potential to emit" 100 tpy or more of a regulated pollutant;[85] or (2) any other source that has a "potential to emit" 250 tpy or more of a pollutant.[86]

The term source is defined broadly in EPA's PSD regulations to include all emission units at "contiguous or adjacent sites," that are subject to "common control," and that belong to the same Standard Industrial Classification ("SIC") code.[87] The term "potential to emit" refers to the maximum capacity of a facility to emit pollution.[88] A source's potential to emit can be restricted, however, by enforceable restrictions placed on facility operations.[89] Historically, only "federally" enforceable restrictions could be taken into account, although this requirement was vacated by the U.S. Court of Appeals for the D.C. Circuit in September 1995.[90]

Major Modification

Once a major source has been built, any "major modification" of that source must be preceded by issuance of a PSD permit. A "major modification" is defined in EPA's PSD rules (as last amended in 2002) as a "physical or operational change" that results in (1) a "significant emissions increase" and (2) a "significant net emissions increase" of a PSD pollutant.[91] What constitutes a "physical or operational change," and how one computes an "emissions increase," have been the subject of much debate over the past years. These topics are addressed at length in Chapter 3 under the "modification" heading. EPA's rules establish "significance" levels for many of the regulated pollutants. For example, the significance level is 40 tpy for SO_2, 15 tpy for coarse particulate matter ("PM"), and 40 tpy for nitrogen oxides ("NOx").[92]

The "significant emissions increase" prong of EPA's rules is related to the project or activity itself that is determined to be a "change." That is, this first step of the emissions increase analysis requires an evaluation of whether the change itself would result in a significant emissions increase. The rules provide two types of tests for making this evaluation (the so-called "actual-to-projected-actual" and "actual-to-potential" tests), and elaborate procedures for applying these tests, depending on the type of emissions unit involved and the source's election.[93]

EPA's rules specify that "[i]f the project causes a significant emissions increase, then the project is a major modification only if it also results in a significant net emissions increase."[94] In this second step of the emissions increase analysis, one must balance out contemporaneous emissions increases and decreases at the source.[95] EPA's rules provide criteria that govern when emissions decreases at existing units at a source can be used to offset emissions increases that result, for example, from the increase in potential emissions associated with the construction of a new emissions unit. This concept is referred to as "emissions netting."

Generally, "contemporaneous" emissions increases and decreases must be aggregated to determine if a significant net emissions increase has taken place. Emissions increases and decreases are "contemporaneous" if they take place within a period starting five years before construction of the proposed facility begins and the time the proposed facility commences operation.[96] Moreover, in order to use emissions decreases to "net out" of PSD review, those decreases (1) must be computed based on emission reductions from the lower of past actual or allowable emissions; (2) must be voluntary reductions (*i.e.,* not otherwise required by law); and (3) must be made enforceable, for example, through a permit condition or SIP revision.[97]

In addition to netting out of new source review, the owner or operator of a source may avoid PSD review under EPA's Plantwide Applicability Limitation ("PAL") program. Under the PAL program, plant changes do not trigger NSR as long as source-wide emissions remain below a certain level specified in the source's PAL permit. The PAL program is summarized below in subsection 6.

Examples of Applicability Determinations

The PSD applicability rules can give rise to numerous difficult questions regarding whether emissions exceed either the "major source" definition or the "significance" thresholds. These questions often involve how one aggregates emission changes over time among the individual emission units that comprise a source.

For example, assume that a source is subject to the 100 tpy "major source" applicability threshold, but has a potential to emit only 90 tpy of SO_2. If an emissions unit that has a potential to emit 90 tpy of SO_2 is added to that source, would it be subject to PSD review?

Under EPA's rules, PSD review would *not* apply, because the new facility is not a "major source," and there is no existing major source for purposes of the "major modification" rule.[98] The addition of the 90 tpy unit, however, would result in an existing source that is "major" for purposes of any future additions (*i.e.,* the potential to emit of the existing source after the addition would be 180 tpy). As a result, the next addition of an emissions unit with the potential to emit 40 tpy or more of SO_2 would trigger PSD review for the new emissions unit (but not the already constructed units).[99]

Determination of what is a significant "net" emissions increase may raise similar questions. For example, expanding on the case described above, assume that the 90 tpy source (1) adds an emissions unit in year one with a potential to emit 30 tpy of SO_2; (2) shuts down a 10 tpy emissions unit in year four; (3) adds a 20 tpy emission unit in year five; and (4) adds a 40 tpy emission unit in year six. When would PSD review be triggered, and which of these facilities would be subject to review?

The source in this example would become "major" in year one, assuming the 100 tpy threshold applies. The addition in year four is not a "major modification" (*i.e.*, emissions are below the 40 tpy significance level), so no PSD permit would be required to construct this unit. The addition of a 40 tpy emissions unit in year six represents a "significant emissions increase," and thus requires an evaluation of "net" emissions to determine whether it constitutes a "major modification." The changes in years four, five and, six are "contemporaneous" and would equal 50 tpy, thus exceeding the 40 tpy significance level. Therefore, PSD review would be triggered in year six. Only the addition in year six, however, would be subject to PSD review, *unless* the projects in years five and six had been intentionally split apart in order to avoid review.[100]

Best Available Control Technology

In order to receive a PSD permit, an applicant must show that it will employ BACT for each pollutant regulated under the Act that it emits in significant amounts. BACT is defined as the "maximum degree of [emission] reduction . . . achievable," taking into account economic, energy, and environmental factors. BACT must be at least as stringent as any new source performance standard ("NSPS") applicable to the source category.

The BACT determination is a matter of judgment for the state permitting authority, based on a balancing of the economic, energy, and environmental impact of alternative control technologies.[101] In December 1987, however, EPA issued guidance (referred to as the "top-down" BACT guidance) that can restrict state discretion in making BACT determinations. The history of the controversy over top-down BACT is discussed in the Chapter 3 review of Clean Air Act control technology requirements. In 2004, the Supreme Court confirmed in *Alaska Department of Environmental Conservation v. EPA*, that "[n]othing in the Act or its implementing regulations mandates top-down analysis,"[102] yet upheld an EPA order based on EPA's determination that the state, which sought to apply the top-down methodology, did not provide a reasoned analysis for rejecting the "top" technology choice under that methodology.[103] Under *Alaska Department of Environmental Conservation*, therefore, while a state may not be required to follow a top-down methodology for determining BACT, the state must nonetheless properly apply that methodology once it has decided to use it in the permitting process.

Air Quality Issues

Although the BACT determination is perhaps the most important and controversial aspect of PSD permitting, a variety of other issues must also be resolved in order to receive a permit to construct a new or modified source. For example, the applicant must show that the proposed source will not cause or contribute to exceedances of either any applicable NAAQS or PSD increments (stringent air quality requirements designed to prevent significant deterioration of air quality in clean air areas). The applicant must also show that the proposed source will not adversely impact other air quality-related values. And the applicant may be required to consider the implications of its control technology proposals for unregulated emissions of air toxics. These issues are discussed below.

NAAQS and PSD Increment Compliance

A permit applicant must demonstrate that the proposed facility will not cause or contribute to an exceedance of any applicable NAAQS or PSD increment. PSD increments have been set for SO_2, PM, and NOx at a fraction of the NAAQS, in order to preserve air quality in clean air areas.[104]

The Act provides three levels of PSD increments. The most stringent (Class I increments) apply in "mandatory Class I areas" (larger wilderness areas and national parks).[105] The rest of the country is subject to Class II PSD increments. States can opt into a less stringent set of increments (Class III increments), as set out in section 164(a) of the Act, but none has elected to do so since enactment of the 1977 Amendments.

Compliance with NAAQS and PSD increments is determined through application of atmospheric dispersion models. EPA continues to refine these models and the related guidance for application of the models. Accordingly, the latest version of EPA's Air Quality Modeling Guidelines[106] and EPA's database for regulatory atmospheric modeling[107] should be consulted. Moreover, since disputes over how modeling should be conducted can delay receipt of a permit, one should consult the state and EPA Regional new source review staffs before filing a permit application in order to develop a protocol that resolves modeling issues. Questions that need to be addressed in this regard include the need for onsite meteorological data, the appropriate years for such data, how background pollution concentration should be defined, the amount of interactive source modeling that must be performed, and the location and density of receptor grids for air quality modeling.

A common issue that arises with respect to air quality modeling concerns whether a PSD permit may be issued for a source where a NAAQS exceedance is predicted in the vicinity of the source based on emissions from nearby, existing sources. Such modeled exceedances may be discovered for the first time in the course of air quality modeling conducted in support of the new source permit. Moreover, such modeled exceedances may be wholly artificial constructs of the modeling process, resulting from application of EPA's rules on "good engineering practice" stack height (which curtail the amount of dispersion credit one may use as input in air quality modeling).[108]

EPA's rules and guidance allow a source to receive a permit under the PSD program in this situation if it can be shown either that the proposed source will not have a "significant" ambient impact (as defined by EPA's nonattainment rules) for the pollutant,[109] or if it can be shown that the predicted ambient impact of the proposed new source will be insignificant at the point of the predicted exceedance.[110] If one of these showings cannot be made, the exceedance will have to be corrected (either through refined modeling or installation of additional controls) before a permit can be issued,[111] or the area in which the source proposes to locate will have to be redesignated as a nonattainment area so that permitting can proceed under the nonattainment program. Each approach can be time-consuming and burdensome.

Air Quality-Related Values and the Federal Land Manager

The PSD program was designed to prevent pollution concentrations in clean air areas from deteriorating to the level of the NAAQS. At the same time, this program was intended to be compatible with reasonable economic growth.[112]

Congress therefore designed the PSD increments to allow a greater margin of growth in urban and industrial areas. By contrast, in the case of certain national parks and wilderness areas (referred to as "mandatory Class I" areas), Congress provided for additional air quality protection, including more stringent PSD increments. Congress also authorized the Federal Land Manager ("FLM") for mandatory Class I areas to participate in the preconstruction permitting process when the area "may be affected by emissions" from the construction or operation of a new source.[113] If the FLM demonstrates to the satisfaction of the state that the "proposed emitting facility will have an adverse impact" on the "air quality related values" ("AQRVs") of the Class I areas,[114] the facility may not receive a permit, even if the allowable increments would not be exceeded.[115] On the other hand, if the FLM is satisfied that there will not be an adverse impact on AQRVs, the permit may be issued even if the allowable increments would be exceeded.[116]

In 2000, the Federal Land Managers' Air Quality Related Values Work Group ("FLAG") (formed by the FLMs for the stated purpose of developing a more consistent approach for reviewing PSD permit applications) published recommendations for evaluating AQRVs and guidelines for completing and evaluating PSD permit applications.[117] According to the FLAG Report, prior to submitting a permit application, the applicant should "consult" with the FLM to confirm preferred procedures for evaluating PSD Class I area impact, and the FLM "may ask . . . an applicant to address any and all of the areas of concern [to the FLM]. The primary areas of concern to the FLMs with respect to air pollution emissions are visibility impairment, ozone effects on vegetation, and effects of pollutant disposition on soils and surface waters."[118]

Since the 1990 Clean Air Act Amendments, the FLMs have become increasingly involved in the PSD permitting process. Based on a relatively rigid application of the FLAG Report, particularly for visibility, FLMs have requested that sources mitigate the impact of their emissions.[119] If sources refuse to mitigate impacts to the satisfaction of the FLM, the FLM may issue an adverse impact finding, in which case the permitting authority will not issue the permit unless it disagrees with the FLM's determination.[120]

Because the FLMs have become more aggressive in the PSD permitting process, one should carefully consider the proximity of Class I areas in making decisions regarding the siting of proposed new facilities.

Consideration of Air Toxics

Air toxics have been considered in two ways in the PSD permitting process. First, prior to the 1990 Amendments, the PSD rules required BACT review for *regulated* hazardous air pollutants emitted in significant amounts. Because EPA never set "significance" levels for several hazardous air pollutants (*e.g.*, arsenic, benzene, and radionuclides), some took the position that *any* emissions of these pollutants should lead to BACT review.

Second, EPA's decision in the "*North County*" permitting case explained that permitting authorities must consider the effects of a control technology on *unregulated* hazardous air pollutants in making BACT determinations for regulated pollutants.[121] Under this doctrine, a technology that controls emissions of an unregulated trace metal or organic compound would be preferable to one that did not, all else being equal. Similarly, a technology producing emissions of a hazardous substance would be less desirable than one that did not, all else being equal.

The 1990 Amendments to the Act changed the law in this area, at least with respect to the first issue noted above. The amendments to section 112 specifically state that substances listed under the new air toxics program are *not* subject to the PSD program.[122] According to EPA, this exemption applies to federal PSD permits issued on or after November 15, 1990.[123] States with an approved

PSD program, however, may continue to regulate air toxics if their PSD regulations provide an independent basis for such regulation.[124]

Because the air toxics list is extensive (187 substances and compounds are currently listed),[125] this provision should obviate the need for BACT review for regulated hazardous air pollutants. Because most states implement their own PSD permitting programs, however, the impact of the federal amendments on BACT considerations for regulated hazardous air pollutants will vary by state. The 1990 Amendments, however, do *not* affect the policy enunciated in the *North County* remand decision regarding consideration of unregulated hazardous air pollutants in the BACT determination for regulated pollutants.

Permissible Preconstruction Activities

Under the PSD rules, one cannot "begin actual onsite construction" of a new source, or of a major modification to an existing source, without obtaining a PSD permit. EPA has addressed in guidance the types of "preconstruction" activities that can be undertaken before receiving a PSD permit. Such preconstruction activities include site preparation, grading, and other work preliminary to laying the foundation of the facility.[126] Concluding contractual arrangements also fall outside the scope of the "actual onsite construction" concept, at least as long as the contracts do not anticipate either onsite construction or offsite construction of unique, site-specific equipment or facilities, before receipt of a permit.

To the extent that construction is begun without a permit, EPA may issue an administrative order to halt construction.[127] Such an order is enforceable in federal district court. In addition, EPA has authority to seek civil penalties for violation of such an order.[128] EPA's enforcement authority is discussed in Chapter 11.

EPA's Role With Respect to State-Issued PSD Permits

Reflecting EPA efforts to impose more uniformity on state BACT decisions through policy guidance, EPA Regions actively review state permit decisions to ensure state conformity with national guidance. The type of review authority exercised by the EPA Regions depends upon whether a state has developed its own PSD program as part of its SIP, or whether the state has been delegated authority by EPA to implement the federal program.[129]

SIP-Approved PSD Programs

When a state has developed its own PSD program and that program has been approved by EPA as part of the SIP, EPA's authority to review state decisions is limited. EPA has authority to revoke its approval of the state's PSD program, based on a showing by EPA that the state program is "substantially inadequate" to carry out the purposes of the PSD program.[130] The burden is on EPA, however, to show substantial inadequacy. Given that Congress intended states to have substantial discretion to implement the PSD program, this burden is a heavy one. By contrast, EPA has used its enforcement authority under sections 167 and 113(a)(5) of the Act to enforce SIP-approved PSD programs. Section 167 authorizes EPA to issue orders, enforceable in district court, halting construction of projects that do not have valid PSD permits. Section 113(a)(5), which was added by the 1990 Amendments to the Act, authorizes the Administrator to issue enforcement orders whenever she finds that "a State is not acting in compliance with any requirement or prohibition of the Act relating to the construction of new sources or the modification of existing sources." Violation of such orders can give rise to the assessment of administrative or civil penalties. Although such orders are clearly appropriate in the cases of clear-cut violations of the PSD program (for example, where construction has begun on a major modification without a PSD permit, or where the state issues a PSD permit that is deficient on its face, such as a permit that contains no BACT determination), EPA has also used these provisions in cases where it merely disagrees with the state's exercise of discretion with respect to specific PSD issues (for example, the choice among alternative control technologies as BACT). Although lower federal courts were initially reluctant to accept this latter assertion of authority,[131] the Supreme Court in 2004 held that "EPA has supervisory authority over the reasonableness of state permitting authorities' BACT determinations and may issue stop construction orders, under §§ 113(a)(5) and 167, if a BACT selection is not reasonable."[132] Because the touchstone of the Supreme Court's holding remains whether the *state's* BACT decision is "reasonable," however, it remains to be seen how far EPA can go to "second guess" state permit decisions in states that have SIP-approved PSD programs.

Delegated PSD Authority

Where a state has been delegated authority by EPA to implement the federal PSD rules, EPA has greater authority to control state decisions. For example, EPA may preserve in the delegation agreement the right to review state decisions. As a result, when seeking a PSD permit in such states, it is important to consult the delegation agreement to ascertain precisely what role EPA may play regarding the PSD permit decision.

Regardless of the terms of the delegation agreement, EPA retains authority under the consolidated permit regulations to review PSD decisions by states that have been delegated permitting authority, based either on a petition from a private party or on its own initiative.[133] Such review authority must be exercised within 30 days of the state permit decision. If review of the decision is sought within 30 days (under 40 C.F.R. § 124.15, permit decisions by states with delegated authority do not become effective until 30 days after the decision is issued), the permit does not become effective until either: (1) the Agency denies the petition to appeal; (2) the petition is settled; or (3) the state responds to a remand decision.[134]

EPA Regions and private citizen groups have actively sought administrative review of the state permit decisions. This has caused delays in obtaining PSD permits in states with delegated authority. In formulating a permitting strategy, therefore, it is critical to know the status of the state's PSD permitting authority and to establish a comprehensive record for the state's permit decision that reduces the risk of administrative appeals.

The Plantwide Applicability Limitation Program

As mentioned above, the owner or operator of an existing source may avoid PSD review under EPA's PAL program.[135] Under the PAL regulations, as under the NSR netting regulations, so long as source-wide emissions do not increase (*i.e.*, so long as any emissions resulting from a change at one emissions unit at the source are offset by decreases at another emissions unit at the same source), PSD does not apply. The PAL program, however, may have an advantage over netting because a PAL is established once every ten years and covers all changes that occur during its term, while netting must be applied separately for every change. According to EPA, the "added flexibility of a PAL allows sources to respond rapidly to market changes consistent with the goals of the NSR program."[136]

What is a PAL?

A PAL is an emission limitation for a major stationary source expressed in tpy and set on a pollutant-by-pollutant basis. It must be enforceable as a practical matter and established source-wide in accordance with EPA's PAL regulations.[137] In other words, a PAL is specific to a particular pollutant, and multiple permits can be established so that emissions of several regulated pollutants are limited. As long as a source is able to comply with its PALs, changes, including alterations to existing emissions units and the addition of new emissions units, may occur at the source without triggering PSD.[138]

Determining the PAL Level

An application for a PAL must demonstrate that the PAL will not cause or contribute to a violation of any applicable NAAQS, will not cause or contribute to an exceedance of a PSD increment, and will not adversely impact visibility or an AQRV in a Class I area.[139] In general, for each covered pollutant, the PAL is determined by summing the baseline actual emissions for all emissions units at the source and adding an amount equal to the applicable significance level for that pollutant. The applicant must determine the baseline actual emissions using the same 24-month period for all units but may use allowable emissions for any emissions unit added to the facility after the selected 24-month period (emissions from permanently shutdown units must be subtracted).

A reviewing authority must provide an opportunity for public participation on the application for a PAL, including a comment period and the opportunity for a public hearing.[140] The application for a PAL must contain a proposed monitoring system, and a facility with a PAL must perform monitoring of all applicable units to demonstrate that the PAL is not exceeded.[141] A facility must determine its actual emissions on a monthly basis and compare them to its PAL on a rolling 12-month total basis.[142] Emission calculations and deviation reports must be submitted to the regulatory agency at least semi-annually.[143]

Term of the PAL

The permitting authority may reduce a PAL during its term but only if a reduction is required due to the promulgation of a new regulatory standard (*e.g.,* a new NSPS or MACT) or if the authority determines that the PAL may cause an exceedance of a NAAQS or have an adverse impact to a federal Class I area.[144] Limits eliminated by a PAL (for example, limits in accordance with 40 C.F.R. § 52.21(r)) do not return upon the expiration of a PAL. Once a PAL is determined and approved, it remains valid for 10 years and is renewable every 10 years.[145]

At the conclusion of the term of a PAL, the permitting authority may renew the PAL at the original PAL level without considering other factors if the sum of the baseline actual emissions for the emissions units at the source (plus significance levels) is equal to or greater than 80 percent of the original PAL level.[146] If the recalculated baseline plus significance level is less than 80 percent of the original PAL level, the permitting authority may set the PAL at a level that it believes is appropriate, taking into account air quality needs, advances in control technology, anticipated economic growth in the area, and other factors identified by the authority.[147] The new PAL level cannot be higher than the potential to emit of the source or the existing PAL (unless PAL increase provisions are met).[148]

The Nonattainment NSR Program

In areas that have not attained the NAAQS for a given pollutant (*i.e.,* "nonattainment" areas), new or modified stationary sources must receive a nonattainment NSR permit before construction of the proposed source or modification may begin. States are responsible for implementing the nonattainment permit program. The state permit program must require, at a minimum, that major new sources or major modifications of existing sources install control technology that will achieve a standard defined as the "Lowest Achievable Emission Rate" ("LAER"). The nonattainment permit must also require that emissions of the nonattainment pollutant from the new or modified source be offset by emission reductions that have a similar air quality impact, that the source owner or operator certify that its other sources are in compliance (or on a schedule to comply) with all applicable air quality requirements, and that the benefits of the proposed source outweigh its costs.

The Applicability Determination

The Act defines a "nonattainment area" as one "which does not meet (or that contributes to ambient air quality in a nearby area that does not meet)" any NAAQS.[149] The designation is made separately for each pollutant, and an area is typically "nonattainment" for some pollutants and "attainment" for others.

SIPs for nonattainment areas must "require permits for the construction and operation of new or modified major stationary sources."[150] A major stationary source is one that has the potential to emit 100 tpy or more of a nonattainment pollutant.[151] In contrast to the PSD program, there is no separate category of 250 tpy sources.

The 1990 Amendments impose a more stringent definition of major source for certain ozone nonattainment areas, depending on the seriousness of the nonattainment areas. For "moderate" ozone nonattainment areas, the applicability threshold remains at 100 tpy.[152] For "serious" nonattainment areas, the threshold is 50 tpy; for "severe" areas, it is 25 tpy; and for "extreme" areas, it is 10 tpy.[153] These more stringent major source thresholds will also apply to NOx emissions in ozone nonattainment areas, unless the state has found that reductions in NOx emissions in the area will not contribute to attainment of the ozone standard.[154]

In serious carbon monoxide ("CO") nonattainment areas where the Administrator determines that stationary sources contribute significantly to CO concentrations, the 1990 Amendments revise the major source threshold from 100 tpy to 50 tpy.[155] In serious PM nonattainment areas, the major source threshold is revised from 100 tpy to 70 tpy.

Like the PSD rules, the nonattainment NSR rules apply to physical or operational changes that result in a "significant" emissions increase.[156] Significance levels are defined in EPA's rules.[157] The 1990 Amendments make certain changes to these significance levels, however. For example, in serious and severe ozone nonattainment areas, an increase in 25 tpy of volatile organic compounds ("VOCs") over a five-year period is defined as significant. In an extreme ozone nonattainment area, *any* increase in VOCs is defined as significant.[158] These significance thresholds also may apply to NOx emitters in certain ozone nonattainment areas.[159]

The definition of "major modification" under the nonattainment NSR program differs somewhat from the PSD program in other respects. Under the nonattainment rules, states have discretion as to whether to allow emissions "netting" in making applicability determinations – *i.e.,* whether to allow a source to avoid review by making contemporaneous emissions decreases at existing emission units to avoid an emission increase from the source as a whole.[160] States generally have two options under the nonattainment program. Under the first option, referred to as the "dual source" definition, emissions from separate emission units at a common site are aggregated to determine whether the major source threshold is met. All proposed new facilities at a site are then aggregated to determine whether the "significant" increase threshold is met, but emissions decreases elsewhere at the source cannot be applied to "net out" of nonattainment NSR review.

A state may reject the "dual source" definition, and adopt an emissions netting approach that is similar to that of the PSD applicability rules, subject to certain special requirements of the 1990 Amendments. For example, the 1990 Amendments specifically address the issue of emissions netting in serious and severe ozone nonattainment areas. For serious and severe areas, sources that have a potential to emit VOCs of less than 100 tpy can avoid triggering the modification rule if emission increases from the proposed facility are offset by emission decreases internal to the source at a ratio of 1.3 to 1 or more.[161] If such an offset is not obtained, the modification rule applies, but BACT can be substituted for the more stringent LAER. Sources in such areas with a potential to emit 100 tpy or more of VOCs can avoid LAER if they obtain 1.3-to-1 internal offsets.[162]

Finally, the nonattainment NSR program is a *state*-implemented program. As a result, there may be important state-to-state variations in nonattainment requirements, including applicability requirements. Some states, for example, have adopted definitions of what is a "significant" emissions increase that are more stringent than the federal minimum. States may adopt different approaches to the control of NOx emissions in ozone nonattainment areas under the 1990 Amendments. It is therefore important to examine closely a state's nonattainment NSR program in developing a new source permitting strategy.

The "Lowest Achievable Emission Rate" Requirement

Like the PSD program, the nonattainment permit program requires the owner or operator of a proposed facility to install stringent control technology. Spe-

cifically, the source owner or operator must demonstrate that the proposed facility will use control technology for nonattainment pollutants emitted in significant
amounts that complies with the "LAER" standard.

LAER is defined as "the most stringent emission limitation" contained in
any SIP, or that is "achieved in practice" by the same or a similar source category, whichever is most stringent. If the owner or operator of the proposed source
can demonstrate the most stringent technology is not feasible for its proposed
facility, a less stringent technology can be established as LAER.

The LAER requirement is discussed further in Chapter 3 of this Handbook
regarding new source control technology requirements.

Air Quality Issues

Besides the LAER determination, several air quality issues must be addressed in a permit for construction of a major source or a major modification in
a nonattainment area. These issues are summarized briefly below, and discussed
in more detail in Chapter 2 regarding the nonattainment program.

Emission Offsets

In order to ensure progress towards attainment of the NAAQS, a proposed
new facility must offset its potential to emit nonattainment pollutants by secur-
ing emission reductions from nearby facilities at a greater than 1-to-1 ratio. Under the 1990 Amendments, varying offset ratios and more inclusive definitions
of "major source" apply to permit programs in ozone, CO, and PM nonattainment areas. Offset ratio requirements in ozone nonattainment areas vary between 1.1 and 1.5 to 1 according to the area's classification.

The Administrator is given authority to set rules for determining the "baseline" against which emission offsets are to be credited.[163] Generally, a new or
modified major stationary source may comply with offset requirements only by
obtaining enforceable emission reductions from the same source or other sources
in the same nonattainment region. States may allow a source to obtain the reductions in another nonattainment area, however, if the second area has a nonattainment classification of greater or equal seriousness and emissions from that
area contribute to nonattainment in the first area.

Offsetting emission reductions must be in effect and enforceable by the time
the new source commences operation, and offsets must be adequate to assure
that the total tonnage of increased emissions are offset by reductions in actual
emissions that are not otherwise required by law.[164]

The Report of the House Committee on Energy and Commerce on the 1990
Amendments notes that a company that received a construction permit under the
current Act is grandfathered and thus need not satisfy any additional offsets to
retain its construction permit, or subsequently to obtain an operating permit.

The Committee Report further states that the Amendments "make no change in current law [regarding the grandfathering of permits]." Given this congressional intent, EPA guidance tied the applicability of the new offset requirements to whether a completed application was filed by the date the state's nonattainment SIP submittal for new source permitting was due (*i.e.*, for VOCs, by November 15, 1992).[165]

Compliance Certification

In order to receive a nonattainment permit, the owner or operator of the proposed facility must certify that all other facilities it owns or operates in the same jurisdiction are in compliance with all air quality control requirements, or subject to an enforceable schedule to come into compliance. Emissions testing to verify compliance may be required in some jurisdictions.

Benefits of the Project and Mitigation Strategies

The 1990 Amendments require that the owner or operator of the proposed facility undertake "an analysis of alternative sites, sizes, production processes, and environmental control techniques" for the proposed facility.[166] In order to receive a permit, that analysis must demonstrate that "the benefits of the proposed source significantly outweigh the environmental and social costs imposed as a result of its location, construction, or modification." The extent of this provision is broad and varies from state to state.

Resource Materials for Permit Applicants

As can be seen from the foregoing discussion, permitting authorities are called upon to make numerous, complex decisions under both the PSD and nonattainment NSR permit programs. These decisions will depend on the facts and circumstances of each case, and will be influenced by EPA's latest NSR and air quality guidance.

In planning for permitting a new facility, therefore, it is important to consult the most recent versions of EPA's guidance documents as well as recent EPA and state permit decisions. Materials that should be consulted in preparing a PSD and/or nonattainment NSR permit application include the following:

- The PSD and nonattainment regulations.[167]
- EPA's 1980 PSD Workshop Manual.[168]
- EPA's 1990 Draft NSR Workshop Manual.[169]
- The latest versions of the Air Quality Modeling Guidelines and EPA's Annual Model Clearinghouse Reports.

- EPA's RACT/BACT/LAER Clearinghouse, which is available at: http://cfpub.epa.gov/RBLC/.
- EPA Region 7 New Source Review Policy and Guidance Database, which is available at: http://www.epa.gov/region07/programs/artd/air/ nsr/nsrpg.htm.
- EPA's Control Technique Guidelines, which are available at: http://www.epa.gov/ttn/caaa/t1ctg.html.
- The PSD program status in the various EPA Regions which is available at: http://www.epa.gov/air/nsr/where.html.

Combined Title V/Preconstruction Permit Programs

Some states have sought to combine the Title V permitting program with their existing PSD and nonattainment NSR permitting programs. The objective is to harmonize the procedural requirements of the two programs so that a source need not engage in two separate permitting processes, for example, when undertaking a modification that triggers NSR and requires a revision of an existing Part 70 permit. In some cases, however, this effort has raised questions about the scope of EPA's permit review authority and its use of Title V veto authority, which may be appropriate for certain Part 70 permit terms but not for state PSD determinations.

Notes

1. Preconstruction permitting is addressed in the Act under the prevention of significant deterioration ("PSD") program of Title I Part C and the nonattainment new source review ("NSR") program of Title I Part D.

2. EPA, Requirements for the Preparation, Adoption, and Submittal of Implementation Plans; Approval and Promulgation of Implementation Plans, 54 Fed. Reg. 27,274 (June 28, 1989).

3. EPA, Operating Permit Program, 57 Fed. Reg. 32,250 (July 21, 1992).

4. EPA, Federal Operating Permits Program, 61 Fed. Reg. 34,202 (July 1, 1996). The federal operating permit program would be administered either by EPA or by the state under a delegation of authority from EPA.

5. *Clean Air Implementation Project v. EPA*, No. 92-1303 and consolidated cases (D.C. Cir. filed July 21, 1992).

6. Although the case has been administratively terminated for lack of activity, any party could seek to resume the case at any time.

7. EPA, Operating Permits Program Rule Revisions, 59 Fed. Reg. 44,460 (Aug. 29, 1994).

8. EPA, Operating Permits Program and Federal Operating Permits Program, 60 Fed. Reg. 45,530 (Aug. 31, 1995).

9. EPA, Prevention of Significant Deterioration and Title V Tailoring Rule, 75 Fed. Reg. 31,514 (June 3, 2010).

10. EPA, Deferral for CO2 Emissions From Bioenergy and Other Biogenic Sources Under the Prevention of Significant Deterioration (PSD) and Title V Programs, 76 Fed. Reg. 43,490 (July 20, 2011).

11. *Center for Biological Diversity v. EPA*, 722 F.3d 401 (D.C. Cir. 2013).

12. 40 C.F.R. § 70.3(b)(1). The rules also provides states with authority to permanently exempt two source categories from Title V: wood stoves and asbestos renovation and demolition projects. *Id.* § 70.3(b)(4).

13. *Id.* § 70.3(b)(2); *see, e.g.*, National Emission Standards for Hazardous Air Pollutants for Source Categories: Gasoline Distribution Bulk Terminals, Bulk Plants, and Pipeline Facilities; and Gasoline Dispensing Facilities, 73 Fed. Reg. 1916 (Jan. 10, 2008); National Emission Standards for Hazardous Air Pollutants for Area Sources: Polyvinyl Chloride and Copolymers Production, Primary Copper Smelting, Secondary Copper Smelting, and Primary Nonferrous Metals: Zinc, Cadmium, and Beryllium, 72 Fed. Reg. 2930 (Jan. 23, 2007); Standards of Performance for New Stationary Sources and Emission Guidelines for Existing Sources: Large Municipal Waste Combustors, Proposed Rule, 70 Fed. Reg. 75,348 (Dec. 19, 2005).

14. 57 Fed. Reg. at 32,273.

15. CAA § 502(c), 42 U.S.C. § 7661a(c); *see* 40 C.F.R. §§ 70.2, 70.3(a).

16. CAA § 504(e), 42 U.S.C. § 7661c(e); 40 C.F.R. § 70.6(e).

17. CAA § 504(d), 42 U.S.C. § 7661c(d); 40 C.F.R. § 70.6(d).

18. 40 C.F.R. § 70.4(d).

19. EPA, Extension of Operating Permits Program Interim Approvals, 62 Fed. Reg. 45,732 (Aug. 29, 1997).

20. *See* 66 Fed. Reg. 27,008 (May 15, 2001).

21. *See generally* 40 C.F.R. § 70.10.

22. CAA § 503(c), 42 U.S.C. § 7661b(c); 40 C.F.R. § 70.5(a)(1)(i). Section 70.5(a)(1)(i) also stipulates, however, that the permitting authority may establish an earlier date for submission of a permit application.

23. 40 C.F.R. § 70.5(a)(1)(ii).

24. *Id.*

25. *Id.* § 70.7(a)(4).

26. CAA § 503(d), 42 U.S.C. § 7661b(d); 40 C.F.R. § 70.7(b).

27. *See* 40 C.F.R. § 70.6(b)(2).

28. *Id.* § 70.5(c)(8)-(9).

29. *Id.* § 70.5(d).

30. Memorandum from L.N. Wegman, Dep. Dir., Office of Air Quality Planning and Standards, EPA, to Dir., Office of Ecosystem Protection, Region I, et al., White Paper Number 2 for Improved Implementation of the Part 70 Operating Permits Program (Mar. 5, 1996); Memorandum from L.N. Wegman, Dep. Dir., Office of Air Quality Planning and Standards, EPA, to Dir., Air, Pesticides and Toxics Management Division, Regions I and IV, et al., White Paper for Streamlined Development of Part 70 Permit Applications (July 10, 1995).

31. 40 C.F.R. § 70.7(a)(2).

32. 57 Fed. Reg. at 32,266.

33. 40 C.F.R. § 70.6(a).

34. *See, e.g.*, EPA, Clean Air Act Final Interim Approval of Operating Permit Programs; State of Tennessee and Memphis-Shelby County, Tennessee, 61 Fed. Reg. 39,335, 39,337 (July 29, 1996).

35. *See* Section II.A of this chapter.

36. *Sierra Club v. EPA*, 536 F.3d 673 (D.C. Cir. 2008).

37. *See also* 40 C.F.R. § 70.8(a).

38. CAA § 505(b)(1), 42 U.S.C. § 7661d(b)(1); 40 C.F.R. § 70.8(c)(1).

39. CAA § 505(c), 42 U.S.C. § 7661d(c); 40 C.F.R. § 70.8(c)(4). Courts interpreting EPA's obligation to issue or deny permits have held that, because the Act provides no explicit deadline for EPA's action, the timing is discretionary and EPA's inaction does not authorize a suit to compel performance of a nondiscretionary duty. *See, e.g., Zen-Noh Grain Corp. v. Jackson*, No. 2:12-cv-02535, 2013 WL 1856084 (E.D. La. Apr. 30, 2013); *WildEarth Guardians v. Jackson*, 885 F. Supp. 2d 1112 (D.N.M. 2012).

40. 40 C.F.R. § 70.7(h).

41. *Id.* § 70.8(d).

42. CAA § 505(b)(2), 42 U.S.C. § 7661d(b)(2). Several U.S. Courts of Appeal have upheld EPA's discretion to determine whether a petitioner has demonstrated that a permit does not comply with the Act and found reasonable EPA's finding that the petitioners had not met that burden. *See, e.g., Sierra Club v. EPA*, 557 F.3d 401 (6th Cir. 2009); *Sierra Club v. Johnson*, 541 F.3d 1257 (11th Cir. 2008); *Citizens Against Ruining the Env't v. EPA*, 535 F.3d 670 (7th Cir. 2008).

43. CAA § 505(a)(2), 42 U.S.C. § 7661d(a)(2); 40 C.F.R. § 70.8(b)(1).

44. 40 C.F.R. § 70.8(b)(2).

45. *Id.* § 70.7(c).

46. *Id.* § 70.5(a)(1)(iii).

47. *Id.* § 70.7(f)(1)(i).

48. *Id.* § 70.7(f)(1)(ii).

49. *Id.* § 70.7(f)(1)(iii)-(iv).

50. *Id.* § 70.7(f)(2).

51. 59 Fed. Reg. at 44,460.

52. 60 Fed. Reg. at 45,530.

53. *See* EPA, Operating Permits Program; Notice of Availability of Draft Rules and Accompanying Information, 62 Fed. Reg. 30,289 (June 3, 1997).

54. 40 C.F.R. § 70.7(d).

55. *Id.* § 70.7(e)(2).

56. *Id.* § 70.7(e)(4).

57. How EPA provides for operational flexibility under the Title V rules has been a subject of intense controversy. Section 502(b)(10) of the Act provides that states shall "allow changes within a permitted facility . . . *without requiring a permit revision*, if the changes are not modifications under any provision of title I and the changes do not exceed the emissions allowable under the permit." (Emphasis added.) The Act further contemplates that sources will provide EPA and the permitting authority notice seven days in advance of implementing the change. The 1992 Title V rule contains provisions that require state programs to provide for these types of changes. 40 C.F.R. § 70.4(b)(12). The 1994 and 1995 proposals would have limited the scope of "Section 502(b)(10) changes" substantially.

58. 40 C.F.R. § 70.6(a)(9).

59. EPA, Operating Permit Programs and Prevention of Significant Deterioration (PSD) and Nonattainment New Source Review (NSR); Flexible Air Permitting Rule, 72 Fed. Reg. 52,206 (Sept. 12, 2007).

60. EPA, Operating Permit Programs; Flexible Air Permitting Rule, 74 Fed. Reg. 51,418 (Oct. 6, 2009).

61. 40 C.F.R. § 70.9(b).

62. *Id.* § 70.9(b)(3).

63. *Id.* § 70.9(b)(2).

64. *Id.*

65. The Title V Task Force, Final Report to the Clean Air Act Advisory Committee on the Title V Implementation Experience (Apr. 2006), *available at* http://www.epa.gov/oar/caaac/titlev.html.

66. CAA § 114(a)(3), 42 U.S.C. § 7414(a)(3).

67. 40 C.F.R. § 64.2. Some emission limitations and standards, including those proposed by the Administrator after November 15, 1990, pursuant to section 111 or 112 of the Act, are exempt from the rule.

68. *Id.* § 64.3.

69. *Id.* § 64.7(d).

70. *Id.* § 64.8.

71. *Id.* § 64.6(c).

72. *Id.* § 64.5.

73. *Natural Res. Def. Council v. EPA*, 194 F.3d 130 (D.C. Cir. 1999).

74. EPA, State and Federal Operating Permits Program: Amendments to Compliance Certification Requirements, 68 Fed. Reg. 38,518 (June 27, 2003).

75. *See generally* 57 Fed. Reg. at 32,259-60.

76. CAA § 112(j)(5), 42 U.S.C. § 7412(j)(5).

77. *Id.* § 112(d)(2), 42 U.S.C. § 7412(d)(2).

78. *Id.* § 112(i)(5), 42 U.S.C. § 7412(i)(5).

79. *Id.* § 112(i)(5)(B), 42 U.S.C. § 7412(i)(5)(B).

80. *Id.* § 506(a), 42 U.S.C. § 7661e(a).

81. H.R. Rep. No. 101-952, Conference Report on S. 1630 at 345 (1990), *reprinted in* 1 Env't and Natural Res. Policy Div., Library of Congress, A Legislative History of the Clean Air Act Amendments of 1990 at 1795 (1998).

82. The PSD Program is contained in Title I Part C of the Act, and the nonattainment program is contained in Title I Part D of the Act.

83. CAA § 502(a) provides that "[n]othing in this subsection shall be construed to alter the applicable requirements of this [Act] that a permit be obtained before construction or modification."

84. *See generally* 40 C.F.R. § 52.21. If an area attains the NAAQS for certain pollutants and not for others, a proposed source may be required to obtain both a PSD and a nonattainment NSR permit. The nonattainment NSR program is discussed below, following the PSD discussion.

85. This list of source categories is contained in Appendix 2 of this Handbook.

86. 40 C.F.R. § 52.21(b)(1)(i).

87. *See id.* § 52.21(b)(5), (6); *see also* EPA, Requirements for Preparation, Adoption, and Submittal of Implementation Plans; Approval and Promulgation of Implementation Plans, 45 Fed. Reg. 52,676, 52,693-96 (Aug. 7, 1980) (preamble to EPA's 1980 PSD rules). All of these terms (*i.e.*, "contiguous or adjacent," "common control," and "SIC code") have been the subject of EPA guidance and policy statements. For example, "common control" has been interpreted to mean the right to make or to veto environmental decisions for a facility. *See, e.g.*, Letter from W.A. Spratlin, Air, Dir., RCRA, and Toxics Div., EPA, to P.R. Hamlin, Chief, Air Quality Bureau, Iowa Dept. of Natural Res. (Sept. 18, 1995). Facilities that do not belong to the same SIC code have been found to be part of the same facility where they are auxiliary or supporting facilities. *See, e.g.*, Letter from W.B. Hathaway, Dir., Air Pesticides and Toxics Div., Region 3, EPA, to J. Salvaggio, Dir. Of Air Quality, Pennsylvania DEP (undated, post 2000). EPA has indicated that facilities separated by some distance may be considered "contiguous" or "adjacent" facilities, where they otherwise have some practical relationship. *See, e.g.*, Memorandum from R.G. Kellam, Acting Dir., Office of Air Quality Planning and Standards, EPA, to R.R. Long, Dir. Air Program, Region 8, EPA, Analysis of the Applicability of Prevention of Significant Deterioration to the Anheuser-Busch, Incorporated Brewery and Nutri-Turf, Incorporated Landfarm at Fort Collins, Colorado (Aug. 27, 1996); Letter from R.R. Long, Dir. Air Programs, Region 8, EPA, to L.R. Menlove, Manager NSR Section, Utah Dept. of Envtl. Quality (Aug. 8, 1997); Letter from R.R. Long, Dir. Air Programs, Region 8, EPA, to D. Myers, Construction Permit Unit Leader, Colorado Dept. of Public Health and Env't (Apr. 20, 1999).

88. 40 C.F.R. § 52.21(b)(4).

89. EPA guidance addresses how operating restrictions must be written in order to be considered "enforceable" as a practical matter. *See* EPA Air Enforcement Division, Office of Enforcement and Compliance Monitoring, Guidance on Limiting Potential to Emit in New Source Permitting (June 13, 1989); *see also* EPA Office of Air Quality Planning and Standards, Guidance for Limiting the Potential to Emit (PTE) of a Stationary Source Under Section 112 and Title V of the Clean Air Act (Jan. 25, 1995).

90. *Chem. Mfrs. Ass'n v. EPA*, 70 F.3d 637 (D.C. Cir. 1995). EPA issued "interim" guidance on January 22, 1996, addressing the types of restrictions that could be taken into account in defining potential to emit, EPA Office of Air Quality Planning and Standards and Office of Regulatory Enforcement, Release of Interim Policy of Federal Enforceability of Limitations on Potential to Emit (Jan. 22, 1996), and has subsequently issued guidance for the potential to emit from specific categories of sources, *see, e.g.*, EPA, Potential to Emit Guidance for Specific Source Categories (Apr. 14, 1998).

91. 40 C.F.R. § 52.21(a)(2)(iv)(*a*), (b)(2).

92. Significance levels for other regulated pollutants can be found at 40 C.F.R. § 52.21(b)(23)(i), and are contained in Appendix 3. States that have developed their own PSD programs may set more stringent significance levels.

93. *Id.* § 52.21(a)(2)(iv)(*b*)-(*c*).

94. *Id.* § 52.21(a)(2)(iv)(*a*).

95. *Id.* § 52.21(b)(3).

96. *Id.* § 52.21(b)(3)(i)(*b*).

97. *Id.* § 52.21(b)(3)(vi).

98. *See* EPA, Requirements for Preparation, Adoption, and Submittal of Implementation Plans; Approval and Promulgation of Implementation Plans, 45 Fed. Reg. 52,676, 52,702 (Aug. 7, 1980).

99. *See id.*

100. *See* EPA Air Enforcement Division, Office of Enforcement and Compliance Monitoring 10-13 (June 13, 1989). More detailed discussion of emissions netting, and examples of how the applicability rules apply in specific cases, are presented in EPA's 1980 PSD Workshop Manual, *see* EPA, EPA-450/2-80-081, Prevention of Significant Deterioration Workshop Manual I-A-25 to I-A-39, II-A-10 to II-A-11 (Oct. 1980) ("1980 PSD Workshop Manual"), and the 1990 draft update of that manual, *see* EPA, New Source Review Workshop Manual: Prevention of Significant Deterioration and Nonattainment Area Permitting A-28 to A-33 (Draft Oct. 1990) ("1990 Draft NSR Workshop Manual").

101. *See, e.g.*, 1980 PSD Workshop Manual I-B-2.

102. 540 U.S. 461, 476 n.7 (2004).

103. *See id.* at 497-99.

104. *See* 40 C.F.R. § 52.21(c). In addition, up to one year of air quality monitoring data may be required for pollutants for which the proposed facility will cause significant ambient concentrations, as defined in EPA's rules. *See id.* § 52.21(m).

105. *Id.* § 52.21(e)(1).

106. EPA, EPA-450/2-78-027R, Office of Air Quality Planning and Standards, Guideline on Air Quality Models (Revised) (July 1986).

107. EPA's database may be accessed at http://www.epa.gov/scram001/.

108. *See* CAA § 123, 42 U.S.C. § 7423; 40 C.F.R. § 52.21(h).

109. *See* 40 C.F.R. pt. 51, Appendix S, § III.A.

110. *See, e.g.*, EPA, Model Clearinghouse: FY88 Summary Report 57 (Oct. 1988).

111. Theoretically, a permit to construct could be issued if a commitment were made: (1) to solve the exceedance problem; and (2) not to commence operation of the

new facility until the problem had been resolved. *See* 40 C.F.R. pt. 51, Appendix S, § III.C.

112. *See, e.g.,* CAA § 160(3), 42 U.S.C. § 7470(c). As numerous legislators indicate through the entire legislative history of the PSD provisions, the PSD program is to be flexible and allow for controlled growth, even in or near Class I areas. *See* Environmental Policy Division of the Congressional Research Service of the Library of Congress, A Legislative History of the Clean Air Act Amendments of 1977, at 318, 367, 369, 726, 1033 (1978). There is to be a "balancing" of the need for clean air against the need for economic growth even in those pristine areas. *See, e.g., id.* at 366, 726, 770, 774, 818, 899, 914, 923, 938, 1041.

113. CAA § 165(d)(2)(A), 42 U.S.C. § 7475(d)(2)(A); 40 C.F.R. § 52.21(p)(1).

114. CAA § 165(d)(2)(B), 42 U.S.C. § 7475(d)(2)(B); 40 C.F.R. § 52.21(p)(2). According to the legislative history of the Act, the term "air quality related values" means the "fundamental purposes for which such lands have been established and maintained by Congress and the responsible Federal Agency." S. Rep. No. 127, 95th Cong., 1st Sess. 36 (1977).

115. CAA § 165(d)(2)(C)(ii), 42 U.S.C. § 7475(d)(2)(C)(ii).

116. *Id.* § 165(d)(2)(C)(iii), 42 U.S.C. § 7475(d)(2)(C)(iii).

117. *See* U.S. Forest Service – Air Quality Program, National Park Service – Air Resources Division, U.S. Fish and Wildlife Serv. – Air Quality Branch, Phase I Report iii (Dec. 2000) ("FLAG Report").

118. *Id.* at iv.

119. For example, the FLMs for the Dolly Sod and Otter Creek Wilderness Areas, both of which are part of the Monongahela National Forest, requested that a West Virginia source agree to a mitigation plan that included providing for offsets of SO2 emissions to reduce impacts on visibility and acid deposition in those Class I areas. *See* West Virginia Dept. of Env't Prot., Final Determination/Fact Sheet for a Major New Source Construction at Longview Power LLC (Mar. 2, 2004).

120. For example, the FLM for the Mingo Wilderness Area issued an adverse impact finding for a new facility in Illinois, but the Illinois Environmental Protection Agency, after reviewing all of the information, disagreed with the FLM and issued the permit. *See* Illinois Envtl. Protection Agency, Responsiveness Summary for the Prairie State Generating Station (Apr. 2005).

121. *See* Memorandum from G.A. Emison, EPA Office of Air Quality Planning and Standards, to EPA Regional Dirs., Implementation of North County Resource Recovery PSD Remand (Sept. 25, 1987).

122. CAA § 112(b)(6), 42 U.S.C. § 7412(b)(6).

123. EPA, State Implementation Plans; General Preamble for the Implementation of Title I of the Clean Air Act Amendments of 1990; Supplemental, 57 Fed. Reg. 18,070, 18,075 (Apr. 28, 1992).

124. *Id.*

125. Information on the air toxics list and revisions to the list are available at http://www.epa.gov/ttnatw01/pollsour.html.

126. *See* EPA, Flambeau Paper Corp., Park Falls, Wisconsin, Final Determination, 46 Fed. Reg. 37,777, 37,778 (July 22, 1981); E. Reich, Dir., Stationary Source Compliance, EPA, to R. DeSpain, Chief, Air Programs, Region VII, EPA (Mar. 28, 1986); R. Strelow, Assistant Adm'r for Air and Waste Management, EPA, Memorandum to EPA Regional Administrators (Dec. 18, 1975).

127. CAA §§ 113(a)(5), 167, 42 U.S.C. §§ 7413(a)(5), 7477.

128. CAA § 113(b)(3), 42 U.S.C. § 7413(b)(3).

129. A state may receive "full" delegation to implement EPA's PSD rules or more limited delegation to conduct certain technical aspects of PSD review. A majority of states, however, have developed PSD programs as part of their SIPs. Information regarding PSD program status can be found on EPA's website at http://www.epa.gov/air/nsr/where.html. The state agency or EPA regional office should be contacted to determine the current status of an individual state's PSD authority.

130. CAA § 110(a)(2)(H), 42 U.S.C. § 7410(a)(2)(H).

131. *See, e.g., United States v. Solar Turbines, Inc.*, 732 F. Supp. 535 (M.D. Pa. 1989); *see also Allsteel v. EPA*, 25 F.3d 312 (6th Cir. 1994); *United States v. AM General Corp.*, 34 F.3d 472 (7th Cir. 1994).

132. *Alaska Dep't of Envtl. Conservation*, 540 U.S. at 502.

133. 40 C.F.R. § 124.19.

134. *Id.* § 124.19(f).

135. *See generally id.* §§ 52.21(aa), et seq. The PAL regulations were promulgated by EPA in December 2002 as part of its comprehensive "NSR Reform" rulemaking. The PAL regulations were upheld by the United States Court of Appeals for the D.C. Circuit in 2005. *See New York v. EPA*, 413 F.3d 3, 36 (D.C. Cir. 2005). The program took effect in March 2003 in "EPA delegated" states; SIP-approved states were required to submit revised rules to EPA in 2006 to implement the program.

136. EPA, Agenda of Regulatory and Deregulatory Actions, 69 Fed. Reg. 38,154, 38,197 (June 28, 2004).

137. *See* 40 C.F.R. § 52.21(aa)(1)(v).

138. *See id.* § 52.21(aa)(1)(ii).

139. *See id.* § 52.21(aa)(7). The application for a PAL must list all emissions units, their size, all federal and state requirements applicable to each emissions unit, and baseline actual emissions for each emissions unit.

140. *See id.* § 52.21(aa)(5).

141. *See id.* § 52.21(aa)(12).

142. *See id.* § 52.21(aa)(14).

143. *See id.*

144. *See id.* § 52.21(aa)(8)(ii).

145. *See id.* § 52.21(aa)(4)(i)(f), (aa)(10).

146. *See id.* § 52.21(aa)(10)(iv)(a).

147. *See id.* § 52.21(aa)(10)(iv)(b).

148. *See id.* § 52.21(aa)(10)(iv)(c). The provisions applicable to increasing a PAL are set forth in 40 C.F.R. § 52.21(aa)(11).

149. CAA §§ 107(d)(1)(A)(i), 171(2), 42 U.S.C. §§ 7407(d)(1)(A)(i), 7501(2).

150. *Id.* § 172(b)(6), 42 U.S.C. § 7502(b)(6).

151. *Id.* § 302(j), 42 U.S.C. § 7602(j).

152. *Id.* § 182(b), 42 U.S.C. § 7511a(b).

153. *Id.* § 182(c)-(e), 42 U.S.C. § 7511a(c)-(e).

154. *Id.* § 182(f), 42 U.S.C. § 7511a(f).

155. *Id.* § 187(c)(1), 42 U.S.C. § 7512a(c)(1).

156. *Id.* § 189(b)(3), 42 U.S.C. § 7513a(b)(3).

157. 40 C.F.R. § 51.165(a)(1)(x). These significance levels are listed in Appendix 3 to this book.

158. CAA § 182(c)(6), (e)(2), 42 U.S.C. § 7511a(c)(6), (e)(2).

159. *Id.* § 182(f), 42 U.S.C. § 7511a(f).

160. *See Chevron U.S.A., Inc. v. Natural Resources Def. Council, Inc.*, 467 U.S. 837 (1984).

161. CAA § 182(c)(7), 42 U.S.C. § 7511a(c)(7).

162. *Id.* § 182(c)(8), 42 U.S.C. § 7511a(c)(8).

163. *Id.* § 173(a)(1)(A), 42 U.S.C. § 7503(a)(1)(A).

164. *Id.* § 173(c), 42 U.S.C. § 7503(c).

165. *See* Memorandum from J. Seitz, Dir., EPA Office of Air Quality Planning and Standards, NSR Program Supplemental Transitional Guidance (Sept. 3, 1992).

166. CAA § 173(a)(5), 42 U.S.C. § 7503(a)(5).

167. EPA's general PSD and nonattainment NSR regulations appear at 40 C.F.R. §§ 52.21 and 52.24, respectively. It is also critical to consult the state's regulations, to determine whether it has adopted additional or different rules.

168. *See* supra note 100.

169. *Id.*

Chapter 5

HAZARDOUS AIR POLLUTANTS

The 1990 Clean Air Act Amendments completely revamped the pre-existing system of hazardous air pollution control. Congress enacted Title III of the 1990 Amendments to respond to perceived problems with the prior risk-based system of hazardous air pollutant regulation. The old regulatory scheme required the U.S. Environmental Protection Agency ("EPA") to establish a list of hazardous air pollutants ("HAPs") and impose health-based emission standards for each pollutant. The new scheme initially identified 190 HAPs, directed EPA to identify the sources of those pollutants, and established a timeframe in which EPA must promulgate technology-based standards for each source category. Although the 1990 Amendments shifted the emphasis of the air toxics program to technology-based standards, Congress did not entirely abandon risk-based standards. The Amendments require EPA to assess the risk to public health likely to remain after implementation of the technology-based standards and to promulgate residual risk-based standards where necessary.

This Chapter presents an overview of the air toxics provisions under the 1990 Amendments, including the pollutants and sources subject to regulation, and how emission standards have been, and continue to be, developed and implemented.

Listed Air Toxics

The 1990 Amendments established a list of 190 HAPs that were to be addressed by the new air toxics program under the Clean Air Act.[1] Through subsequent congressional action and EPA de-listing actions, there are now 187 regulated pollutants.[2] The list includes organics, metals, and chemical compounds common to many industrial processes. The list does not include lead or precursors to pollutants subject to regulation under section 108(a).[3] A copy of the HAP list appears in Appendix 3 to this handbook.

The Amendments also provide that "[n]o substance, practice, process or activity regulated under [Title VI of this Act regarding stratospheric ozone] shall be subject to regulation under this section solely due to its adverse effects on the environment."[4] As noted in Chapter 4, the 1990 Amendments provided that air toxics will no longer be regulated under the Prevention of Significant Deterioration program.[5] Therefore, the 187 HAPs currently listed under section 112(b) are not considered "regulated pollutants" for purposes of Part C of Title I.

Additions/Deletions by EPA

The 1990 Amendments require the EPA Administrator to review the list of HAPs periodically and revise it by rule as necessary.[6] Based on this review, the Administrator may add a pollutant to the list if it "present[s], or may present, through inhalation or other routes of exposure, a threat of adverse human health effects . . . ."[7] These substances include those that are "carcinogenic, mutagenic, teratogenic, neurotoxic, which cause reproductive dysfunction, or which are acutely or chronically toxic . . . ."[8]

The Administrator may also add a substance to the list that presents, or may present, adverse environmental effects through ambient concentrations, bioaccumulation, deposition, or other means. The 1990 Amendments define "adverse environmental effect" to mean "any significant and widespread adverse effect, which may reasonably be anticipated, to wildlife, aquatic life, or other natural resources, including adverse impacts on populations of endangered or threatened species or significant degradation of environmental quality over broad areas."[9]

The current standard for listing HAPs is different from the standard that existed under the Act prior to the passage of the 1990 Amendments. The 1990 Amendments include a broader category of effects, including "adverse environmental effects."[10] Under the current standard, more substances could qualify for regulation as HAPs.

Petitions to Modify

Any person may petition the Administrator to add a substance to or delete a substance from the list.[11] The petitioner must show that "there is adequate data on the health or environmental effects of the pollutant or other evidence" to support the addition or deletion of the substance.[12]

EPA has noted, in denying a petition to delist, that "as a general matter, when EPA determines that a petition submitted under section 112(b)(3) is deficient or incomplete, EPA intends to return the petition . . . along with a brief description of the deficiency or missing information."[13] Rather than formally deny a deficient petition, EPA "will afford the petitioner an opportunity to remedy the deficiency or supply the missing information prior to formal action on the petition."[14]

The Amendments specify that the Administrator's decision to grant a petition to add or delete a pollutant must be based on the petitioner's showing "or on the Administrator's own determination."[15] In making this decision, the Administrator can use any authority available to acquire the information she needs if she does not have sufficient information on the health or environmental effects of a substance.[16] The Administrator, however, is prohibited from "deny[ing] a petition solely on the basis of inadequate resources or time for review."[17]

The Administrator has 18 months within which to grant or deny the petition and to publish her reasons for doing so.[18] The 1990 Amendments do not address what happens if the Administrator fails to respond to the petition to list or delist. Presumably, a suit could be brought in federal district court to compel EPA action.

A decision by the Administrator to add a pollutant to the list is not final agency action subject to judicial review. That action becomes reviewable under section 307 of the Act only after EPA issues emission standards regulating that pollutant.[19]

Sources Covered

In July 1992, EPA promulgated the initial list of categories and subcategories of "major" and "area" sources of HAPs for regulation under the air toxics provisions.[20] In the preamble to the original list, EPA made clear that "the Agency considers the listing of source categories under section 112(c)(1) to be an ongoing process."[21] The statute requires EPA to revise the list of source categories from time to time, if appropriate, but no less than every eight years.[22] After establishing the original list, the Administrator has added categories and subcategories to the list based on the same criteria used to designate the original list.[23] Current major source and area source categories are listed in Appendix 2.

EPA's listing of a source category is not final agency action subject to judicial review. A listing decision becomes reviewable only after EPA issues emissions standards for that source category.[24] The Act required EPA to promulgate regulations for all listed categories and subcategories within ten years of enactment.[25] As detailed below, this deadline was not met, which prompted legal challenge. The availability of judicial review for a decision by EPA not to list a source category is not explicitly addressed by section 112(e)(4) of the Act.

The following discussion summarizes the statutory standards governing the definition of "major" and "area" sources of air toxics and also discusses the special rules that govern several specific industrial source categories.[26]

Major Sources

In general, a "major source" is

> any stationary source or group of stationary sources located within a contiguous area and under common control that emits or has the potential to emit . . . 10 tons per year or more of any hazardous air pollutant or 25 tons per year or more of any combination of hazardous air pollutants.[27]

A "stationary source" in this section has the same meaning ascribed to it in section 111(a), which is "any building, structure, facility, or installation which emits or may emit any air pollutant."[28] The 1990 Amendments did not indicate whether there was any restriction on grouping together different types of pollutant-emitting activities, for example, whether the facilities in question need to be within the same Standard Industrial Classification code. In *National Mining Association v. EPA*, however, the U.S. Court of Appeals for the D.C. Circuit upheld EPA's approach of aggregating all HAP emissions from different sources at a plant to determine if the facility (and all its components) were a "major source," even if the component sources fell into different industrial categories.[29]

The Administrator can establish a lesser quantity cutoff for defining a major source based on "the potency of the air pollutant, persistence, potential for bio-accumulation, other characteristics of the air pollutant, or other relevant factors."[30] The Administrator also may establish different criteria than "tons per year" for determining whether facilities that emit radionuclides are "major sources."[31]

Area Sources

An "area source" is any stationary source that is not a major source. Area sources do not have Title V obligations, and the modification, construction, and reconstruction provisions of section 112(g) also do not apply to them.[32]

The 1990 Amendments require the Administrator to include on the source category list each category and subcategory of area sources "which the Administrator finds presents a threat of adverse effects to human health or the environment (by such sources individually or in the aggregate) warranting regulation under this section."[33] The Amendments also require EPA to list "sufficient categories or subcategories of area sources to ensure that area sources representing 90 percent of the area source emissions of the 30 hazardous air pollutants that present the greatest threat to public health in the largest number of urban areas are subject to regulation under this section."[34] In determining appropriate urban area sources, EPA was to develop a "comprehensive strategy to control emissions of hazardous air pollutants from area sources in urban areas" and transmit that strategy to Congress by November 1995.[35] In 1999, EPA published the final Urban Air Toxics Strategy pursuant to section 112(k) and 112(c)(3).[36] In that strategy, which addressed area and mobile sources (regulated under Title II of the Act), EPA identified the 33 HAPs presenting the "greatest potential threat to public health," 30 of which are emitted by area sources. EPA also identified 70 area source categories that "emit a substantial portion of these HAPs, and which are being considered for regulation under section 112(d),"[37] but explained that additional action was needed to meet EPA's section 112(c)(3) duties.[38] After legal challenge of EPA's delay to meet those obligations, and subsequent court-imposed rulemaking deadlines, then-EPA Administrator Lisa Jackson announced on March 21, 2011, that EPA had promulgated all of the required area source rules to meet its section 112(c)(3) obligations.[39]

As shown in Appendix 2, there are currently 71 area source categories. In the June 4, 2010 "Area Source Rule Implementation Guidance" developed for section 112-delegated authorities, EPA recommended prioritized implementation of the various area source standards.[40]

Specific Sources

The Amendments contain special provisions governing several types of sources, including electric utility boilers, oil and gas wells, and facilities subject to the Resource Conservation and Recovery Act ("RCRA").

Electric Utility Steam Generating Units

Electric utility steam generating unit ("EGU") is defined in the air toxics program to mean "any fossil fuel fired combustion unit of more than 25 megawatts that serves a generator that produces electricity for sale."[41] It also includes a "unit that cogenerates steam and electricity and supplies more than one-third of its potential electric output capacity and more than 25 megawatts electrical output to any utility power distribution system for sale."[42]

These electric utility boilers were exempt from regulation under the air toxics provisions unless EPA conducted a study of their air toxics emissions and associated health risks and, through that study, determined regulation of EGUs to be "appropriate and necessary."[43] Congress specified that the study should examine the hazards to public health reasonably anticipated to occur as a result of air toxic emissions from fossil fuel-fired power plants "after imposition of the requirements of this [Act]."[44] If EPA determined that regulation of power plants under the air toxics provisions was "appropriate and necessary," the report was required to describe "alternative control strategies" for those emissions that warrant regulation.[45]

EPA submitted its final Utility Study to Congress in 1998. Following the completion of the 1998 study, EPA determined that it would defer the determination of whether regulation of EGU HAP emissions was "appropriate and necessary." In mid-December 2000, then-EPA Administrator Carol Browner made a determination under section 112(n)(1)(A) that regulation of mercury from coal-fired EGUs and nickel emissions from oil-fired units was "appropriate and necessary" and listed those units under section 112(c).[46]

The December 2000 listing was challenged in federal court because it was made without notice and opportunity for public comment and did not otherwise comply with the rulemaking requirements of the Administrative Procedure Act.

The D.C. Circuit dismissed the challenge as premature, citing CAA § 112(e)(4), 42 U.S.C. § 7412(e)(4).[47]

In March 2005, EPA promulgated a final rule in which EPA concluded "it is neither appropriate nor necessary to regulate coal- and oil-fired Utility Units under section 112 [of the CAA]."[48] EPA therefore removed coal- and oil-fired EGUs from the section 112(c) list based on information developed and received since the December 2000 determination. EPA promulgated the Clean Air Mercury Rule ("CAMR") to regulate mercury EGU emissions under section 111 of the Act through a market-based cap-and-trade program.[49] In February 2008, the D.C. Circuit vacated EPA's 2005 delisting rule because the court found that EPA had not made findings required by section 112(c)(9).[50] Because EGUs were subject to section 112 regulation after vacatur of the delisting determination, and EPA interprets section 112 regulation as precluding section 111(d) regulation, the court also vacated CAMR.[51]

In 2011, the Utility Air Regulatory Group filed a section 112(c)(9) petition for delisting. In early 2012, EPA denied that petition and finalized section 112 emission standards for EGUs.[52] Those standards are subject to ongoing legal challenge in the D.C. Circuit.[53]

Oil and Gas Wells

According to the 1990 Amendments, "emissions from any oil or gas exploration or production well . . . [and] its associated equipment . . . and from any pipeline compressor or pump station [cannot] be aggregated with emissions from other similar units" to determine if they are major sources.[54] In 1999, EPA promulgated emissions standards for oil and natural gas production major sources,[55] and defined "associated equipment" as "equipment associated with an oil or natural gas exploration or production well, . . . includ[ing] all equipment from the wellbore to the point of custody transfer, except glycol dehydration units and storage vessels *with the potential for flash emissions*."[56] In August 2012, EPA finalized a rule that, among other things, narrowed the definition of "associated equipment" by deleting the italicized phrase.[57] That revision rule is subject to pending legal challenge.[58]

Oil and gas production and exploration wells (and their "associated equipment") were statutorily excluded from the list of *area* sources, unless the Administrator established "an area source category for oil and gas production wells located in any metropolitan . . . area with a population in excess of 1 million" because HAP emissions from these wells are found to "present more than a negligible risk of adverse effects to public health."[59] EPA proposed to list oil and natural gas production as an area source category in 1998 but did not finalize that proposed listing.[60] Oil and natural gas production was instead listed as an area source category pursuant to the Urban Air Toxics Strategy.[61] EPA published final standards for oil and natural gas production area sources on January 3, 2007.[62]

The 1990 Amendments to the Clean Air Act also required the Administrator "to assess the [risks] to public health and the environment resulting from the emission of hydrogen sulfide associated with the extraction of oil and natural gas ... [and] to report to Congress."[63] EPA published its final report in 1993.[64] In its study, EPA found that while routine emissions of hydrogen sulfide from oil and gas wells created the potential for human and environmental exposure, insufficient evidence existed to suggest that these exposures presented any significant threat.[65] Thus, EPA did not recommend further legislation pertaining to routine hydrogen sulfide emissions or accidental releases from oil and gas wells.[66]

Publicly Owned Treatment Works

Although the 1990 Amendments required the Administrator to promulgate control technology standards for publicly owned treatment works ("POTWs") not later than five years after the enactment of the 1990 Amendments,[67] EPA did not promulgate final maximum achievable control technology ("MACT") standards for POTWs until October 1999.[68]

RCRA Facilities

In developing emission standards for categories or subcategories of sources whose air emissions are regulated under the hazardous waste provisions of Subtitle C of RCRA, the Administrator is to take the applicable RCRA requirements into account, to the maximum extent practicable, in order to ensure the consistency of requirements under RCRA and the Clean Air Act.[69] This provision anticipates application of concurrent and consistent requirements under both of these regulatory programs.[70] EPA has attempted to harmonize its responsibilities under the Clean Air Act and RCRA. For example, EPA promulgated so-called "Subpart CC" rules under RCRA that allow certain covered facilities to meet Clean Air Act regulations in lieu of complying with some provisions of the Subpart CC rules.[71]

Deleting Sources from the List of Source Categories

EPA may delete any source category from the list of source categories to be regulated upon petition or on the Administrator's own motion if: (1) in the case of a carcinogen, no source in the category emits pollutants that may cause a lifetime risk of cancer greater than "one in one million" to the most exposed individual; or (2) in the case of pollutants that may cause an adverse health effect (other than cancer) or may cause adverse environmental effects, public health will be protected with an ample margin of safety and no adverse environmental effects will occur as a result of emissions of the pollutant.[72] EPA has deleted source categories on its own motion,[73] but never upon receipt of a petition.[74] The Administrator cannot exempt or delist a *sub*category (*i.e.*, part of a category) from section 112 requirements. The D.C. Circuit struck down EPA's risk-based exemption for a subcategory of plywood and composite wood products sources in 2007 because EPA had "failed to make the required statutory determination that *no source* in the *category*, rather than in the low-risk subcategory emits HAPs 'in quantities which may cause a lifetime risk of cancer greater than one in one million to the individual in the population who is most exposed to emissions . . . .'"[75] EPA had previously deleted source categories without making a section 112(c)(9) finding.[76] In dicta in *New Jersey v. EPA*, however, the D.C. Circuit suggested that in light of the Act's "plain text," EPA cannot "correct[] its own listing 'errors' except through section 112(c)(9)'s delisting process or court-sanctioned vacatur."[77]

Standards for Regulation of Air Toxics

The 1990 Amendments provide for different types of emissions standards under the air toxics program. These include: (1) technology-based standards, known as MACT (maximum achievable control technology) and generally available control technologies ("GACT") standards; (2) work practice standards; and (3) residual risk-based standards. This section discusses the statutory criteria governing development of these standards. EPA's standard-setting methodology, especially for MACT, has evolved considerably.

Technology-Based Standards

MACT Standards

Under section 112(d), EPA engages in a two-step MACT standard-setting process for listed HAPs unless EPA determines that GACT or work practice standards are appropriate. Step 1 is to set the "MACT floors" for new and existing major sources pursuant to section 112(d)(3) – that is, the emissions levels actually achieved by the best-performing sources in a category or subcategory.[78] For a new source category or subcategory, the MACT floor is "the emission control that is achieved in practice by the best controlled similar source, as determined by the Administrator."[79] Calculation of an existing source MACT floor depends on the number of sources in the category or subcategory.[80] For an existing source category or subcategory with 30 or more major sources, the MACT floor is the average emission limitation achieved by the best performing 12 percent of the existing sources in the same source category or subcategory.[81] If there are fewer than 30 existing sources in the source category or subcategory, the MACT floor must be at least as stringent as the average emission limitation achieved by the best performing five sources in that category or subcategory.[82]

In Step 2 of the MACT standard-setting process, EPA conducts a "beyond-the-floor" analysis to determine whether to make the emissions standards even more stringent. Under section 112(d)(2), EPA evaluates "the cost of achieving such emission reduction, and any non-air quality health and environmental impacts and energy requirements" in assessing the need for a more stringent standard.[83]

EPA has sought to employ a variety of MACT standard-setting methodologies, with considerable pushback from the D.C. Circuit. Through these challenges, several clarifications of, and constraints on, EPA's MACT methodology has developed:

- EPA must determine a MACT limit for all listed HAPs that a category or subcategory emits, not just those HAPs "controlled with technology";[84]
- In setting MACT standards for each HAP, EPA may use a surrogate pollutant (for example, particulate matter),[85] *but only* provided that EPA demonstrates a correlation between surrogate emissions and regulated HAP emissions and indicates for which HAPs a surrogate is used;[86]

- In determining the emissions *achieved* by the best-performing sources under section 112(d)(3), it is not necessary that EPA determine that the MACT floor is *achievable* by all sources,[87] and indeed EPA cannot design a MACT solely to ensure that all sources that use a given technology can achieve the floor;[88]

- Any existing source MACT pool (*i.e.*, group of best performing sources used to determine a MACT floor) is to be identified using available "emissions information." The D.C. Circuit has concluded that regulatory data, such as compliance testing data, can qualify as suitable "emissions information."[89] If actual emissions information about the best performing sources is not available, only a "reasonable estimate" of emission control *achieved* by the best performing sources may be used to determine the MACT floor;[90]

- Although the control technology employed by the best performing source(s) may determine those source(s)' emissions, and therefore the MACT floor, if factors *other than* control technology affect the best performing source(s)' emissions (for example, access to cleaner raw material due to an owner's/operator's geographic location), EPA is obligated to consider those factors in setting the MACT floor, even if they are not deliberate on the part of the owner/operator;[91]

- In accounting for emissions variability of the best performing unit(s), EPA must demonstrate that its analysis is "a reasonable estimate of emissions achieved by the best-performing sources,"[92] and cannot, for example, use emissions data from worst performing units that use the same control technology as the best performing units to account for the best performing units' variability unless EPA shows that those data "actually predict" the best performers' emissions;[93] and

- In making any beyond-the-floor determination, EPA is required to consider *each* of those factors set forth in section 112(d)(2).[94]

The D.C. Circuit has also looked to section 129, added to the Act in 1990, in evaluating MACT floors issued by EPA under section 112.[95] Section 129 governs regulation of emissions resulting from "solid waste incineration units" and uses a standard-setting approach that is extremely similar to MACT standard-setting under section 112(d)(2) and (d)(3).[96] As sections 112 and 129 are "mutually exclusive" in their applicability to sources,[97] the question of which sources are subject to regulation under which section remains a subject of ongoing litigation.[98] In 2011, EPA finalized rules that defined "commercial and industrial solid waste incineration units" ("CISWI"), as well as non-hazardous secondary materials that are solid waste, and thereby delineated which units are subject to regulation under section 129 and which are subject to regulation under section 112.[99] The CISWI rule was reconsidered and recently issued in final form.[100] Judicial challenges to the 2011 CISWI rule and 2013 CISWI rule have been consolidated and are pending in the D.C. Circuit.[101]

Although the section 112 air toxics program relies principally on technology-based regulation, there is some room for consideration of public health effects. For "pollutants for which a health threshold has been established, the Administrator may consider such threshold level, with an ample margin of safety, when establishing emission standards under this subsection."[102] EPA has invoked section 112(d)(4) in only a limited number of rulemakings, however.[103]

GACT

EPA can promulgate area source standards or requirements "which provide for the use of [GACT] or management practices by such sources to reduce emissions of hazardous air pollutants" in lieu of setting MACT standards.[104] This provision reflects the potential inapplicability of the MACT concept to area sources and the need for separate control requirements. GACT may take the form of numerical emission limits, use of certain pollution control equipment, or employment of other types of management practices.[105]

Interim Technology-Based Standards

To ensure that emission standards for major sources are implemented, Congress added a "hammer" provision to section 112.[106] If the Administrator "fails to promulgate a standard for a category or subcategory of majors sources" pursuant to section 112(e)(1) and (3) within 18 months after the statutory deadline, the statute requires states to establish MACT standards for the affected sources on a case-by-case basis.[107] In those circumstances, the owner or operator of a major source must submit "a timely and complete [permit] application" to the state, and the state will establish a source-specific MACT limit.[108] That application must "demonstrate how an emission unit will obtain the degree of emission reduction that the Administrator or the State has determined is at least as stringent as the emission reduction that would have been obtained had the relevant emission standard been promulgated according to the source category schedule."[109]

If an applicable MACT standard is promulgated after a permit application has been filed but before it is approved, the new federal standard will apply instead of the source-specific limitation.[110] If the new standard is promulgated after the permit is approved, however, the new standard will be included in the next renewal of the permit, and the source will be provided reasonable time to comply with that limit (but no longer than eight years from promulgation of the standard or permit renewal, whichever is earlier).[111]

Issued initially in 1994 and amended in 2002, the implementing regulations for section 112(j) set forth a two-part process for applications.[112] Those amended regulations were challenged by Sierra Club, and under a settlement agreement, EPA agreed to amend the regulations further. In 2010, EPA proposed revisions that clarified the applicability of section 112(j) to situations in which MACT standards are completely vacated because EPA interpreted complete vacatur as "[f]ailure to promulgate a standard" under section 112(j)(2).[113] In its proposal, EPA also reminded that section 112(j) only applied to "initially listed" categories and subcategories (*i.e.*, those initially listed in 1992[114]), and amended obsolete portions of the regulations. EPA has never finalized these revisions.

Under section 112(g), Congress created another interim program, which requires MACT standards to be applied on a case-by-case basis to newly constructed, reconstructed, and modified major sources until general, category-wide MACT standards are promulgated under section 112(d). This interim program was included in the 1990 Amendments because Congress recognized that the most cost-effective time for implementing MACT standards is during the construction, modification, or reconstruction of a facility, but that category-wide MACT standards could not quickly be developed for all source categories. Facilities that are subject to case-by-case MACT under section 112(g) may be given up to eight additional years to come into compliance with a category-wide MACT standard once that standard is promulgated pursuant to section 112(d).

EPA promulgated regulations implementing section 112(g) in December 1996.[115] Those regulations narrowed the scope of the program to cover only the construction or reconstruction of a facility. Modifications of a facility do not trigger section 112(g) MACT standards. EPA explained that construction of a major source could trigger the applicability of section 112(g) in one of two ways. First, section 112(g) is triggered by the construction of a major emitting source on a greenfield site. Second, section 112(g) would become applicable to the construction of a new "'process or production unit' at an existing site where the process or production unit is itself major emitting."[116]

A reconstruction of a source takes place when there is a:

replacement of components at an existing process or production unit that in and of itself emits or has the potential to emit 10 tons per year of any HAP or 25 tons per year of any combination of HAP, whenever:

(1) The fixed capital cost of the new components exceeds 50 percent of the fixed capital cost that would be required to construct a comparable process or production unit; and

(2) It is technically and economically feasible for the reconstructed major source to meet the applicable maximum achievable control technology emission limitation for new sources established under this subpart.[117]

Work Practice Standards

If the Administrator determines that it is "not feasible . . . to prescribe or enforce an emission standard" for a hazardous air pollutant, she may "in lieu thereof, promulgate a design, equipment, work practice, or operational standard, or combination thereof, which in the Administrator's judgment is consistent" with MACT/GACT reductions or, in the case of risk-based standards (discussed below), the ample margin of safety standard.[118] These alternative standards are to be promulgated as numerical emission standards where feasible. The standards must include requirements that "will assure the proper operation and maintenance of any such element of design or equipment."[119]

The infeasibility requirement is met if the Administrator determines either: (A) "a hazardous air pollutant or pollutants cannot be emitted through a conveyance designed and constructed to emit or capture such pollutant, or that any requirement for, or use of, such a conveyance would be inconsistent with any Federal, State or local law"; or (B) "the application of measurement methodology to a particular class of sources is not practicable due to technological and economic limitations."[120]

If an owner or operator can demonstrate that an alternative means of emission limitation will achieve an emission reduction equal to the reduction required under a work practice standard, the Administrator must permit the use of that alternative.[121]

Residual Risk Standards

One of the most significant section 112 developments in the last ten years is EPA's residual risk-rulemaking program. The 1990 Amendments do not completely abandon the concept of risk-based emission standards that existed before 1990. By November 1996, the Administrator was required to investigate and report to Congress on the risks to public health remaining, or likely to remain, after the application of MACT standards.[122] The report was to identify: (1) the significance of these risks; (2) the technologically and commercially available methods and costs of reducing these risks; and (3) the "actual health effects with respect to persons living in the vicinity of sources, any available epidemiological or other health studies, risks presented by background concentrations of hazardous air pollutants, any uncertainties in risk assessment methodology or other health assessment techniques, and any negative health consequences to the community of efforts to reduce such risks." The Administrator also was required to make recommendations for legislation regarding those risks. EPA submitted its residual risk report to Congress in 1999 and did not set forth any legislative recommendations.[123]

Unless Congress took legislative action pursuant to EPA's recommendation (which it did not), the Act directs EPA to make a decision on risk-based standards within eight years after promulgation of MACT standards for a major source category (or within nine years if a MACT standard was required within two years of enactment of the 1990 Amendments) to protect the public health with an "ample margin of safety" and to prevent adverse environmental effects.[124] If MACT standards applicable to sources "emitting a pollutant (or pollutants) classified as a known, probable or possible human carcinogen do not reduce lifetime excess cancer risks to the individual most exposed to emissions from a source in the category or subcategory to less than one in one million," the Administrator is to "promulgate standards under this subsection for such source category."[125]

But a health-based standard need not reduce risks to all exposed individuals to one-in-one million, as clarified by the D.C. Circuit.[126] In *Natural Resources Defense Council v. EPA*, environmental groups argued that EPA's Risk and Technology Review ("RTR") rule for the synthetic organic chemicals category violated section 112(f) because it did not reduce lifetime cancer risks to less than one-in-one million. The court held that while the statute requires EPA to "promulgate standards," "it says nothing about the substantive content of those standards."[127] Therefore, "[i]f EPA determines that the existing technology-based standards already provide 'an ample margin of safety,' then the agency is free to readopt those standards during a residual risk rulemaking."[128]

In that case, the court found that EPA reasonably interpreted "ample margin of safety" in the same way as it did before the 1990 Amendments. As the court observed, that interpretation—set forth in the benzene rulemaking conducted under the 1970 version of section 112[129]—grew out of the D.C. Circuit's holding in an earlier case also called *Natural Resources Defense Council v. EPA*.[130] That 1987 decision set forth "a two-step process for EPA to follow in making [ample margin of safety] judgments: first, determine a 'safe' or 'acceptable risk' level, and then set standards at the level—which may be equal to or lower, but not higher than, the 'safe' or 'acceptable' level—that protects public health with an ample margin of safety."[131] In the first step, which evaluates only health effects, a one in ten thousand lifetime risk of cancer for the maximally exposed individual is, generally speaking, presumptively "acceptable," though EPA may determine an alternate "acceptable" level.[132] In the second step, EPA determines the "ample margin of safety" through consideration of "other relevant factors *including costs and economic impacts*, technological feasibility, and other factors relevant to each particular decision."[133] This "ample margin" cannot be higher than the "acceptable" level (i.e., floor) determined at step 1. Under this standard-setting process, reduction to a one in one million lifetime risk of cancer is "an aspirational goal," not a requirement.[134]

Through the RTR Program, EPA has combined its rulemaking duties under section 112(f) and section 112(d)(6). EPA set forth its RTR Program methodology in a 2009 draft report,[135] which was then reviewed by EPA's Science Advisory Board.[136] EPA has conducted residual risk reviews of more than 30 major source categories and will conduct more reviews under schedules set forth by a consent decree.[137]

Residual risk standards are generally effective upon promulgation.[138] These standards, however, do not apply to existing sources until 90 days after the standards' effective date.[139] The Administrator is authorized to grant waivers for up to two years for existing sources to come into compliance with these standards if the Administrator finds that it is necessary to install controls and if steps are taken to protect the health of persons from imminent endangerment during the waiver period.[140]

Pre-Existing Standards

The 1990 Amendments contain a savings clause that preserves the effectiveness of air toxics emission standards promulgated prior to the 1990 Amendments.[141] The savings clause provides that the amendments to section 112 will not affect existing standards that were promulgated before enactment (whether in effect at that time or not), unless they are modified under the pre-1990 section 112 or the new section 112. The savings provision contains a special rule for radionuclide emissions. Under this rule, no standard will be established under the new air toxics program "for radionuclide emissions from (A) elemental phosphorous plants, (B) grate calcination elemental phosphorous plants, (C) phosphogypsum stacks, or (D) any subcategory of the foregoing."[142] Regulatory decisions under the old section 112 will remain in effect for emissions from these sources. The savings provision also addresses radionuclide emissions from certain source categories.[143]

Timing for Development of Standards Under 1990 Amendments

The 1990 Amendments imposed general deadlines on EPA to establish technology-based standards for source categories.[144] The Amendments also required EPA to establish a regulatory schedule for promulgating standards for each source category consistent with the statutory schedule.[145] Failure to promulgate a standard according to its regulatory schedule could (and did) result in citizen suits pursuant to section 304 to establish court-ordered schedules for development of standards.[146] Under section 112(d)(6), EPA must review and revise all section 112 standards at least every 8 years, "taking into account developments in practices, processes, and control technologies." In undertaking this review, EPA does not need to recalculate the prior MACT determination.[147] As discussed above, EPA has combined the section 112(d)(6) review process with development of residual risk standards under section 112(f).

Compliance Deadlines Under Standards

A new source must comply with any emissions standards (as well as limitations or other regulatory requirements) in proposed or final form at the time that the new source "commences or recommences reconstruction."[148] A new source will be given three years after promulgation for compliance, however, if (1) the requirement is "more stringent" in final form than in the proposed form in which it was written at the time the new source commenced construction or reconstruction, and (2) the source complies with the proposed version during the interim three-year period.[149] Once emission standards are promulgated, existing sources can have up to three years to comply.[150] EPA, however, may require compliance sooner.

An existing source may obtain a one-year compliance extension from EPA or the source's Title V permitting authority if needed for "installation of controls."[151] Sources can also defer compliance with otherwise applicable MACT standards by participating in the early reductions program.[152] If, prior to proposal of an applicable MACT standard, an existing source reduces its hazardous air emissions by 90 percent (95 percent for particulates), it may qualify for a six-year compliance extension. A source that qualifies for the extension will be subject to an alternative emission limitation that will be included in the source's Title V operating permit.[153]

The President can exempt *any* stationary source from any standard or limitation, including MACT, for up to two years if the President determines that the "technology to implement such standard is not available" and "it is in the national security interests of the United States to do so."[154] This exemption can be extended by the President for additional two-year periods. To date, no President has invoked this option.

Implementation of The Air Toxics Program

EPA issued General Provisions regulations that govern the air toxics program, unless superseded by implementing regulations issued for individual standards. Air toxics requirements are implemented and enforced through the Title V operating permit program. States may develop and implement their own air toxics programs pursuant to section 112(*l*).[155]

General Provisions

EPA first promulgated the General Provisions for HAP regulation in 1994.[156] These provisions are meant to create basic, common standards and requirements for stationary sources that emit (or have the potential to emit) one or more of the 187 listed HAPs. As source-specific standards are promulgated, General Provisions are superseded where they conflict with source-specific standards. Where source-specific standards do not address a requirement contained in the General Provisions, the General Provisions remain in effect.

The General Provisions provide procedures and criteria for implementing all section 112 standards. These include administrative procedures related to: (1) applicability determinations, such as definitions of "major source" and "potential to emit"; (2) compliance extensions; and (3) requests to use alternative means of compliance. In addition, compliance-related provisions outline the responsibilities of owners and operators to comply with relevant emission standards, such as: (1) compliance dates; (2) operation and maintenance requirements; (3) methods for determining compliance with standards; (4) procedures for emission performance testing and monitoring; and (5) reporting and record-keeping requirements. Some of the issues addressed in the General Provisions are discussed below.

Potential To Emit

In determining whether any stationary source or a group of stationary sources located within a contiguous area and under common control is a major source, EPA considers that site's "potential to emit" HAPs.[157] In the General Provisions, EPA defines "potential to emit" as "the maximum capacity of a stationary source to emit a pollutant under its physical and operational design."[158] Moreover, "[a]ny physical or operational limitation on the capacity of the stationary source to emit a pollutant, including air pollution control equipment and restrictions on hours of operation or on the type or amount of material combusted, stored, or processed, shall be treated as part of its design *if the limitation or the effect it would have on emissions is federally enforceable.*"[159] In response to a judicial challenge of that italicized requirement, the D.C. Circuit mandated that EPA must explain its decision to consider only federally enforceable limitations, and not, for example, "effective" emission limitations imposed by state or local regulations.[160] In 1995, after suit was brought but before the D.C. Circuit issued its opinion, EPA issued guidance setting out a transition policy that provided means to sources for treatment as non-major sources if they did not have federally enforceable limits in effect.[161] In that memorandum, EPA indicated that it intended to conduct rulemaking on the issue. EPA has since issued a number of guidance documents, but has never conducted a rulemaking.[162]

Monitoring and Testing Requirements

The General Provisions also detail "monitoring and performance testing requirements" for major and area sources.[163] When EPA issued the General Provisions in 1994, EPA noted that it would incorporate the concept of "enhanced monitoring" directly into all new rules promulgated in section 112 standards for specific source categories.[164] As a result, in the Compliance Assurance Monitoring rule,[165] EPA exempted those "emission limitations or standards proposed by the Administrator after November 15, 1990 pursuant to section 111 or 112 of the Act."[166] Thus, "enhanced monitoring" requirements for emission standards under section 112 are determined in individual rulemakings under section 112.

With regard to the performance testing requirements, the General Provisions stipulate when these tests must be conducted, the operating conditions under which the tests must be conducted, the content of the site-specific test plan, how long the agency has to review the test plan, how many runs are needed, procedures for applying for the use of an alternative test method, and procedures for requesting a waiver of the performance test, among other things.[167] In 2010, EPA added to the General Provisions a requirement for analysis of audit samples as part of each performance test as soon as such samples are commercially available.[168]

Operation and Maintenance Requirements[169]

Of note, the General Provisions mandated that sources develop a "startup, shutdown, and malfunction plan" containing procedures for operating and maintaining the source during periods of startup, shutdown, and malfunction ("SSM")[170] and exempted sources from complying with section 112(d) standards during SSM. The D.C. Circuit vacated the exemption provisions, however, as contrary to the Clean Air Act, finding the Act requires that "some section 112 standard apply continuously" to sources regulated under the HAP program.[171] EPA published a letter in the wake of the court's decision that indicated how the vacatur would affect section 112 implementation.[172] EPA is still in the process of revising source category standards that use similar SSM exemption language and has not yet revised the General Provisions that were vacated.

Recordkeeping and Reporting Requirements

The General Provisions also contain requirements for recordkeeping and reporting.[173] These provisions detail information regarding dates and timelines for various requirements arising under the statute. The provisions also specify how notifications are to be sent to the Administrator, rules regarding record retention, and procedures for filing quarterly reports regarding the status of emissions and monitoring systems.

Title V Permits

All sources subject to regulation under section 112, including area sources, must apply for and operate in compliance with a Title V operating permit.[174] Operating permits issued pursuant to Title V must contain all of the Clean Air Act requirements applicable to a given source, including air toxics standards and limitations. The Title V operating permit program is discussed in more detail in Chapter 4.

State Air Toxics Programs

EPA is responsible for implementing and enforcing the air toxics program until a state seeks EPA approval of a program for implementing and enforcing emission standards and other requirements for HAPs, including requirements for the prevention and mitigation of accidental releases under section 112(r).[175] In this regard, the 1990 Amendments provide for either partial or complete delegation of the Administrator's authority and responsibilities to implement and enforce the air toxics program. There is no deadline for a state to apply for such delegation of authority.[176]

The Administrator must disapprove a state program if she finds one of the following:

- "[T]he authorities contained in the program are not adequate to assure compliance by all sources . . .";
- Adequate authority or resources "do[] not exist . . . to implement the program";
- "[T]he schedule for implementing the program and assuring compliance . . . is not sufficiently expeditious"; or

- "[T]he program is otherwise not in compliance" with the Administrator's guidance or will not satisfy the objectives of the Act.[177]

If the Administrator disapproves a state program, she must notify the state of the reasons for disapproval, and the state can revise and resubmit the program.[178] Moreover, the Administrator can withdraw her approval of a state program, after public hearing and notice to the state, if the state is not administering and enforcing the program in accordance with EPA's guidance.[179] The state has 90 days after notification to take action to assure "prompt compliance" before the approval will be withdrawn.[180] Finally, the Amendments make clear that, even if a state has been delegated authority to implement and enforce the air toxics program, the Administrator will retain independent enforcement authority.[181]

The Administrator may also approve programs developed and submitted by a local pollution control agency (after consultation with the state). The local agency can implement its approved program and take any action authorized to be taken by a state under this section.[182] As with state programs, the Administrator retains the authority to enforce any applicable emission standard or requirement even if she approves a local program.

The Administrator initially published rules to implement section 112(*l*) in 1993, with revisions in 2000 and 2003.[183] Those rules allow states to assume enforcement responsibility either for federal standards or, alternatively, to enforce state laws that are "no less stringent" than federal law. The option of allowing states to displace federal law under section 112(*l*) by making state laws federally enforceable has been controversial. EPA's regulations were challenged by environmental groups and industry alike, contending that EPA exceeded its authority. Both groups argued that the requirement that state law be "no less stringent" was ambiguous and would be difficult to apply in practice. As a result, environmental groups feared that state standards that were actually less stringent would be made federally enforceable, and industry feared that more stringent state standards would become federally enforceable even though EPA would be barred from adopting those standards on its own. The D.C. Circuit declined to resolve the issue because at that time no state had attempted to federalize a state law under section 112(*l*).[184] In its December 2000 revisions of Subpart E, EPA clarified its view that it "always retain[s] the right to enforce and implement" under section 112(*l*)(7) "Federal rules, including the [state, local, and tribal] rules or programs that are substituted for [EPA's] Federal rules and become the Federal rules."[185]

Accidental Release Prevention

Section 112(r) of the 1990 Amendments created a new set of provisions that address accidental air releases of hazardous substances that have significant off-site consequences to human health and the environment. The accidental release prevention program covers owners and operators of stationary sources producing, processing, handling, or storing listed hazardous substances. The scope and content of this program are discussed below. A state may be delegated section 112(r) authority pursuant to section 112(*l*)(1).[186]

Substances Covered

Within 24 months of enactment, EPA was required to promulgate a list of not less than 100 substances that "in the case of an accidental release, are known to cause or may reasonably be anticipated to cause death, injury, or serious adverse effects to human health or the environment." In developing the list, EPA was to use as a starting point the list of "extremely hazardous substances" ("EHS") developed under section 302 of the Emergency Planning and Community Right-To-Know Act of 1986 ("EPCRA").[187] Section 112(r) also required EPA to include 16 specific substances in the initial list of regulated substances, including chlorine, ammonia, and sulfur trioxide.[188]

Section 112(r) lists factors that EPA must consider in establishing the list of regulated substances. Among other things, no substance for which a primary NAAQS has been established is to be included on the list.[189] EPA may revise the list and must review it at least every five years.[190]

When the Administrator lists a substance, she must establish by rule a threshold quantity for the substance, "taking into account the toxicity, reactivity, volatility, dispersibility, combustibility, or flammability of the substance and the amount of the substance which, as a result of an accidental release, is known to cause or may reasonably be anticipated to cause death, injury or serious adverse effects to human health for which the substance was listed."[191] In contrast to the emergency release notification provisions of CERCLA, the statute establishes no default threshold quantity that would apply in the absence of action by EPA.[192]

In January 1994, EPA promulgated a list of section 112(r)-regulated substances and threshold quantities.[193] Subsequent to that initial listing determination, EPA deleted Division 1.1 explosives listed in Department of Transportation regulations in 49 C.F.R. § 172.101 from the section 112(r) list.[194] EPA also amended the listing for hydrochloric acid to include only those solutions that contain at least a 37 percent concentration of hydrogen chloride.[195] The current list includes 77 toxic substances and 63 flammable substances. Sources that have one or more of the listed substances on site in quantities *greater than the threshold* established by this rule will be subject to *specific regulations* under section 112(r)(7) for prevention and detection of and response to accidental releases.

The General Duty Clause

Section 112(r)(1) of the accidental release prevention program imposes on owners and operators a general duty "to prevent the accidental release and to minimize the consequences of any such release of any substance listed pursuant to [section 112(r)(3)] *or any other extremely hazardous substance.*"[196] In doing this, *any* facility that has extremely hazardous substances is required to "identify hazards which may result from [accidental] releases using appropriate hazard assessment techniques, to design and maintain a safe facility taking such steps as are necessary to prevent releases, and to minimize the consequences of accidental releases which do occur."[197] This "general duty" is self-implementing. That is, it can be used as a basis for enforcement actions by EPA,[198] even in the absence of any implementing regulations defining what steps are needed to comply with this "general duty."[199] The general duty clause, however, cannot be used as the basis for citizen suits or for suits seeking to recover for personal injury or property damage.[200]

Accidental Release Regulations

Statutory Requirements for Regulations

Section 112(r)(7) provides EPA with the authority to promulgate two sets of regulations. Under section 112(r)(7)(A), the Administrator *may* promulgate release prevention, detection, and correction requirements that would include monitoring, recordkeeping, reporting, training, vapor recovery, secondary containment, and other design, equipment, work practice, and operational requirements. Under section 112(r)(7)(B), EPA *must* promulgate within three years of enactment "reasonable regulations and appropriate guidance" regarding the prevention and detection of accidental releases from stationary sources of the listed substances and for response to such releases by owners and operators.

The latter set of regulations must require owners and operators of sources at which a regulated substance is present in more than a threshold quantity to prepare and implement a "risk management plan" ("RMP") to detect and prevent or minimize accidental releases and to provide a prompt emergency response to any such releases in order to protect human health and the environment.[201] The RMPs must include a hazard assessment that evaluates the off-site consequences of accidental releases of covered substances. *Id.* They also must cover the use, operation, repair, replacement, and maintenance of equipment to monitor, detect, inspect, and control releases. *Id.* Finally, RMPs must address training and provide procedures and measures for emergency response after an accidental release. *Id.* The RMPs must be registered with EPA and submitted to the Chemical Safety and Hazard Investigation Board ("CSB"),[202] the state in which the facility is located, and its local emergency planning and response agency.[203] The RMPs also must be made available to the public. *Id.*

In developing these regulations, EPA also was required to consider, as appropriate, "differences in size, operations, processes, class and categories of sources and the voluntary actions of such sources to prevent such releases and respond to such releases."[204]

EPA's Regulations – 40 C.F.R. Part 68

In June 1996, EPA first promulgated regulations (which it has subsequently revised) implementing the requirements of section 112(r)(7)(B).[205] Part 68, which now applies to approximately 13,000 facilities,[206] regulates any "stationary source" that has a regulated substance present in a "process" above threshold quantities.[207] A "stationary source" is defined as "any building, structures, equipment, installations, or substance emitting stationary activities which belong to the same industrial group, which are located on one or more contiguous properties, which are under the control of the same person (or persons under common control), and from which an accidental release may occur," with some limited exceptions.[208] The regulations also specify that properties are "not . . . considered contiguous solely because of a railroad or gas pipeline right-of-way."[209]

The term "process" means "any activity involving a regulated substance including any use, storage, manufacturing, handling or on-site movement of such substances, or combination of these activities."[210] The term "process" also includes "any group of vessels that are interconnected, or separate vessels that are located such that a regulated substance could be involved in a potential release."[211]

Each covered facility is required to develop an RMP by the later of: June 21, 1999, or whenever a regulated substance is initially present above the threshold quantity in a process at the facility. RMPs are filed through a central system[212] and must be made available to the public.[213] Sources are required to update their RMPs at least once every five years, unless certain circumstances dictate an earlier update.[214] The RMPs are subject to periodic audits.[215]

The rule established three levels of compliance, depending on the relative risk a covered source poses for accidental releases of hazardous substances that have off-site consequences.[216] The three compliance levels are called "Program 1," "Program 2," and "Program 3." Program 1, which contains the fewest requirements, applies to facilities that are considered to pose a relatively low risk for accidental releases with off-site consequences.[217] Program 3, which requires the highest level of compliance, applies to facilities that are considered to pose the greatest risk of accidental releases.[218] Program 2 is a somewhat streamlined version of Program 3 and is the default level for all covered sources that do not fall under Program 1 or Program 3.[219]

RMPs generally include three basic elements: (1) hazard assessment; (2) accidental release prevention program information; and (3) accidental release emergency response plan. The hazard assessment requirement of the RMP requires each covered source to evaluate the risk of catastrophic accidental releases of regulated substances from its facility and to estimate the likely impacts such releases would have on off-site receptors of concern (human health and sensitive environments). A hazard assessment must include a five-year history of accidental releases that resulted in significant off-site consequences.[220] The hazard assessment must also include analyses of a "worst-case" release scenario, as well as other alternative release scenarios, for each regulated substance present in a process above the threshold quantity.[221] The worst-case release analysis evaluates the off-site impacts that are likely to result from the accidental release of the largest quantity of a regulated substance from a vessel or process, taking into account administrative controls and passive mitigation.[222] The alternative release scenarios cover those releases that the source determines are more likely to occur than a worst-case release.[223] All covered facilities must conduct a hazard assessment, regardless of whether they fall under Program 1, Program 2, or Program 3.[224] Program 1 facilities are required, however, to analyze only their worst-case release scenarios and are not required to analyze any alternative release scenarios.[225]

The accidental release prevention program requirement of the RMP requires covered sources to develop and implement procedures designed to prevent catastrophic accidental releases from occurring. The rule outlines specific prevention program requirements, which generally parallel the requirements in the OSHA PSM.[226] The primary difference between the section 112(r)(7) rule and the OSHA PSM rule is that OSHA PSM addresses the prevention of accidental releases that have on-site impacts, whereas the section 112(r)(7) rule addresses the prevention of accidental releases that have off-site impacts.

Facilities that qualify for Program 1 regulation are not subject to the prevention program requirements.[227] Facilities in Program 2 have the option of complying with the specifically outlined prevention program requirements or developing their own prevention program according to general guidelines set out in the rule.[228] Program 3 facilities must comply with the fully outlined requirements.[229] Any facility that already is complying with OSHA PSM, however, need not undertake additional measures to be in compliance with the prevention program requirements of the section 112(r)(7) rule.[230]

The emergency response plan requirement of the RMP requires covered sources to develop procedures to respond to catastrophic accidental releases if they occur and to mitigate off-site consequences of those releases. Specific emergency response plan requirements are outlined in the rule and are the same for Program 2 and Program 3.[231] Facilities in Program 1 are not required to comply with these requirements but need only certify that emergency response procedures have been coordinated with the appropriate local agency.[232] A covered facility in Program 2 or Program 3 is not required to undertake additional measures to comply with the emergency response requirements of the section 112(r) rule if it can demonstrate that it already has a plan that complies with another comparable federal contingency plan regulation or is otherwise consistent with the National Response Team's Integrated Contingency Plan Guidance.[233] The rule also exempts a covered facility from the emergency response plan requirements if the facility can demonstrate that (1) its employees will not respond to accidental releases, (2) the facility has coordinated with local emergency response agencies for accidental releases, and (3) measures are in place for notifying the local emergency response agencies.[234]

Imminent and Substantial Endangerment

Whenever the Administrator determines that there may be "an imminent and substantial endangerment to the human health or welfare or the environment" from a listed substance, "the Administrator may secure such relief as may be necessary to abate such danger or threat . . . ."[235]

The federal district court in the area of the endangerment will have the jurisdiction "to grant such relief as the public interest and the equities of the case may require." The Administrator may take other actions, including "issuing such orders as may be necessary to protect human health."[236]

Chemical Process Safety Management

Section 304(a) of the 1990 Amendments required the Secretary of Labor, in coordination with the EPA Administrator, to promulgate a chemical process safety standard to protect employees from hazards associated with accidental releases of highly hazardous chemicals in the workplace. Section 304(b) of the Amendments required the Secretary of Labor to develop a list of such hazardous chemicals and include that list in the standard.

In 1992, the Secretary of Labor published the PSM rule.[237] The rule applies to any process involving a listed highly hazardous chemical at or above specified threshold quantities. The elements of the rule are largely replicated in the accidental release prevention program requirements under section 112(r)(7) and include requirements to develop process information, process hazard analyses, standard operating procedures, training, pre-startup review procedures, mechanical integrity requirements, management of change requirements, accident investigation procedures, safety audits, and emergency response procedures.

Chemical Safety Hazard Investigation Board

The 1990 Amendments established an independent safety council called the Chemical Safety and Hazard Investigation Board, or CSB, which has up to five members appointed by the President of the United States.[238] The CSB is a non-enforcement agency, which is independent and non-regulatory, with its main office in Washington, D.C. and a regional office in Denver. The purposes of the

CSB are to: (1) investigate or cause to be investigated "any accidental release resulting in a fatality, serious injury or substantial property damages"; (2) issue periodic reports recommending measures to reduce the likelihood of these accidents and proposing corrective steps; and (3) establish by regulation requirements directing persons to report such accidental releases.[239] The CSB is one of the entities that receives risk management plans developed and submitted by facilities covered by EPA's regulations under section 112(r)(7).[240]

The President did not begin the appointment process of the CSB until 1997, after EPA and OSHA had promulgated the accidental release/risk management regulations. Consequently, the CSB did not participate in the rulemaking process for those regulations as contemplated by the statute.[241] Since the CSB began operations in January 1998, it has coordinated with other agencies, including EPA and OSHA. The CSB has screened thousands of incidents, deployed to more than 100 incidents, published more than 70 investigation reports after conducting investigations (which routinely last six months to one year), issued more than 600 recommendations, and produced more than 25 safety videos since its inception. The CSB is currently operating under its 2012-2016 strategic plan.[242]

Study Provisions

Section 112 of the Act contains a number of study provisions, several of which have already been mentioned (including the electric utility study and oil and gas study). The Amendments also require EPA to study mercury emissions and their health and environmental effects, atmospheric deposition of air toxics to the Great Lakes and other water bodies, and the potential hazards of hydrofluoric acid to human health and the environment. The Amendments also mandate a comprehensive study of risk assessment methodology, its uses, and policy implications. These studies are discussed below.

The Mercury Studies

Section 112(n) requires EPA to study the rate of mercury emissions from electric utilities, municipal waste incinerators, and other sources, the health and environmental effects of those emissions, and technologies available to control them. This study focused on both direct and indirect human health effects and environmental effects from mercury emissions. EPA released its eight-volume study in December 1997.[243]

Section 112(n) also mandated a companion study by the National Institute of Environmental Health Science "to determine the threshold level of mercury exposure below which adverse human health effects are not expected to occur." This report was submitted to Congress in 1993 and did not establish a health threshold for mercury.[244]

The Great Waters Study

Section 112(m) of the Act requires EPA to study atmospheric deposition of air toxics to the Great Lakes, Lake Champlain, the Chesapeake Bay, and coastal waters, and to determine whether additional emissions standards or control measures are necessary to prevent serious adverse health and environmental effects. This provision contains an ongoing reporting requirement. EPA was to submit its first report to Congress by November 1993 and to update that report every two years. If EPA determined, based on the results of the study, that additional controls are necessary, it was to promulgate regulations by 1995.

EPA released its First Great Waters Study in May 1994, but declined to make a determination as to whether it needed additional regulatory authority to protect the Great Waters because of deficiencies in the data available.[245] EPA released its Second Great Waters Study in June 1997[246] and then issued proposed findings that section 112 authorities are adequately protecting the Great Waters and that no additional regulations were "necessary and appropriate" under section 112(m)(6).[247] EPA finalized those findings in March 1998.[248] In June 2000, EPA issued its Third Great Waters Study, in which it evaluated more recent data and also committed to development of a work plan regarding air deposition problems.[249] EPA's Office of Air and Radiation and Office of Water released an *Air-Water Interface Work Plan* on January 18, 2001, that provided for collaborative efforts under the Clean Air Act and Clean Water Act. In December 2007, EPA then issued a "Survey of New Findings in Scientific Literature Related to Atmospheric Deposition to the Great Waters," which focused on deposition of polycyclic aromatic hydrocarbons[250] and polychlorinated biphenyls.[251]

Hydrofluoric Acid

Section 112(n)(6) required the Administrator to complete a study of the potential hazards of hydrofluoric acid and make recommendations to Congress for the reduction of such hazards if appropriate. In September 1993, EPA published its final report.[252] EPA's report did not recommend that Congress take any action to reduce the hazards associated with hydrofluoric acid. EPA found that the primary risk of exposure stemmed from potential accidental releases and that government agencies' authority, as well as the accidental release provisions of the Clean Air Act Amendments, presented an appropriate framework for addressing that risk. The report did recommend, however, that EPA continue its Chemical Safety Audit program, investigate any chemical accidents associated with hydrofluoric acid, and investigate whether additional regulations are needed.

Risk Assessment and Management Commission

Section 303 of the Clean Air Act Amendments of 1990[253] established an independent commission called the Risk Assessment and Management Commission, which was required to "make a full investigation of the policy implications and appropriate uses of risk assessment and risk management in regulatory programs under various Federal laws to prevent cancer and other chronic human health effects which may result from exposure to hazardous substances."

The Commission was required to consider the National Academy of Sciences' report on risk assessment methodologies required under section 112(o) of the Act, and to evaluate the use and limitations of risk assessment in setting standards, the most appropriate methods for measuring and describing risks, methods for reflecting uncertainties, and various risk management policy issues. The Commission also was required to comment on the possibility or desirability of developing "a consistent risk assessment methodology, or a consistent standard of acceptable risk, among various Federal programs." The two-volume report was made available in 1997.[254]

Notes

1. CAA § 112(b)(1), 42 U.S.C. § 7412(b)(1).

2. Hydrogen sulfide was inadvertently included as a HAP but removed through a joint resolution by the House and Senate in 1991. *See* Clean Air Act Technical Corrections Bill, Pub. L. No. 102-187, 105 Stat. 1285 (1991). Hydrogen sulfide is still regulated under section 112(r), discussed below. Methyl ethyl ketone and caprolactam have been deleted through EPA actions. EPA, List of Hazardous Air Pollutants, Petition Process, Lesser Quantity Designations, Source Category List; Final Rule, 70 Fed. Reg. 75,047 (Dec. 19, 2005); EPA, Hazardous Air Pollutant List: Modification; Final Rule, 61 Fed. Reg. 30,816 (June 18, 1996). The compound of ethylene glycol monobutyl ether is also no longer part of the listed glycol ethers group. EPA, List of Hazardous Air Pollutants, Petition Process, Lesser Quantity Designations, Source Category List: Petition To Delist of Ethylene Glycol Monobutyl Ether; Final Rule, 69 Fed. Reg. 69,320 (Nov. 29, 2004).

3. *See* CAA § 108(a), 42 U.S.C. § 7408(a).

4. *Id.* § 112(b)(2), 42 U.S.C. § 7412(b)(2).

5. *Id.* § 112(b)(6), 42 U.S.C. § 7412(b)(6).

6. *Id.* § 112(b)(2), 42 U.S.C. § 7412(b)(2).

7. *Id.*

8. *Id.*

9. *Id.* § 112(a)(7), 42 U.S.C. § 7412(a)(7).

10. *See id.* § 112(b)(2), 42 U.S.C. § 7412(b)(2).

11. *Id.* § 112(b)(3)(A), 42 U.S.C. § 7412(b)(3)(A). Deletion of caprolactam was prompted by a section 112(b)(3)(A) petition. 61 Fed. Reg. at 30,816.

12. CAA § 112(b)(3)(A), 42 U.S.C. § 7412(b)(3)(A).

13. EPA, Hazardous Air Pollutants List; Notice of Denial, 58 Fed. Reg. 4164, 4165 (Jan. 13, 1993).

14. *Id.*

15. CAA § 112(b)(3)(B), (C), 42 U.S.C. § 7412(b)(3)(B), (C).

16. *Id.* § 112(b)(4), 42 U.S.C. § 7412(b)(4).

17. *Id.* § 112(b)(3)(A), 42 U.S.C. § 7412(b)(3)(A).

18. *Id.*

19. *Id.* § 112(e)(4), 42 U.S.C. § 7412(e)(4).

20. EPA, Initial List of Categories of Sources Under Section 112(c)(1) of the Clean Air Act Amendments of 1990; Notice of Initial List of Categories of Major and Area Sources, 57 Fed. Reg. 31,576, 31,591-92 (July 16, 1992).

21. *Id.* at 31,576.

22. CAA § 112(c)(1), 42 U.S.C. §7412(c)(1).

23. *See id.* § 112(c)(5), 42 U.S.C. §7412(c)(5).

24. *Id.* § 112(e)(4), 42 U.S.C. §7412(e)(4).

25. *Id.* § 112(e)(1)(E), 42 U.S.C. § 7412(e)(1)(E).

26. EPA maintains an applicability determinations index regarding source-specific determinations under section 112. *See* EPA, Search Applicability Determination Index, http://cfpub.epa.gov/adi/.

27. CAA § 112(a)(1), 42 U.S.C. § 7412(a)(1). EPA interpreted the pre-1990 Act to require regulation only of source categories that pose significant public health risks. Environmental groups, by contrast, argued that standards should be set for all sources of a HAP, no matter how small. The 1990 Amendments take a middle ground – defining a tonnage threshold as the trigger for categorization and regulation, regardless of health risk.

In 2000, EPA issued "Guidance on the Major Source Determination for Certain Hazardous Air Pollutants" (signed Aug. 14, 2000), which clarified the application of the tonnage thresholds to listed aggregate groups of HAPs, such as xylenes and dibenzofurans.

28. *See* CAA § 111(a)(3), 42 U.S.C. § 7412(a)(3).

29. *Nat'l Mining Ass'n v. EPA*, 59 F.3d 1351, 1354-55 (D.C. Cir. 1995).

30. CAA § 112(a)(1), 42 U.S.C. § 7412(a)(1).

31. *Id.*

32. *Nat'l Mining Ass'n*, 59 F.3d at 1354.

33. CAA § 112(c)(3), 42 U.S.C. § 7412(c)(3).

34. *Id.*

35. *Id.* § 112(k)(3), 42 U.S.C. § 7412(k)(3).

36. EPA, National Air Toxics Program: The Integrated Urban Strategy; Notice, 64 Fed. Reg. 38,706, 38,706 (July 19, 1999).

37. *Id.*

38. *Id.* at 38,720.

39. EPA, Completion of the Requirement To Promulgate Emission Standards; Notice, 76 Fed. Reg. 15,308 (Mar. 21, 2011). A compiled list of area source rules is available on EPA's Air Toxics Website. *See* EPA, Compilation of Area Source Rules, http://www.epa.gov/ttn/atw/area/compilation.html.

40. EPA, Area Source Rule Implementation Guidance at 2-4 (June 4, 2010), *available at* http://www.epa.gov/compliance/resources/policies/monitoring/caa/ areasource.pdf.

41. CAA § 112(a)(8), 42 U.S.C. § 7412(a)(8).

42. *Id.*

43. *Id.* § 112(n)(1), 42 U.S.C. § 7412(n)(1).

44. *Id.* § 112(n)(1)(A), 42 U.S.C. § 7412(n)(1)(A).

45. *Id.*

46. EPA, Regulatory Finding on the Emissions of Hazardous Air Pollutants From Electric Utility Steam Generating Units; Notice of Regulatory Finding, 65 Fed. Reg. 79,825, 79,826 (Dec. 20, 2000).

47. *See Utility Air Regulatory Group v. EPA*, No. 01-1074, 2001 WL 936363, at *1 (D.C. Cir. July 26, 2001).

48. EPA, Revision of December 2000 Regulatory Finding on the Emissions of Hazardous Air Pollutants From Electric Utility Steam Generating Units and the Removal of Coal- and Oil-Fired Electric Utility Steam Generating Units From the Section 112(c) List; Final Rule, 70 Fed. Reg. 15,994, 15,994 (Mar. 29, 2005).

49. EPA, Standards of Performance for New and Existing Stationary Sources: Electric Utility Steam Generating Units; Final Rule, 70 Fed. Reg. 28,606, 28,606 (May 18, 2005).

50. *New Jersey v. EPA*, 517 F.3d 574, 583 (D.C. Cir. 2008).

51. *Id.*

52. EPA, National Emission Standards for Hazardous Air Pollutants From Coal- and Oil-Fired Electric Utility Steam Generating Units and Standards of Performance for Fossil-Fuel-Fired Electric Utility, Industrial-Commercial-Institutional, and Small Industrial-Commercial-Institutional Steam Generating Units; Final Rule, 77 Fed. Reg. 9304, 9364 (Feb. 16, 2012). EPA subsequently granted reconsideration of a limited set of issues and has finalized changes to certain new source issues. EPA, Reconsideration of Certain New Source Issues: National Emission Standards for Hazardous Air Pollutants From Coal- and Oil-Fired Electric Utility Steam Generating Units and Standards of Performance for Fossil-Fuel-Fired Electric Utility, Industrial-Commercial-Institutional, and Small Industrial-Commercial-Institutional Steam Generating Units; Final Rule; Notice of Final Action on Reconsideration, 78 Fed. Reg. 24,073 (Apr. 24, 2013). EPA has proposed, but not yet taken final action on, changes to the startup and shutdown provisions in the February 16, 2012 rule. EPA, Reconsideration of Certain New Source and Startup/Shutdown Issues: National Emission Standards for Hazardous Air Pollutants From Coal- and Oil-Fired Electric Utility Steam Generating Units and Standards of Performance for Fossil-Fuel-Fired Electric Utility, Industrial-Commercial-Institutional, and Small Industrial-Commercial-Institutional Steam Generating Units; Proposed Rules; Notice of Public Hearing, 77 Fed. Reg. 71,323 (Nov. 30, 2012).

53. *White Stallion Energy Ctr., LLC v. EPA*, No. 12-1100 (D.C. Cir.) (primary litigation); *White Stallion Energy Ctr., LLC v. EPA*, No. 12-1272 (D.C. Cir.) (severed case concerning new source issues); *White Stallion Energy Ctr., LLC v. EPA,* No. 13-1106

(D.C. Cir.) (severed case regarding work practice standards applicable during startup and shutdown).

54. CAA § 112(n)(4)(A), 42 U.S.C. § 7412(n)(4)(A).

55. *See* 40 C.F.R. pt. 63, subpt. HH.

56. EPA, National Emission Standards for Hazardous Air Pollutants: Oil and Natural Gas Production and National Emission Standards for Hazardous Air Pollutants: Natural Gas Transmission and Storage; Final Rules, 64 Fed. Reg. 32,610, 32,629 (June 17, 1999) (emphasis added).

57. EPA, Oil and Natural Gas Sector: New Source Performance Standards and National Emission Standards for Hazardous Air Pollutants Reviews; Final Rule, 77 Fed. Reg. 49,490, 49,569 (Aug. 16, 2012).

58. *Am. Petroleum Inst. v. EPA*, No. 12-1409 & consol. cases (D.C. Cir.).

59. CAA § 112(n)(4), 42 U.S.C. § 7412(n)(4).

60. EPA, National Emission Standards for Hazardous Air Pollutants: Oil and Natural Gas Production and Natural Gas Transmission and Storage; Proposed Rules and Notice of Public Hearing, 63 Fed. Reg. 6288 (Feb. 6, 1998); 64 Fed. Reg. at 32,610 (final rule).

61. *See* 64 Fed. Reg. at 38,706.

62. EPA, National Emission Standards for Hazardous Air Pollutants for Source Categories From Oil and Natural Gas Production Facilities; Final Rule, 72 Fed. Reg. 26 (Jan. 3, 2007).

63. CAA § 112(n)(5), 42 U.S.C. § 7412(n)(5).

64. EPA, EPA 453/R-93-045, Report to Congress on Hydrogen Sulfide Air Emissions Associated with the Extraction of Oil and Natural Gas (Oct. 1993), *available at* http://nepis.epa.gov/Exe/ZyPURL.cgi?Dockey=00002WG3.txt.

65. *Id.* at iii.

66. *Id.*

67. *See* CAA § 112(e)(5), 42 U.S.C. § 7412(e)(5).

68. *See* EPA, National Emission Standards for Hazardous Air Pollutants: Publicly Owned Treatment Works; Final Rule, 64 Fed. Reg. 57,572, 57,579 (Oct. 26, 1999); 40 C.F.R. pt. 63, subpt. VVV.

69. CAA § 112(n)(7), 42 U.S.C. § 7412(n)(7).

70. *See* EPA Region IV, CAA and RCRA Overlap Provisions in Subparts AA, BB, and CC of 40 CFR Parts 264 and 265, at vii (Oct. 2000); *see also Cement Kiln Recycling Coal. v. EPA*, 255 F.3d 855, 858 (D.C. Cir. 2001) (discussing overlap between RCRA and CAA).

71. EPA, Hazardous Waste Treatment, Storage, and Disposal Facilities and Hazardous Waste Generators; Organic Air Emission Standards for Tanks, Surface Impoundments, and Containers; Final Rule, 61 Fed. Reg. 59,932, 59,938 (Nov. 25, 1996).

72. CAA § 112(c)(9)(B), 42 U.S.C. § 7412(c)(9)(B).

73. *See, e.g.,* EPA, National Emission Standards for Hazardous Air Pollutants: Revision of Source Category List Under Section 112 of the Clean Air Act; Notice of Revisions to the List of Categories of Major and Area Sources, 67 Fed. Reg. 6521 (Feb. 12, 2002); EPA, National Emission Standards for Hazardous Air Pollutants: Revision of Source Category List and Schedule for Standards Under Section 112 of the Clean Air Act; Notice of Revisions to the List of Categories of Major and Ares Sources, 66 Fed. Reg. 8220 (Jan. 30, 2001); EPA, National Emission Standards for Hazardous Air Pollutants: Revision of Source Category List and Schedule for Standards Under Section 112 of the Clean Air Act; Notice of Revisions to the List of Categories of Major and Area Sources and Revisions to the Promulgation Schedule for Standards, 64 Fed. Reg. 63,025 (Nov. 18, 1999); EPA, National Emission Standards for Hazardous Air Pollutants; Revision of List of Categories of Sources and Schedule for Standards Under Section 112 of the Clean Air Act; Notice of Revisions to the List of Categories of Major and Area Sources and Revisions to the Promulgation Schedule for Standards, 63 Fed. Reg. 7155 (Feb. 12, 1998); EPA, Delisting of Source Category and Revision of Initial List of Categories of Sources and Schedule for Standards Under Section 112(c) of the Clean Air Act; Removal of the Asbestos Processing Area Source Category from the Initial List of Categories of Sources and Schedule for Standards for Major and Area Sources of Hazardous Air Pollutants, 60 Fed. Reg. 61,550 (Nov. 30, 1995).

74. *See, e.g.,* 77 Fed. Reg. at 9364 (denying petition to delist EGU source category). EPA issued guidance entitled "Information on EPA's Delisting Process" for use by potential petitioners. Memorandum from Sally L. Shaver, Dir., EPA, to Potential Petitioners Seeking Delisting of Hazardous Air Pollutants or Source Categories, Regarding "Information on EPA's Delisting Process" (undated).

75. *Natural Res. Def. Council v. EPA*, 489 F.3d 1364, 1372 (D.C. Cir. 2007) (quoting CAA § 112(c)(9)(B)(i), 42 U.S.C. § 7412(c)(9)(B)(i)) (emphases added).

76. *E.g.,* EPA, National Emission Standards for Hazardous Air Pollutants; Revision of Initial List of Categories of Sources and Schedule for Standards Under Sections 112(c) and (e) of the Clean Air Act Amendments of 1990; Notice of Revisions to Initial List of Categories of Major and Area Sources, and Revisions to Promulgation Schedule of Standards, 61 Fed. Reg. 28,197, 28,200 (June 4, 1996) ("The Agency is not invoking the authority within Section 112(c)(9) for deleting source categories . . . . Instead, in today's notice, the Agency is simply contending that the data originally used for listing were erroneous, and that, based on newer data, the original listings are not warranted.").

77. *New Jersey v. EPA*, 517 F.3d at 583.

78. CAA § 112(d)(3), 42 U.S.C. § 7412(d)(3).

79. *Id.*

80. *See id.* § 112(d)(3)(A), (B), 42 U.S.C. § 7412(d)(3)(A), (B).

81. *Id.* § 112(d)(3)(A), 42 U.S.C. § 7412(d)(3)(A).

82. *Id.* § 112(d)(3)(B), 42 U.S.C. § 7412(d)(3)(B).

83. *Id.* § 112(d)(2), 42 U.S.C. § 7412(d)(2).

84. *Nat'l Lime Ass'n v. EPA*, 233 F.3d 625, 633-34 (D.C. Cir. 2000) (rejecting EPA's "no control" floors for certain HAPs); *see also Sierra Club v. EPA*, 479 F.3d 875, 883 (D.C. Cir. 2007) (same).

85. *Nat'l Lime Ass'n*, 233 F.3d at 637.

86. *Mossville Envtl. Action Now v. EPA*, 370 F.3d 1232,1242-43 (D.C. Cir. 2004).

87. *Sierra Club,* 479 F.3d at 880-81.

88. *See Cement Kiln*, 255 F.3d at 861 ("EPA may not deviate from section [112(d)(3)'s] requirement that floors reflect what the best performers actually achieve by claiming that floors must be achievable by all sources using MACT technology.").

89. *See id.* at 867 (citing *Sierra Club v. EPA*, 167 F.3d 658, 662, 665 (D.C. Cir. 1999)).

90. *Mossville*, 370 F.3d at 1240-42; *Cement Kiln*, 255 F.3d at 866.

91. *Sierra Club*, 479 F.3d at 882-83.

92. *Mossville*, 370 F.3d at 1241 (quoting *Cement Kiln*, 255 F.3d at 865).

93. *Sierra Club*, 479 F.3d at 882.

94. *Nat'l Lime Ass'n,* 233 F.3d at 634.

95. *See, e.g., id.* at 632.

96. CAA § 129(a)(2), 42 U.S.C. § 7429(a)(2); *Ne. Md. Waste Disposal Auth. v. EPA*, 358 F.3d 936, 944 (D.C. Cir. 2004) (summarizing MACT analysis under section 129).

97. *Natural Res. Def. Council v. EPA*, 489 F.3d at 1256 (quoting section 129(h)(2)) ("no solid waste incineration unit subject to performance standards under [sections 129 and 111] . . . shall be subject to standards under section 7412(d)") (internal quotation marks omitted).

98. In 2007, the D.C. Circuit vacated an EPA rule that defined "commercial and industrial waste" for purposes of section 129. *Id.* at 1254. The under-inclusiveness of EPA's definition caused some industrial boilers to be subject to section 112 rather than section 129 standards, and so the court also vacated the industrial boiler section 112 standards. *Id.* at 1261-62. EPA has also vacated section 112 standards promulgated for Portland cement facilities because of interdependence issues between sections 112 and section 129. *Portland Cement Ass'n v. EPA*, 665 F.3d 177 (D.C. Cir. 2011). In setting section 112 MACT standards for those facilities, EPA had considered *all* facilities, even though it was likely that some kilns would ultimately be subject to section 129 standards. *Id.* at 185-86. Because EPA did not propose a definition of "commercial and industrial waste" (which would determine which kilns would be subject to section 129) until after the end of the comment period for the section 112 rule, and EPA then refused to revise its MACT calculations after the section 129 waste definition rule was finalized, the D.C. Circuit held EPA's actions to be arbitrary and capricious. *Id.* at 185, 188.

99. EPA, Standards of Performance for New Stationary Sources and Emission Guidelines for Existing Sources: Commercial and Industrial Solid Waste Incineration

Units; Final Rule, 76 Fed. Reg. 15,704 (Mar. 21, 2011); EPA, Identification of Non-Hazardous Secondary Materials That Are Solid Waste; Final Rule, 76 Fed. Reg. 15,456 (Mar. 21, 2011).

100. EPA, Commercial and Industrial Solid Waste Incineration Units: Reconsideration and Final Amendments; Non-Hazardous Secondary Materials That Are Solid Waste; Final Rule; Notice of Final Action on Reconsideration, 78 Fed. Reg. 9112, 9116-17 (Feb. 7, 2013) (discussing division between sections 112 and 129).

101. *Portland Cement Ass'n v. EPA*, No. 13-1111 (D.C. Cir.).

102. CAA § 112(d)(4), 42 U.S.C. § 7412(d)(4).

103. *See* EPA, National Emission Standards for Hazardous Air Pollutants From Coal- and Oil-Fired Electric Utility Steam Generating Units and Standards of Performance for Fossil-Fuel-Fired Electric Utility, Industrial-Commercial-Institutional, and Small Industrial-Commercial-Institutional Steam Generating Units; Proposed Rule, 76 Fed. Reg. 24,976, 25,050 (May 3, 2011) (discussing EPA's historical use of section 112(d)(4)).

104. CAA § 112(d)(5), 42 U.S.C. § 7412(d)(5).

105. *See, e.g.,* EPA, National Emission Standards for Hazardous Air Pollutants for Area Sources: Electric Arc Furnace Steelmaking Facilities; Final Rule, 72 Fed. Reg. 74,088, 74,089-91 (Dec. 28, 2007) (summarizing GACT requirements for electric arc furnace steelmaking facilities that are area sources).

106. CAA § 112(j), 42 U.S.C. § 7412(j).

107. *Id.* § 112(j)(2), 42 U.S.C. § 7412(j)(2).

108. *Id.* § 112(j)(2), (3), 42 U.S.C. § 7412(j)(2), (3). The application must be reviewed and approved or disapproved according to the Title V operating permit procedures discussed in Chapter 5. *Id.* § 112(j)(4), 42 U.S.C. § 7412(j)(4).

109. 40 C.F.R. § 63.53.

110. CAA § 112(j)(6), 42 U.S.C. § 7412(j)(6).

111. *Id.*

112. 40 C.F.R. §§ 63.50-63.56.

113. EPA, Requirements for Control Technology Determinations for Major Sources in Accordance With Clean Air Act Sections, Sections 112(g) and 112(j); Proposed Rule, 75 Fed. Reg. 15,655, 15,657 (Mar. 30, 2010).

114. 57 Fed. Reg. at 31,576.

115. 40 C.F.R. §§ 63.40-63.44; *see also* EPA, Hazardous Air Pollutants: Regulations Governing Constructed or Reconstructed Major Sources; Final Rule, 61 Fed. Reg. 68,384 (Dec. 27, 1996); EPA, Hazardous Air Pollutants: Regulations Governing Constructed or Reconstructed Major Sources; Direct Final Rule, 64 Fed. Reg. 35,029 (June 30, 1999) (extending period of time for EPA to make case-by-case determination if permitting authority does not yet have section 112(g) procedures in place).

116. 61 Fed. Reg. at 68,388.

117. 40 C.F.R. § 63.41.

118. CAA § 112(h)(1), 42 U.S.C. § 7412(h)(1).

119. *Id.*

120. *Id.* § 112(h)(2), 42 U.S.C. § 7412(h)(2); *see also Sierra Club*, 479 F.3d at 884 (holding that lack of emissions data alone is not sufficient basis for invocation of need for work practice standards).

121. CAA § 112(h)(3), 42 U.S.C. § 7412(h)(3).

122. *Id.* § 112(f)(1), 42 U.S.C. § 7412(f)(1).

123. EPA, EPA-453/R-99-001, Residual Risk: Report to Congress (Mar. 1999).

124. CAA § 112(f)(2), 42 U.S.C. § 7412(f)(2). The Administrator is not required to conduct any review or promulgate any emission limitations based on residual risk for area source categories or subcategories for which GACT emission standards have been promulgated. *Id.* § 112(f)(5), 42 U.S.C. § 7412(f)(5).

125. *Id.* § 112(f)(2)(A), 42 U.S.C. § 7412(f)(2)(A). In residual risk rulemaking, EPA may use any reasonable data source, including industry-supplied data. *See Natural Res. Def. Council v. EPA*, 529 F.3d 1077, 1086 (D.C. Cir. 2008).

126. *Natural Res. Def. Council,* 529 F.3d at 1077.

127. *Id.* at 1081.

128. *Id.* at 1083.

129. EPA, National Emission Standards for Hazardous Air Pollutants; Benzene Emissions From Maleic Anhydride Plants, Ethylbenzene/Styrene Plants, Benzene Storage Vessels, Benzene Equipment Leaks, and Coke By-Product Recovery Plants; Final Rule, 54 Fed. Reg. 38,044 (Sept. 14, 1989).

130. *Natural Res. Def. Council v. EPA*, 824 F.2d 1146 (D.C. Cir. 1987).

131. 54 Fed. Reg. at 38,048.

132. *Id.* at 38,045.

133. *Natural Res. Def. Council,* 529 F.3d at 1083 (quoting 54 Fed. Reg. at 38,045) (emphasis in original).

134. *Id.* at 1082.

135. EPA, EPA-452/R-09/006, RTR Risk Assessment Methodologies: For Review by the EPA's Science Advisory Board with Case Studies – MACT I Petroleum Refining Sources and Portland Cement Manufacturing (June 2009).

136. Letter from Drs. Deborah L. Swackhamer & Jana Milford, Chairs, Science Advisory Board, to Lisa Jackson, Adm'r, EPA (May 7, 2010) (transmitting Science Advisory Board's review of draft RTR report).

137. EPA maintains a website of all residual risk regulatory actions at http://www.epa.gov/ttn/atw/rrisk/rtrpg.html.

138. CAA § 112(f)(3), 42 U.S.C.§ 7412(f)(3).

139. *Id.* § 112(f)(4)(A), 42 U.S.C.§ 7412(f)(4)(A).

140. *Id.* § 112(f)(4)(B), 42 U.S.C.§ 7412(f)(4)(B).

141. *Id.* § 112(q)(1), 42 U.S.C. § 7412(q)(1).

142. *Id.* § 112(q)(2), 42 U.S.C. § 7412(q)(2).

143. *Id.* § 112(q)(3), 42 U.S.C. § 7412(q)(3).

144. *Id.* § 112(e)(1), 42 U.S.C. § 7412(e)(1).

145. *Id.* § 112(e)(3), 42 U.S.C. § 7412(e)(3).

146. Those deadlines were generally not met, resulting in litigation and revised court-ordered promulgation deadlines.

147. *Ass'n of Battery Recyclers, Inc. v. EPA*, 716 F.3d 667, 672 (D.C. Cir. 2013).

148. CAA §112(i)(2), 42 U.S.C.§ 7412(i)(2).

149. *Id.* § 112(i)(2)(A),(B), 42 U.S.C. § 7412(i)(2)(A), (B).

150. *Id.* § 112(i)(3)(A), 42 U.S.C.§ 7412(i)(3)(A).

151. *Id.* § 112(i)(3)(A), (B), 42 U.S.C. § 7412(i)(3)(A). The Part 63 General Provisions, discussed below in further detail, provide additional information regarding the application for and the approval of section 112(i)(3)(B) compliance extensions. *See* 40 C.F.R. § 63.6(i).

152. CAA § 112(i)(5), 42 U.S.C. § 7412(i)(5).

153. *See* 40 C.F.R. pt. 63, subpt. D.

154. CAA § 112(i)(4), 42 U.S.C. § 7412(i)(4).

155. EPA has conducted four National Air Toxics Assessments – in 1996, 1999, 2002, and 2005 – to assist EPA and delegated authorities in section 112 implementation and to prioritize regulation by pollutant, source type, and geographic location. These assessments evaluate cancer and non-cancer risks associated with HAP inhalation.

156. *See* 40 C.F.R. pt. 63, subpt. A.

157. CAA § 112(a)(1), 42 U.S.C. § 7412(a)(1).

158. 40 C.F.R. § 63.2.

159. *Id.* (emphasis added).

160. *Nat'l Mining Ass'n*, 59 F.3d at 1363-64 ("What EPA has not explained is how its refusal to consider limitations other than those that are 'federally enforceable' serves the statute's directive to 'consider[] controls' when it results in a refusal to credit controls imposed by a state or locality even if they are unquestionably effective.").

161. John S. Seitz, Director, Office of Air Quality Planning and Standards, and Robert Van Heuvelen, Director, Office of Regulatory Enforcement, Options for Limiting the Potential to Emit (PTE) of a Stationary Source Under Section 112 and Title V of the Clean Air Act (Act) (Jan. 25, 2005).

162. *See, e.g.,* John S. Seitz, Director, EPA Office of Air Quality Planning and Standards, and Eric Schaeffer, Director, EPA Office of Regulatory Enforcement, Third Extension of January 25, 1995 Potential to Emit Transition Policy (Dec. 20, 1999); John S. Seitz, Director, EPA Office of Air Quality Planning and Standards, and Eric Schaeffer, Director, EPA Office of Regulatory Enforcement, Potential to Emit for Specific Source Categories (Apr. 14, 1998); *see also* Bruce Buckheit, Director, EPA Air Enforcement

Division, and Lydia Wegman, Deputy Director, EPA Office of Air Quality Planning and Standards, Memorandum: Discussion Paper on Options for the Potential to Emit Rulemaking (Nov. 3, 1997).

163. 40 C.F.R. §§ 63.7, 63.8. With regard to monitoring issues, whether under the General Provisions or specific MACT standards, courts are generally deferential to EPA. *See, e.g., Nat'l Lime Ass'n v. EPA*, 233 F.3d at 634.

164. EPA, National Emission Standards for Hazardous Air Pollutants for Source Categories: General Provisions; Final Rule, 59 Fed. Reg. 12,408, 12418 (Mar. 16, 1994).

165. *See* EPA, Compliance Assurance Monitoring; Final Rule; Final Rule Revisions, 62 Fed. Reg. 54,900 (Oct. 22, 1997). This rule is discussed in more detail in Chapter 4.

166. *See* 40 C.F.R. § 64.2(b)(i).

167. 59 Fed. Reg. at 12,419.

168. EPA, Restructuring of the Stationary Source Audit Program, 75 Fed. Reg. 55,636 (Sept. 13, 2010).

169. *See* 40 C.F.R. § 63.6.

170. *Id.* § 63.6(e)(3).

171. *Sierra Club v. EPA*, 551 F.3d 1019, 1028 (D.C. Cir. 2008).

172. Letter from Adam M. Kushner, Dir., EPA Office of Civil Enforcement, regarding Vacatur of Startup, Shutdown, and Malfunction Exemption (40 C.F.R. §§ 63.6(f)(1) and 63.6(h)(1)) (July 22, 2009).

173. *See* 40 C.F.R. §§ 63.9, 63.10.

174. 40 C.F.R. § 70.3(a)(3); EPA, Operating Permit Program; Final Rule, 57 Fed. Reg. 32,250, 32,295, 32,297 (July 21, 1992). The Title V permit rules allow states to exempt area sources from the permitting requirement for five years. 40 C.F.R. § 70.3(b)(1); 57 Fed. Reg. at 32,261, 32,297.

175. CAA § 112(*l*)(1), 42 U.S.C. § 7412(*l*)(1). The accidental release provisions of section 112(r) are discussed in the following section of this chapter.

176. *See* 40 C.F.R. § 63.99 (listing states and their delegation status).

177. CAA § 112(*l*)(5), 42 U.S.C. § 7412(*l*)(5).

178. *Id.*

179. *Id.* § 112(*l*)(6), 42 U.S.C. § 7412(*l*)(6).

180. *Id.*

181. *Id.* § 112(*l*)(7), 42 U.S.C. § 7412(*l*)(7).

182. *Id.* § 112(*l*)(8), 42 U.S.C. § 7412(*l*)(8).

183. 40 C.F.R. pt. 63, subpt. E.

184. *La. Envtl. Action Network v. Browner*, 87 F.3d 1379 (D.C. Cir. 1996).

185. EPA, Hazardous Air Pollutants: Amendments to the Approval of State Programs and Delegation of Federal Authorities; Final Rule, 65 Fed. Reg. 55,810, 55,814 (Sept. 14, 2000).

186. 40 C.F.R. § 63.95.

187. *See* 42 U.S.C. § 11002. The EHS list is published at 40 C.F.R. part 355.

188. CAA § 112(r)(3), 42 U.S.C. § 7412(r)(3).

189. *Id.*

190. *Id.*

191. *Id.* § 112(r)(5), 42 U.S.C. § 7412(r)(5).

192. *See* Comprehensive Environmental Response, Compensation, and Liability Act ("CERCLA") §§ 102, 103, 42 U.S.C. §§ 9602, 9603. Section 102(b) of CERCLA establishes a default reportable quantity value of one pound unless EPA specifies otherwise by rule.

193. EPA, List of Regulated Substances and Thresholds for Accidental Release Prevention; Requirements for Petitions Under Section 112(r) of the Clean Air Act as Amended; Final Rule, 59 Fed. Reg. 4478 (Jan. 31, 1994) (codified at 40 C.F.R. § 68.130). These substances are listed in Appendix 3 to this Handbook. In the January 1994 rule, EPA also promulgated the applicability provisions and definitions for the section 112(r)(7) regulations (discussed below), which EPA promulgated in full in June 1996.

194. EPA, List of Regulated Substances and Thresholds for Accidental Release Prevention; Amendments; Final Rule, 63 Fed. Reg. 640 (Jan. 6, 1998).

195. EPA, List of Regulated Substances and Thresholds for Accidental Release Prevention; Final Rule, 62 Fed. Reg. 45,130 (Aug. 25, 1997).

196. Thus, the general duty clause applies regardless of whether that substance is listed under section 112(r)(3).

197. *Id.* EPA has issued guidance regarding the "general duty" clause. *See, e.g.,* EPA, EPA 550-B99-002, Guidance for Implementation of the General Duty Clause, Clean Air Act Section 112(r)(1) (May 2000).

198. For an example of EPA enforcement action under the "general duty" clause, see EPA, Office of Regulatory Enforcement, EPA 300-N-98-006, Enforcement Alert: Owners, Operators of Stationary Sources Must Comply with Clean Air Act's General Duty Clause (Aug. 1998).

199. This result was suggested by the citation to the Department of Labor's Office of Health and Safety Administration's ("OSHA") general duty clause (29 U.S.C. § 654) in the legislative language. The OSHA general duty clause was interpreted by the D.C. Circuit to be self-implementing. *Int'l Union v. Gen. Dynamics Land Sys. Div.*, 815 F.2d 1570 (D.C. Cir. 1987).

200. CAA § 112(r)(1), 42 U.S.C. § 7412(r)(1).

201. *Id.* § 112(r)(7)(B)(i), 42 U.S.C. § 7412(r)(7)(B)(i).

202. Section 112(r)(6) of the CAA, 42 U.S.C. § 7412(r)(6), directs the President to appoint five members to this independent safety board. The CSB is discussed below.

203. *Id.* § 112(r)(7)(B)(iii), 42 U.S.C. § 7412(r)(7)(B)(iii).

204. *Id.* § 112(r)(7)(B)(i), 42 U.S.C. § 7412(r)(7)(B)(i).

205. 40 C.F.R. pt. 68. EPA has issued several guidance documents regarding the Risk Management Program under section 112(r). *See, e.g.,* EPA, EPA 550-K-11-001, Guidance for Conducting Risk Management Program Inspections Under Clean Air Act Section 112(r) (Jan. 2011); EPA, EPA-555-B-04-001, General Guidance on Risk Management Programs for Chemical Accident Prevention (40 CFR Part 68) (Mar. 2009); EPA, Risk Management Programs Under Clean Air Act Section 112(r): Guidance for Implementing Agencies (Feb. 1998). EPA has also issued guidance for specific types of facilities, including ammonia refrigeration, propane storage facilities, waste water treatment plants, warehouses, and chemical distributors.

206. EPA, EPA 550-K-11-001, Guidance for Conducting Risk Management Program Inspections Under Clean Air Act Section 112(r) at 5 (Jan. 2011).

207. Certain exemptions apply in making the threshold determination. *See* 40 C.F.R. § 68.115.

208. *Id.* § 68.3.

209. *Id.*

210. *Id.*

211. *Id.*

212. *Id.* § 68.150.

213. *Id.* § 68.210. In 1997, EPA began considering the development of an electronic filing system that would place RMPs on the internet to allow access by EPA, the CSB, the states, local agencies, and the public. EPA has since released RMP*eSubmit, an online reporting tool.

214. *Id.* §§ 68.150, 68.190.

215. *Id.* § 68.220.

216. *Id.* § 68.10. EPA has issued off-site consequence analysis guidance. EPA, EPA 550-B-99-009, Risk Management Program Guidance for Offsite Consequence Analysis (Mar. 2009). A program called RMP*Comp also allows an owner/operator to complete off-site consequence analysis for planning purposes.

217. To qualify for Program 1 regulation, a facility must demonstrate that: (1) a worst-case release from a covered process would not impact any public receptors of concern; (2) the facility has not had any accidental releases with significant off-site consequences within the previous five years; and (3) the facility has coordinated emergency response procedures with local emergency planners and responders. 40 C.F.R. § 68.10(b).

218. Facilities subject to Program 3 requirements include those that are not eligible for Program 1 and are either subject to the OSHA Process Safety Management ("PSM") standard or fall within North American Industry Classification System code 32211, 32411, 32511, 325181, 325188, 325192, 325199, 325211, 325311, or 32532. *Id.* § 68.10(d). OSHA PSM is discussed further below.

219. *Id.* § 68.10(c).

220. *Id.* § 68.42.

221. *Id.* §§ 68.25, 68.28.

222. *Id.* § 68.25.

223. *Id.* § 68.28.

224. *Id.* § 68.12.

225. *Id.* § 68.12(b)(1).

226. *Id.* §§ 68.65-68.87. The OSHA PSM rule is codified at 29 C.F.R. § 1910.119.

227. 40 C.F.R. § 68.12.

228. *Id.* §§ 68.12, 68.48-68.60.

229. *Id.* §§ 68.12, 68.65-68.87.

230. EPA, Accidental Release Prevention Requirements: Risk Management Programs Under Clean Air Act Section 112(r)(7); Final Rule, 61 Fed. Reg. 31,668, 31,670, 31,672 (June 20, 1996). EPA and OSHA have entered into agreements to address potential conflicts in accident investigation and enforcement authority over the similar and overlapping requirements of section 112(r)(7) and OSHA PSM: (1) Strategy for Coordinated EPA/OSHA Implementation of the Chemical Accident Prevention Requirements of the Clean Air Act Amendments of 1990 (Aug. 8, 1996); and (2) Memorandum of Understanding Between EPA (Office of Solid Waste and Emergency Response; Office of Enforcement and Compliance Assurance) and OSHA (Occupational Safety and Health Administration) on Chemical Accident Investigation (Nov./Dec. 1996).

231. 40 C.F.R. § 68.95.

232. *Id.* § 68.12.

233. *Id.* § 68.95(b). The Integrated Contingency Plan Guidance, also known as the One Plan, was developed by a multi-agency group called the National Response Team. The One Plan was published at 61 Fed. Reg. 28,642 (June 5, 1996), with corrections published shortly thereafter at 61 Fed. Reg. 31,103 (June 19, 1996).

234. 40 C.F.R. § 68.90.

235. CAA § 112(r)(9)(A), 42 U.S.C. § 7412(r)(9)(A).

236. *Id.*

237. OSHA, Process Safety Management of Highly Hazardous Chemicals; Explosives and Blasting Agents; Final Rule, 57 Fed. Reg. 6356 (Feb. 24, 1992) (codified at 29 C.F.R. § 1910.119).

238. CAA § 112(r)(6), 42 U.S.C. § 7412(r)(6).

239. *Id.* § 112(r)(6)(C), 42 U.S.C. § 7412(r)(6)(C).

240. *Id.* § 112(r)(7)(B)(iii), CAA § 7412(r)(7)(B)(iii).

241. *See, e.g., id.* § 112(r)(6)(K), 42 U.S.C. § 7412(r)(6)(K).

242. CSB, 2012-2016 Chemical Safety Board Strategic Plan (June 2012).

243. EPA, EPA-452/R-97-003, Mercury Study Report to Congress (Dec. 1997).

244. National Institute of Environmental Health Sciences, Report to Congress on Methylmercury (1993).

245. EPA, EPA-453/R-93-055, Deposition of Air Pollutants to the Great Waters: First Report to Congress (1994).

246. EPA, EPA-453/R-97-011, Deposition of Air Pollutants to the Great Waters: Second Report to Congress (1997).

247. EPA, Draft Determination of Adequacy of Section 112 Authorities And Draft Determination of Need for Additional Standards; Notice of Draft Determinations, 62 Fed. Reg. 36,436 (July 7, 1997).

248. EPA, Determination of Adequacy of Section 112 Authorities and Determination of Need for Additional Standards; Notice of Determinations, 63 Fed. Reg. 14,090 (Mar. 24, 1998).

249. EPA, EPA-453/R-00-005, Deposition of Air Pollutants to the Great Waters: Third Report to Congress (2000).

250. EPA, EPA-452/R-07-011, Survey of New Findings in Scientific Literature Related to Atmospheric Deposition to the Great Waters: Polycyclic Aromatic Hydrocarbons (PAH) (Dec. 2007).

251. EPA, EPA-452/R-07-012, Survey of New Findings in Scientific Literature Related to Atmospheric Deposition to the Great Waters: Polychlorinated Biphenyls (PCB) (Dec. 2007).

252. EPA, EPA-550-R-93-001, Hydrogen Fluoride Study – Report to Congress: Section 112(n)(6) Clean Air Act as Amended (1993).

253. Clean Air Act Amendments of 1990, Pub. L. No. 101-549, § 303, 104 Stat. 2399, 2574-76 (1990).

254. The Presidential/Congressional Commission on Risk Assessment and Risk Management, Framework for Environmental Health Management (1997).

Chapter 6

VISIBILITY PROTECTION

Background

The 1977 Clean Air Act Amendments declared as a national goal "the prevention of any future, and the remedying of any existing, impairment of visibility in mandatory class I Federal areas which impairment results from manmade air pollution."[1] Pursuant to the Act, EPA identified 156 mandatory Federal Class I areas, which include large national parks and wilderness areas. To implement the 1977 Amendments, EPA in 1980 adopted a "Phase I" visibility program addressing "plume blight" (*i.e.*, visible plumes) that impact Class I areas.[2] Citing uncertainties in monitoring and modeling techniques for evaluating regional visibility impairment (*i.e.*, regional haze), EPA decided at that time to postpone development of a "Phase II" program addressing regional haze.

The Phase I visibility program was difficult for states to implement and was therefore only rarely used. The most notable example of its use was the regulation of the Navajo Generating Station ("NGS") to reduce the visibility impacts of that source's plume in Grand Canyon National Park.[3]

In 1990, Congress amended the Act in response to EPA's continued deferral of a regional haze regulatory program. New CAA § 169B required research on monitoring and modeling of regional haze, established a Grand Canyon Visibility Transport Commission, and set a new deadline for EPA to adopt the regional haze regulatory program called for by CAA § 169A.

The Regional Haze Regulatory Program

In 1999, EPA adopted final rules to implement the regional haze regulatory program,[4] including the two main components of the program: the reasonable progress requirement and the "best available retrofit technology" ("BART") requirement. The 1999 regional haze rules were challenged in the D.C. Circuit by both industry and environmental groups. The reasonable progress program survived judicial review, but the court vacated the BART rules and remanded

176

them to EPA for further rulemaking.[5] The D.C. Circuit remanded EPA's BART rules because the court determined that the Agency had impermissibly constrained the states' "broad authority over BART determinations."[6]

EPA undertook a BART remand rulemaking and issued revised BART rules in 2005.[7] Those rules include the so-called "BART Guidelines," which are legally binding with respect to state BART determinations for power plants exceeding 750 megawatts ("MW").[8] For other sources, the Guidelines provide only guidance to the states.[9] States generally have followed that guidance, however. With the final BART program in place, the regional haze program shifted to the implementation stage.

States must implement the regional haze rules pursuant to CAA § 110(a)(2)(J), which requires each state to develop a state implementation plan ("SIP") to address the CAA's visibility protection requirements. States develop regional haze SIPs and submit them to EPA for approval. Regional haze SIPs for the first implementation period of the program (which addresses regional haze requirements through 2018) were due to EPA by December 17, 2007,[10] although most states did not meet that deadline. Future regional haze SIPs will cover every ten-year period beyond 2018, until at least 2064, which is the non-binding target date for completion of the program.[11] The following sections describe the regional haze program, the implementation process undertaken by states, the resulting SIP requirements, and legal challenges to various aspects of the program.

The Regional Planning Organizations

The regional haze rules require an expensive and intensive implementation effort by the states. The states must analyze air quality monitoring data collected by the so-called "IMPROVE" (Interagency Monitoring of Protected Visual Environments) monitoring network for the Class I areas within their borders,[12] determine reasonable progress goals for those areas through air quality modeling and consideration of other factors,[13] determine BART emission limitations for applicable sources,[14] and adopt emission control strategies, known as each state's "long-term strategy," that are designed to achieve the reasonable progress goals and BART.[15] The 1999 rules encouraged states to join together in doing much of the analysis and technical work needed for implementation of the rules, and the 2005 rules and BART Guidelines retained this recommendation.

States implemented these recommendations by forming and participating in five "regional planning organizations" ("RPOs"), each covering a different area of the country. These RPOs are: (1) the Mid-Atlantic/Northeast Visibility Union (commonly known as "MANE-VU"), (2) the Visibility Improvement State and Tribal Association of the Southeast (known as "VISTAS"), (3) the Midwest Regional Planning Organization ("MRPO"), (4) the Central Regional Air Planning Association ("CENRAP"), and (5) the Western Regional Air Partnership ("WRAP"). Each of these RPOs undertook a multi-year research effort involving monitoring and modeling to assist its member states in developing their regional haze SIPs.

BART

The BART program requires states to review stationary sources in 26 source categories and determine which of those sources are both "BART-eligible" and "subject to BART."[16] BART eligibility for specific sources in these source categories is determined by the size of the source (potential emissions of a visibility-impairing pollutant must be at least 250 tons per year) and by the date that the source began operation (the source must have been in existence on August 7, 1977, but must not have begun operation before August 7, 1962).[17] A BART-eligible source is "subject to BART" if it may reasonably be anticipated to cause or contribute to visibility impairment in a Class I area.[18] EPA's rules allow a state either to assume that all BART-eligible sources in that state are subject to BART or to perform (or to have the source perform) source-specific modeling to evaluate whether the source "causes or contributes to" visibility impairment in a Class I area.[19] EPA's BART Guidelines indicate that, for source-specific modeling, any source whose emissions contribute 1.0 (or more) "deciviews"[20] of visibility impairment in a Class I area normally would be deemed to cause visibility impairment and any source whose emissions contribute 0.5 (or more) deciviews of visibility impairment in a Class I area normally would be deemed to contribute to visibility impairment.[21]

If a source is both BART-eligible and subject to BART, then the state must make a BART determination for that source.[22] In making the BART determination, the state must consider five factors. These are: (1) the costs of compliance; (2) the energy and nonair-quality environmental impacts of compliance; (3) any existing pollution control technology in use at the source; (4) the remaining useful life of the source; and (5) the degree of visibility improvement that may reasonably be anticipated to result from the use of the proposed BART control technology.[23]

EPA's BART Guidelines also contain "presumptive BART limits" for NOx and SO$_2$ for a variety of electric generating unit ("EGU") boiler types that are premised on a generalized assessment of the BART factors for various types of

EGUs. Although states have discretion to deviate from the presumptive limits based on an source-specific evaluation of the BART factors, EPA's BART Guidelines state that the presumptive limits are "highly cost-effective" and "are extremely likely to be appropriate for all greater than 750 MW power plants subject to BART."[24]

After an evaluation of the relevant information, a state or, in some cases, EPA must make a BART determination for each facility that is subject to BART. The BART determination for a source is expressed as an emission limitation for that source, for each of the visibility-impairing pollutants that the source emits (above de minimis levels). These emission limitations are included in the source's Title V permit.

Reasonable Progress

The regional haze program's other major component is the reasonable progress requirement. The regional haze rules reflect an objective of attaining the goal of no manmade visibility impairment (so-called "natural conditions") in Class I areas by the year 2064. EPA has issued guidance for states to use in determining natural conditions for each Class I area.[25] The rules instruct the states to define interim reasonable progress goals between a baseline period (2000-2004) and 2064, with the first reasonable progress goal occurring in the year 2018. The rules indicate that the state should initially calculate the reasonable progress goals by extrapolating, in a linear fashion, progress in visibility improvement in each Class I area between the 2000-2004 baseline conditions (the average annual visibility impairment for the annual worst 20% of days in that baseline period, based on IMPROVE monitoring data) and the estimated natural conditions level, assuming that that level will be reached in 2064.[26] Once the state determines the 2018 reasonable progress goal for each Class I area, the state must then identify and analyze the emission measures that would satisfy that goal. If the state determines that those measures are "reasonable," then the state submits them to EPA for approval as part of the SIP. To assess whether they are reasonable, the state must consider several statutory factors that are almost identical to the statutory factors used in determining BART.[27] If the state determines that those measures are unreasonable, the state may set a less ambitious goal. A state must justify such a goal as reasonable based on the statutory factors. A state may also set a goal that is *more* ambitious than the "linear" rate of progress if it finds that such a goal is reasonable based on those factors.

When EPA promulgated the regional haze rules in 1999, EPA stated that it expected already-existing CAA requirements and BART to be sufficient for satisfying the 2018 reasonable progress requirement for many Class I areas. Many of the regional haze SIPs submitted to EPA have been consistent with that expectation, but, in some cases, states and EPA have included additional emission controls pursuant to the CAA's reasonable progress provisions.

Implementation Plan Rulemaking Actions

Beginning in 2009 and with the bulk of EPA's rulemaking action taking place between 2011 and 2012, EPA has now proposed – and in many cases taken final action on – regional haze SIPs submitted by each of the fifty states and the U.S. territories. In addition, where states (or territories) have failed to submit regional haze SIPs and in other special circumstances under which EPA has primary jurisdiction to implement the regional haze program, EPA has also proposed, and in some cases promulgated, Federal Implementation Plans ("FIPs") that include BART determinations for subject-to-BART sources and reasonable progress goals. EPA has also promulgated regional haze FIPs where the Agency has decided that a submitted SIP would have inadequately controlled visibility-impairing emissions. A number of these rulemaking actions have been controversial. A summary of EPA's key rulemakings and litigation challenging EPA's actions follows.

EPA's 2009 "Finding of Failure"

EPA's first significant regional haze program implementation rulemaking was its January 15, 2009 "Finding of Failure To Submit State Implementation Plans Required by the 1999 Regional Haze Rule."[28] This finding of failure stated that 37 states, the District of Columbia, and the U.S. Virgin Islands had failed to submit regional haze SIPs for EPA review by the applicable deadline of December 17, 2007. The publication of that finding triggered CAA § 110(c), which empowers EPA to promulgate a regional haze FIP at any time within 2 years after: (1) the Administrator determines that a state has failed to submit a required SIP; (2) the Administrator determines that a submitted SIP does not satisfy the CAA's minimum criteria; or (3) the Administrator disapproves a SIP in whole or in part. EPA's authority to issue a FIP under section 110(c) terminates if "the State corrects the deficiency, and the Administrator approves the plan or plan revision, before the Administrator promulgates such [FIP]."[29]

Accordingly, EPA's 2009 finding of failure triggered an EPA obligation to promulgate FIPs for those jurisdictions that did not submit approvable regional haze SIPs to EPA by January 15, 2011.

Regional Haze Rulemakings for Facilities on Tribal Lands

EPA's first regional haze FIP-related rulemaking action was the August 28, 2009 Advanced Notice of Proposed Rulemaking ("ANPR") for two western coal-fired power plants, Four Corners Power Plant ("FCPP") and NGS, both of which are located on the Navajo Nation.[30] The ANPR did not address regional haze for a jurisdiction that had failed to submit a SIP, such as those identified in EPA's 2009 finding of failure. Rather, EPA claimed primary regulatory jurisdiction for purposes of implementing the regional haze program for FCPP and NGS under EPA's Tribal Authority Rule ("TAR")[31] due to their location on tribal lands. In the ANPR, EPA sought comment on a number of issues central to the manner in which the regional haze program should be implemented, and EPA also shed some light on the manner in which EPA might evaluate various elements of the program, such as the BART and reasonable progress factors. For instance, EPA suggested in the ANPR that, when assessing BART, visibility impacts of various controls should be evaluated on a "cumulative" basis (*i.e.*, visibility impacts at multiple Class I areas should be added together), rather than evaluated on a "maximum impact area" basis (*i.e.*, visibility impacts at the Class I area that is most affected by the emissions of a particular source should be assessed). The BART Guidelines and the CAA, on the other hand, grant states considerable discretion as to how visibility impacts can be taken into account, and the Guidelines suggest that the "maximum impact area" approach to visibility assessment is appropriate.[32] Similarly, in the ANPR, EPA indicated that it would seek to evaluate the costs of compliance in assessing BART by relying exclusively on the methodology provided in the Agency's *Control Cost Manual*, even though the BART Guidelines state that the *Manual* is only one source of information regarding costs.[33]

Over a year later, on October 19, 2010, EPA published in the *Federal Register* its proposed FIP for FCPP.[34] EPA's proposed rule largely adhered to the BART evaluation methodologies that the Agency set forth in the ANPR. EPA's proposed BART determinations for FCPP included emission limits for nitrogen oxides ("NOx") and particulate matter ("PM"). The NOx BART limit was viewed as particularly controversial, as it was based on installation and operation of selective catalytic reduction ("SCR") technology, a post-combustion control that, according to the presumptive BART limits, is a category of emission controls that is generally more stringent than BART.[35] On February 25, 2011, EPA published a proposed supplement to its FIP for FCPP.[36] The supplemental proposed rule contained an alternative emission control strategy proposed by FCPP's operator and part owner. That alternative involved shutting down three of the five units at FCPP and installing SCR on the two remaining units by the end of 2018. EPA promulgated a FIP on August 24, 2012, that contained its

BART determinations as it had originally proposed them and that also included the BART alternative as an option for compliance.[37]

EPA's NOx BART Rule for New Mexico's San Juan Generating Station

EPA's next proposed major regional haze rulemaking action, which was published in the *Federal Register* on January 5, 2011, addressed NOx BART for the San Juan Generating Station ("SJGS") in New Mexico.[38] In the proposed rule, EPA sought to disapprove a portion of New Mexico's interstate transport SIP, a plan submitted to address interstate obligations related to the 1997 ozone and PM national ambient air quality standards pursuant to CAA § 110(a)(2)(D). A subsection of that provision, section 110(a)(2)(D)(i)(II), requires that SIPs contain provisions to prevent interference by their sources of emissions with the provisions included in the SIP of another state for the purpose of protecting visibility. Because EPA was subject to a consent decree deadline to take action on the interstate transport SIP for New Mexico, the Agency also proposed to take action on BART for SJGS at that time in order to avoid a succession of conflicting visibility-related requirements and, as EPA stated, to provide the owners and operator of SJGS with certainty.

EPA's proposed NOx BART FIP included an especially stringent NOx limit for SJGS of 0.05 pounds per million British Thermal Units ("lb/mmBtu") based on installation and operation of SCR. At the time EPA proposed its NOx BART FIP for SJGS, New Mexico had not submitted a regional haze SIP for EPA review and approval. The state was, however, nearing completion of its own rulemaking process to finalize its regional haze SIP and requested that EPA delay action on its proposed FIP until the Agency had considered New Mexico's SIP for approval. EPA received New Mexico's regional haze SIP submittal on July 5, 2011.[39] The state's SIP contained a markedly different NOx BART determination for SJGS: an emission limit of 0.23 lb/mmBtu based on selective noncatalytic reduction ("SNCR") technology.[40] Despite receipt of New Mexico's contradictory regional haze SIP, EPA proceeded, on August 22, 2011, to publish its final NOx BART FIP for SJGS.[41]

The Governor of New Mexico, the New Mexico Environment Department, and the operator (and part owner) of SJGS, filed petitions for review of EPA's NOx BART FIP for SJGS in the U.S. Court of Appeals for the Tenth Circuit, raising a number of challenges to the final rule. The court heard oral argument in October 2012 but had not issued a decision in the case at the time this Handbook went to publication.

EPA Rulemakings for Additional States

After its initial regional haze rulemakings actions, EPA proposed and in some cases took final action on a number of relatively noncontroversial regional haze SIPs.[42] EPA took considerable time to act on regional haze SIPs and FIPs for the majority of states, prompting environmental organizations to file suit in several federal courts seeking to compel EPA to perform its nondiscretionary duty under CAA § 110(k)(2)[43] either to approve or disapprove each state's submitted regional haze SIP or to promulgate a FIP within the two year period required under CAA § 110(c).[44] These lawsuits each resulted in consent decrees negotiated with the Agency establishing deadlines for action on SIPs and/or FIPs for the states covered by the litigation.

Many of the rulemakings that followed raised controversial issues like EPA's earlier FIP actions for FCPP, NGS, and SJGS. In many rulemakings, EPA rejected state BART determinations and imposed more stringent emission limits based on more advanced and expensive emission control technologies than the states determined to be reasonable, and EPA frequently rejected state BART evaluations that failed to examine and rely on "cumulative" visibility impacts across all Class I areas potentially affected by a source's emissions.[45] On the other hand, environmental groups often opposed EPA decisions to allow sources five years – the maximum compliance period allowable under the CAA – to comply with BART and argued that some of the Agency's decisions imposed or let stand state determinations that allowed for too lenient BART requirements.[46] A number of these rulemaking actions have been challenged in federal court, but no decisions had been issued at the time of publication.[47]

Reliance on Other EPA Rules To Satisfy BART Obligations

EPA's regional haze rules allow states to adopt a "BART alternative" in lieu of requiring BART provided the alternative emission controls "will achieve greater reasonable progress toward natural visibility conditions" than BART.[48] EPA's authority to approve BART alternatives was specifically upheld by the D.C. Circuit.[49] BART alternatives have been approved for individual power plants and in rulemakings specific to individual states.[50] EPA has also approved state reliance on other broadly applicable EPA regulations as valid BART alternatives. First, in conjunction with EPA's promulgation of the Clean Air Interstate Rule ("CAIR"), a NOx and sulfur dioxide ("SO_2") emission trading program applicable to 28 eastern states and the District of Columbia, EPA promulgated a rule declaring that states subject to CAIR's emission trading programs could rely on compliance with CAIR's requirements instead of requiring source-by-source BART for EGUs within those states. This rule is often called the "CAIR=BART" rule.[51] CAIR was challenged in the U.S. Court of Appeals for the D.C. Circuit, and after EPA promulgated the CAIR=BART rule, the court found CAIR invalid and remanded the rule to EPA.[52] The court did decide, however, to leave CAIR in place until EPA could promulgate a valid replacement rule.[53]

On August 8, 2011, EPA promulgated the Cross-State Air Pollution Rule (known as "CSAPR" or the "Transport Rule") as a replacement for CAIR. Like CAIR, CSAPR is a NOx and SO_2 emissions trading program. After promulgation of CSAPR, EPA promulgated a final rule[54] that: (1) deemed CSAPR a valid BART alternative for states covered by CSAPR and promulgated a "CSAPR=BART" rule; (2) removed EPA's CAIR=BART determination from its regulations; (3) finalized "limited disapprovals" of the SIPs of fourteen states[55] that relied on the CAIR=BART rule; and (4) promulgated FIPs for twelve states[56] replacing their reliance on the CAIR=BART rule with reliance on the CSAPR=BART rule. After EPA's promulgation of the CSAPR=BART rule, the D.C. Circuit ruled on challenges that had been filed against CSAPR and vacated CSAPR.[57] The court ordered that CAIR continue in effect until such time as EPA could promulgate a valid replacement rule, creating considerable uncertainty over the status of the CSAPR=BART rule and SIPs and FIPs related to that rule.[58]

Several parties challenged the CSAPR=BART rule in a number of different courts.[59] Those cases have all been transferred to the D.C. Circuit where they have been consolidated and placed into abeyance pending the outcome of the Supreme Court's decision on the petitions for writ of certiorari in the CSAPR litigation.[60]

Notes

1. Clean Air Act ("CAA") § 169A(a)(1), 42 U.S.C. § 7491(a)(1).
2. EPA, Visibility Protection for Federal Class I Areas 45 Fed. Reg. 80,084 (Dec. 2, 1980).
3. *See Central Arizona Water Conservation District v. EPA*, 990 F.2d 1531 (9th Cir. 1993).
4. EPA, Regional Haze Regulations, 64 Fed. Reg. 35,714 (July 1, 1999).
5. *Am. Corn Growers Ass'n v. EPA*, 291 F.3d 1 (D.C. Cir. 2002).
6. *Id.* at 8.

7. EPA, Regional Haze Regulations and Guidelines for Best Available Retrofit Technology (BART) Determinations; Final Rule, 70 Fed. Reg. 39,104 (July 6, 2005).

8. *Id.* at 39,108.

9. *Id.* at 39,158.

10. 40 C.F.R. § 51.308(b).

11. *Id.* § 51.308(f). States have considerable discretion to extend their target dates for achieving "natural" visibility conditions. *Id.* § 51.308(d)(1)(i), (d)(1)(ii).

12. *Id.* § 51.308(d)(4).

13. *Id.* § 51.308(d)(1).

14. *Id.* § 51.308(e).

15. *Id.* §§ 51.306, 51.308(d)(3).

16. *See id.* § 51.301.

17. *See id.*

18. *Id.* § 51.308(e).

19. 70 Fed. Reg. at 39,107.

20. A deciview is defined as "a measurement of visibility impairment" that is "derived from calculated light extinction, such that uniform changes in haziness correspond to uniform incremental changes in perception across the entire range of conditions, from pristine to highly impaired." 40 C.F.R. § 51.301.

21. 70 Fed. Reg. at 39,161.

22. 40 C.F.R. § 51.308(e)(1)(ii).

23. *Id.* § 51.308(e)(1)(A).

24. 70 Fed. Reg. at 39,131.

25. EPA, Office of Air Quality Planning and Standards, *Guidance for Setting Reasonable Progress Goals Under the Regional Haze Program* (revised July 1, 2007), *available at* http://www.epa.gov/ttn/caaa/t1/memoranda/ reasonable_progress_guid071307.pdf.

26. 40 C.F.R. § 51.308(d)(1)(i)(B). EPA's BART Guidelines refer to this linear improvement in visibility conditions as the "uniform rate of progress." 70 Fed. Reg. at 39,143.

27. 40 C.F.R. § 51.308(d)(1). These factors are "the costs of compliance, the time necessary for compliance, the energy and non-air quality environmental impacts of compliance, and the remaining useful life of any potentially affected sources . . . ." *Id.* The reasonable progress factors largely mirror the factors states must consider in determining BART. *See id.* § 51.308(e)(1)(A). Accordingly, EPA guidance indicates that compliance with any BART requirement during the first regional haze planning period will likely satisfy any reasonable progress requirement for that planning period as well. EPA, Office of Air Quality Planning and Standards, *Guidance for Setting Reasonable Progress Goals Under the Regional Haze Program* at 4-1 (revised July 1, 2007).

28. EPA, Finding of Failure To Submit State Implementation Plans Required by the 1999 Regional Haze Rule, 74 Fed. Reg. 2392 (Jan. 15, 2009).

29. CAA § 110(c)(B), 42 U.S.C. §7410(c)(B).

30. EPA, Assessment of Anticipated Visibility Improvements at Surrounding Class I Areas and Cost Effectiveness of Best Available Retrofit Technology for Four Corners Power Plant and Navajo Generating Station: Advanced Notice of Proposed Rulemaking, 74 Fed. Reg. 44,313 (Aug. 28, 2009).

31. 40 C.F.R. §§ 49.1-49.11.

32. 70 Fed. Reg. at 39,170 (stating that analyses at areas other than the most impacted area need not be performed and may be "unwarranted").

33. *Id.* at 39,127 ("[T]he Control Cost Manual provides a good reference tool for cost calculations, but if there are elements or sources that are not addressed by the Control Cost Manual or there are additional cost methods that could be used, we believe that these could serve as useful supplemental information.").

34. EPA, Source Specific Federal Implementation Plan for Implementing Best Available Retrofit Technology for Four Corners Power Plant: Navajo Nation, 75 Fed. Reg. 64,221 (Oct. 19, 2010).

35. The BART Guidelines state that with the exception of cyclone units, the presumptive BART limits for NOx are based on combustion controls or in extreme cases advanced combustion controls. 70 Fed. Reg. at 39,134. These controls are generally much less expensive, and thus more cost-effective from the perspective of a BART analysis, than post-combustion controls like SCR.

36. EPA, Supplemental Proposed Rule of Source Specific Federal Implementation Plan for Implementing Best Available Retrofit Technology for Four Corners Power Plant: Navajo Nation, 76 Fed. Reg. 10,530 (Feb. 25, 2011).

37. EPA, Source Specific Federal Implementation Plan for Implementing Best Available Retrofit Technology for Four Corners Power Plant: Navajo Nation, 77 Fed. Reg. 51,620 (Aug. 24, 2012).

38. EPA, Approval and Promulgation of Implementation Plans; New Mexico; Federal Implementation Plan for Interstate Transport of Pollution Affecting Visibility and Best Available Retrofit Technology Determination, 76 Fed. Reg. 491 (Jan. 5, 2011).

39. The New Mexico SIP addressed all elements of the regional haze program for the State of New Mexico including NOx BART for SJGS. EPA took final action approving all elements of that SIP except for the SJGS NOx BART determination on November 27, 2012. EPA, Approval and Promulgation of State Implementation Plans; State of New Mexico; Regional Haze Rule Requirements for Mandatory Class I Areas, 77 Fed. Reg. 70,693 (Nov. 27, 2012). At the time this chapter was submitted for publication, EPA had not taken any action on that element of New Mexico's regional haze SIP.

40. SNCR is generally less expensive control technology than SCR. It is, however, considered a more advanced technology than the combustion controls that comprise the basis for the presumptive NOx limits in the BART Guidelines that apply to SJGS. An emission rate of 0.23 lb/mmBtu is the presumptive limit for the types of units present at SJGS.

41. EPA, Approval and Promulgation of Implementation Plans; New Mexico; Federal Implementation Plan for Interstate Transport of Pollution Affecting Visibility and Best Available Retrofit Technology Determination, 76 Fed. Reg. 52,388 (Aug. 22, 2011).

42. *See, e.g.*, EPA, Approval and Promulgation of Air Quality Implementation Plans; State of California; Interstate Transport, 76 Fed. Reg. 34,608 (June 14, 2011) (final

approval of California's regional haze SIP); EPA, Approval and Promulgation of Implementation Plans; State of Idaho; Regional Haze State Implementation Plan and Interstate Transport Plan, 76 Fed. Reg. 36,329 (June 22, 2011) (final approval of Idaho's regional haze SIP).

43. CAA § 110(k)(2), 42 U.S.C. § 7410(k)(2), requires EPA to approve or disapprove a SIP within 12 months after the SIP has been determined or deemed by operation of law to be complete pursuant to CAA § 110(k)(1)(B), 42 U.S.C. § 7410(k)(1)(B).

44. *See, e.g., Nat'l Parks Conservation Ass'n v. EPA*, No. 11-1548 (D.D.C.); *WildEarth Guardians v. Jackson*, No. 11-0001 (D. Colo.).

45. *See, e.g.*, EPA, Approval and Promulgation of Implementation Plans; Oklahoma; Federal Implementation Plan for Interstate Transport of Pollution Affecting Visibility and Best Available Retrofit Technology Determinations, 76 Fed. Reg. 81,728 (Dec. 28, 2011) (final rule disapproving Oklahoma's SO_2 BART determinations and imposing an SO_2 BART FIP); EPA, Approval, Disapproval and Promulgation of Air Quality Implementation Plans; Arizona; Regional Haze State and Federal Implementation Plans, 77 Fed. Reg. 72,512 (Dec. 5, 2012) (final rule disapproving Arizona's NOx BART determinations and promulgating a FIP for three facilities).

46. *See, e.g.*, EPA, Approval and Promulgation of Implementation Plans; North Dakota; Regional Haze State Implementation Plan; Federal Implementation Plan for Interstate Transport of Pollution Affecting Visibility and Regional Haze, 77 Fed. Reg. 20,894 (Apr. 6, 2012) (final rule for North Dakota allowing a higher-than-proposed NOx limit); EPA, Approval and Promulgation of Air Quality Implementation Plans; Nevada; Regional Haze State and Federal Implementation Plans; BART Determination for Reid Gardner Generating Station, 77 Fed. Reg. 50,936 (Aug. 23, 2012) (final rule for EGU in Nevada allowing a relatively high NOx emission rate of 0.20 lb/mmBtu as BART).

47. *See, e.g., Oklahoma v. EPA*, No. 12-9526 (10th Cir.); *Public Service Co. of Oklahoma v. EPA*, No. 12-9525 (10th Cir.); *North Dakota v. EPA*, No. 12-1844 (8th Cir.); *PPL Montana v. EPA*, No. 12-73757 (9th Cir.); *Nevada Power Co. v. EPA*, No. 12-73411 (9th Cir.); *Moapa Band of Paiute Indians v. EPA*, No. 12-73388 (9th Cir.); *WildEarth Guardians v. EPA*, No. 12-73417 (9th Cir.).

48. 40 C.F.R. § 51.308(e). Specific criteria for determining whether an alternative measure achieves greater reasonable progress than source-specific BART are set out at 40 C.F.R. § 51.308(e)(3).

49. *Utility Air Regulatory Group v. EPA*, 471 F.3d 1333 (D.C. Cir. 2006).

50. *See, e.g.*, EPA, Source Specific Federal Implementation Plan for Implementing Best Available Retrofit Technology for Four Corners Power Plant: Navajo Nation, 77 Fed. Reg. 51,619 (Aug. 24, 2012) (final rule allowing a BART alternative for FCPP).

51. 70 Fed. Reg. at 39,106.

52. CAIR and the legal challenge to CAIR are discussed in more detail in Chapter 2.

53. *North Carolina v. EPA*, 531 F.3d 896; *modified by* 550 F.3d 1176 (D.C. Cir. 2008).

54. EPA, Regional Haze: Revisions to Provisions Governing Alternatives to Source-Specific Best Available Retrofit Technology (BART) Determinations, Limited

SIP Disapprovals, and Federal Implementation Plans, 77 Fed. Reg. 33,642 (June 7, 2012).

55. The fourteen states are Alabama, Georgia, Indiana, Iowa, Louisiana, Michigan, Mississippi, Missouri, North Carolina, Ohio, Pennsylvania, South Carolina, Texas, and Virginia. In separate rulemaking proceedings, EPA also finalized limited disapprovals of the regional haze SIPs of Kentucky, Tennessee, and West Virginia because of their reliance on the CAIR=BART rule.

56. The twelve states are Georgia, Indiana, Iowa, Kentucky, Michigan, Missouri, Ohio, Pennsylvania, South Carolina, Tennessee, Virginia, and West Virginia. EPA did not promulgate FIPs for Alabama, Louisiana, Mississippi, North Carolina, and Texas because those states were legally entitled to time to revise their SIPs. In addition, EPA had separately proposed a limited disapproval and FIP for Florida but ended up not finalizing either proposal because EPA had changed Florida's status under CSAPR subsequent to CSAPR's promulgation and the Agency determined it was appropriate to allow Florida time to revise its SIP as well.

57. CSAPR and the litigation related to that rule are discussed in Chapter 2.

58. *EME Homer City Generation, L.P. v. EPA*, 696 F.3d 7 (D.C. Cir. 2012).

59. *See, e.g., Utility Air Regulatory Group v. EPA*, No. 12-3772 (6th Cir.); *Luminant Generation Company, et al. v. EPA*, No. 12-60617 (5th Cir.).

60. *Utility Air Regulatory Group v. EPA*, No. 12-1342 and consolidated cases (D.C. Cir.).

Chapter 7

CLIMATE CHANGE

Addressing climate change was not a focus of Congress when it enacted the Clean Air Act and made major amendments to it between 1970 and 1990. As climate change began to become a larger concern and as congressional efforts to address climate change stalled, however, advocacy groups turned to the Clean Air Act as a vehicle to limit greenhouse gas ("GHG") emissions and address climate change, despite the fact that climate change, with its global causes and impacts, does not fit neatly into the Act's statutory construct. Every step along the road to regulating GHGs under the Act has been highly controversial, with each attempt yielding record-setting comment submissions, followed by multiple legal challenges.

With little congressional appetite to adopt mandatory restrictions on GHG emissions, regulatory action under the Clean Air Act may comprise one of the few – if only – mandatory restrictions on GHG emissions facing the U.S. economy for the foreseeable future. This area of regulation under the Clean Air Act did not even exist when the last edition of the *Clean Air Handbook* was published. The length and breadth of this new chapter is testament to the rapid development of this area of law.

Background

In the late 1990s and early 2000s, dueling memoranda and statements by three general counsels of the U.S. Environmental Protection Agency ("EPA") considered the question of the Agency's authority to regulate GHGs under the Clean Air Act. Two general counsels interpreted the Clean Air Act as giving the Agency authority to regulate carbon dioxide, while one did not.[1] Even though not legally binding, these statements expressed the changing policy views of the Agency on the question of whether it could regulate GHG emissions under the Act and served as the foundation for a petition for rulemaking filed with EPA by the International Center for Technology Assessment ("ICTA") and 18 other entities in 1999.

The ICTA petition asked EPA to regulate emissions of carbon dioxide ("CO_2") and three other GHGs (methane ("CH_4"), nitrous oxide ("N_2O"), and hydrofluorocarbons ("HFCs")) from new motor vehicles and new motor vehicle engines under section 202(a)(1) of the Clean Air Act to address global climate change.[2] As discussed in Chapter 8, section 202(a)(1) authorizes the EPA Administrator to:

> [B]y regulation prescribe (and from time to time revise) in accordance with the provisions of this section, standards applicable to the emission of any air pollutant from any class or classes of new motor vehicles or new motor vehicle engines, which in his judgment cause, or contribute to, air pollution which may reasonably be anticipated to endanger public health or welfare.[3]

EPA asked for public comment on the ICTA petition in 2001[4] but then did not take final action on the petition. In 2002, ICTA filed suit in the United States District Court for the District of Columbia to enforce their right to a reasonably timely response to the petition.[5] In response to the lawsuit, EPA acted on the ICTA petition, denying it.[6] EPA denied the petition on three separate grounds: (1) the Clean Air Act did not provide EPA with authority to regulate GHGs to address climate change;[7] (2) even if the Agency did have such authority under the Act, it would nevertheless decline to regulate GHGs at this time for numerous policy reasons, which was within its discretion under the Act;[8] and (3) because the only way for EPA to regulate GHG emissions from new motor vehicles and new motor vehicle engines was to increase fuel economy, regulation of GHGs would conflict impermissibly with Congress's directive in the Energy Policy and Conservation Act that the Department of Transportation solely regulate fuel economy from motor vehicles.[9]

Numerous parties challenged EPA's denial of the ICTA petition in the U.S. Court of Appeals for the D.C. Circuit. In a divided three-part opinion, the D.C. Circuit upheld EPA's denial of the rulemaking petition.[10] Petitioners filed a petition for a writ of certiorari with the Supreme Court seeking review of the D.C. Circuit's decision. The Supreme Court granted the petition in June 2006.[11]

Massachusetts V. EPA

On April 2, 2007, the U.S. Supreme Court issued its landmark decision in *Massachusetts v. EPA*,[12] which held that GHGs are within the scope of "air pollutants" as defined by the Clean Air Act and that section 202(a)(1) authorizes EPA to regulate GHG emissions from new motor vehicles if EPA were to determine that such emissions meet the "endangerment" test for regulation under section 202(a)(1).[13] The Court found that EPA failed to provide a legally adequate justification for its denial of the ICTA petition because it improperly considered factors outside the scope of the Clean Air Act.[14]

The Supreme Court held that GHGs are air pollutants covered by the Clean Air Act, that the definition of "air pollutant" under the Act is "sweeping," encompassing "all airborne compounds of whatever stripe,"[15] and that EPA must determine whether GHG emissions from new motor vehicles cause or contribute to endangerment of public health or welfare.[16] With regard to the question raised by EPA of whether the Department of Transportation has exclusive jurisdiction over fuel economy standards, the Court found "no reason to think the two agencies cannot both administer their obligations and yet avoid inconsistency."[17]

The Court made clear that EPA could regulate under section 202(a)(1) only "[i]f EPA makes a finding of endangerment" and that "EPA no doubt has significant latitude as to the manner, timing, [and] content" of any regulations.[18] The Court added, however, that "EPA can avoid taking further action only if it determines that GHGs do not contribute to climate change or if it provides some reasonable explanation as to why it cannot or will not exercise its discretion to determine whether they do."[19] It also explicitly stated that it did not "reach the question whether on remand EPA must make an endangerment finding, or whether policy concerns can inform EPA's actions in the event that it makes such a finding."[20] The Court simply sent the matter back to EPA for further consideration.

A dissent authored by Chief Justice Roberts and joined by Justices Scalia, Thomas, and Alito stated that those justices would not have found standing by any petitioner.[21] A separate dissent authored by Justice Scalia and joined by the Chief Justice and Justices Thomas and Alito addressed the merits of the case and argued that the majority substituted "its own desired outcome for the reasoned judgment of the responsible agency."[22]

EPA's First Efforts to Regulate GHG Emissions Under The Clean Air Act

The GHG Reporting Rule

In 2007, following the Supreme Court's decision in *Massachusetts*, Congress included a provision in an appropriations bill requiring EPA to adopt a mandatory GHG reporting rule for large stationary and certain mobile sources.[23] EPA adopted this rule in October 2009,[24] and has periodically revised it since.[25] With few exceptions, the rule generally requires stationary sources emitting more than 25,000 metric tons of carbon dioxide equivalent ("CO_2e") per year[26] to report to EPA their annual GHG emissions for the prior year. It also requires reporting from manufacturers and suppliers of certain products, including mobile sources, that would result in GHG emissions if released, combusted, or oxidized. The first emission reports under the rule were submitted in September 2011 for the 2010 emissions year. Most reported data are available to the public electronically.[27]

EPA's Advance Notice of Proposed Rulemaking

Following the Supreme Court's decision in *Massachusetts*, EPA published an Advance Notice of Proposed Rulemaking ("ANPR") regarding how it might regulate GHGs under the Clean Air Act.[28] In the ANPR, EPA sought comment on a broad array of issues relevant to EPA's possible regulation of GHGs under various Clean Air Act programs and how the Agency should respond to the *Massachusetts* decision. Recognizing that GHG emissions, particularly CO_2 emissions, are ubiquitous, EPA noted that "[t]he potential regulation of greenhouse gases under any portion of the Clean Air Act could result in an unprecedented expansion of EPA authority that would have a profound effect on virtually every sector of the economy and touch every household in the land."[29]

The Endangerment Finding

In December 2009, EPA made two distinct findings: first, that the combination of "well-mixed GHGs" of CO_2, CH_4, N_2O, HFCs, perfluorocarbons ("PFCs"), and sulfur hexafluoride ("SF_6") "in the atmosphere may reasonably be anticipated both to endanger public health and to endanger public welfare,"[30] and that the combined emissions of four of those GHGs (CO_2, CH_4, N_2O, and HFCs) from new motor vehicles and new motor vehicle engines contribute to that endangering air pollution.[31] EPA made clear that the findings "are in response to the Supreme Court's decision in *Massachusetts v. EPA*," and that they "are for purposes of [Clean Air Act] section 202(a)."[32] It also stated, in response to public comments, that the test for endangerment does not require that any resulting regulations be able to "fruitfully attack" the endangerment: "EPA's belief one way or the other regarding whether regulation of greenhouse gases from new motor vehicles would be 'effective' is irrelevant in making the endangerment and contribution decisions before EPA."[33] These findings were finalized in the *Federal Register* on December 15, 2009, and were effective January 14, 2010.[34]

The findings were a prerequisite for EPA's regulation of GHG emission standards for light-duty vehicles, proposed together with the Department of Transportation in September 2009.[35] Once EPA finalized GHG emission standards for motor vehicles, it then said that it was compelled to regulate GHGs from stationary sources under the Prevention of Significant Deterioration ("PSD") and Title V permitting programs of the Act.[36]

Numerous petitions for administrative reconsideration were filed with EPA, including a petition by nine members of the U.S. House of Representatives, asking EPA to reconsider the endangerment finding. Several petitions for review were also filed in the U.S. Court of Appeals for the D.C. Circuit, challenging the endangerment finding.[37] The petitions to reconsider EPA's endangerment finding focused on the validity of the climate science on which the Agency had relied on in its determination. In July 2010, EPA denied the petitions for administrative reconsideration.[38] Petitions for review were filed by numerous parties challenging the denial of the reconsideration petitions.[39] These petitions for review were consolidated with the petitions filed challenging the endangerment finding itself.[40] The legal challenges to the endangerment finding and the denial of reconsideration of the endangerment finding are discussed in Section IV.

Regulation of GHG Emissions From Mobile Sources and Fuels Under Title II of the Clean Air Act

California's Actions

Although EPA was initially hesitant to regulate GHG emissions under the Clean Air Act and did not attempt to do so until after the Supreme Court's 2007 decision in *Massachusetts*, California's first attempts to limit such emissions from mobile sources date back to 2004. The Clean Air Act generally preempts state regulation of mobile source emissions, but section 209(b) of the Act permits California to implement state emissions standards that are more protective of public health and welfare than federal standards if EPA grants the state a waiver to do so.[41] In September 2004, the California Air Resources Board ("CARB") adopted standards to regulate GHG emissions from new passenger cars, light-duty trucks, and medium-duty vehicles, which California's Office of Administrative Law approved in September 2005.[42] On December 21, 2005,

CARB submitted a waiver request to EPA for its motor vehicle GHG standards under section 209(b).[43]

EPA denied CARB's waiver request in 2008.[44] Shortly after taking office, however, President Barack Obama directed EPA to reconsider the request.[45] On June 30, 2009, EPA reversed course and granted California's request for a waiver of Clean Air Act preemption for its GHG emissions standards.[46]

Federal-State-Automobile Manufacturers' Agreement

In the intervening period, twelve other states and the District of Columbia adopted California's GHG emissions standards for light-duty motor vehicles as permitted by section 177 of the Act, potentially subjecting approximately 40 percent of the national market for new light-duty vehicles to California's standards.[47] Faced with the prospect of having to comply with two sets of motor vehicle emissions standards, auto manufacturers joined environmental groups in calling for federal action to develop a uniform national regulatory scheme for GHG emissions from motor vehicles. In a May 2009 Rose Garden ceremony attended by representatives of several major auto manufacturers, President Obama announced the establishment of a National Fuel Efficiency Policy to coordinate the efforts of EPA, the Department of Transportation, and the State of California in developing harmonized regulations governing GHG emissions from light-duty vehicles.[48] The new policy was supported by auto manufacturers, environmental groups, the United Auto Workers, and several states.[49] The Department of Transportation, which establishes motor vehicle fuel economy standards through the National Highway Traffic Safety Administration ("NHTSA"), was an important part of this coordinated approach because reducing fuel consumption through greater fuel economy is the primary method of reducing GHG emissions from motor vehicles.

Light-Duty Vehicle Tailpipe Rule (Model Years 2012-2016)

Seven months after President Obama announced the National Fuel Efficiency Policy, EPA finalized the endangerment finding. Once EPA made its December 2009 endangerment finding, it was then required to regulate GHG emissions from motor vehicles under section 202(a).[50] Section 202(a) requires EPA to regulate the emission of air pollutants from "any class or classes of new motor vehicles or new motor vehicle engines, which ... cause, or contribute to, air pollution which may reasonably be anticipated to endanger public health or welfare."[51]

In May 2010, EPA and NHTSA jointly published what is known as the "Tailpipe Rule," which implemented the National Fuel Efficiency Policy and fulfilled EPA's requirements under section 202(a).[52] In the Tailpipe Rule, EPA enacted GHG emissions standards under section 202(a) of the Clean Air Act, and NHTSA enacted Corporate Average Fuel Economy ("CAFE") standards under the Energy Policy and Conservation Act and the Energy Independence and Security Act of 2007 ("EISA").[53] These standards apply to model year 2012-2016 passenger cars, light-duty trucks, and medium-duty passenger vehicles.[54] Under the rule, vehicles in these model years face increasingly stringent GHG emission limits each year. EPA's rule requires a manufacturer's light-duty vehicle fleet to meet a combined average CO_2 emissions rate of 250 grams/mile ("g/mi") in model year 2016, while NHTSA's CAFE standards require the manufacturer's fleet to meet a combined average fuel economy of 34.1 miles per gallon ("mpg") in model year 2016 (37.8 mpg for passenger cars, 28.8 mpg for light trucks).[55] EPA also adopted caps on emissions of other GHGs, including N_2O (0.010 g/mi) and CH_4 (0.030 g/mi).[56] Although the CO_2 standards call for greater reductions than those afforded by meeting the CAFE standards alone, EPA will allow manufacturers to achieve full compliance by earning CO_2e credits for reducing emissions of HFCs and CO_2 from vehicle air conditioning systems.[57]

EPA expects manufacturers to achieve these standards through the use of technologies such as gasoline direct injection, downsized engines, advanced transmissions, increased use of start-stop technology, improvements in tire rolling resistance, reductions in vehicle weight, increased use of hybrid technologies, and the commercialization of electric vehicles and plug-in hybrids.[58] EPA and NHTSA predicted that these standards will result in 960 million metric tons of total CO_2e emissions reductions over the lifetime of model year 2012-2016 vehicles, and that fuel savings would offset the estimated increase in the average vehicle cost.[59]

Consistent with the National Fuel Efficiency Policy, California took steps to harmonize its light-duty vehicle standards with the Tailpipe Rule. In 2009, CARB adopted provisions allowing manufacturers to pool vehicle sales across California and other states that adopt its standards and to submit federal CAFE program data for compliance determinations.[60] In 2010, California adopted amendments providing that compliance with EPA's GHG standards will be deemed compliance with the California standards for model years 2012-2016.[61]

Numerous states and industry groups challenged the Tailpipe Rule and that litigation is discussed in Section IV.[62]

Light-Duty Vehicle Rule (Model Years 2017-2025)

In October 2012, EPA and NHTSA built on the Tailpipe Rule by enacting GHG emissions and CAFE standards for model year 2017-2025 light-duty vehicles.[63] Like the Tailpipe Rule, the 2012 Light-Duty Rule requires manufacturers to meet increasingly stringent standards for each model year. EPA's GHG emissions limits require manufacturers' light-duty vehicle fleets to achieve an emissions rate of 163 g/mi of CO_2 in model year 2025.[64] Light-duty trucks will initially face a lower rate of annual reductions in CO_2 emissions than passenger cars in order to preserve their utility while transitioning into these stricter standards.[65] Because NHTSA is authorized to issue fuel economy standards for periods of only five model years at a time, the 2012 Light-Duty Rule includes final CAFE standards only for model years 2017-2021.[66] Those vehicles must achieve a combined average fuel economy of 40.3 to 41 mpg in model year 2021 (46.1 to 46.8 mpg for passenger cars, 32.6 to 33.3 mpg for light-duty trucks).[67] NHTSA also published projected standards for model years 2022-2025 that would require manufacturers to achieve a combined average fuel economy of 48.7 to 49.7 mpg in model year 2025 (55.3 to 56.2 mpg for passenger cars, 39.3 to 40.3 for light-duty trucks).[68] This second phase of CAFE standards, however, is not legally binding and merely reflects NHTSA's current estimate of the maximum levels of stringency that will be feasible in those model years.[69]

The 2012 Light-Duty Rule provides flexible compliance options. Manufacturers may earn credits for achieving greater improvements in GHG emissions or fuel economy than required in a given model year, which may be carried forward or traded.[70] EPA will continue to give manufacturers credit for GHG emission reductions from air conditioning systems, but will cap those credits at 18.8 g/mi of CO_2e for cars and 24.4 g/mi of CO_2e for trucks.[71] In addition, the rule provides incentives for the production of electric vehicles, plug-in hybrid electric vehicles, and fuel cell vehicles sold in model years 2017-2021 in the form of an incentive multiplier for CO_2 emissions compliance purposes.[72] EPA estimates that its emissions standards will reduce GHG emissions by approximately 2 billion metric tons over the lifetimes of model year 2017-2025 light-duty vehicles, and that the average cost increase of $1,800 to new light-duty vehicles in model year 2025 will be offset by reduced spending on fuel.[73]

Heavy-Duty Vehicles

Following on the example of the light-duty National Fuel Efficiency Policy, in May 2010, President Obama held another Rose Garden ceremony during which he signed a presidential memorandum directing EPA and NHTSA to cooperate again in developing fuel economy and GHG emissions standards for commercial medium- and heavy-duty vehicles beginning with model year 2014.[74] As with the light-duty vehicle regulations, this coordinated regulatory approach to heavy-duty vehicles was supported by California and by the automobile and truck manufacturing industry.[75]

EPA and NHTSA adopted GHG emissions and CAFE standards for heavy-duty vehicles in 2011.[76] These standards apply to "all vehicles with a gross vehicle weight rating above 8,500 pounds and to the engines that power them," excluding medium-duty passenger vehicles.[77] To reflect the significant diversity of heavy-duty vehicles and engines, EPA and NHTSA divided these vehicles into three groups—Combination Tractors, Heavy-Duty Pickup Trucks and Vans, and Vocational Vehicles (such as buses and dump trucks)—and developed GHG emissions and CAFE standards for subcategories within each group based on gross vehicle weight and design.[78] The 2011 Heavy-Duty Rule also limits emissions of other GHGs from some types of heavy-duty vehicles, such as nitrous oxide and methane from engines and hydrofluorocarbons from air conditioning system leakage.[79] Although EPA's GHG emission standards for heavy-duty vehicles take effect in model year 2014, NHTSA's CAFE standards are voluntary in model years 2014 and 2015 (and model year 2016 for diesel engines) to provide the four full model years of regulatory lead time required by the EISA.[80] EPA estimates that these standards will reduce CO_2 emissions by 273 million metric tons over the lifetime of all model year 2014-2018 heavy-duty vehicles.[81]

Petitions for review of the Heavy-Duty Rule were pending in the D.C. Circuit at the time of publication.[82]

Renewable Fuel Standard Program

The Energy Policy Act of 2005 amended the Clean Air Act to establish a Renewable Fuel Standard ("RFS") program requiring that a minimum volume of renewable fuel be used in gasoline sold in the United States each year, ramping up from 4 billion gallons in 2006 to 7.5 billion gallons in 2012.[83] To achieve these goals, EPA is required to determine and publish the applicable renewable fuel obligation for fuel refineries, blenders, and importers for each calendar year by November 30 of the preceding year, expressed as a volume percentage of transportation fuel sold or introduced into commerce in the United States.[84] In 2007, EPA enacted regulations to implement and enforce the RFS program and established the 2007 renewable fuel obligation for refiners, blenders, and importers.[85]

In the 2007 EISA, Congress amended the RFS program by substantially increasing the volumes of renewable fuel required to be used each year, extending the time frame over which those volumes ramp up through at least 2022, and expanding the program to cover nearly all transportation fuels.[86] The total minimum volume of required renewable fuels will gradually increase from 4.7 billion gallons in 2007 to 36 billion gallons in 2022.[87] In addition, the EISA divided renewable fuels into four categories: total renewable fuels, advanced biofuel, cellulosic biofuel, and biomass-based diesel.[88] Each category faces a separate annual statutory minimum volume, and EPA must determine the applicable renewable fuel obligation for fuel refineries, blenders, and importers to meet these requirements for each category.[89] EPA may waive or reduce these minimum volumes if the Administrator determines that there is an inadequate domestic supply of any fuel or that the requirements would cause severe economic or environmental harm.[90] Due to the embryonic nature of cellulosic biofuel production and the potential for price volatility in the biomass-based diesel market, EPA is required to reduce the applicable volume requirement for these categories in response to projected fuel unavailability (for cellulosic biofuel) or price shocks (for biomass-based diesel).

Furthermore, to qualify for inclusion in the RFS program, renewable fuels must meet certain GHG emission thresholds demonstrating that their lifecycle GHG emissions—the aggregate direct and indirect emissions related to the fuel, from feedstock generation through its final use—are sufficiently less than those of the gasoline or diesel fuel they would replace.[91] Advanced biofuel and biomass-based diesel must achieve lifecycle GHG emission reductions of at least 50 percent compared to the gasoline or diesel baseline.[92] Cellulosic biofuel must achieve 60 percent lifecycle GHG emission reductions, while the threshold for other renewable fuels from new sources is 20 percent.[93] Eligible renewable fuels must also be made from feedstocks that qualify as "renewable biomass" based on their type and source.[94]

In March 2010, EPA adopted a new set of RFS regulations, known as RFS2, to implement these amendments.[95] The Agency identified several types of renewable fuels as meeting the applicable lifecycle GHG emissions thresholds based on EPA's modeling, including: ethanol and biobutanol from corn starch (20 percent renewable fuels threshold); ethanol from sugarcane (50 percent advanced biofuel threshold); biodiesel and renewable diesel from soy oil or waste oils, fats, and greases (50 percent biomass-based diesel threshold); and cellulosic ethanol and cellulosic diesel (60 percent cellulosic biofuel threshold).[96] The rule also established mechanisms for renewable fuel producers to verify that their feedstocks qualify as renewable biomass.[97] Since enacting RFS2, EPA has identified other renewable fuels that meet the applicable lifecycle GHG emissions thresholds.[98]

EPA published the renewable fuel obligations and associated percentage standards that apply to transportation fuel refiners, blenders, and importers in each category of renewable fuels for 2010, 2011, and 2012.[99] The D.C. Circuit, however, struck down the Agency's 2012 renewable fuel obligation for cellulosic biofuel in 2013.[100] The Clean Air Act required the use of 500 million gallons of cellulosic biofuel in 2012, but EPA adjusted that year's renewable fuel obligation downward under the Act's waiver provision to 8.65 million gallons because the industry was still incapable of producing that fuel at a commercial scale.[101] The court held that the reduced obligation was still impermissibly high, noting that while other parts of the RFS program may be technology-forcing, EPA must base its annual cellulosic biofuel requirement on a projection that "aims at accuracy" and is not merely "aspirational."[102]

Regulating GHGs Under the Act's Prevention of Significant Deterioration and Title V Permitting Programs

As discussed in greater detail in Chapter 4, new and modified major stationary sources of regulated air pollutants must obtain preconstruction permits to prevent significant deterioration of air quality in those areas. EPA's PSD regulations require newly constructed or modified major sources that emit one or more "regulated [new source review ("NSR")] pollutant[s]"[103] above certain thresholds to obtain a PSD permit and to install "best available control technology" ("BACT") for those regulated NSR pollutants.[104] The definition of "regulated NSR pollutant" includes "any pollutant that otherwise is subject to regulation under the Act."[105]

In re: Deseret Power Electric Cooperative

Four months after the *Massachusetts v. EPA* decision, EPA's Region 8 issued a PSD permit to Deseret Power Electric Cooperative to allow it to build a new waste-coal-fired electric generating unit in Bonanza, Utah.[106] The permit did not contain any limits for the plant's eventual CO_2 emissions and Sierra Club petitioned EPA's Environmental Appeals Board ("EAB") for review of the decision to issue the permit, arguing that Region 8 erred in failing to require BACT for the plant's CO_2 emissions.[107]

Sierra Club argued that CO_2 is a pollutant "subject to regulation" under the Act for PSD purposes through Section 821 of the 1990 Amendments to the Clean Air Act. Section 821 requires electric generating units ("EGUs") subject to the Act's Acid Rain Program to monitor and report their CO_2 emissions. Sierra Club took issue with EPA's position that "subject to regulation" for PSD purposes means subject to emission controls or other emission standards.[108] Under Sierra Club's interpretation, CO_2 became subject to the PSD permitting program as early as 1993 when certain EGUs were required to monitor and report their CO_2 emissions under Section 821.

In November 2008, the EAB rejected the Sierra Club's argument that the language of the Act clearly renders CO_2 "subject to regulation" under the Act for purposes of the PSD program and its requirement for an analysis of BACT based on the CO_2 monitoring and reporting requirements of the Act. At the same time, however, the EIB found clear error in the Region's assertion that it had no authority to subject CO_2 to BACT based on EPA's asserted historical interpretation of "subject to regulation" under the Act as requiring actual control of emissions.[109] In other words, the EIB found that EPA had not been "sufficiently clear and consistent" on this issue to bind the Regions in responding to permit applications.[110] The EAB remanded the permit back to Region 8 to "reconsider whether or not to impose a CO_2 BACT limit in light of the Agency's discretion to interpret, consistent with the Clean Air Act, what constitutes a 'pollutant subject to regulation under this Act.'"[111]

The PSD Interpretive Memorandum and "Timing Rule"

The EAB's *Deseret* opinion left PSD permitting decisions in a state of uncertainty. In response, EPA Administrator Stephen Johnson issued a memorandum stating with immediate effect that a pollutant becomes "subject to regulation" under the Act when "a provision of the Clean Air Act or regulation adopted by EPA under the Clean Air Act . . . requires actual control of emissions of that pollutant."[112] This statement distinguished pollutants that "are subject only to monitoring and reporting requirements," which the memorandum made clear were not subject to PSD.[113] EPA expressly left open for the future the question of whether the Agency should take action to subject CO_2 and other GHGs to emission controls under the Clean Air Act.

In February 2009, the Agency, under a new administration, granted a petition filed by Sierra Club to reconsider the interpretation contained in the December 2008 memorandum, but denied a request to stay the interpretation during the reconsideration period.[114] In October 2009, EPA proposed a rule to reconsider that interpretation[115] and, in April 2010, finalized EPA's position on the matter, maintaining the interpretation contained in the December 2008 memorandum that requires "actual control of emissions of a pollutant" to subject that pollutant to PSD permitting requirements for certain stationary sources. The reconsideration further stated that the PSD permitting requirements "will not apply to a newly regulated pollutant [like GHGs] until a regulatory requirement to control emissions of that pollutant 'takes effect.'"[116] The reconsideration specifically provided that GHG emissions from stationary sources were to become "subject to regulation" on the first date a model year 2012 light-duty vehicle could become available, which was January 2, 2011.[117] EPA's final rule on reconsideration of the PSD Interpretive Memorandum is sometimes referred to as the "Timing Rule." Numerous states and industry groups filed petitions for review of the Timing Rule and that litigation is discussed in Section IV.[118]

The Tailoring Rule

In October 2009, EPA proposed the Prevention of Significant Deterioration and Title V Greenhouse Gas Tailoring Rule (commonly called the Tailoring Rule), which aimed to "tailor" statutory provisions of the Clean Air Act so that the PSD and Title V permitting programs would initially apply only to the largest-emitting stationary sources of GHGs.[119] Under the Act, any stationary source emitting as few as 100 or 250 tons per year ("tpy") of one or more GHGs would be required to obtain such permits, a threshold that many churches, hospitals, and office buildings would easily surpass. EPA stated the action was necessary because direct application of the statutory PSD and Title V thresholds (which were written with traditional pollutants in mind) to sources of GHG emissions would "greatly increas[e] the number of required permits, impos[e] undue costs on small sources, overwhelm[] the resources of permitting authorities, and severely impair[] the functioning of the [PSD and Title V] programs."[120] EPA estimated that, without the Tailoring Rule, six million sources would need to obtain Title V operating permits[121] (compared to only 15,500 with the rule),[122] and 82,000 PSD permits would need to be written each year[123] (compared to 1,600 per year with the rule).[124]

In June 2010, EPA finalized the Tailoring Rule. Under the final rule, EPA decided to phase in the statutory applicability thresholds in two steps.[125] The first step applied beginning January 2, 2011, to projects with existing Title V and PSD permits for non-GHG pollutants (or to new sources obtaining Title V or PSD permits) that would increase GHG emissions by at least 75,000 tpy of CO_2e, but "only if the project also significantly increases emissions of at least one non-GHG pollutant."[126] The second step took effect on July 1, 2011, and requires PSD pre-construction and Title V operating permits for sources undertaking new projects that would emit at least 100,000 tpy of GHGs (measured as CO_2e).[127] Modifications at existing facilities that would result in an increase in GHG emissions of 75,000 tpy of CO_2e would also require a PSD permit. Title V permits would be required for sources emitting at least 100,000 tpy of CO_2e.

GHG emissions above these thresholds would trigger PSD and Title V requirements even if the source did not exceed permitting thresholds for other non-GHG pollutants.

EPA conducted a rulemaking in 2012 as step 3 of the Tailoring Rule and determined at that time not to lower further the applicability thresholds established in steps one and two.[128] EPA also committed to completing a study on the administrative burdens associated with PSD and Title V permitting by April 30, 2015, and to complete a step 4 rulemaking to determine whether to lower the applicability thresholds further by April 30, 2016.[129]

EPA relied on deference it is given in interpreting the Clean Air Act,[130] as well as the judicial doctrines of "absurd results," "administrative necessity," and "one-step-at-a-time" in promulgating the Tailoring Rule and phasing in the applicability requirements.[131] EPA described the "absurd results" doctrine as "authoriz[ing] agencies to apply statutory requirements differently than a literal reading would indicate, as necessary to effectuate congressional intent and avoid absurd results."[132] It described the "administrative necessity doctrine" as "authoriz[ing] agencies to apply statutory requirements in a way that avoids impossible administrative burdens."[133] EPA also relied on the so-called "one-step-at-a-time" doctrine, which, as the name would suggest, "authorizes agencies to implement statutory requirements a step at a time."[134] EPA also cited section 301(a) of the Act, "which authorizes the Administrator 'to prescribe such regulations as are necessary to carry out his functions under [the Clean Air Act].'"[135]

Numerous states and industry groups filed petitions for review challenging the Tailoring Rule and that litigation is discussed in Section IV.[136]

Litigation Challenging The Endangerment Finding, The GHG Emission Standards for Model Year 2012-2016 Light-Duty Motor Vehicles, The Timing Rules, and The Tailoring Rule

Several dozen states and industry group parties filed numerous petitions for review in the U.S. Court of Appeals for the D.C. Circuit challenging EPA's first suite of GHG rules. These ended up being consolidated into four separate cases as follows: (1) petitions for review challenging EPA's endangerment finding, consolidated with petitions for review of EPA's denial of petitions for administrative reconsideration of the endangerment finding;[137] (2) petitions for review of the Tailpipe Rule;[138] (3) petitions for review of the Timing Rule, consolidated with petitions for review challenging the Tailoring Rule;[139] and (4) petitions for review challenging EPA's past PSD rulemakings on the basis of "grounds arising after."[140] The D.C. Circuit heard oral argument in all four cases over two days, on February 28 and 29, 2012.

On June 26, 2012, the D.C. Circuit issued a *per curiam* opinion in the four cases.[141] The court upheld all of EPA's rules, finding that petitioners lacked standing to challenge the Timing and Tailoring Rules, and that while the petitioners did have standing to challenge the endangerment finding and Tailpipe Rule, those rules were not arbitrary or capricious. The court further held that EPA's interpretation of the Clean Air Act in promulgating those rules (and its prior PSD regulations) was "unambiguously correct."[142]

With regard to the endangerment finding and the denial by EPA of the petitions for administrative reconsideration of that finding, petitioners argued in part that EPA failed to consider the "absurd results" that would stem from EPA's action, as the Agency was required to do under section 202(a)(1).[143] Petitioners said that the endangerment finding would likely (and in fact did) lead to regulation of GHG emissions from even very small, non-industrial stationary sources under the PSD provisions of the Act, something Congress could not have intended.[144] Petitioners also challenged the record on which EPA relied in promulgating the endangerment finding, and accused the Agency of "improperly delegat[ing] its judgment" to the authors of secondary studies it relied on in making the finding.[145] Petitioners further alleged that EPA's failure to "quantify" the risks created by climate change was incorrect, and that EPA erred in defining the term "air pollutant" in the finding as the aggregate of six GHGs.[146]

The court found that EPA properly relied on "substantial record evidence"[147] in making the finding and that the finding was consistent with both *Massachusetts* and the Clean Air Act.[148] It held that EPA did not improperly rely on scientific evidence compiled by others: "EPA is not required to re-prove the existence of the atom every time it approaches a scientific question."[149] The court further held that EPA was not required to do anything more than make a "'scientific judgment' about the potential risks greenhouse gas emissions pose to public health and welfare,"[150] and that "[t]he statute speaks in terms of endangerment, not in terms of policy, and EPA has complied with the statute."[151] The court further found that the absurdity of what might result from a finding is "irrelevant to the endangerment inquiry."[152] EPA is also not required to make a quantitative determination of risk or harm in its endangerment finding process, the court held.[153] With regard to the argument that EPA was arbitrary and capricious in determining that the aggregate of six "well-mixed" GHGs was the "air pollutant" at issue in the endangerment finding, the D.C. Circuit found that no petitioner had shown any injury-in-fact in making the argument, and therefore did not have standing to do so.[154]

Petitioners also challenged EPA's interpretation that the Tailpipe Rule necessarily triggered regulation of GHGs from stationary sources, and that EPA improperly failed to consider and justify the cost impacts of this triggering.[155] The court upheld the Tailpipe Rule, stating that once the Agency made its endangerment finding for GHG emissions from motor vehicles, "EPA lacked discretion to defer promulgation of the Tailpipe Rule" on the basis of its triggering other Clean Air Act requirements or its overlapping authority with NHTSA to regulate fuel economy.[156]

The court found that EPA's interpretation of the term "any air pollutant" in the PSD provisions of the Act to include GHGs was reasonable, because that term "unambiguously" includes "any pollutant regulated under the [Clean Air Act]."[157] Industry petitioners listed a number of reasons why the PSD program should not be construed to require permitting for GHG emissions. On these points, the court said that it is "crystal clear that PSD permittees must install BACT for greenhouse gases," despite petitioners' contentions to the contrary.[158] The court also said that despite the traditionally local and regional focus of the PSD program, nothing in the Act limits the PSD provisions to such a focus and, indeed, Congress, according to the court, apparently intended for the program to address broad public health and welfare impacts.[159]

Industry petitioners further argued that PSD permits are required only of facilities that emit pollutants for which the area where the facility is located has reached attainment. In other words, a facility is subject to PSD permitting requirements for fine particulate matter when that area where the facility is located has reached attainment under the NAAQS program for fine particulate matter, since the PSD program is of course aimed at "preventing significant deterioration" of attainment with NAAQS standards.[160] Because EPA has chosen not to regulate GHGs under the NAAQS program, this "situs" argument leads to the conclusion that GHGs cannot be regulated under the PSD program. The court disposed of this argument by stating that it agreed with EPA's longstanding interpretation of the PSD program to mean that as long as a source is located in an area that is either unclassified or classified as in attainment with the NAAQS program generally, it must obtain a PSD permit for *any* pollutant the source will emit (in significant amounts) that is regulated under the Act.[161]

In finding that the petitioners lacked standing to challenge the Timing and Tailoring Rules, the court said that they had failed to demonstrate injury-in-fact, "much less injury that could be redressed by the Rules' vacatur."[162] The court said that it was not EPA's action in the Tailoring and Timing Rules that imposed the administrative burdens of the PSD and Title V permitting programs on certain Petitioners' stationary sources, but rather that the statute itself "automatic[ally] operat[ed]" to impose these burdens once EPA made the endangerment finding.[163] The court also stated that the Timing and Tailoring Rules "actually mitigate" the impacts of the imposition of the PSD program on stationary sources because the Act's thresholds for application are much lower than the thresholds EPA established in the Tailoring Rule.[164]

Petitioners filed petitions for rehearing *en banc*, which the court denied in December 2012. Judges Brown and Kavanaugh each filed lengthy dissents to the denial of rehearing.[165] Judge Brown started her dissent with a personal story of her experience with Los Angeles air pollution, and argued that despite the *Massachusetts* opinion, Congress never intended to address climate change through the statute. She further argued that EPA had not made the requisite determination regarding the "nexus" between the air pollutant CO_2 and the object of the harm – in other words, that CO_2 had not yet been found to *directly* harm public health and welfare.[166] She concluded that *Massachusetts* does not apply and should not apply to the PSD and Title V programs. Judge Kavanaugh's dissent focused on EPA's "strange" interpretation of the statute in rewriting the 100 and 250-ton thresholds to arrive at the Tailoring Rule, arguing that the PSD program should be limited to the NAAQS pollutants and not extended to GHG emissions.[167] Like Brown, Kavanaugh would not have found that the holding in *Massachusetts* extended to the PSD and Title V programs.[168] He concluded that "the ultimate clincher in this case is one simple point: EPA chose an admittedly absurd reading over a perfectly natural reading of the relevant statutory text. An agency cannot do that."[169]

In responding to the dissents, Chief Judge Sentelle, joined by Judges Rogers and Tatel (the original panel in the case), argued that while "the stakes here are high, . . . [t]he legal issues presented . . . are straightforward, requiring no more than the application of clear statutes and binding Supreme Court precedent."[170] Chief Judge Sentelle also argued that despite Judge Brown's contentions, EPA *did* find the requisite nexus between CO_2 and the alleged harms to public health and welfare, and alleged that Judge Brown's real "quarrel is with the Supreme Court['s]" decision in *Massachusetts*.[171] As to Judge Kavanaugh's point, Chief Judge Sentelle said that Congress's use of the term "any air pollutant" was meant to encompass *any* air pollutant in the PSD program, not just the NAAQS pollutants.[172]

Nine petitions for a writ of certiorari were filed with the United States Supreme Court seeking review by that Court of the D.C. Circuit's decision. On October 15, 2013, the Supreme Court granted six of the petitions, limiting its review to the Timing and Tailoring Rules by directing the parties to address the following issue: "Whether EPA permissibly determined that its regulation of greenhouse gas emissions from new motor vehicles triggered permitting requirements under the Clean Air Act for stationary sources that emit greenhouse gases."[173] The Court denied those petitions that sought solely to review the D.C. Circuit's decision upholding the endangerment finding and EPA's model year 2012-2016 light-duty vehicle GHG emission standards.

Litigation Involving State Implementation Plans and Federal Implementation Plans Regarding Regulation of GHGs Under the PSD Permitting Program

After EPA finalized the Tailoring Rule, it proposed two rules in September 2010 to address potential issues with states' implementation of their PSD programs for sources of GHGs. In the first proposed rule, EPA proposed to find that all or parts of 13 states' EPA-approved state implementation plans ("SIPs") for their PSD programs were substantially inadequate to meet the Clean Air Act's requirements because those SIPs did not appear to authorize application of PSD requirements to GHG-emitting sources.[174] Through a "SIP-Call," EPA proposed to require each of these 13 states[175] to revise its SIP as necessary to correct the alleged deficiencies. EPA proposed an expedited schedule for states to submit their corrective SIP-revision because the Agency claimed that GHG-emitting sources that trigger PSD on January 2, 2011, or July 1, 2011, may not be able to obtain PSD permits to construct or modify unless and until their state has an adequate and approved SIP authorizing such permitting.[176] Other states with approved SIP PSD programs were asked to submit comments on whether their PSD programs would or would not apply to GHG-emitting sources by the threshold applicability dates in 2011.[177] If, based on this information and other analyses, EPA were to conclude that the SIP for each such state would not authorize PSD permits for GHG-emitting sources, then EPA would proceed to issue a finding of substantial inadequacy and a SIP call for that state. In the second proposed rule, EPA proposed a federal implementation plan ("FIP") to apply in any state that is unable to submit, by its deadline, a corrective SIP revision to ensure that the state has authority to issue PSD permits to sources of GHG emissions consistent with the Tailoring Rule.[178]

On December 13, 2010, EPA published its final PSD SIP Call rule.[179] In the final rule, EPA found that the PSD provisions in EPA-approved SIPs for all or part of 13 states are "substantially inadequate" to meet Clean Air Act requirements because they do not authorize application of PSD requirements to sources' GHG emissions. The final rule established the deadline for each state's submission of SIP revisions to incorporate GHGs into the state's PSD program. Seven of the states chose to accept the earliest SIP submittal deadline of December 22, 2010.[180] EPA stated in the final SIP Call rule that it would issue a FIP for any of these states on December 23, 2010 (i.e., the date after the submittal deadline) if the state did not submit a SIP revision before then.[181] Five of the states (or local agencies in those states) selected SIP submittal deadlines after December 22, 2010,[182] and EPA noted that it would also issue a FIP for these jurisdictions if they failed to meet their deadline dates.[183] Texas did not select a SIP submittal date, and EPA stated in the final SIP Call rule that it was "planning additional actions to ensure that GHG sources in Texas can be issued permits as of January 2, 2011."[184]

On December 23, 2010, EPA issued a final rule finding that the seven states that had agreed to a PSD SIP submittal deadline of December 22, 2010, had failed to meet that deadline.[185] EPA simultaneously issued a final FIP for those seven states.[186] On that same day, EPA also issued a proposed SIP Call and FIP rule for Texas,[187] along with an interim final rule.[188] In the interim final rule, EPA partially disapproved Texas's PSD SIP under EPA's interpretation of the Clean Air Act's "error correction" provisions of section 110(k)(6) of the Clean Air Act. EPA asserted in the interim rule that it made an error when it previously approved Texas's PSD SIP because Texas did not address how its program would apply to pollutants newly subject to regulation and did not provide assurances that the program has adequate legal authority to apply to such pollutants.[189] Because EPA, in the interim final rule, disapproved Texas's PSD SIP in this respect, EPA also issued a FIP to take over PSD permitting of large sources of GHGs in Texas immediately.[190] The proposed SIP Call and FIP reiterated the rationale EPA had laid out in the interim final rule and sought public comment. The interim final rule expired on its own terms on April 30, 2011, and EPA published its final rule disapproving Texas's PSD SIP and imposing a FIP on Texas on May 3, 2011.[191]

Petitions for review were filed in the D.C. Circuit challenging all of these rules, and the court issued its opinion in the cases on July 26, 2013.[192] The court dismissed all of the petitions for review for lack of jurisdiction, finding that none of the petitioners had standing to challenge EPA's actions.[193] In finding that petitioners lacked standing, the court relied on its decision upholding EPA's suite of rules to regulate GHGs under the PSD and Title V permitting programs (discussed above in Section IV). The court stated that "[b]ecause we now hold that under the plain text of [sections 165(a) and 167 of the Clean Air Act] the permitting requirements are self-executing without regard to previously approved SIPs, industry petitioners fail to show how they have been injured in fact by the rules enabling issuance of necessary permits."[194] The court also held that Texas and Wyoming lacked standing because they could not show "in the face of Congress's mandate in [section] 165(a) . . . how vacating the rules would redress their purported injuries."[195]

Judge Kavanaugh filed a dissenting opinion. He would have vacated all of EPA's rules and said that "[i]n [his] view, this case is straightforward. The relevant EPA regulation [40 C.F.R. § 51.166(a)(6)] plainly gives States three years to revise their SIPs whenever new pollutants, like [GHGs], are regulated under EPA's PSD regulations."[196] He stated that "[d]uring that time, States may still issue PSD construction permits."[197] Judge Kavanaugh also rejected EPA's alternative theory for the Texas FIP—correction of an error in the Texas SIP under section 110(k)(6)—as flawed because Texas's SIP was valid when approved in 1992 and was not "in error."[198] He also rejected EPA's alternative theory for the PSD SIP Call, Finding of Failure, and FIP rules, which was that those states' SIPs could be retroactively disapproved because they failed to update automatically to include GHGs. Judge Kavanaugh noted that it is not a requirement of either the Clean Air Act or EPA's regulations that SIPs update automatically to include new pollutants.[199]

Petitioners have obtained an extension of time to file petitions for rehearing in these cases pending the Supreme Court's decision in *Utility Air Regulatory Group v. EPA*, which is discussed above in Section IV, and the cases are in abeyance awaiting that Court's decision.[200]

EPA's Second Wave or Regulatory Efforts: Performance Standards Under Section 111

Proposed New Source Performance Standards Under Section 111(b)

Section 111(b) of the Act provides for EPA to issue standards of performance for new and modified sources.[201] Under the process set out in section 111, EPA first defines the source category that will be regulated and then sets the standard applicable to that category. It also typically will set different standards for different sub-categories within that category. Once set, all sources across the country that construct or make major modifications after the date of *proposal* must meet the standard.[202]

In 2006, EPA issued new source performance standards ("NSPS") for new EGUs and under section 111(b) of the Clean Air Act and decided at that time not to establish GHG emission standards for new EGUs.[203] EPA's rationale for not setting GHG emission standards was that the Agency did not have authority to regulate GHGs under the Clean Air Act.[204] EPA also declined to establish GHG emission standards for new petroleum refineries when it issued NSPS for those sources in 2008.[205] Several states and environmental groups challenged those decisions in the D.C. Circuit, claiming that EPA was required to set GHG emission standards as part of the NSPS.[206] The D.C. Circuit entered an order remanding the EGU NSPS rulemaking to EPA after the Supreme Court's 2007 decision in *Massachusetts*,[207] and placed the litigation regarding the petroleum refineries NSPS in abeyance pending administrative reconsideration of that rule.[208] EPA ultimately entered into settlement agreements in the cases wherein it agreed to propose and finalize NSPS under section 111(b) of the Act for GHG emissions from new and modified EGUs and petroleum refineries by May 26, 2012, and November 10, 2012, respectively.[209] EPA also agreed to issue emission guidelines for existing EGUs and petroleum refineries under section 111(d) of the Act.

EPA missed these deadlines and first proposed an NSPS for new EGUs in April 2012.[210] The proposed rule addressed only CO_2 (not all GHGs)[211] and addressed only new sources.[212] The proposed source category included all new oil-, gas-, and coal-fired EGUs over 73 MW in capacity and designed to meet baseload or intermediate demand.[213] The proposal also was unusual in that it set a single standard across all EGUs – 1,000 pounds of CO_2 per megawatt hour ("lbs CO_2/MWh") of electricity generated on a gross basis per megawatt-hour – an emissions rate achievable only by a natural gas combined cycle facility.[214] Thus, in essence, no new coal-fired EGUs could be built. EPA did propose an alternative method to meet the standard, however. If the facility uses coal or petroleum coke as fuel, it could comply with the standard by emitting as much as 1,800 lbs CO_2/MWh for the first ten years of the facility's operation, and then emitting no more than 600 lbs CO_2/MWh for the following twenty years of its operation.[215] On a 30-year average basis, the unit would not be able to emit more than 1,000 lbs CO_2/MWh.[216] EPA noted that the 1,800 lbs CO_2/MWh rate could be met with supercritical steam conditions, integrated gasification combined cycle ("IGCC") facilities, and pressurized circulating fluidized bed boilers.[217] The 600 lbs CO_2/MWh standard was designed to be met by a carbon capture and storage ("CCS") facility.[218]

Several industry parties filed suit in the D.C. Circuit challenging the proposed rule on the basis that the proposal constituted final agency action with immediate effect because it prevented the construction of new coal-fired EGUs as of April 13, 2012—the date of proposal. Under section 111(a)(2) of the Act, NSPS must be adhered to by all new sources that commence construction after the date of proposal—not the date of the final rule.[219] In December 2012, the D.C. Circuit dismissed the challenge saying it was unripe because the proposal did not constitute final agency action.[220]

Because of concerns that had been raised regarding the April 2012 rule's legality, President Obama directed EPA to withdraw the rule and issue a new proposed rule setting NSPS for CO_2 emissions from new EGUs as part of his Climate Action Plan. The President's Climate Action Plan, which was released in June 2013, specifically directed EPA to do the following: (1) repropose NSPS addressing CO_2 emissions from new EGUs by no later than September 20, 2013; (2) issue final NSPS for new EGUs "in a timely fashion" thereafter;[221] (3) "issue proposed carbon pollution standards, regulations, or guidelines, as appropriate, for modified, reconstructed, and existing power plants by no later than June 1, 2014"; (4) "issue final standards, regulations, or guidelines, as appropriate for modified, reconstructed, and existing power plants by no later than June 1, 2015"; and (5) require states to submit section 111(d) plans by no later than June 30, 2016.[222]

EPA did release its reproposed NSPS addressing CO_2 emissions from new EGUs on September 20, 2013 (the deadline specified in the Climate Action Plan) but the proposal was not published in the Federal Register until January 8, 2014.[223] The reproposed rule proposed separate standards for fossil fuel-fired steam generating boilers and IGCC units, and for natural gas-fired stationary combustion turbines. With regard to fossil fuel-fired steam generating boilers and IGCC units, EPA proposed: (1) a rate of 1,100 lbs CO_2/MWh (on a 12-operating-month rolling average) or a rate of between 1,000 and 1,050 lbs CO_2/MWh (on an 84-operating-month rolling average); and (2) a determination that the best system of emission reduction ("BSER") that has been adequately demonstrated for these units is "partial implementation of CCS."[224]

With regard to natural gas-fired stationary combustion turbines, the reproposed rule proposed: (1) a rate of 1,000 lbs CO_2/MWh for larger units (those with a heat input rating greater than 850 million British thermal units per hour ("mmBtu/hour")); (2) a rate of 1,100 lbs CO_2/MWh for smaller units (those with a heat input rating less than or equal to 850 mmBtu/hour); and (3) a determination that BSER for these units is natural gas combined cycle without CCS.[225]

The reproposed NSPS rule for EGUs exempted or otherwise did not include: (1) modified and reconstructed sources; (2) simple-cycle "peaking" stationary combustion turbines that sell less than one-third of potential electrical output to the grid; (3) EGUs that primarily fire biomass and oil; and (4) three specific plants that might be exempted because they were under development or construction.[226] The reproposed rule was accompanied by a notice that formally rescinded the April 2012 proposed rule.[227] The only GHG covered by the reproposed rule is CO_2.[228] EPA also specifically noted in the reproposed GHG NSPS rule that "this proposal does not have any direct applicability on the determination of [BACT] for existing EGUs that require PSD permits to authorize a major modification of the EGU," and that "[i]t is important to note that a proposed NSPS does not establish the BACT Floor for affected facilities seeking a PSD permit."[229]

Existing Source Performance Standards

Section 111(d) of the Clean Air Act governs the regulation of emissions from existing sources of air pollutants that are not listed as criteria air pollutants pursuant to section 108 of the Act or listed as hazardous air pollutants under section 112.[230] Regulation of existing sources under this provision rarely occurs. Section 111(d) does not directly authorize EPA to establish standards of performance for existing sources. Rather, that section of the Clean Air Act directs EPA to issue regulations governing the procedure by which states are to submit plans to EPA regarding how the states will regulate existing sources within their borders. EPA issued such regulations in 1975.[231] EPA's regulations set forth a process that is much like the one used by states to develop SIPs.[232]

In September 2013, as part of its preparation of the proposed guidelines to address GHG emissions from existing EGUs under section 111(d), EPA issued a five-page document containing a list of questions for stakeholders to respond to regarding EPA's ongoing effort to prepare the proposed guidelines. In the document, EPA asked four main questions: (1) what is state and stakeholder experience with programs that reduce CO_2 emissions in the electric power sector?; (2) how should EPA set the performance standard for state plans?; (3) what requirements should state plans meet, and what flexibility should be provided by states in developing their plans?; and (4) what can EPA do to facilitate state plan development?[233] EPA also announced plans for a series of "listening sessions" throughout the country where stakeholders could raise with EPA issues that they thought the Agency should consider as part of the section 111(d) guideline development process.[234]

Pending Petitions for Rulemaking Under Other Clean Air Act Provisions

EPA has been petitioned by environmental groups a number of times to initiate additional rulemakings to regulate GHG emissions under the Clean Air Act. These petitions, none of which have been acted upon by EPA, are discussed below.

In December 2009, the Center for Biological Diversity and an organization called 350.org (based on the parts per million level that they believe is the safe upper limit for CO_2 in the atmosphere) filed a petition for rulemaking with EPA seeking to have seven GHGs (CO_2, CH_4, N_2O, HFCs, PFCs, SF_6, and nitrogen trifluoride) listed as criteria air pollutants under section 108 of the Clean Air Act.[235] If, as a result of this petition for rulemaking, EPA chooses to (or is required to, as the petition argues) list these GHGs as criteria air pollutants, EPA would then have to establish a NAAQS for those pollutants.[236]

In February 2013, the New York University School of Law's Institute for Policy Integrity petitioned EPA to make certain findings and to regulate GHG emissions under sections 111, 115, 615, and Title II of the Clean Air Act.[237] Pursuant to section 111 (NSPS), the petition requests EPA to list additional source categories that "contribute significantly to greenhouse gas pollution" including agricultural sources and coal mines.[238] The petition also asks EPA to revise performance standards for already-listed categories to cover significant GHG emissions (including landfills, natural gas and petroleum systems, iron and steel producers, cement producers, nitric acid plants, wastewater treatment facilities, and manufacturing).[239]

Pursuant to Title II of the Act (mobile sources), the petition restates the Institute for Policy Integrity's 2009 request to EPA to establish a cap-and-trade system for vehicle fuels, and newly petitions EPA, in the alternative, to promulgate emissions standards for mobile sources not yet regulated for their GHG emissions, including motorcycles, trailers of heavy-duty trucks, aircraft, marine vessels, buses, and locomotives.[240] With regard to section 115 (international air pollution) of the Act, the petition asks EPA (i) to find that all prerequisites under section 115 for controlling GHG emissions have been satisfied; (ii) to require states to revise their SIPs to control GHG emissions to meet the requirements of section 115; and (iii) to advise states on their options under section 115, "including flexible regulatory tools like market incentives"[241] such as "an integrated, nationwide cap-and-auction control system."[242]

Pursuant to section 615 of the Clean Air Act (stratospheric ozone), the petition asks EPA to "initiate a public call for information under Title VI regarding the effect of GHGs on the stratosphere and ozone in the stratosphere," to issue an endangerment finding under section 615 if warranted,[243] and then to control GHG emissions "through flexible regulatory tools like markets."[244] The petition notes that simultaneous regulation under all four of these sections is not necessary, and that regulation under one of the more "comprehensive" sections 115 and 615 might be sufficient.[245]

Notes

1. *See* Memorandum from Jonathan Z. Cannon, General Counsel, EPA, to Carol M. Browner, Adm'r, EPA, regarding EPA's Authority to Regulate Pollutants Emitted by Electric Power Generation Sources (Apr. 10, 1998) (concluding that carbon dioxide is a "pollutant" subject to regulation under the Clean Air Act); Letter from Gary S. Guzy, General Counsel, EPA, to David M. McIntosh, Chairman, Subcomm. on Nat'l Econ. Growth, Natural Resources & Regulatory Affairs, Comm. on Gov't Reform, U.S. House of Representatives (Dec. 1, 1999) (stating that carbon dioxide may be regulated under the Clean Air Act if other requirements of Act are met); Memorandum from Robert E. Fabricant, General Counsel, EPA, to Marianne L. Horinko, Acting Adm'r, EPA, regarding EPA's Authority to Impose Mandatory Controls to Address Global Climate Change Under the Clean Air Act (Aug. 28, 2003) (concluding Clean Air Act does not authorize EPA to regulate GHGs to address global climate change); *see also Joint Hearing of the Subcomm. on Nat'l Econ. Growth, Natural Res. & Regulatory Affairs of the Comm. on Gov't Reform & the Subcomm. on Energy & Env't of the Comm. on Science, U.S. House of Representatives*, 106th Congress (Oct. 6, 1999) (testimony of Gary S. Guzy, General Counsel, EPA).

2. Petition for Rulemaking and Collateral Relief Seeking the Regulation of Greenhouse Gas Emissions from New Motor Vehicles Under § 202 of the Clean Air Act, *Int'l Ctr. for Tech. Assessment v. Browner*, Air & Radiation Docket No. A-2000-04 (EPA Oct. 20, 1999).

3. CAA § 202(a)(1), 42 U.S.C. § 7521(a).

4. Control of Emissions From New and In-use Highway Vehicles and Engines; Notice; request for comment, 66 Fed. Reg. 7486 (Jan. 23, 2001).

5. Comp. for Declaratory Relief & Writ of Mandamus or Other Order, *Int'l Ctr. for Tech. Assessment v. Whitman*, No. 1:02-cv-02376-PBW (D.D.C. filed Dec. 5, 2002).

6. EPA, Control of Emissions from New Highway Vehicles and Engines, Notice of Denial of Petition for Rulemaking, 68 Fed. Reg. 52,922 (Sept. 8, 2003).

7. *Id.* at 52,925-29.

8. *Id.* at 52,929-31.

9. *Id.* at 52,929.

10. *Massachusetts v. EPA*, 415 F.3d 50 (D.C. Cir. 2005), *rev'd* 549 U.S. 497 (2007).

11. *Massachusetts v. EPA*, 548 U.S. 903 (2006).

12. *Massachusetts v. EPA*, 549 U.S. 497 (2007).

13. *Id.* at 528-32.

14. *Id.* at 532-35.

15. *Id.* at 528-29.

16. *Id.* at 552 (citing CAA § 202(a)(1), 42 U.S.C. § 7521(a)(1)); *see also id.* at 514, 528, 532-33, 543-44.

17. *Id.* at 532.

18. *Id.* at 533.

19. *Id.*

20. *Id.* at 534-35.

21. *Id.* at 535-36, 543-44 (Roberts, C.J., dissenting).

22. *Id.* at 560 (Scalia, J., dissenting).

23. Consolidated Appropriations Act of 2008, Pub. L. No. 110-161, tit. II, 121 Stat. 1844, 2128 (2007).

24. EPA, Mandatory Reporting of Greenhouse Gases, 74 Fed. Reg. 56,260 (Oct. 30, 2009) (adopting 40 C.F.R. part 98 and amending 40 C.F.R. part 86).

25. The GHG reporting rule has been amended multiple times. A full list of amendments can be found on EPA's website at: http://www.epa.gov/climate/ ghgreporting/reporters/notices/index.html.

26. "Carbon dioxide equivalent" or "CO2e" is a reference that enables the expression of the volumes of different GHGs in a single metric relative to carbon dioxide. It is calculated based on how potent each gas is in terms of its ability to accelerate global warming (the gas's "global warming potential"). For instance, one ton of nitrous oxide is roughly equivalent to 300 tons of carbon dioxide according to its global warming potential.

27. *See* EPA, Greenhouse Gas Reporting Program, http://www.epa.gov/ climate/ghgreporting/ghgdata/reported/index.html.

28. EPA, Regulating Greenhouse Gas Emissions Under the Clean Air Act, 73 Fed. Reg. 44,354 (July 30, 2008).

29. *Id.* at 44,355.

30. EPA, Endangerment and Cause or Contribute Findings for Greenhouse Gases Under Section 202(a) of the Clean Air Act; Final Rule, 74 Fed. Reg. 66,496, 66,496, 66,497 (Dec. 15, 2009).

31. *Id.* at 66,499 (finding that section 202 sources as a whole contribute "just over 23% of the United States well-mixed greenhouse gas emissions" and "about 4% of total global well-mixed greenhouse gas emissions").

32. *Id.*

33. *Id.* at 66,507.

34. *Id.* at 66,546.

35. Section III.D discusses mobile source GHG emissions regulation under the Clean Air Act.

36. Section III.E discusses regulation of GHGs under the PSD and Title V permitting programs.

37. *Coal. for Responsible Regulation, Inc. v. EPA*, No. 09-1322 (and consolidated cases) (D.C. Cir.).

38. EPA's Denial of the Petitions To Reconsider the Endangerment and Cause or Contribute Findings for Greenhouse Gases Under Section 202(a) of the Clean Air Act, 75 Fed Reg. 49,556 (Aug. 13, 2010).

39. *Coal. for Responsible Regulation, Inc. v. EPA*, No. 10-1234 (and consolidated cases) (D.C. Cir.).

40. Order, *Coal. for Responsible Regulation, Inc. v. EPA*, No. 09-1322 (D.C. Cir. Nov. 15, 2010).

41. CAA § 209(b), 42 U.S.C. § 7543(b). Other states may adopt the California emission standards if they prefer those to the federal standards. *Id.* § 177, 42 U.S.C. § 7507.

42. EPA, California State Motor Vehicle Pollution Control Standards; Notice of Decision Granting a Waiver of Clean Air Act Preemption for California's 2009 and Subsequent Model Year Greenhouse Gas Emission Standards for New Motor Vehicles, 74 Fed. Reg. 32,744, 32,746 (July 8, 2009).

43. *Id.* at 32,747.

44. EPA, California State Motor Vehicle Pollution Control Standards; Notice of Decision Denying a Waiver of Clean Air Act Preemption for California's 2009 and Subsequent Model Year Greenhouse Gas Emission Standards for New Motor Vehicles, 73 Fed. Reg. 12,156 (Mar. 6, 2008).

45. Memorandum of January 26, 2009, State of California Request for Waiver Under 42 U.S.C. 7543(b), the Clean Air Act, Presidential Documents, 74 Fed. Reg. 4905 (Jan. 28, 2009).

46. 74 Fed. Reg. at 32,744.

47. *See* CAA § 177, 42 U.S.C. § 7507 (permitting state adoption of California standards in nonattainment areas); 74 Fed. Reg. 24,007, 24,008 (May 22, 2009) (noting adoption of California standards by other states).

48. Press Release, Office of the Press Secretary, The White House, President Obama Announces National Fuel Efficiency Policy (May 19, 2009), *available at* http://www.whitehouse.gov/the-press-office/president-obama-announces-national-fuel-efficiency-policy.

49. *See, e.g.*, Letter from Dave McCurdy, President and CEO, Alliance of Auto. Mfrs., to Ray LaHood, Sec'y of Transp., and Lisa P. Jackson, Adm'r, EPA (May 18, 2009), *available at* http://www.epa.gov/omswww/climate/letters.htm.

50. 74 Fed. Reg. at 66,497.

51. CAA § 202(a)(1), 42 U.S.C. § 7521(a)(1).

52. EPA, Light-Duty Vehicle Greenhouse Gas Emission Standards and Corporate Average Fuel Economy Standards; Final Rule, 75 Fed. Reg. 25,324 (May 7, 2010).

53. *Id.*

54. *Id.* at 25,328.

55. *Id.* at 25,330.

56. *Id.* at 25,396.

57. *Id.* at 25,399 & n.161.

58. *Id.* at 25,332.

59. *Id.* at 25,328.

60. *See* EPA, California State Motor Vehicle Pollution Control Standards; Within-the-Scope Determination for Amendments to California's Motor Vehicle Greenhouse Gas Regulations; Notice of Decision, 76 Fed. Reg. 34,693, 34,693 (June 14, 2011) (approving amendments to California standards as consistent with 2009 preemption waiver).

61. *Id.*

62. *Coal. for Responsible Regulation, Inc. v. EPA*, No. 10-1092 (and consolidated cases) (D.C. Cir.).

63. EPA, 2017 and Later Model Year Light-Duty Vehicle Greenhouse Gas Emissions and Corporate Average Fuel Economy Standards, 77 Fed. Reg. 62,624 (Oct. 15, 2012) ("2012 Light-Duty Rule").

64. *Id.* at 62,638.

65. *Id.*

66. *Id.* at 62,639.

67. *Id.* at 62,640.

68. *Id.*

69. *Id.* at 62,639.

70. *Id.* at 62,628.

71. *Id.*

72. *Id.*

73. *Id.* at 62,631.

74. Memorandum of May 21, 2010, Improving Energy Security, American Competiveness and Job Creation, and Environmental Protection Through a Transformation of Our Nation's Fleet of Cars and Trucks, Presidential Documents, 75 Fed. Reg. 29,399 (May 26, 2010).

75. *See, e.g.*, Letter from Dave McCurdy, President and CEO, Alliance of Auto. Mfrs., to Ray LaHood, Sec'y of Transp. & Lisa P. Jackson, Adm'r, EPA (May 20, 2010), *available at* http://www.epa.gov/omswww/climate/letters.htm.

76. EPA, Greenhouse Gas Emissions Standards and Fuel Efficiency Standards for Medium- and Heavy-Duty Engines and Vehicles, 76 Fed. Reg. 57,106 (Sept. 15, 2011) ("2011 Heavy-Duty Rule").

77. *Id.* at 57,109.

78. *See id.* at 57,117 (model year 2017 standards for Combination Tractors); *id.* at 57,121-22 (model year 2017 standards for Vocational Vehicles).

79. *Id.* at 57,117.

80. *Id.* at 57,110.

81. *Id.* at 57,126.

82. *Delta Constr. Co. v. EPA*, No. 11-1428 (and consolidated cases) (D.C. Cir.).

83. Energy Policy Act of 2005, Pub. L. No. 109-58, § 1501, 119 Stat. 594, 1067, 1069 (codified as amended at CAA § 211(o), 42 U.S.C. 7545(o)).

84. CAA § 211(o)(3)(B), 42 U.S.C. § 7545(o)(3)(B).

85. EPA, Regulation of Fuels and Fuel Additives: Renewable Fuel Standard Program, 72 Fed. Reg. 23,900 (May 1, 2007).

86. Energy Independence and Security Act of 2007, Pub. L. No. 110-140, §§ 201-210, 121 Stat. 1492, 1519-32 (codified at CAA § 211(o), 42 U.S.C. § 7545(o)).

87. CAA § 211(o)(2)(B)(i)(I), 42 U.S.C. § 7545(o)(2)(B)(i)(I).

88. *Id.* § 211(o)(2)(B)(i), 42 U.S.C. § 7545(o)(2)(B)(i).

89. *Id.* § 211(o)(2)(B), (3)(B), 42 U.S.C. § 7545(o)(2)(B), (3)(B).

90. *Id.* § 211(o)(7)(A), 42 U.S.C. § 7545(o)(7)((A).

91. *Id.* § 211(o)(1)(H), 42 U.S.C. § 7545(o)(1)(H) (defining lifecycle GHG emissions).

92. *Id.* § 211(o)(1)(B), (D), 42 U.S.C. § 7545(o)(1)(B), (D).

93. *Id.* § 211(o)(1)(E), (2)(A)(i), 42 U.S.C. § 7545(o)(1)(E), (2)(A)(i).

94. *Id.* § 211(o)(1)(I)-(J), 42 U.S.C. § 7545(o)(1)(I)-(J).

95. EPA, Regulation of Fuels and Fuel Additives: Changes to Renewable Fuel Standard Program, 75 Fed. Reg. 14,670 (Mar. 26, 2010).

96. *Id.* at 14,677.

97. *Id.* at 14,681.

98. *See* EPA, Supplemental Determination for Renewable Fuels Produced Under the Final RFS2 Program From Grain Sorghum, 77 Fed. Reg. 74,592, 74,593, 74,603 (Dec. 17, 2012) (grain sorghum ethanol from natural gas-burning facilities meets 20% renewable fuel threshold; grain sorghum ethanol from certain biomass-burning facilities meets 50% advanced biofuel threshold); EPA, Supplemental Determination for Renewable Fuels Produced Under the Final RFS2 Program From Canola Oil, 75 Fed. Reg. 59,622, 59,622 (Sept. 28, 2010) (canola oil biodiesel meets 50% biomass-based diesel and advanced biofuel thresholds).

99. *See* 75 Fed. Reg. at 14,670 (adopting renewable fuel standards for 2010); EPA, Regulation of Fuels and Fuel Additives: 2011 Renewable Fuel Standards, 75 Fed. Reg. 76,790, 76,790 (Dec. 9, 2010) (renewable fuel standards for 2011); EPA, Regulation of Fuels and Fuel Additives: 2012 Renewable Fuel Standards, 77 Fed. Reg. 1,320 (Jan. 9, 2012) (renewable fuel standards for 2012).

100. *Am. Petroleum Inst. v. EPA*, 706 F.3d 474 (D.C. Cir. 2013).

101. *Id.* at 476. Despite Energy Information Administration projections that production would reach 5 million and 3.9 million gallons in 2010 and 2011, respectively, the domestic industry was unable to produce any cellulosic biofuel in those years. *Id.* at 478.

102 *Id.* at 480.

103. 40 C.F.R. § 52.21(b)(50) (2012) (defining "regulated NSR pollutant").

104. *Id.* § 52.21(j)(3); *see also* CAA §§ 165, 169, 42 U.S.C. §§ 7475, 7479.

105. 40 C.F.R. § 52.21(b)(50)(iv).

106. EPA, Region 8, Final Air Pollution Control Prevention of Significant Deterioration (PSD) Permit to Construct, Permit No. PSD-OU-0002-04.00, Deseret Power Electric Cooperative, at 1, 2 (Aug. 30, 2007), *available at* www.epa.gov/region8/air/pdf/FinalStatementOfBasis.pdf.

107. Order Granting Review, *In re: Deseret Power Electric Coop.*, PSD Appeal No. 07-03 (EAB Nov. 21, 2007).

108. In January 2008, the EAB had denied review of a similar challenge in the *In re Christian County Generation* case, *see* Order Denying Review, *In re Christian County Generation, LLC*, PSD Appeal No. 07-01, 13 E.A.D. 449 (EAB Jan. 28, 2008), *available at* http://yosemite.epa.gov/oa/EAB_Web_Docket.nsf/ Appeal~Number/F39D157BEB42E111852573DF005F4398/$File/Christian%20County.pdf, where Sierra Club had also raised the BACT CO2 issue. In its *Christian County* ruling, the EAB determined that Sierra Club had waived that issue by failing to raise it in its initial comments on the Christian County permit. The EAB further noted *Massachusetts v. EPA* did not address the BACT CO2 issue, so that issue "remains a matter of considerable dispute." *Id.* at 461.

109. Order Denying Review In Part and Remanding In Part, *In re Deseret Power Electric Cooperative*, PSD Appeal No. 07-03 (EAB Nov. 13, 2008).

110. *Id.* at 37, 43.

111. *Id.* at 63.

112. Memorandum from Stephen L. Johnson, Adm'r, to EPA Regional Adm'rs, Regarding EPA's Interpretation of Regulations That Determine Pollutants Covered by Federal Prevention of Significant Deterioration (PSD) Permit Program at 1 (Dec. 18, 2008) ("PSD Interpretive Memorandum"); *see also* 73 Fed. Reg. 80,300 (Dec. 31, 2008) (public notice of memorandum). The PSD Interpretive Memorandum sometimes is also referred to as the "Johnson Memorandum."

113. PSD Interpretive Memorandum at 1.

114. Letter from Lisa P. Jackson, EPA Adm'r, to David Bookbinder, Chief Climate Counsel, Sierra Club (Feb. 17, 2009) (responding to amended petition for reconsideration dated Jan. 6, 2009).

115. EPA, Prevention of Significant Deterioration (PSD): Reconsideration of Interpretation of Regulations That Determine Pollutants Covered by the Federal PSD Permit Program; Proposed Rule; Reconsideration, 74 Fed. Reg. 51,535 (Oct. 7, 2009).

116. EPA, Reconsideration of Interpretation of Regulations That Determine Pollutants Covered by Clean Air Act Permitting Programs, Final Action on Reconsideration of Interpretation, 75 Fed. Reg. 17,004, 17,004 (Apr. 2, 2010).

117. *Id.* at 17,004, 17,007, 17,015.

118. *Coal. for Responsible Regulation, Inc. v. EPA*, No. 10-1073 (and consolidated cases) (D.C. Cir.).

119. EPA, Prevention of Significant Deterioration and Title V Greenhouse Gas Tailoring Rule; Proposed Rule, 74 Fed. Reg. 55,292 (Oct. 27, 2009).

120. EPA, Prevention of Significant Deterioration and Title V Greenhouse Gas Tailoring Rule; Final Rule, 75 Fed. Reg. 31,514, 31,514 (June 3, 2010).

121. *Id.* at 31,536.

122. EPA, Summary of Clean Air Act Permitting Burdens With and Without the Tailoring Rule ("EPA Summary of Permitting Burdens"), *available at* http://www.epa.gov/NSR/documents/20100413piecharts.pdf.

123. 75 Fed. Reg. at 31,556.

124. EPA Summary of Permitting Burdens.

125. 75 Fed. Reg. at 31,514.

126. *Id.* at 31,516.

127. *Id.*

128. EPA, Prevention of Significant Deterioration and Title V Greenhouse Gas Tailoring Rule Step 3 and GHG Plantwide Applicability Limits; Final Rule, 77 Fed. Reg. 41,051, 41,051 (July 12, 2012).

129. *Id.* at 41,054.

130. *See Chevron, U.S.A., Inc. v. Natural Res. Def. Council*, 467 U.S. 837 (1984).

131. 75 Fed. Reg. at 31,517.

132. *Id.* at 31,516.

133. *Id.*

134. *Id.*

135. *Id.*

136. *Southeastern Legal Found., Inc. v. EPA*, No. 10-1131 (and consolidated cases) (D.C. Cir.).

137. *See* supra notes 37, 39, 40.

138. *See* supra note 62.

139. *See* supra notes 118, 136; Order, *Coal. for Responsible Regulation, Inc. v. EPA*, No. 10-1073 (D.C. Cir. Nov. 16, 2010).

140. *Am. Chemistry Council v. EPA*, No. 10-1167 (and consolidated cases) (D.C. Cir.).

141. *Coal. for Responsible Regulation, Inc. v. EPA*, 684 F.3d 102 (D.C. Cir. 2012), *cert. granted sub nom Utility Air Regulatory Group v. EPA*, 134 S. Ct. 418 (2013).

142. *Id.* at 113-14.

143. *Id.* at 118-19.

144. *Id.* at 119.

145. *Id.*

146. *Id.* at 117.

147. *Id.* at 121.

148. *Id.* at 122.

149. *Id.* at 120.

150. *Id.* at 117-18.

151. *Id.* at 118.

152. *Id.* at 119.

153. *Id.* at 122-23.

154. *Id.* at 123-24.

155. *Id.* at 126.

156. *Id.* at 126-27.

157. *Id.* at 136; *see also id.* at 134-35.

158. *Id.* at 137.

159. *Id.* at 137-38.

160. *See id.* at 138-41.

161. *Id.* at 143.

162. *Id.* at 146.

163. *Id.*

164. *Id.*

165. *Coal. for Responsible Regulation, Inc. v. EPA,* No. 09-1322, 2012 WL 6621785 (D.C. Cir. Dec. 20, 2012) (denial of rehearing).

166. *Id.* at *7-8.

167. *Id.* at *15 (Kavanaugh, J., dissenting).

168. *Id.* at *19 (Kavanaugh, J., dissenting).

169. *Id.* at *21 (Kavanaugh, J., dissenting).

170. *Id.* at *3 (Sentelle, C.J.).

171. *Id.* at *1 (Sentelle, C.J.).

172. *Id.* at *2 (Sentelle, C.J.)

173. *Utility Air Regulatory Group v. EPA*, 134 S. Ct. 418 (2013).

174. EPA, Action To Ensure Authority To Issue Permits Under the Prevention of Significant Deterioration Program to Sources of Greenhouse Gas Emissions: Finding of Substantial Inadequacy and SIP Call; Proposed Rule, 75 Fed. Reg. 53,892 (Sept. 2, 2010).

175. The 13 states are: Alaska, Arizona, Arkansas, California, Connecticut, Florida, Idaho, Kansas, Kentucky, Nebraska, Nevada, Oregon, and Texas. *Id.* at 53,899, Table IV-1.

176. *Id.* at 53,896.

177. *Id.*

178. Action To Ensure Authority To Issue Permits Under the Prevention of Significant Deterioration Program to Sources of Greenhouse Gas Emissions: Federal Implementation Plan; Proposed Rule, 75 Fed. Reg. 53,883 (Sept. 2, 2010).

179. Action To Ensure Authority To Issue Permits Under the Prevention of Significant Deterioration Program to Sources of Greenhouse Gas Emissions: Finding of Substantial Inadequacy and SIP Call; Final Rule, 75 Fed. Reg. 77,698 (Dec. 13, 2010).

180. *Id.* at 77,705. The seven states are: Arizona, Arkansas, Florida, Idaho, Kansas, Oregon, and Wyoming.

181. *Id.* at 77,717.

182. *Id.* at 77,705.

183. *Id.* at 77,716.

184. *Id.* at 77,700.

185. Action To Ensure Authority To Issue Permits Under the Prevention of Significant Deterioration Program to Sources of Greenhouse Gas Emissions: Finding of Failure To Submit State Implementation Plan Revisions Required for Greenhouse Gases; Final Rule, 75 Fed. Reg. 81,874 (Dec. 29, 2010).

186. Action To Ensure Authority To Issue Permits Under the Prevention of Significant Deterioration Program to Sources of Greenhouse Gas Emissions: Federal Implementation Plan; Final Rule, 75 Fed. Reg. 82,246 (Dec. 30, 2010).

187. Determinations Concerning Need for Error Correction, Partial Approval and Partial Disapproval, and Federal Implementation Plan Regarding Texas Prevention of Significant Deterioration Program; Proposed Rule, 75 Fed. Reg. 82,365 (Dec. 30, 2010).

188. Determinations Concerning Need for Error Correction, Partial Approval and Partial Disapproval, and Federal Implementation Plan Regarding Texas Prevention of Significant Deterioration Program; Interim Final Rule, 75 Fed. Reg. 82,430 (Dec. 30, 2010).

189. *Id.* at 82,431.

190. *Id.*

191. Determinations Concerning Need for Error Correction, Partial Approval and Partial Disapproval, and Federal Implementation Plan Regarding Texas's Prevention of Significant Deterioration Program; Final Rule, 76 Fed. Reg. 25,178 (May 3, 2011).

192. *Texas v. EPA*, 726 F.3d 180 (D.C. Cir. 2013).

193. *Id.* at 183.

194. *Id.*

195. *Id.*

196. *Id.* at 200 (Kavanaugh, J., dissenting).

197. *Id.*

198. *Id.* at 204 (Kavanaugh, J., dissenting).

199. *Id.*

200. Amending Order, *Texas v. EPA*, No. 10-1425 (D.C. Cir. Nov. 12, 2013).

201. CAA § 111(b), 42 U.S.C. § 7411(b).

202. *Id.* § 111(a)(2), 42 U.S.C. § 7411(a)(2).

203. EPA, Standards of Performance for Electric Utility Steam Generating Units for Which Construction Is Commenced After September 18, 1978; Standards of Performance for Industrial-Commercial-Institutional Steam Generating Units, and Small Industrial-Commercial-Institutional Steam Generating Units; and Standards of Performance for Small Industrial-Commercial-Institutional Steam Generating Units; Final Rule; Amendments, 71 Fed. Reg. 9866 (Feb. 27, 2006).

204. *Id.* at 9869.

205. EPA, Standards of Performance for Petroleum Refineries; Final Rule, 73 Fed. Reg. 35,838 (June 24, 2008).

206. *New York v. EPA*, No. 06-1322 (D.C. Cir. Sept. 13, 2006) (challenge to EGU NSPS); *Am. Petroleum Institute v. EPA*, No. 08-1277 (D.C. Cir.) (challenge to petroleum refinery NSPS).

207. Order, *New York v. EPA*, No. 06-1322 (D.C. Cir. Sept. 24, 2007) (*per curiam* order remanding to EPA)).

208. Order, *Am. Petroleum Institute v. EPA*, No. 08-1277 (D.C. Cir. Dec. 15, 2008) (holding cases in abeyance).

209. Proposed Settlement Agreement by and between Petitioners and EPA at 3-4 (last dated Dec. 21, 2010), http://www.epa.gov/carbonpollutionstandard/ settlement.html

(settlement involving EGUs); Proposed Settlement Agreement by and between Petitioners and EPA at 4-5 (last dated Dec. 21, 2010) http://www.epa.gov/carbonpollutionstandard/settlement.html (settlement involv-ing petroleum refineries).

210. EPA, Standards of Performance for Greenhouse Gas Emissions for New Stationary Sources: Electric Utility Generating Units; Proposed Rule, 77 Fed. Reg. 22,392 (Apr. 13, 2012).

211. *Id.* at 22,406.

212. *Id.* at 22,395, 22,421.

213. *Id.* at 22,405, 22,436.

214. *Id.* at 22,394.

215. *Id.* at 22,398.

216. *Id.*

217. *Id.* at 22,406.

218. This is sometimes also referred to as carbon capture and sequestration. The terms are used interchangeably.

219. CAA § 111(a)(2), 42 U.S.C. § 7411(a)(2).

220. Order Granting Motions to Dismiss, *Las Brisas Energy Center v. EPA*, No. 12-1248 (and consolidated cases) (D.C. Cir. Dec. 13, 2012) ("The challenged proposed rule is not final agency action subject to judicial review.").

221. Under the Clean Air Act, NSPS are to be finalized within one year from the date of publication of the proposed NSPS in the Federal Register. CAA § 111(a)(2), 42 U.S.C. § 7411(a)(2).

222. The President's Climate Action Plan, Executive Office of the President (June 2013), *available at* http://www.whitehouse.gov/sites/default/files/image/ president27sclimateactionplan.pdf (June 2013).

223. Standards of Performance for Greenhouse Gas Emissions From New Stationary Sources: Electric Utility Generating Units; Proposed Rule, 79 Fed. Reg. 1430 (Jan. 8, 2014).

224. *Id.* at 1433.

225. *Id.*

226. *Id.* at 1433, 1434, 1435 n.8, 1446 n.83, 1461-62.

227. Withdrawal of Proposed Standards of Performance for Greenhouse Gas Emissions From New Stationary Sources: Electric Utility Generating Units, 79 Fed. Reg. 1352 (Jan. 8, 2014).

228. 79 Fed. Reg. at 1432.

229. *Id.* at 1487, 1489.

230. The above interpretation of section 111(d) is how the statute has traditionally been interpreted by EPA. A legal argument exists, however, that section 111(d) does not apply to *source categories* that are regulated under section 112 (rather than *hazardous air pollutants* regulated under that provision). This issue has never been resolved by a court.

231. State Plans for the Control of Certain Pollutants From Existing Facilities, 40 Fed. Reg. 53,340 (Nov. 17, 1975).

232. SIPs are discussed in more detail in Chapter 2.

233. EPA, Considerations in the Design of a Program to Reduce Carbon Pollution from Existing Power Plants (Sept. 23, 2013), *available at* http://www2.epa.gov/sites/production/files/2013-09/documents/20130923statequestions.pdf.

234. *See* EPA, Outreach on Reducing Carbon Pollution from Existing Power Plants, http://www2.epa.gov/carbon-pollution-standards/outreach-reducing-carbon-pollution-existing-power-plants.

235. Petition to Establish National Pollutant Limits for Greenhouse Gases Pursuant to the Clean Air Act (Dec. 2, 2009), *available at* http://www.biological diversity.org/programs/climate_law_institute/global_warming_litigation/clean_air_act/pdfs/Petition_GHG_pollution_cap_12-2-2009.pdf.

236. The NAAQS program is discussed in detail in Chapter 2.

237. Institute for Policy Integrity at New York University School of Law, Petition for Rulemakings and Call for Information under Section 115, Title VI, Section 111, and Title II of the Clean Air Act to Regulate Greenhouse Gas Emissions (Feb. 19, 2013), *available at* http://policyintegrity.org/what-we-do/update/epa-petition-to-curb-greenhouse-gas-emissions/.

238. *Id.* at 18.

239. *Id.*

240. *Id.* at 30.

241. *Id.* at 1.

242. *Id.* at 15.

243. *Id.* at 2.

244. *Id.* at 31

245. *Id.*

Chapter 8

MOBILE SOURCES

The reach of the Clean Air Act is perhaps at its broadest with respect to the regulation of mobile sources of air pollution. Although the regime principally focuses on motor vehicles, it extends far beyond them. Almost any mobile source, no matter how big or how small, potentially falls within EPA's regulatory domain. The list of regulated mobile sources is both extensive and impressive, including cars, trucks, buses, motorcycles, construction equipment, off-road recreational vehicles, locomotives, aircraft, marine vessels, and lawn and garden equipment.

The source of EPA's authority to regulate mobile sources is Title II of the Act, which essentially establishes two different forms of regulation. The first form of regulation involves the establishment of performance standards for emissions from the subset of mobile sources considered to be significant sources of air pollution. These standards limit the amount of certain pollutants that can be emitted by the source. The pollutants typically covered by these emission standards are carbon monoxide, volatile organic carbons ("VOCs"), nitrogen oxides ("NOx"), and particulate matter ("PM"). In recent years, EPA has also begun to regulate greenhouse gas emissions from mobile sources, including carbon dioxide, methane, nitrous oxide, and hydrofluorocarbons. The emission standards for mobile sources, usually expressed in terms of a mass of emissions per unit measurement (*e.g.*, grams per mile), are technology-forcing. Emission control systems consist of several components, which, for cars and light trucks, generally include three-way catalytic converters, on-board diagnostic computers, and oxygen sensors. As emission standards are tightened, these and other emission-related components must be developed or improved.

The second form of regulation involves the fuels upon which mobile sources operate. The purpose of the fuel provisions is twofold. They are designed either to (1) reduce further the emission of various pollutants from mobile sources; or (2) require an assessment of the public health implications of the fuel's use. If information indicates that a particular fuel can result in emission reductions, the use of the fuel in certain mobile sources can be mandated. Conversely, if information indicates that the fuel will adversely affect the operation of emission control systems or present a significant risk to public health, the use of the fuel can be limited or prohibited.

The discussion below tracks these two forms of regulation. The first section provides an overview of the mobile source emission standards either developed or proposed by EPA. The focus of this section is on the cross-cutting, common elements of the various emission control programs EPA has developed for each category of mobile sources. The second section, which focuses on fuel regulation, summarizes a series of complex regulations developed by EPA to regulate the composition of gasoline and other fuels and to assess their potential impact on public health.

Mobile Source Emission Standards

Primary Contributors: Cars and Light Trucks

The principal focus of the mobile source regulatory program has long been the control of emissions from cars and light trucks, the primary contributors to mobile source pollution.[1] The basic framework for this regulatory program was laid out in the 1970 Clean Air Act. In the 1990 amendments to the Clean Air Act, this framework was largely retained but was revised to be substantially more prescriptive and stringent.

EPA's general authority to regulate mobile sources comes from section 202(a) of the Act, which directs the Administrator to prescribe "standards applicable to the emission of any air pollutant from any class or classes of new motor vehicles or new motor vehicle engines, which in his judgment cause, or contribute to, air pollution which may reasonably be anticipated to endanger public health or welfare."[2] These standards are to be applicable for the entire "useful life" of the vehicle, as determined by the Administrator.[3] Mobile source standards promulgated under section 202(a) are intended to be technology-forcing, but feasible: EPA must allow sufficient time for the "development and application of the requisite technology" before such standards take effect, considering the cost of compliance within that period.[4] To support its prediction that its standards are feasible, EPA must "answer[] any theoretical objections . . . , identif[y] the major steps necessary in refinement of the [technology], and offer[] plausible reasons for believing that each of those steps can be completed in the time available."[5]

The 1990 Clean Air Act amendments specified detailed emission standards for "light-duty vehicles" (*i.e.*, cars) and "light-duty trucks" (*i.e.*, light trucks) to be phased in beginning with model year 1994.[6] These standards are commonly known as the "Tier 1" standards. In addition, the amendments laid out a framework for EPA to adopt more stringent "Tier 2" standards for model years 2004 and later. Congress directed EPA to study whether further emission reductions would be required from light-duty vehicles and certain light-duty trucks in order to attain or maintain the national ambient air quality standards.[7] Based on this study, EPA was required to promulgate more stringent standards if: (1) further emission reductions were needed; (2) the necessary technology would be available, considering the costs, lead time, energy, and safety impacts; and (3) further reductions would be cost-effective.[8]

EPA submitted the required study to Congress in 1998 concluding that all three criteria were satisfied.[9] In 2000, the Agency promulgated Tier 2 standards for light-duty vehicles and trucks to be phased in beginning with model year 2004.[10] EPA was able to adopt substantially more stringent emission limitations due to advances in control technologies and EPA's simultaneous adoption of limits on the content of sulfur in gasoline, which interferes with the effectiveness of these technologies.[11] This "system" approach, in which the engine and its fuel are regulated together, has been a fundamental part of EPA's recent mobile source standards. The Tier 2 standards establish a system of certification "bins," each with its own set of increasingly stringent emission requirements.[12] Manufacturers have the choice to certify particular vehicles to any one of these bins, but must meet a fleetwide average NOx standard.[13] In addition, EPA expanded its emission standards to include a new class of "medium-duty passenger vehicles," such as minivans and sport utility vehicles, which had previously been subject to less stringent limitations.[14]

In May 2013, EPA took further steps to limit emissions from mobile sources by proposing Tier 3 standards for light-duty vehicles and trucks beginning in model year 2017.[15] Unlike the Tier 2 standards, which were guided by strict directions from Congress, the proposed new Tier 3 limits are based on EPA's general authority over mobile source emissions under section 202(a). Like the Tier 2 standards, the Tier 3 proposal relies on a "system" approach, in which EPA regulates both the vehicle's emissions and the content of the fuel used to simultaneously reduce the sulfur content of fuels and thereby make the proposed emission standards feasible. EPA estimates that its proposed Tier 3 standards for light-duty vehicles and trucks and medium-duty passenger vehicles would reduce fleet average emissions of non-methane organic gases and NOx by 80 percent and reduce per-vehicle PM emissions by 70 percent.[16]

In addition to limits on tailpipe emissions generally, EPA also operates several other regulatory programs addressing pollutants from mobile sources. Sections 202(a)(6) and 202(k) require the control of evaporative emissions from fuel during refueling, running, and nonoperation.[17] In response to these provisions, EPA promulgated rules requiring onboard vapor recovery systems to address evaporative emissions from refueling[18] and adopted new test procedures for other evaporative emissions.[19] The Agency has adopted special limits for emissions of carbon monoxide at temperatures below 20 degrees Fahrenheit because of research showing that such emissions are significantly higher at very cold temperatures.[20] In addition, pursuant to Congress's mandate in section 202(m), EPA requires manufacturers to install onboard diagnostics systems on light-duty vehicles and trucks to assess whether a vehicle's emissions control equipment is functioning properly.[21]

More recently, EPA has significantly expanded the scope of its mobile source regulatory regime by promulgating standards for the emission of greenhouse gases. In 2010, EPA adopted its first suite of greenhouse gas emission standards for light-duty vehicles and trucks for model years 2012 through 2016.[22] In 2012, the Agency followed up these first-time greenhouse gas emission standards with a set of more stringent greenhouse gas emission standards for model years 2017 through 2025.[23] EPA's mobile source greenhouse gas standards are also discussed in Chapter 7 on Climate Change.

Heavy-Duty Vehicles and Engines

Heavy-duty vehicles and engines, such as large trucks and buses, are regulated under a scheme similar to that for light-duty vehicles and trucks. Emission standards for these mobile sources must reflect "the greatest degree of emission reduction achievable through the application of technology which the Administrator determines will be available for the model year to which such standards apply," considering cost, energy, and safety.[24] In adopting these standards, EPA may differentiate heavy-duty vehicles or engines into classes based on gross vehicle weight, horsepower, type of fuel used, or other factors.[25] EPA allows manufacturers to comply with these standards by averaging emissions across different engine families or by banking emission credits.[26]

As with the standards for light-duty vehicles and trucks, the 1990 Clean Air Act amendments led EPA to significantly tighten its requirements for heavy-duty vehicles and engines. The first round of new emission standards for these mobile sources imposed new standards for NOx emissions from new heavy-duty trucks for model years 1998 and later.[27] EPA followed up with stricter emission standards for heavy-duty diesel engines starting in model year 2004[28] and for heavy-duty gasoline engines in model year 2005.[29]

In 2001, EPA adopted a set of substantially tighter emission limitations for heavy-duty vehicles known as the Phase 2 rule.[30] Like the Tier 2 standards for light-duty vehicles and trucks, the Phase 2 rule relied on the "system" approach to make its significant further cuts in tailpipe emissions achievable by simultaneously requiring reductions in the sulfur content of diesel fuel. The new standards were phased in beginning in model year 2007 for diesel engines and 2008 for gasoline engines.

Further limits on certain heavy-duty vehicle emissions are included in EPA's proposed Tier 3 regulations.[31] The proposed standards would apply to heavy-duty vehicles and engines under 14,000 pounds gross vehicle weight rating ("GVWR") beginning in model year 2018. EPA estimates that these limits would reduce emissions of PM and combined NOx and non-methane organic gases from such sources by 60 percent compared to the Phase 2 standards.[32]

Over time, EPA has also extended numerous supplemental requirements applicable to light-duty vehicles and trucks to include heavy-duty vehicles. For example, in 2000 EPA promulgated a rule requiring onboard diagnostics systems for heavy-duty vehicles and engines under 14,000 pounds GVWR,[33] and later extended that requirement to the entire heavy-duty fleet.[34] In addition, EPA has promulgated evaporative emission standards for heavy-duty vehicles and engines[35] and requires onboard refueling vapor recovery systems in heavy-duty gasoline vehicles under 10,000 pounds GVWR.[36]

In 2011, EPA adopted greenhouse gas emission standards for heavy-duty vehicles and engines over 8,500 pounds GVWR beginning in model year 2014.[37] These standards are also discussed in Chapter 7.

Nonroad Sources: From Chainsaws and Lawnmowers to Planes and Trains

EPA has developed emission standards for several other mobile sources of air pollution as well, in recognition of their increasing impact on the national emissions inventory. This category of "nonroad engines" includes any internal combustion engine that is not used in a motor vehicle.[38] These "other" sources employ a far more diverse array of engine sizes and specifications, fuel-metering methods, and emission control systems than cars and trucks.

Congress granted EPA the authority to regulate nonroad engines in the 1990 Clean Air Act amendments. Section 213(a) directs EPA to determine whether emissions of carbon monoxide, NOx, and VOCs from nonroad engines are significant contributors to ozone or carbon monoxide concentrations in more than one nonattainment area for those pollutants.[39] If so, EPA must promulgate standards applicable to emissions of those pollutants from the classes of nonroad engines that contribute to such pollution that provide "the greatest degree of emission reduction achievable," considering cost and noise, energy, and safety factors.[40] EPA published the requisite finding in 1994.[41]

EPA may also regulate other pollutants from nonroad engines if they significantly contribute to air pollution that may reasonably be anticipated to endanger public health or welfare.[42] In addition, the Act directs EPA to promulgate emission standards for locomotives[43] and aircraft.[44]

The regulated categories of nonroad engines include construction equipment,[45] off-road recreational vehicles,[46] marine vessels,[47] lawn and garden equipment,[48] locomotives and locomotive engines,[49] and aircraft.[50] Notwithstanding these regulations, which now encompass all nonroad engines, the relative contribution of pollutants from these mobile sources has steadily increased, owing in part to the increasing populations of nonroad engines.

Cross-Cutting Approach to Emission Reductions

Although the emission standards for each mobile source may be different, the primary elements of the regulatory programs that implement and enforce the standards are essentially the same. Each program contains three core components: (1) certification; (2) assembly line testing; and (3) in-use testing and recall authority.[51] These components are designed to ensure compliance by the source with the applicable emission standards over the life cycle of the source.

Certification

Certification refers to a process in which manufacturers of the regulated mobile source demonstrate to EPA's satisfaction that a prototype engine will meet applicable emission control standards. The process occurs in advance of full-scale production of the mobile source, whether it be a leaf blower or a bulldozer. Based on test procedures established by EPA, the manufacturer submits detailed information about the design, operation, and emission performance of the regulated source in an application for certification. If the manufacturer meets the specified requirements, EPA issues a "certificate of conformity" signi-

230 • CHAPTER 8

fying that the source complies with applicable emission standards. Once the manufacturer obtains the necessary certification, full-scale production can begin. The sale of sources not covered by a certificate of conformity is strictly prohibited, punishable by a fine of up to $37,500 per day of violation.[52]

The test procedures used in the certification process have been the subject of substantial attention and revision. Since 1999, test procedures for motor vehicles, for example, have been promulgated, challenged, vacated, revised, then challenged again. Prior to 1999, EPA had imposed a relatively proscriptive series of test procedures to be used in the motor vehicle certification process. To demonstrate the long-term durability of emission control systems, manufacturers were required to accumulate a substantial amount of mileage on a prototype vehicle over a prescribed standard road cycle, then to test that vehicle's emissions at periodic intervals.[53] As time passed, however, EPA became increasingly concerned that this fixed cycle was too expensive, too time-consuming, and too outdated.[54] The Agency therefore began to vest manufacturers with increasing discretion to determine what test procedures to use to demonstrate compliance with emission standards.[55] Eventually, this trend manifested itself in what is commonly referred to as the "CAP2000" rule, which allowed manufacturers to customize their own test procedures, subject to EPA approval.[56]

Soon after CAP2000's issuance, however, a fuel additive manufacturer petitioned for its review on the basis that it did not comport with EPA's statutory obligation to establish test procedures "by regulation."[57] In 2002, the D.C. Circuit agreed and vacated the CAP2000 program, prompting EPA to respond with yet another revision to the test procedures.[58] The revised procedures, in turn, were again challenged in the D.C. Circuit.[59] That case is currently being held in abeyance pending EPA's response to the petitioner's administrative petition for reconsideration of the revised procedures.[60]

Assembly Line Testing

Because the certification process focuses on the performance of a prototype engine, EPA has established a program to ensure that the sources actually coming off the assembly line also conform to emission standards. In the case of motor vehicles, section 206(b) authorizes EPA to test, or to require manufacturers to test, samples of new vehicles or engines covered by a certificate of conformity.[61] EPA implements this mandate through the "selective enforcement audit" or "SEA" program, which allows the Agency to sample randomly motor vehicle assembly lines using specified test procedures.[62] If a sufficient sampling fails to comply with applicable emission standards, EPA can suspend or revoke the applicable certificate of conformity, forcing the manufacturer to remedy related deficiencies before it can be reinstated. Although EPA appears to be reducing its reliance on SEAs in favor of in-use testing,[63] the program may continue to serve a deterrent value, spurring manufacturers to perform their own self-audits to ensure compliance. Somewhat surprisingly, however, EPA's regulations allow up to 40 percent of vehicles to fail emission standards before the certificate of conformity will be suspended or revoked.[64]

In-Use Testing and Recall Authority

The Clean Air Act typically requires manufacturers of regulated mobile sources to design and produce sources that will remain in compliance with emission standards throughout their useful lives, or else face potential recall. The "useful life" is an administratively defined period of source operation during which the source is subject to emission control standards.[65] The useful life for a car, for example, is 10 years or 120,000 miles of operation, whichever is reached first.[66] If in-use testing indicates a problem with the emissions performance of a particular make and model within this period, then it may be subject to recall by EPA. As provided in section 207(c)(1):

> If the Administrator determines that a substantial number of any class or category of vehicles or engines, although properly maintained and used, do not conform to [emission standards] when in actual use throughout their useful life . . . he shall immediately notify the manufacturer thereof of such nonconformity, and he shall require the manufacturer to submit a plan for remedying the nonconformity . . . .[67]

Courts have interpreted the requirement of a "substantial number" of nonconforming vehicles to mean "any number large enough to show that a 'systematic or pervasive problem in a particular class or category of vehicles' exists."[68] A "plan for remedying the nonconformity" must include, among other things, a description of how the vehicle owners subject to the recall will be notified and a description of the specific remedial measures to be undertaken at the manufacturer's expense.[69]

Most emission-related motor vehicle recalls, however, are now executed voluntarily by manufacturers in connection with EPA's "in-use verification program" ("IUVP"). The IUVP is the primary program by which EPA implements its recall authority. The IUVP requires manufacturers to conduct their own in-use emissions performance testing[70] and to report the results of such testing to EPA.[71] Manufacturers that discover potential noncompliance issues or defects during IUVP testing often initiate voluntary recalls to circumvent, among other things, an EPA-mandated recall. Voluntary recalls play a key role in mobile source enforcement. In 2009, manufacturers voluntarily recalled over 2.6 million vehicles targeting 39 different emission-related problems,[72] up from 1 million recalls targeting 44 emission-related problems in the previous year.[73]

State Regulatory Authority: California and the Preemption Waiver

The preemptive scope of the Clean Air Act's regulatory regime for mobile sources is unique from any other program in the Act. Although section 209 broadly and explicitly preempts any state regulation of mobile sources, it simultaneously provides a highly deferential waiver of that prohibition for the state of California.[74] California was leading national efforts to regulate motor vehicle emissions long before the adoption of the Clean Air Act. In recognition of the state's "pioneering efforts" in emission control,[75] Congress directed EPA to waive the Act's preemptive effect with regard to mobile source standards adopted by California if the state submits a request and determines that its standards "will be, in the aggregate, at least as protective of public health and welfare as applicable Federal standards."[76] Where such a waiver is granted, EPA must treat compliance with the California standard as compliance with applicable federal standards.[77] As a result of this dual system of regulatory authority, motor vehicle manufacturers face the prospect of having to produce a "second vehicle" for each model: one for sale in California that will comply with its state standards, and one for sale in the rest of the United States that will comply with federal mobile source standards.

Courts have recognized that the purpose of the Act's waiver provision is "to afford California the broadest possible discretion in selecting the best means to protect the health of its citizens and the public welfare."[78] Traditionally, EPA has granted California substantial discretion to develop its own regulatory regime for mobile sources. Section 209(b) permits EPA to deny a preemption waiver only in very limited circumstances, including if California's determination that its standards are at least as protective as the federal standards is arbitrary and capricious.[79] The most notable recent example of EPA's deferential approach is the Agency's 2009 approval of a waiver for California's mobile source greenhouse gas regulations.[80]

In addition, Congress allows other states containing nonattainment areas to opt into California's regime under section 177.[81] Any state standards adopted under section 177 must be completely identical to their California counterparts in order to avoid requiring manufacturers to produce a "third vehicle."[82] Several states have availed themselves of the section 177 authority for various California emission requirements, including Connecticut, Maryland, Maine, Massachusetts, New Jersey, New York, Pennsylvania, Rhode Island, Vermont, and Washington.[83]

The Regulation of Fuels

A comprehensive framework governing both mobile sources and the fuels upon which they operate is essential for a sound regulatory program. According to EPA, "[t]he systems approach of combining the engine and fuel standards into a single program is critical to the success of our overall efforts to reduce emissions, because the emission standards will not be feasible without the fuel change."[84] The emission products of fuels and fuel additives can not only impair the efficacy of emission control systems, but can independently cause or contribute to tailpipe emissions. EPA's fuel regulations therefore impact nearly every aspect of fuel production and use in the United States. The bulk of EPA's authority to regulate fuels arises under section 211.[85]

Registration and Testing

Section 211(a) requires the "registration" of "designated" fuels and fuel additives prior to introduction of the fuel or additive into commerce.[86] Designated fuels and fuel additives generally include commercially produced motor vehicle gasoline and diesel fuel and the additives produced or sold for use in them.[87] Registration requires, among other things, the submission of information, including the name of any additive that will or may be used in the fuel, the "range of concentration," "purpose-in-use," and "chemical composition" of any such additive, and the test data and other information required in the testing process.[88]

Section 211(b) requires that designated fuels and fuel additives be tested for registration purposes "to determine potential health and environmental effects of the fuel or additive."[89] The "primary purpose" of this registration program, according to EPA, is "to establish registration requirements which will provide information for identifying and evaluating the potential adverse effects of designated [fuel and fuel additive] emissions and for guiding the direction of related regulatory actions in the future . . . ."[90] The regulations that implement section

211(b) set forth three tiers of testing, each of which is designed to assess whether the combustion or evaporative emissions of the fuels and fuel additives present a significant risk to public health:

- Tier 1 requires the fuel or fuel additive manufacturer to conduct tests to characterize the nature of the emissions (both combustion and evaporative) associated with use of the fuel or fuel additive, and to perform a literature search on health and welfare effects.[91]
- Tier 2 sets forth a battery of biological testing for specific health effect endpoints, including carcinogenic or mutagenic effects, teratogenic and reproductive effects, general toxicity and pulmonary effects, and neurotoxic effects.[92] EPA may, at its discretion, require Alternative Tier 2 testing[93] in lieu of the standard Tier 2 if EPA concludes that, among other things: (1) available information caused EPA to be concerned about "potential health effects unrelated to an endpoint not specifically addressed in Tier 2"; or (2) EPA identifies a "potentially significant public health risk related to a Tier 2 endpoint, such that EPA knows that more definitive testing will be required . . . ."[94]
- Tier 3 testing authorizes EPA to impose additional testing requirements on a case-by-case basis depending upon the results of testing from Tiers 1 and 2.[95] According to EPA, a decision to impose testing under its Tier 3 authority requires the exercise of "expert scientific judgment" and depends upon "the availability of adequate data to enable a health risk evaluation and the need for more definitive information for developing regulatory decisions."[96] The scope of Tier 3 tests is determined at EPA's discretion as well.

To alleviate some of the burden associated with the health effects testing regulations, EPA developed a framework that allows manufacturers of similar fuel products to "group" their resources to conduct the necessary testing.[97] EPA's goal was to reduce duplicative testing and to reduce the cost burden for individual fuel product manufacturers.

Controls and Prohibitions

In addition to EPA's "pre-clearance" authority under section 211(a) and (b), EPA has a broad grant of authority under section 211(c) to control or prohibit the use of certain fuels or fuel additives. As interpreted by EPA, the Agency's authority to control or prohibit the use of certain fuels or fuel additives "must be read in conjunction with" its testing authority.[98] As a result, "[t]he purpose of obtaining data on fuels and fuel additives is," according to EPA, "to provide a basis for further risk characterization and possible regulation under section 211(c)."[99] Section 211(c) provides EPA with the authority to control or prohibit the use of fuels or fuel additives based on either of two criteria:

- "[I]f, in the judgment of the Administrator, any . . . emission product of [a] fuel or fuel additive causes, or contributes, to air pollution or water pollution . . . that may reasonably be anticipated to endanger the public health or welfare"; or

- "[I]f emission products of [a] fuel or fuel additive will impair to a significant degree the performance of any emission control device or system which is in general use, or which the Administrator finds has been developed to a point where in a reasonable time it would be in general use were such regulation to be promulgated."[100]

EPA has availed itself of its section 211(c) authority in the context of lead and sulfur, among other pollutants. The steps taken to control lead have been a true success story. By EPA estimates, U.S. blood-lead levels decreased 78 percent from 1978 to 1991 as a result of EPA-imposed fuel controls, five years before the statutory prohibition on leaded gasoline set forth in section 211(n) even took effect.[101] More recently, EPA has been aggressively targeting sulfur in fuels as a key part of its "system" approach to limiting mobile source emissions, based on the Agency's finding that "gasoline sulfur degrades the effectiveness of catalytic converters" and that "high sulfur levels in commercial gasoline could affect the ability of future automobiles – especially those designed for very low emissions – to meet more stringent standards in use."[102] The current gasoline sulfur standards impose an annual average standard of 30 parts per million ("ppm") and a per-gallon cap of 80 ppm.[103] EPA's proposed Tier 3 rule would require further cuts in gasoline sulfur content by lowering the annual average standard to 10 ppm beginning in 2017 for large refiners and 2020 for small refiners.[104]

The Reformulated Gasoline and Anti-Dumping Programs

Faced with the repeated difficulties that metropolitan areas were experiencing in meeting air quality goals, Congress established the Reformulated Gasoline ("RFG") and Anti-Dumping programs in the 1990 Clean Air Act amendments.[105] The RFG program seeks to improve air quality by requiring refiners to reformulate the gasoline used in certain areas to make it burn more completely and, thereby, reduce motor vehicle emissions.[106] The program is based upon the understanding that changes in the composition of the gasoline (*i.e.*, its "reformulation") will reduce emissions of certain "air toxics,"[107] VOCs, and NOx from motor vehicles.[108] To achieve the goal of cleaner burning gasoline, section 211(k) imposes both composition and performance requirements for RFG. Conversely, the companion Anti-Dumping program prohibits refiners, blenders, and importers from "dumping" relatively dirtier fuel components generated from the production of RFG into "conventional" gasoline sold in all other areas of the nation not using RFG.[109]

The RFG program, which commenced January 1, 1995, imposes VOC and air toxics standards based on either a fuel formula or an emission reduction performance standard.[110] The fuel formula includes controls on benzene and aromatic hydrocarbons, a lead prohibition, and a requirement to add detergents to prevent the accumulation of deposits in engines or vehicle fuel supply systems. The emission reduction performance standard requires the aggregate emissions of ozone-forming VOCs and air toxics from baseline vehicles when using RFG to be 25 percent below (on a mass basis) the aggregate emissions of these materials from vehicles using conventional gasoline. EPA has the discretion to provide for a lesser (but not below 20 percent) or greater reduction based on "technological feasibility" and "considering the cost of achieving such reductions in VOC emissions."[111]

To achieve these targets, EPA developed two statistical "models" to be used by refiners to evaluate how changes in the composition of the gasoline they produce will affect motor vehicle emissions. The first model, applicable in the early years of the program, is known as the "simple model."[112] The second model, applicable today, is known as the "complex model."[113] EPA developed both models after extensive discussions with fuel and fuel additive manufacturers, the automotive industry, and several other stakeholders based on emission data derived from extensive vehicle testing using a wide range of different fuel parameters. Using these models, a refiner can mix and match different fuel parameters in keeping with refiner-specific technological and economic constraints to achieve the RFG emission reduction targets in a cost-effective manner. The models allow the formula for RFG to vary from one refiner to the next so long as the underlying emission reduction targets are achieved.

RFG "covered areas" include the nation's nine largest metropolitan areas with the most severe summertime ozone levels.[114] Congress also authorized certain other areas to "opt-in" to the RFG program, provided those areas were classified as marginal, moderate, serious, or severe ozone nonattainment areas.[115] As of July 2013, certain counties in the following states are included in the RFG program: California, Connecticut, Delaware, Illinois, Indiana, Kentucky, Maryland, Massachusetts, Missouri, New Hampshire, New Jersey, New York, Pennsylvania, Rhode Island, Texas, Virginia, and Wisconsin.[116] The District of Columbia is also part of the program.[117]

The Anti-Dumping program, which applies everywhere else in the country, was essentially designed to protect conventional gasoline from the potential adverse impacts associated with the RFG refining process. Section 211(k)(8) directs that motor vehicle emissions associated with the use of conventional gasoline after January 1, 1995, must meet refiner-specific "baseline" emission standards attributable to gasoline sold in the year 1990.[118] EPA's regulations direct refiners to apply statistical models corresponding to the simple and complex models to calculate both their 1990 baseline emission limitations for conventional gasoline and subsequent compliance with those standards for all conventional gasoline produced after January 1, 1995.

Renewable Fuels Mandate

With the enactment of the Energy Policy Act of 2005, Congress wrought considerable changes in fuel and fuel additive regulation by introducing a national renewable fuels mandate, which was incorporated into the Clean Air Act as section 211(o).[119] In its original version, the renewable fuel standard ("RFS") program required that a minimum volume of renewable fuel be used in gasoline sold in the United States each year, ramping up from 4 billion gallons in 2006 to 7.5 billion gallons in 2012.[120] In the Energy Independence and Security Act of 2007, Congress strengthened the RFS program by substantially increasing the volumes of renewable fuel required to be used each year, extending the time frame over which those volumes ramp up through at least 2022, differentiating renewable fuels into four nested categories, and expanding the program to cover nearly all transportation fuels.[121] To carry out the program's mandate, EPA must determine and publish the applicable renewable fuel obligation for fuel refineries, blenders, and importers for each calendar year by November 30 of the preceding year, expressed as a volume percentage of transportation fuel sold or introduced into commerce in the United States.[122] EPA has the discretion to waive the mandate if the Agency determines that it would "severely harm the economy or environment" or that there is an "inadequate domestic supply."[123]

The RFS program is discussed in greater detail in Chapter 7 on Climate Change. EPA's implementation of the program has been the subject of significant controversy as the Agency's annual renewable fuel obligations have routinely exceeded the production capacity of the nation's renewable fuel suppliers.

Notes

1. The regulations controlling emissions from cars and light trucks are located at 40
2. CAA § 202(a)(1), 42 U.S.C. § 7521(a)(1).
3. *Id.*
4. *Id.* § 202(a)(2), 42 U.S.C. § 7521(a)(2).
5. *Natural Res. Def. Council v. EPA*, 655 F.2d 318, 332 (D.C. Cir. 1981).
6. CAA § 202(g), (h), 42 U.S.C. § 7521(g), (h).
7. *Id.* § 202(i)(1), (2), 42 U.S.C. § 7521(i)(1), (2).
8. *Id.* § 202(i)(3)(C), 42 U.S.C. § 7521(i)(3)(C).
9. EPA, EPA 420-R-98-008, Tier 2 Report to Congress (July 31, 1998).
10. EPA, Control of Air Pollution From New Motor Vehicles: Tier 2 Motor Vehicle Emissions Standards and Gasoline Sulfur Control Requirements, 65 Fed. Reg. 6698 (Feb. 10, 2000).
11. EPA's regulation of fuel content is addressed in Section II below.
12. 40 C.F.R. § 86.1811-04(c)(6).
13. *Id.* § 86.1811-04(d).
14. 65 Fed. Reg. at 6751.
15. EPA, Control of Air Pollution From Motor Vehicles: Tier 3 Motor Vehicle Emission and Fuel Standards, 78 Fed. Reg. 29,816 (May 21, 2013).
16. *Id.* at 29,819.
17. CAA § 202(a)(6), (k), 42 U.S.C. § 7521(a)(6), (k).
18. EPA, Control of Air Pollution From New Motor Vehicles and New Motor Vehicle Engines; Refueling Emission Regulations for Light-Duty Vehicles and Light-Duty Trucks, 59 Fed. Reg. 16,262 (Apr. 6, 1994).
19. EPA, Control of Air Pollution From New Motor Vehicles and New Motor Vehicle Engines; Evaporative Emission Regulations for Gasoline- and Methanol-Fueled Light-Duty Vehicles, Light-Duty Trucks and Heavy-Duty Vehicles, 58 Fed. Reg. 16,002 (Mar. 24, 1993).
20. CAA § 202(j), 42 U.S.C. § 7521(j); EPA, Control of Air Pollution From New Motor Vehicles and New Motor Vehicle Engines; Cold Temperature Carbon Monoxide Emissions From 1994 and Later Model Year Gasoline-Fueled Light-Duty Vehicles and Light-Duty Trucks, 57 Fed. Reg. 31,888 (July 17, 1992).
21. CAA § 202(m), 42 U.S.C. § 7521(m); EPA, Control of Air Pollution From New Motor Vehicles and New Motor Vehicle Engines; Regulations Requiring On-Board Diagnostic Systems on 1994 and Later Model Year Light-Duty Vehicles and Light-Duty

Trucks, 58 Fed. Reg. 9468 (Feb. 19, 1993); EPA, Control of Air Pollution From Motor Vehicles and New Motor Vehicle Engines; Modification of Federal Onboard Diagnostic Regulations for Light-Duty Vehicles and Light-Duty Trucks; Extension of Acceptance of California OBD II Requirements, 63 Fed. Reg. 70,681 (Dec. 22, 1998).

22. EPA, Light-Duty Vehicle Greenhouse Gas Emission Standards and Corporate Average Fuel Economy Standards, 75 Fed. Reg. 25,324 (May 7, 2010).

23. EPA, 2017 and Later Model Year Light-Duty Vehicle Greenhouse Gas Emissions and Corporate Average Fuel Economy Standards, 77 Fed. Reg. 62,624 (Oct. 15, 2012).

24. CAA § 202(a)(3), 42 U.S.C. § 7521(a)(3).

25. *Id.* § 202(a)(3)(ii), 42 U.S.C. § 7521(a)(3)(ii).

26. 40 C.F.R. §§ 86.004-15, 86.007-15.

27. EPA, Control of Air Pollution From New Motor Vehicles and New Motor Vehicle Engines; Particulate Emission Regulations for 1993 Model Year Buses, Particulate Emission Regulations for 1994 and Later Model Year Urban Buses, Test Procedures for Urban Buses, and Oxides of Nitrogen Emission Regulations for 1998 and Later Model Year Heavy-Duty Engines, 58 Fed. Reg. 15,781 (Mar. 24, 1993).

28. EPA, Control of Emissions of Air Pollution From Highway Heavy-Duty Engines, 62 Fed. Reg. 54,694 (Oct. 21, 1997).

29. EPA, Control of Emissions of Air Pollution from 2004 and Later Model Year Heavy-Duty Highway Engines and Vehicles; Revision of Light-Duty On-Board Diagnostics Requirements, 65 Fed. Reg. 59,896, 59,926 (Oct. 6, 2000).

30. EPA, Control of Air Pollution from New Motor Vehicles: Heavy-Duty Engine and Vehicle Standards and Highway Diesel Fuel Sulfur Control Requirements, 66 Fed. Reg. 5002 (Jan. 18, 2001).

31. 78 Fed. Reg. at 29,816.

32. *Id.* at 29,819.

33. 65 Fed. Reg. at 59,916, 59,929.

34. EPA, Control of Air Pollution From New Motor Vehicles and New Motor Vehicle Engines; Regulations Requiring Onboard Diagnostic Systems on 2010 and Later Heavy-Duty Engines Used in Highway Applications Over 14,000 Pounds; Revisions to Onboard Diagnostic Requirements for Diesel Highway Heavy-Duty Vehicles Under 14,000 Pounds, 74 Fed. Reg. 8310 (Feb. 24, 2009).

35. 66 Fed. Reg. at 5044.

36. 65 Fed. Reg. at 59,924.

37. EPA, Greenhouse Gas Emissions Standards and Fuel Efficiency Standards for Medium- and Heavy-Duty Engines and Vehicles, 76 Fed. Reg. 57,106 (Sept. 15, 2011).

38. CAA § 216(10), 42 U.S.C. § 7550(10).

39. *Id.* § 213(a), 42 U.S.C. § 7547(a).

40. *Id.* § 213(a)(3), 42 U.S.C. § 7547(a)(3).

41. EPA, Control of Air Pollution; Determination of Significance for Nonroad Sources and Emission Standards for New Nonroad Compression-Ignition Engines At or Above 37 Kilowatts, 59 Fed. Reg. 31,306 (June 17, 1994).

42. CAA § 213(a)(4), 42 U.S.C. § 7547(a)(4).

43. *Id.* § 213(a)(5), 42 U.S.C. § 7547(a)(5).

44. *Id.* § 231, 42 U.S.C. § 7571.

45. 40 C.F.R. pt. 1039; *see also* EPA, Control of Emissions of Air Pollution From Nonroad Diesel Engines and Fuel, 69 Fed. Reg. 38,958 (June 29, 2004).

46. 40 C.F.R. pt. 1051; *see also* EPA, Control of Emissions From Nonroad Large Spark-Ignition Engines, and Recreational Engines (Marine and Land-Based), 67 Fed. Reg. 68,242 (Nov. 8, 2002).

47. 40 C.F.R. pts. 89 & 94; *see also* EPA, Control of Emissions of Air Pollution From Locomotive Engines and Marine Compression-Ignition Engines Less Than 30 Liters per Cylinder; Republication, 73 Fed. Reg. 37,096 (June 30, 2008); EPA, Control of Emissions From Nonroad Spark-Ignition Engines and Equipment, 73 Fed. Reg. 59,034 (Oct. 8, 2008); EPA, Control of Emissions From Nonroad Spark-Ignition Engines and Equipment, 75 Fed. Reg. 22,896 (Apr. 30, 2010).

48. 40 C.F.R. pt. 90; *see also* EPA, Phase 2 Emission Standards for New Nonroad Spark-Ignition Handheld Engines At or Below 19 Kilowatts and Minor Amendments to Emission Requirements Applicable to Small Spark-Ignition Engines and Marine Spark-Ignition Engines, 65 Fed. Reg. 24,268 (Apr. 25, 2000).

49. 40 C.F.R. pt. 92; *see also* EPA, 73 Fed. Reg. at 37,096.

50. 40 C.F.R. pt. 87.

51. EPA establishes emission standards for aircraft, but the Federal Aviation Administration of the U.S. Department of Transportation enforces the standards. For this reason, the regulation of aircraft emission control standards is somewhat different from the other mobile source programs discussed here.

52. CAA § 205(a), 42 U.S.C. § 7524(a); 40 C.F.R. § 19.4.

53. *See, e.g.*, EPA, Emission Durability Procedures for New Light-Duty Vehicles, Light-Duty Trucks and Heavy-Duty Vehicles, 71 Fed. Reg. 2810, 2811 (Jan. 17, 2006) (providing a history of the durability demonstration process).

54. *Id.*

55. *See, e.g.*, Letter from Robert E. Maxwell, Director, EPA Office of Mobile Sources, to automobile manufacturers (July 29, 1994) (providing manufacturers with alternative durability guidance for model years 1994 through 1998).

56. EPA, Control of Air Pollution From New Motor Vehicles; Compliance Programs for New Light-Duty Vehicles and Light-Duty Trucks, 64 Fed. Reg. 23,906 (May 4, 1999) (adopting CAP2000, which established emissions compliance procedures for new light-duty vehicles and trucks).

57. *Ethyl Corp. v. EPA*, 306 F.3d 1144 (D.C. Cir. 2002) (holding that EPA's CAP2000 rulemaking did not satisfy the requirements of section 206(d) of the Act to establish methods and procedures "by regulation").

58. 71 Fed. Reg. at 2810 (revising the methods used to determine emissions deterioration for the purposes of certification in light of the *Ethyl Corp.* decision).

59. *Afton Chem. Corp. v. EPA*, No. 06-1095 (D.C. Cir. filed Mar. 17, 2006).

60. *See* Status Report, *Afton Chem. Corp. v. EPA*, No. 06-1095, Dkt. No. 1444380 (D.C. Cir. filed Mar. 17, 2006).

61. CAA § 206(b), 42 U.S.C. § 7525(b).

62. 40 C.F.R. pt. 86, subpt. G.

63. *See, e.g.*, EPA, Control of Emissions of Air Pollution From New Motor Vehicles: In-Use Testing for Heavy-Duty Diesel Engines and Vehicles, 70 Fed. Reg. 34,594, 34,615 (June 14, 2005) (anticipating that a "robust, mature manufacturer-run in-use program would significantly reduce the role SEA plays in EPA's compliance program").

64. 40 C.F.R. § 86.610-98.

65. *Id.* § 86.1803-01.

66. *Id.* § 86.1805-12.

67. CAA § 207(c)(1), 42 U.S.C. § 7541(c)(1).

68. *Chrysler Corp. v. EPA*, 631 F.2d 865, 891 n.133 (D.C. Cir. 1980).

69. *See* 40 C.F.R. § 85.1803.

70. *See, e.g., id.* § 86.1845-04.

71. *Id.* § 86.1847-01.

72. EPA, Office of Transportation and Air Quality, 2009 Annual Summary of Emission-Related Recall and Voluntary Service Campaigns Performed on Light-Duty Vehicles and Light-Duty Trucks, http://www.epa.gov/otaq/cert/recall/ 420b10007b.pdf (June 2010).

73. EPA, Office of Transportation and Air Quality, 2008 Annual Summary of Emission-Related Recall and Voluntary Service Campaigns Performed on Light-Duty Vehicles and Light-Duty Trucks, http://www.epa.gov/otaq/cert/recall/ 420b09016.pdf (Apr. 2009).

74. CAA § 209(b), 42 U.S.C. § 7543(b).

75. S. REP. NO. 90-403, at 33 (1967).

76. CAA § 209(b)(1), 42 U.S.C. § 7543(b)(1).

77. *Id.* § 209(b)(3), 42 U.S.C. § 7543(b)(3).

78. *Motor & Equip. Mfrs. Ass'n v. EPA*, 627 F.2d 1095, 1110 (D.C. Cir. 1979).

79. CAA § 209(b)(1), 42 U.S.C. § 209(b)(1).

80. EPA, California State Motor Vehicle Pollution Control Standards; Notice of Decision Granting a Waiver of Clean Air Act Preemption for California's 2009 and Subsequent Model Year Greenhouse Gas Emission Standards for New Motor Vehicles, 74 Fed. Reg. 32,744 (July 8, 2009). This grant reversed EPA's original decision to deny California's waiver request. EPA, California State Motor Vehicle Pollution Control Standards; Notice of Decision Denying a Waiver of Clean Air Act Preemption for California's 2009 and Subsequent Model Year Greenhouse Gas Emission Standards for New Motor Vehicles, 73 Fed. Reg. 12,156 (Mar. 6, 2008).

81. CAA § 177, 42 U.S.C. § 7507.

82. *Id.*

83. 78 Fed. Reg. at 29,820 (listing states that have adopted California's Low-Emission Vehicle (LEV III) emissions program).

84. 66 Fed. Reg. at 5005.

85. Other provisions of the Act address fuel issues either directly or indirectly, including section 104 (research relating to fuels and vehicles), section 212 (loans, appropriations, and grants for renewable fuel research and development), and sections 241 to 246 (clean-fueled vehicle fleet requirements for promoting use of "clean" alternative fuels).

86. CAA § 211(a), 42 U.S.C. § 7545(a)(1).

87. 40 C.F.R. §§ 79.30-79.33.

88. *Id.* §§ 79.10-79.24.

89. CAA § 211(b), 42 U.S.C. § 7545(b).

90. EPA, Fuels and Fuel Additives Registration Regulations, 59 Fed. Reg. 33,042 (June 27, 1994).

91. 40 C.F.R. § 79.52.

92. *Id.* § 79.53.

93. *Id.* § 79.58(c).

94. 59 Fed. Reg. at 33,081.

95. 40 C.F.R. § 79.53.

96. 59 Fed. Reg. at 33,082.

97. 40 C.F.R. § 79.56.

98. EPA, Fuels and Fuel Additives Registration Regulations, 57 Fed. Reg. 13,168, 13,173 (Apr. 15, 1992).

99. 59 Fed. Reg. at 33,174.

100. CAA § 211(c)(1), 42 U.S.C. § 7545(c)(1).

101. EPA, EPA-420-R-05-011, Toward A Cleaner Future – Progress Report 2005, at 31 (Nov. 2005).

102. 65 Fed. Reg. at 6703.

103. 40 C.F.R. § 80.195.

104. 78 Fed. Reg. at 29,825.

105. CAA § 211(k), 42 U.S.C. § 7545(k).

106. The requirements of the RFG program are set forth in 40 C.F.R. pt. 80, subpt. D.

107. Air toxics emissions are defined as the emission of benzene, 1,3-butadiene, polycyclic organic matter, acetaldehyde, and formaldehyde. CAA § 211(k)(10)(C), 42 U.S.C. § 7545(k)(10)(C).

108. VOC and NOx emissions can contribute to the formation of ozone, causing certain areas – particularly urban areas – to fall into ozone nonattainment.

109. The requirements of the Anti-Dumping program are set forth in 40 C.F.R. pt. 80, subpt. E.

110. Notably, the RFG program initially contained a two percent oxygen content requirement, which was repealed in the Energy Policy Act of 2005. Although this require-

ment was a core element of the original design of the RFG program, numerous factors – including advanced fuel technologies, a renewable fuels mandate (described below), and groundwater contamination associated with the use of Methyl Tertiary Butyl Ether ("MTBE") (one of the two most predominantly used oxygenates) – led to its eventual repeal. Congress left in place, however, the "Oxyfuels" program set forth in section 211(m), which relies on the use of oxygenated fuels to limit carbon monoxide emissions as opposed to ozone.

111. CAA § 211(k)(3)(B), 42 U.S.C. § 7545(k)(3)(B).

112. *See* 40 C.F.R. § 80.42.

113. *See id.* § 80.45.

114. CAA § 211(k)(10)(D), 42 U.S.C. § 7545(k)(10)(D).

115. *Id.* § 211(k)(6), 42 U.S.C. § 7545(k)(6).

116. 40 C.F.R. § 80.70.

117. *Id.*

118. CAA § 211(k)(8), 42 U.S.C. § 7545(k)(8).

119. Energy Policy Act of 2005, Pub. L. No. 109-58, § 1501, 119 Stat. 594, 1067, 1069 (codified as amended at CAA § 211(o), 42 U.S.C. 7545(o)).

120. *Id.*

121. Energy Independence and Security Act of 2007, Pub. L. No. 110-140, §§ 201-210, 121 Stat. 1492, 1519-32 (codified at CAA § 211(o), 42 U.S.C. § 7545(o)).

122. CAA § 211(o)(3)(B), 42 U.S.C. § 7545(o)(3)(B).

123. *Id.* § 211(o)(7), 42 U.S.C. § 7545(o)(7).

Chapter 9

THE ACID DEPOSITION CONTROL PROGRAM

Title IV of the Clean Air Act ("CAA"), added by the 1990 Amendments, established a sweeping new program to control electric utility emissions of sulfur dioxide ("SO_2") and nitrogen oxides ("NOx"), air pollutants that are believed to be major contributors to acid deposition. Congress designed this title to reduce electric utility SO_2 emissions by ten million tons and achieve substantial reductions in NOx emissions from 1980 levels by the year 2000.[1]

EPA published most of the regulations required for the SO_2 emission reduction program and the acid rain permitting program in 1993 (the "Title IV Core rules").[2] EPA published the principal regulations to implement the NOx program in 1994, 1995, and 1996.[3] The acid rain rules – contained in 40 C.F.R. parts 72 through 78 – have undergone several revisions, particularly on emission monitoring requirements (discussed below).

This chapter first reviews the two-phase program applicable to SO_2 emissions. It then discusses the NOx control requirements of the acid deposition program, the treatment of specific types of utility and non-utility facilities under Title IV, and the permitting and compliance requirements applicable to affected facilities.

SO_2 Emissions Limitations

The basic feature of the Title IV SO_2 program is a system of SO_2 emission allowances, which imposes a cap on total SO_2 emissions from the electric utility industry. Each allowance entitles the allowance holder to emit one ton of SO_2. These allowances can be freely traded among affected facilities and others. The following sections describe the allowance system and how that system is put in place through a two-phase system of SO_2 control.

The Allowance Allocation and Trading System

Allowances

Rather than mandating traditional "command and control" regulation of SO_2, which would dictate absolute emission limits for each regulated source, Title IV provides for a market-based approach to SO_2 emission control. Under this approach, each existing affected facility is allocated a certain number of allowances to emit SO_2 each year, based on a prescribed emission limit. These allowances can be used in that year, saved for future years, or sold to other sources. Thus, allowance holders can buy and sell allowances on the open market, encouraging reduction of emissions in the most cost-effective manner.

Title IV defines an "allowance" as "an authorization, allocated to an affected unit by the Administrator under [Title IV], to emit, during or after a specified calendar year, one ton of sulfur dioxide."[4] (A "unit" is a "fossil fuel-fired combustion device," such as a boiler or a turbine that is connected to an electric generator.[5]) Although allowance holders may not use an allowance before the calendar year for which EPA issued it, allowances can be carried forward and banked for use in future years or sold to others for their use in the future.[6]

Under Title IV, allowance holders may trade allowances freely. Although some proposed versions of the 1990 Amendments considered by Congress would have restricted trading for existing units to allowance holders within two major geographic regions, the enacted statute did not restrict trading in any way.[7] Allowance transfers are not effective, however, until EPA receives and records a written certification of the transfer signed by a responsible official representing each party to the transaction.[8] In addition, allowance holders may transfer allowances before the calendar year in which they become effective even though the allowances may not actually be used before that year.

EPA issued SO_2 emission allowances to affected units in two phases.[9] For Phase I units – units that first became subject to the allowance-holding requirement in 1995 – EPA issued a certain number of annual allowances, as specified in section 404 of the Act. For both Phase I units and Phase II units – units that first became subject to the allowance-holding requirement in 2000 – allowances are allocated for Phase II (2000 and later) according to 28 specific allowance allocation formulas set out in section 405 of the Act. With limited exceptions, only existing affected units (basically, electric utility units that began commercial operation before November 15, 1990) are entitled to allowance allocations; most "new units" (units that commenced commercial operation after November 15, 1990) must acquire allowances in the market.[10] Allowances are allocated to an existing affected unit even if it was removed from commercial operation after November 15, 1990.

Except for 50,000 annual allowances for Phase I units in certain states and up to 530,000 "bonus allowances" annually for 2000-2009 for certain Phase II units, the total number of allowances is limited by statute to 8.9 million each year in Phase II.[11] If the total of annual Phase II allowances that would be provided through application of the statutory allocation formulas would exceed this 8.9 million "cap," EPA must reduce the number of allowances on a pro rata basis; EPA in fact did this when it allocated allowances in 1993.

Title IV specifies that an allowance is not a property right and that "[n]othing in this title or in any other provision of law shall be construed to limit the authority of the United States to terminate or limit such authorization [to emit]."[12] In addition, issuance of allowances in no way alters the compliance requirements imposed under other sections of the Act, including the national ambient air quality standard and state implementation plan programs.

Allowance Trading

Under Title IV, allowance holders can trade allowances without restriction on a nationwide basis.[13] Although EPA may issue allowances only to the owners or operators of affected units, allowances can be transferred to any person, whether or not that person owns or operates an affected unit. The regulations addressing allowance tracking and trading are in 40 C.F.R. part 73.

Allowances may be traded for compliance purposes for a given calendar year as late as 60 days after the end of the year.[14] The purpose of this 60-day "true-up period" following the end of a calendar year is to allow completion of allowance trades after a full year of emissions data has been obtained, thereby permitting determination of each unit's allowance needs for that year.

In keeping with the statutory scheme, EPA's allowance trading rules provide for minimal EPA involvement in allowance transfers, other than the recording and certification functions contemplated by the statute. For example, the price and other terms of allowance transactions need not be disclosed to EPA. In drafting the rules, EPA recognized the importance of fostering the development of an open and flexible allowance market.

Applicability

The Title IV SO_2 requirements apply to affected utility units. An "affected unit" is "a unit that is subject to emission reduction requirements or limitations under this title."[15] The SO_2 allowance program, in turn, applies to "existing" and "new" "utility units." An "existing unit" is "a unit . . . that commenced commercial operation before November 15, 1990."[16] A "new unit" is "a unit that commences commercial operation on or after November 15, 1990."[17] A "utility unit" is "(i) a unit that serves a generator in any State that produces electricity for sale, or (ii) a unit that, during 1985, served a generator in any State that produced electricity for sale."[18]

The statute carves out several exceptions to this general definition. For example, a unit that cogenerates steam and electricity is not a "utility unit" unless the unit supplies more than one-third of its potential electric output capacity and more than 25 MW of electrical output to any utility power distribution system for sale.[19] EPA's rules, at 40 C.F.R. § 72.6, elaborate on these and other applicability requirements, which should be reviewed carefully in individual cases to determine whether Title IV requirements apply to a facility. 40 C.F.R. § 72.6 addresses applicability criteria for various categories of facilities, including cogeneration facilities, independent power production facilities, and solid waste incinerators. Moreover, 40 C.F.R. § 72.6(c) establishes a procedure by which a binding applicability determination can be requested and obtained from EPA.

In addition, EPA's rules provide for a "de minimis" exemption for new units that serve one or more generators that have a total capacity of 25 MW or less and that use fuels with a sulfur content less than or equal to 0.05 percent by weight.[20] EPA's rules also provide a means to obtain an exemption from Title IV requirements for units that are permanently retired.[21]

NOx Emissions Limitations

Title IV also addresses emissions of NOx by directing EPA to set NOx emission limitations for coal-fired utility boilers in two phases.[22] Under EPA's rules, in 40 C.F.R. part 76, the first phase began in 1996 and the second in 2000. Part 76 sets out specific NOx emission limitations for various categories of coal-fired utility boilers. Unlike the SO_2 part of Title IV, the Title IV NOx provisions do not include emission allowances and allowance trading. These provisions offer some flexibility, however, through options for averaging of NOx emissions rates,[23] and, subject to certain restrictions, alternative emission limitations.[24]

Permits, Penalties, and Monitoring

Title IV Permits

Title IV contains permitting and compliance plan requirements that are in addition to the general operating permit requirements of Title V of the Act.[25] EPA must implement the Title IV permitting requirements in accordance with Title V, except in cases where the requirements of these titles conflict; in such cases, Title IV requirements govern.

Under Title IV, owners and operators of units subject to SO_2 and NOx emission requirements must prepare and submit acid rain permit applications and compliance plans. Unless certain specific compliance options are chosen, a simple statement that the unit will hold enough allowances to cover its SO_2 emissions and will meet any applicable NOx emission limit will satisfy the compliance plan requirement.[26]

A Title IV permit is applicable for five years.[27] For Phase I units, EPA issued the Phase I permit.[28] For Phase II, designated state permitting authorities[29] issue permits.[30] A new unit must submit a Phase II permit application and compliance plan to the permitting authority no later than 24 months before it begins operation.[31]

Excess Emissions Penalty

Section 411 of the Act imposes a penalty of $2,000 per ton (increased yearly for inflation) for a unit's SO_2 emissions that exceed the number of allowances held in the applicable source's compliance account[32] as of the applicable allowance transfer deadline and for NOx emissions that exceed the level of emissions permissible under section 407.[33] Very few units have had to pay this penalty because there have been very few cases in which units have had emission exceedances under Title IV. In addition, a unit must have deducted from its allowance account (generally for the year following the exceedance) one allowance for each ton of excess SO_2 emissions.[34] The rules governing excess emission penalties and offsets are in 40 C.F.R. part 77. Moreover, any violation of Title IV requirements is potentially subject to the Act's other enforcement provisions discussed in Chapter 11 of this Handbook.[35]

Monitoring, Reporting, and Recordkeeping Requirements

The owner or operator of an affected unit under Title IV must install and operate continuous emission monitoring systems ("CEMS"), and must quality-assure the data, for SO_2, NOx, opacity, and volumetric flow.[36] The Act, however, authorizes EPA to allow use of alternative monitoring systems with the same precision, reliability, accessibility, and timeliness as CEMS.[37] The highly technical and complex rules implementing the CEMS provisions and the associated reporting and recordkeeping requirements are in 40 C.F.R. part 75.

Notes

1. CAA § 401(b), 42 U.S.C. § 7651.
2. EPA, Acid Rain Program: General Provisions and Permits, Allowance System, Continuous Emissions Monitoring, Excess Emissions and Administrative Appeals; Final Rule, 58 Fed. Reg. 3590 (Jan. 11, 1993) (promulgating 40 C.F.R. parts 72, 73, 75, 77, 78).
3. EPA, Acid Rain Program: Nitrogen Oxides Emission Reduction Program; Final Rule, 59 Fed. Reg. 13,538 (Mar. 22, 1994) (promulgating certain provisions in 40 C.F.R. part 76); EPA, Acid Rain Program: Nitrogen Oxides Emission Reduction Program; Direct Final Rule; Response to Court Remand, 60 Fed. Reg. 18,751 (Apr. 13, 1995) (promulgating revisions to 40 C.F.R. part 76); EPA, Acid Rain Program: Nitrogen Oxides Emission Reduction Program; Final Rule, 61 Fed. Reg. 67,112 (Dec. 19, 1996) (promulgating further revisions to 40 C.F.R. part 76).
4. CAA § 402(3), 42 U.S.C. § 7651a(3).
5. 40 C.F.R. § 72.2.
6. CAA § 403(g), 42 U.S.C. § 7651b(g).
7. A 2000 New York law that restricted allowance transfers on a geographic basis was struck down as unconstitutional. *Clean Air Markets Grp. v. Pataki*, 194 F. Supp. 2d 147, 158, 159-60 (N.D.N.Y. 2002), *aff'd* 338 F.3d 82, 88 (2d Cir. 2003).
8. CAA § 403(b), 42 U.S.C. § 7651b(b).
9. The allowances are listed in tables in 40 C.F.R. § 73.10.
10. CAA § 402(10), 42 U.S.C. § 7651a(10). *But see id.* § 405(g), 42 U.S.C. § 7651d(g) (authorizing allowance allocations for certain new units that commenced operation between 1986 and December 31, 1995).
11. *Id.* §§ 403(a)(1), 405(a)(2), (3), 42 U.S.C. §§ 7651b(a)(1), 7651d(a)(2), (3).
12. *Id.* § 403(f), 42 U.S.C. § 7651b(f).
13. *Id.* § 403(b), 42 U.S.C. § 7651b(b).

14. *See* 40 C.F.R. § 72.2 (definition of "allowance transfer deadline").

15. CAA § 402(2), 42 U.S.C. § 7651a(2).

16. *Id.* § 402(8), 42 U.S.C. § 7651a(8). The definition does *not* include existing simple combustion turbines or existing units that serve a generator with a nameplate capacity of 25 megawatts ("MW") or less.

17. *Id.* § 402(10), 42 U.S.C. § 7651a(10).

18. *Id.* § 402(17)(A)(i)-(ii), 42 U.S.C. § 7651a(17)(A)(i)-(ii).

19. *Id.* § 402(17)(C), 42 U.S.C. § 7651a(17)(C).

20. 40 C.F.R. § 72.7(1), (3).

21. *Id.* § 72.8.

22. CAA § 407, 42 U.SC. § 7651f.

23. 40 C.F.R. § 76.11.

24. *Id.* § 76.10.

25. CAA § 408, 42 U.S.C. § 7651g. The Title IV permitting rules are contained in 40 C.F.R. part 72.

26. *Id.* § 408(b), 42 U.S.C. § 7651g(b).

27. *Id.* § 408(a), 42 U.S.C. § 7651g(a).

28. *Id.* § 408(c), 42 U.S.C. § 7651g(c).

29. *Id.* § 402(11), 42 U.S.C. § 7651a(11), defines "permitting authority" as "the Administrator, or the State or local air pollution control agency, with an approved permitting program."

30. *Id.* § 408(d), 42 U.S.C. § 7651g(d).

31. *Id.* § 408(e), 42 U.S.C. § 7651g(e).

32. As initially promulgated, the SO2 allowance program was implemented on a unit-by-unit basis using individual unit allowance accounts. In 2005, EPA revised the program to implement the SO2 allowance holding requirement on a source-by source basis effective July 1, 2006. EPA, Rule To Reduce Interstate Transport of Fine Particulate Matter and Ozone (Clean Air Interstate Rule); Revisions to Acid Rain Program; Revisions to the NOx SIP Call; Final Rule, 70 Fed. Reg. 25,162, 25,335 (May 12, 2005). Under this approach, a unit at a source may use allowances from any other unit at the same source without transferring allowances between individual unit accounts. *Id.* at 25,296.

33. CAA § 411(a), (c), 42 U.S.C. § 7651j(a), (c). As a result of cumulative annual inflation adjustments, the per-ton penalty amount for 2012 emissions is $3,636. EPA, Acid Rain Program: Notice of Annual Adjustment Factors for Excess Emissions Penalty, 76 Fed. Reg. 71,559, 71,559 (Nov. 18, 2011).

34. CAA § 411(b), 42 U.S.C. § 7651j(b).

35. *Id.* §§ 411(e), 414, 42 U.S.C. §§ 7651j(e), 7651m.

36. *Id.* § 412, 42 U.S.C. § 7651k.

37. *Id.* § 412(a), 42 U.S.C. § 7651k(a).

Chapter 10

STRATOSPHERIC OZONE PROTECTION

The 1990 Clean Air Act Amendments incorporate into the Act the goals of the Montreal Protocol on Substances that Deplete the Ozone Layer ("Protocol").[1] The Protocol, which has been amended several times since its adoption in 1987, requires its signatories (including the United States) to restrict the production and consumption (defined not as "use," but as production plus imports minus exports of bulk chemicals) of chlorofluorocarbons ("CFCs"), halons, methyl chloroform, carbon tetrachloride, and hydrochlorofluorocarbons ("HCFCs"). As amended in November 1992, the Protocol required the complete phaseout of all listed CFCs, methyl chloroform, and carbon tetrachloride by 1996, and of halons by 1994. The phaseout of HCFCs is to be accomplished over a longer period stretching out from 2020 to 2040. Finally, the 1992 amendments to the Protocol required that production and consumption of hydrobromofluorocarbons ("HBFCs") be phased out beginning in 1996 and added methyl bromide to the list of controlled substances.

In 1988, EPA issued final rules implementing the Protocol in the United States.[2] These rules established a system for allocating production and consumption allowances for ozone-depleting substances based on 1986 levels of production and imports, and established a system for trading these allowances. In 1989, this regulatory system was supplemented with an excise tax on most sales of CFCs and other ozone-depleting chemicals.

Although Title VI of the Clean Air Act ("CAA") largely mirrors the requirements of the Montreal Protocol as they existed in 1990, it contains more stringent interim targets and an earlier phaseout of methyl chloroform. In December 1993, EPA took final action to accelerate these targets in response to new scientific information, the 1992 amendments to the Montreal Protocol, and petitions to the Agency.[3] Title VI also requires EPA to promulgate regulations to: (1) ensure the "lowest achievable levels" of emissions in all user sectors; (2) ban nonessential products; (3) limit the use of harmful substitutes; (4) establish standards and requirements regarding the use, recycling, and disposal of CFCs and certain other substances in appliances and industrial process refrigeration; (5) establish standards and requirements for servicing motor vehicle air conditioners; (6) mandate warning labels; and (7) establish a safe alternatives program.

This chapter sets forth the provisions of Title VI and discusses key implementing regulations.

The Listing and Phaseout of Ozone-Depleting Substances

The provisions of the Montreal Protocol and of Title VI of the Act are directed at reducing and discontinuing the production and consumption of ozone-depleting substances. The statute lists the substances that are to be controlled and mandates that their production and consumption be phased out over a specified time period depending on the ozone-depletion potential of the substances. In addition, Title VI immediately bans specific uses of controlled substances that Congress deemed to be nonessential and authorizes the EPA Administrator to promulgate rules banning additional nonessential uses.

Listing

Under the terms of Title VI, the Administrator was required to publish an initial list of "class I" and "class II" ozone-depleting substances within 60 days of the enactment of the 1990 CAA Amendments. Congress enumerated the substances that were to be included in the initial lists, all of which were contained in the London Amendments to the Montreal Protocol.

A class I substance is any substance that "causes or contributes significantly to harmful effects on the stratospheric ozone layer . . . [and] all substances that the Administrator determines have an ozone depletion potential of 0.2 or greater."[4] "Ozone-depletion potential" is defined in section 601(10) of the Act. The statutory class I substances are divided into five groups that include two groups of CFCs, a group consisting of three halons, and single-substance groups for carbon tetrachloride and methyl chloroform.

A class II substance is any substance "that the Administrator finds is known or may reasonably be anticipated to cause or contribute to harmful effects on the stratospheric ozone layer."[5] Regulations promulgating the lists exactly as given in the statute were published in January 1991.[6]

The Administrator is empowered to add, by rulemaking, any substance to the class I or class II lists that meets the criteria for inclusion. In addition, anyone may petition to have a substance added to the lists. Finally, the Administrator may remove a substance from the class II list by adding it to the class I list; no substance listed in the statute in class I may be removed from that list, however.[7] In response to changes in the Montreal Protocol, and to petitions filed with the Administrator after passage of the 1990 Amendments, EPA added methyl bromide and HBFCs to the class I list in 1993,[8] and added chlorobromomethane to that list in 2003.[9] Each of these new substances is listed in its own group.

Phaseout

Title VI provides for the total elimination of production and consumption of class I substances by January 1, 2000 (January 1, 2002, for methyl chloroform).[10] In each year from 1991 to 2000, production and consumption of class I substances was restricted to a declining percentage of the amount of each substance that was produced in the baseline year, which is defined in the statute.[11]

The statute provides exceptions for essential uses of methyl chloroform, for the essential use of class I substances in medical devices, and for the use of class I halons for aviation safety. These exceptions are capped at amounts equal to 10 percent of the baseline allowance for the specified substance.[12] The Administrator may also grant limited exceptions for production solely for export to developing countries that are parties to the Montreal Protocol, for national security, and for fire suppression and explosion prevention.[13]

Accelerated Schedule

Section 606 of the Act permits the Administrator to promulgate a more stringent phaseout schedule for both class I and class II substances if: (1) based on an assessment of credible scientific information, the Administrator determines an accelerated phaseout is necessary to protect human health and the environment from harmful effects on the stratospheric ozone layer; (2) based on the availability of substitutes for listed substances, a more stringent schedule is practicable, "taking into account technological achievability, safety, and other relevant factors"; or (3) the Montreal Protocol is modified to include an accelerated phaseout schedule.[14] In addition, anyone can petition the Administrator to promulgate regulations under this section.[15]

On February 11, 1992, President George H.W. Bush announced that the United States would phase out production of listed ozone-depleting substances by December 31, 1995. To effectuate this change in policy, as well as to respond to petitions to EPA from both environmental and industry groups seeking an accelerated schedule, the Administrator published a notice of proposed rulemaking on March 18, 1993, proposing an accelerated phaseout of ozone-depleting substances.[16] Under this proposed schedule, production and consumption of all class I substances listed in Title VI, except halons, was to occur by January 1, 1996, and listed halons were to be phased out by January 1, 1994.[17]

EPA proposed to accelerate the phaseout schedule for certain class II HCFCs on a compound-specific basis depending on the ozone depletion potential of each substance. The earliest phaseout date was to be January 1, 2003, for HCFC-141b. Production and consumption of other HCFCs were to be frozen as of January 1, 2010, or January 1, 2015, and complete phaseout would be required by either January 1, 2020, or January 1, 2030, depending on which HCFC is involved.[18]

In the same notice of proposed rulemaking, the Agency proposed adding methyl bromide to the list of class I substances. This addition to the class I list was prompted by the 1992 amendments to the Montreal Protocol and by a petition to EPA under section 602(c)(3) of the Act.[19] In 1998, Congress amended the CAA and directed EPA to conform the phaseout schedule for methyl bromide to what other industrialized nations were doing under the Protocol.[20] In response, EPA issued regulations requiring: (1) a 50 percent reduction from baseline levels beginning January 1, 2001; (2) a 70 percent reduction from baseline levels beginning January 1, 2003; and (3) complete phaseout beginning January 1, 2005.[21]

Finally, to codify the other 1992 amendment to the Montreal Protocol, EPA proposed adding HBFCs to the list of class I substances. The Agency proposed a production and consumption freeze at 1991 baseline levels beginning January 1, 1994, and a January 1, 1996 phaseout date.[22]

In December 1993, EPA promulgated a final rule that implemented the accelerated phaseouts along the lines initially proposed.[23] In addition, in the final rule, EPA made certain minor revisions to its regulatory definition of "production" and implemented a ban on bulk exports of certain specified ozone-depleting substances to countries that are not signatories to the Montreal Protocol.

Nonessential Product Ban

In addition to mandating the gradual elimination of ozone-depleting substances, Title VI also requires the Administrator to promulgate regulations within one year of the enactment of Title VI that identify nonessential products that release class I substances into the environment.[24] In determining that a product is non-essential, the Administrator is directed to consider "the purpose or intended use of the product, the technological availability of substitutes for such product and for such class I substance, safety, health, and other relevant factors."[25] At the least, nonessential products are to include CFC-propelled plastic party streamers and noise horns, and CFC-containing cleaning fluids for noncommercial electronic and photographic equipment. The Administrator is also directed to include any other nonessential consumer products that release class I substances during manufacture, use, storage, or disposal. Regulations banning the sale or distribution in interstate commerce of such products were effective 24 months from the enactment of Title VI.[26]

Title VI also includes a ban on the sale or distribution of nonessential products that release class II substances, including aerosol products or pressurized dispensers containing class II substances and foam products that contain or are manufactured with class II substances.[27] The Administrator may exempt any aerosol product or pressurized dispenser that is essential given flammability or worker safety concerns, where the only available alternative would be a class I substance.[28]

EPA published final regulations implementing the nonessential product ban on class I substances on January 15, 1993, elucidating the specific product bans listed in the statute.[29] CFC-propelled noise horns listed in the regulations include marine safety horns, sporting event horns, personal safety horns, wall-mounted alarms used in factories or other work areas, and intruder alarms used in homes or cars. These items may not be sold, distributed, or offered for sale or distribution in interstate commerce after February 16, 1993. The ban on CFC-containing cleaning fluid for electronic or photographic equipment (except for sale to a commercial purchaser) is effective the same date. The ban on products containing class II products was promulgated on December 30, 1993.[30]

Production and Consumption Allowance Program

The gradual elimination of ozone-depleting substances under the Montreal Protocol and Title VI has been implemented by establishing allowances based on past production and consumption of these substances. These allowances are to decrease each year by a fixed percentage of the original allowance, according to the phaseout schedule for each substance. These allowances may be transferred among producers and consumers and may be increased under certain carefully defined circumstances with the approval of EPA. The rules governing this allowance trading system for class I substances were initially promulgated in 1992[31] and extensively revised in 1995.[32] Rules establishing an allowance system to control HCFCs were promulgated in 2003.[33]

Allocation of Allowances

Title VI provides for the establishment of both production and consumption allowances, which are to be based on baseline production, import, and export level reports that are to be filed with EPA as directed by section 603 of the Act.[34] Regulations promulgated under Title VI in 1992 prohibit persons from producing or importing controlled substances in excess of production and consumption allowances established in those regulations.[35] Production and consumption allowances are specific to individual producers and importers and are allocated by substance.[36] Under this system, to produce any quantity of a controlled substance, a producer must have both production and consumption allowances sufficient to cover the amount of controlled substances produced. An importer need hold only consumption allowances equal to the amount imported.[37]

Allowance Transfer Program

In authorizing the issuance of production and consumption allowances, Title VI specifies that allowances may be transferred so long as such transactions "result in greater total reductions in the production in each year of class I and class II substances than would occur in that year in the absence of such transactions."[38] Transfers may involve either an exchange between two or more persons of production or consumption allowances, or the exchange of allowances for one substance for those of another substance. Any person holding consumption or production allowances, potential production allowances, or authorization to convert potential production allowances to actual production allowances may "transfer" such an allowance to another person, subject to EPA's determination that the transferor has sufficient allowances remaining in that year to effect the transfer. To effectuate the statutory directive that such transfers must result in greater total reductions than would occur otherwise, EPA requires a one percent offset from the transferor's unexpended balance of allowances.[39]

Recycling Programs

Beyond introducing measures directed toward the eventual phaseout of the production and consumption of class I and class II substances, Title VI also imposes requirements intended to promote the recapture and safe disposal of such substances that have already been introduced into the product stream. To this end,

Title VI requires the establishment of programs addressing industrial refrigeration, appliances, and automobile air conditioning.

National Recycling and Emission Reduction Program

Title VI provides for a three-part recycling and emission reduction program.[40] First, by January 1, 1992, EPA was required to have in place regulations establishing standards and requirements regarding the use and disposal of class I substances during the service, repair, or disposal of appliances and industrial process refrigeration.[41] These regulations, commonly referred to as the "refrigerant recycling rules," are to be designed to reduce the use and emission of class I substances to their "lowest achievable level" and to maximize the recapture and recycling of such substances.[42] Similar regulations are to be promulgated for class II substances.[43] As defined broadly by the Act, "appliance" includes "any device which contains and uses a class I or class II substance as a refrigerant and which is used for household or commercial purposes, including any air conditioner, refrigerator, chiller, or freezer."[44]

Second, these regulations are to contain standards for safe disposal. In particular, provisions must require that: (1) class I and class II substances contained in bulk in appliances, machines, or other goods be removed prior to the disposal of such items; (2) any appliance, machine, or other good containing a class I or class II substance in bulk be equipped with a servicing aperture or an equally effective design feature that will facilitate the recapture of such substances; and (3) products in which a class I or class II substance is an "inherent element" be disposed of in a manner that reduces, "to the maximum extent practicable," the release of such substances into the environment.[45]

Third, section 608 contains a self-effectuating prohibition on the venting of class I or class II substances (and, eventually, their substitutes) during servicing of air conditioning and refrigeration equipment. Specifically, effective July 1, 1992, it became unlawful for any person

> in the course of maintaining, servicing, repairing, or disposing of an appliance or industrial process refrigeration, to knowingly vent or otherwise knowingly dispose of any class I or class II substances used as a refrigerant in such appliance (or industrial process refrigeration) in a manner which permits such substance to enter the environment.[46]

"De minimis releases associated with good faith attempts to recapture and recycle or safely dispose of" any class I or class II substance are not subject to this prohibition.[47]

EPA promulgated regulations to implement the refrigerant recycling program on May 14, 1993.[48] Key elements of the regulations include service requirements for the evacuation of air conditioning and refrigeration equipment to established vacuum levels; recovery and recycling equipment certification standards; a voluntary technician certification program; mandatory certification requirements for owners of recycling or recovery equipment, including outside contractors; and standards for safe disposal.

Servicing Motor Vehicle Air Conditioners

In addition to mandating recycling for class I substances used in appliances and industrial process refrigeration, Title VI requires that, as of January 1, 1992:

> [N]o person repairing or servicing motor vehicles for consideration may perform any service on a motor vehicle air conditioner involving the refrigerant for such air conditioner without properly using approved refrigerant recycling equipment and no such person may perform such service unless such person has been properly trained and certified.[49]

Title VI defines "refrigerant" to mean any class I or class II substance used in a motor vehicle air conditioner and, as of 1995, any substitute substances.[50]

Regulations promulgated on July 14, 1992, define "for consideration" to include any form of payment and any service not performed for free.[51] The regulations apply to the person performing the service, not to the owner of the vehicle; therefore, a company that owns its own fleet of vehicles is covered by the regulations because any employee who services the air conditioner is compensated for that service. The regulations define "motor vehicle" as the term is defined in Title II of the Act. This definition excludes "off-road vehicles," but covers other vehicles even if they are used off-road, such as at construction sites and on farms.[52]

These regulations have two major components. The first governs the equipment that may be used to service motor vehicle air conditioners. The second governs the training and certification of service technicians. All technicians who service motor vehicle air conditioners must attend a training and certification program approved, in advance, by EPA. Companies whose business it is to service motor vehicle air conditioners or companies that service their own fleets of motor vehicles may establish their own training and certification programs, but these programs must be approved in advance by EPA.[53] As of January 1, 1993, all persons repairing or servicing motor vehicle air conditioners for consideration must certify to the Administrator that they have purchased approved equipment and that any person authorized to use the equipment is properly trained and certified.[54]

Section 609 of the Act also makes it unlawful to sell, distribute, or offer for sale or distribution any class I or class II substance that may be used as a refrigerant for a motor vehicle air conditioner in a container holding less than 20 pounds of refrigerant. This section became effective by law on November 15, 1992.[55] EPA's regulations require proof that any sales of such small containers were made only to properly certified technicians and to those who intend to re-sell such containers.[56]

Labeling

To promote consumer awareness, section 611 of the Act requires that, effective May 15, 1993, all containers containing class I and class II substances, products containing class I substances, and products manufactured with class I substances that are introduced into interstate commerce bear a warning statement indicating that the product contains or is manufactured with an ozone-depleting substance.[57] Section 611 further provides that after May 15, 1993, products containing or manufactured with class II substances must be labeled if the EPA Administrator determines that safe alternatives are available. By January 1, 2015, all products manufactured with, or containing, class I or class II substances must be labeled.[58]

EPA issued a final rule implementing the labeling provisions of Title VI on February 11, 1993.[59] The rule's important features include: (1) an exemption from the labeling requirement for manufacturers that have reached a total use reduction of 95 percent or greater from 1990 use levels for products manufactured using CFC-113 and methyl chloroform as solvents;[60] (2) an exclusion from the labeling requirements for products manufactured for export outside the U.S.;[61] and (3) limitations on the need for labeling information to be "passed through" by manufacturers to ultimate consumers.[62]

Safe Alternatives Policy

Title VI provides that, to the greatest extent possible, substitutes that are developed for controlled ozone-depleting substances must "reduce overall risks to human health and the environment."[63] To implement this policy, EPA must promulgate rules that make it illegal to replace any class I or II substance with a substitute that the Administrator determines may present adverse effects to human health or the environment, where the Administrator has identified an alternative to such replacement that: (1) reduces the overall risk to human health and the environment; and (2) is currently or potentially available.

The Administrator is to publish a list of prohibited alternatives and a list of safe alternatives.[64] Anyone may petition the Administrator to add a substance to or remove a substance from either the safe alternatives list or the prohibited list.[65] Finally, anyone who produces a substitute for a class I substance must provide the Administrator with any unpublished health and safety studies and must notify the Administrator not less than 90 days before the substance is placed on the market.[66]

EPA published on March 18, 1994, a rule to implement section 612, called the Significant New Alternatives Policy ("SNAP") program.[67] The rule included a list of alternative substances being considered for review under the SNAP program. To evaluate the overall risk of substitutes for controlled substances, EPA considers toxicity and exposure, chlorine loading, ozone-depletion potential, global warming potential, and flammability. EPA also considers economic feasibility, the context of the risk, and the risk as measured by the intended use.

In December 2011, EPA promulgated a rule listing isobutane (R-600a) and R-441A as acceptable, subject to use conditions, as substitutes for CFC-12 and HCFC-22 in household refrigerators, freezers, and combination refrigerators and freezers.[68] In that same action, EPA also listed propane (R-290) as an acceptable substitute for CFC-12, HCFC-22, and R-502 in retail food refrigerators and freezers (standalone units only), subject to use conditions.

Notes

1. Montreal Protocol on Substances that Deplete the Ozone Layer, Sept. 16, 1987, S. Treaty Doc. No. 100-10 (1987),1522 U.N.T.S. 3.
2. See EPA, Protection of Stratospheric Ozone, 53 Fed. Reg. 30,566, 30,598 (Aug. 12, 1988) (codified at 40 C.F.R. pt. 82).
3. EPA, Protection of Stratospheric Ozone, 58 Fed. Reg. 65,018 (Dec. 10, 1993).
4. CAA § 602(a), 42 U.S.C. § 7671a(a).
5. Id. § 602(b), 42 U.S.C. § 7671a(b).
6. See EPA, Protection of Stratospheric Ozone, 56 Fed. Reg. 2420 (Jan. 22, 1991) (codified at 40 C.F.R. pt. 82, App. A).
7. CAA § 602(c)(4), 42 U.S.C. § 7671a(c)(4).
8. See 58 Fed. Reg. at 65,017.
9. See EPA, Protection of Stratospheric Ozone: Phaseout of Chlorobromomethane Production and Consumption, 68 Fed. Reg. 42,884 (July 18, 2003).
10. CAA § 604(a), 42 U.S.C. § 7671c(a).
11. Id. § 601(2), 42 U.S.C. § 7671(2).
12. Id. § 604(d), 42 U.S.C. § 7671c(d).

13. *Id.* § 604(e), (f), (g), 42 U.S.C. § 7671c(e), (f), (g).

14. *Id.* § 606(a), 42 U.S.C. § 7671e(a).

15. *Id.* § 606(b), 42 U.S.C. § 7671e(b).

16. *See* EPA, Protection of Stratospheric Ozone, 58 Fed. Reg. 15,014 (Mar. 18, 1993).

17. *Id.* at 15,022.

18. *Id.* at 15,027.

19. *Id.* at 15,030.

20. CAA § 604(h), 42 U.S.C. § 7671c(h).

21. EPA, Protection of Stratospheric Ozone: Incorporation of Clean Air Act Amendments for Reductions in Class I, Group VI Controlled Substances, 65 Fed. Reg. 70,795 (Nov. 28, 2000). In September 2011, EPA promulgated rules identifying the specific parameters of the "critical use exemption" for methyl bromide and amount of methyl bromide that may be produced, imported, or supplied from pre-phaseout inventory for those uses in 2011. EPA, Protection of Stratospheric Ozone: The 2011 Critical Use Exemption from the Phaseout of Methyl Bromide, 76 Fed. Reg. 60,736 (Sept. 30, 2011).

22. *See* 58 Fed. Reg. at 15,038.

23. 58 Fed. Reg. at 65,018.

24. CAA § 610(b), 42 U.S.C. § 7671i(b).

25. *Id.*

26. *Id.* § 610(c), 42 U.S.C. § 7671i(c).

27. *Id.* § 610(d)(1), 42 U.S.C. § 7671i(d)(1).

28. The ban on plastic foam products does not include foam insulation products or "an integral skin, rigid or semi-rigid foam utilized to provide for motor vehicle safety," if there is no adequate substitute. *Id.* § 610(d)(3), 42 U.S.C. § 7671i(d)(3).

29. EPA, Protection of Stratospheric Ozone, 58 Fed. Reg. 4768 (Jan. 15, 1993).

30. EPA, Protection of Stratospheric Ozone, 58 Fed. Reg. 69,638 (Dec. 30, 1993).

31. EPA, Protection of Stratospheric Ozone, 57 Fed. Reg. 33,754 (July 30, 1992).

32. EPA, Protection of Stratospheric Ozone: Administrative Changes to Final Rule to Phase Out Ozone-Depleting Chemicals, 60 Fed. Reg. 24,970 (May 10, 1995).

33. EPA, Protection of Stratospheric Ozone: Allowance System for Controlling HCFC Production, Import and Export, 68 Fed. Reg. 2820 (Jan. 21, 2003). Additional rules adjusting the allowance system for HCFCs were subsequently promulgated in December 2009 and in August 2011. *See* EPA, Protection of Stratospheric Ozone: Adjustments to the Allowance System for Controlling HCFC Production, Import, and Export, 74 Fed. Reg. 66,412 (Dec. 15, 2009); EPA, Protection of Stratospheric Ozone: Adjustments to the Allowance System for Controlling HCFC Production, Import, and Export, 76 Fed. Reg. 47,451 (Aug. 5, 2011).

34. CAA § 603(b), 42 U.S.C. § 7671b(b).

35. As initially promulgated, the rules provided exceptions for: (1) the production of carbon tetrachloride for feedstock; (2) coincidental, unintentional by-product carbon tetrachloride that is immediately contained and destroyed using maximum available control technology; and (3) coincidentally produced, incinerated methyl chloroform. *See* 57 Fed. Reg. at 33,759, 33,766.

36. 40 C.F.R. §§ 82.5, 82.6.

37. *Id.* § 82.4.

38. CAA § 607(a), 42 U.S.C. § 7671f(a).

39. 40 C.F.R. § 82.12(a).

40. CAA § 608, 42 U.S.C. § 7671g.

41. *Id.* § 608(a)(1), 42 U.S.C. § 7671g(a)(1).

42. *Id.* § 608(a)(3), 42 U.S.C. § 7671g(a)(3).

43. *Id.* § 608(a)(2), 42 U.S.C. § 7671g(a)(2).

44. *Id.* § 601(1), 42 U.S.C. § 7671(1).

45. *Id.* § 608(b), 42 U.S.C. § 7671g(b).

46. *Id.* § 608(c)(1), 42 U.S.C. § 7671g(c)(1).

47. *Id.*

48. EPA, Protection of Stratospheric Ozone; Refrigerant Recycling, 58 Fed. Reg. 28,660 (May 14, 1993). Revisions to the regulations were adopted in the form of a supplemental rule effective August 8, 1995. EPA, Protection of Stratospheric Ozone: Supplemental Rule to Amend Leak Repair Provisions Under Section 608 of the Clean Air Act, 60 Fed. Reg. 40,420 (May 10, 1995).

49. CAA § 609(c), 42 U.S.C. § 7671h(c).

50. *Id.* § 609(b)(1), 42 U.S.C. § 7671h(b)(1).

51. EPA, Protection of Stratospheric Ozone, 57 Fed. Reg. 31,242, 31,261 (July 14, 1992) (codified at 40 C.F.R. § 82.32(g)).

52. *Id.* at 31,261 (codified at 40 C.F.R. § 82.32(c)).

53. *Id.* at 31,263 (codified at 40 C.F.R. § 82.40).

54. *Id.* (codified at 40 C.F.R. § 82.42(a)).

55. CAA § 609(e), 42 U.S.C. § 7671h(e).

56. *See* 57 Fed. Reg. at 31,263 (codified at 40 C.F.R. § 82.42(b)(3)).

57. CAA § 611(b), 42 U.S.C. § 7671j(b).

58. *Id.* § 611(d), 42 U.S.C. § 7671j(d).

59. EPA, Protection of Stratospheric Ozone; Labeling, 58 Fed. Reg. 8136 (Feb. 11, 1993).

60. 40 C.F.R. § 82.106(b)(4).

61. *Id.* § 82.106(b)(5).

62. *Id.* § 82.116.

63. CAA § 612(a), 42 U.S.C. § 7671k(a).

64. *Id.* § 612(c), 42 U.S.C. § 7671k(c).

65. *Id.* § 612(d), 42 U.S.C. § 7671k(d).

66. *Id.* § 612(e), 42 U.S.C. § 7671k(e).

67. EPA, Protection of Stratospheric Ozone: Final Rule, 59 Fed. Reg. 13,043 (Mar. 18, 1994).

68. EPA, Protection of Stratospheric Ozone: Listing of Substitutes for Ozone-Depleting Substances—Hydrocarbon Refrigerants, 76 Fed. Reg. 78,832 (Dec. 20, 2011).

Chapter 11

ENFORCEMENT AND JUDICIAL REVIEW

Environmental enforcement has undergone rapid and significant changes since the 1990s, and the federal government continues to bring a large number of environmental enforcement cases each year. EPA has reported that the combined total of all criminal, civil, and administrative fines and penalties assessed for violations of environmental laws in fiscal year ("FY") 2012 exceeded $250 million, and combined sentences for environmental crimes reached 79 years.[1]

Factors that have contributed to the Agency's enforcement activities include the Pollution Prosecution Act of 1990, which increased the number of Agency criminal investigators with a commensurate increase in support staff.[2] EPA reported that 320 new environmental criminal cases were opened during FY 2012, down from the 371 opened in FY 2011 and 346 in FY 2010.[3] According to EPA, 231 defendants were charged with environmental crimes in FY 2012, down from 250 in FY 2011 and 289 in FY 2010.[4] EPA reported that the value of fines, restitution, and court-ordered environmental projects increased from a combined total of $37 million in FY 2011 to $58 million in FY 2012.[5] EPA also reported that it initiated a total of 3027 judicial and administrative civil enforcement cases in FY 2012 and concluded a total of 3012.[6] EPA reported that in FY 2012, "EPA enforcement actions required companies to invest more than $9 billion in actions [and] equipment to control pollution (injunctive relief)."[7]

A second factor contributing to significant enforcement activity since 1990 is the reorganization of the Agency's Office of Enforcement, to create in 1994 the Office of Enforcement and Compliance Assurance. According to the Agency, the reorganization, which integrates technical and legal enforcement personnel, was undertaken to "further strengthen enforcement capability and place increased emphasis on compliance assurance."[8] More importantly, by locating the enforcement function outside of the program offices responsible for implementing the environmental statutes, the EPA enforcers have been given more ability to shape environmental policy through enforcement.

A third reason for significant enforcement activity is the enforcement tools provided by the 1990 Amendments to the Clean Air Act ("CAA"). Chief among these is the Title V operating permit program, which requires increased compliance monitoring and periodic certification of source compliance status.

264

Finally, the CAA has been in place in one form or another for over 40 years, and many of the basic CAA programs are mature. With the maturation of these programs, the Agency's focus has shifted to enforcement.

In 1999, EPA launched an initiative targeting several industrial sectors for enforcement of the Act's new source review programs. Among those targeted were wood product manufacturers, ethanol manufacturers, coal-fired power plants, and petroleum refineries. In 2007, EPA nominated other sectors for enforcement including cement plants, glass manufacturers, and acid producers.[9] In 2010, EPA indicated that work under this initiative would continue in 2011 to 2013 to focus on large refineries, coal-fired power plants, cement manufacturing facilities, sulfuric and nitric manufacturing facilities, and glass manufacturing facilities.[10] EPA's current enforcement priorities are discussed later in this chapter.

Background

Historically, the statutory provision primarily used by EPA for enforcing the Act was section 113,[11] which authorizes the EPA Administrator to go to court to seek civil or criminal penalties and to issue administrative enforcement orders requiring noncomplying sources to meet CAA requirements.[12] Section 113 of the pre-1990 Act, however, was narrowly drawn. The pre-1990 Act limited the Administrator's authority to assess penalties in cases where violations were not continuous, or where it was unclear exactly how long a source had operated in violation of a statutory provision. Furthermore, the Agency was required to obtain permission of the Department of Justice to go to court before it could collect penalties.

The 1990 Amendments gave the Administrator and the courts broader powers to enforce the substantive provisions of the Act. The amended Act provided for wider applicability of civil sanctions, increased criminal penalties, broader emergency powers, broader inspection powers, and increased citizen involvement in enforcement and administrative decisionmaking. The amended Act also contained an administrative penalty regime that allows EPA to use streamlined procedures to assess administrative penalties of up to $200,000 (or more, in some cases) and to issue on-the-spot citations to violators of the Act.[13]

Furthermore, the Debt Collection and Improvement Act of 1996 ("DCIA") required each federal agency to issue regulations adjusting for inflation the maximum civil monetary penalties that can be imposed pursuant to such agency's statutes. The DCIA requires adjustments to be made at least once every four years. Effective January 30, 1997, the maximum statutory civil and administrative fines for CAA violations increased 10 percent under the Agency's Civil

Penalty Inflation Adjustment rule.[14] CAA penalty amounts were again adjusted in 2004, raising the cap on penalties assessed under section 113(d)(1) to $32,500 per day of violation, and the cap on fines assessed under the administrative penalty scheme was increased to $270,000.[15] Most recently, the 2008 Penalty Inflation Rule, which became effective on January 12, 2009, raised the cap to $37,500 per day of violation and the cap on administrative penalties to $295,000 under section 113(d)(1).[16]

In February 1997, EPA promulgated a rule, known as the "credible evidence" rule, that significantly expands the kinds of emissions information that can be used to enforce compliance with CAA emission standards. As discussed further in this chapter, this rule and related guidance have been the subject of much litigation, and they have raised complex legal questions regarding a source's compliance status and compliance certification obligations.

This chapter summarizes the enforcement provisions of the CAA, addressing the administrative penalty regime, the civil and criminal enforcement provisions, the impact of voluntary environmental compliance audit programs on enforcement under the Act, provisions regarding public involvement in enforcement proceedings, and judicial review provisions.

The Administrative Penalty Regime

The pre-1990 Act did not authorize EPA to use administrative procedures to assess monetary penalties. Section 113(d) of the 1990 Act changed that by allowing the EPA Administrator to assess administrative penalties for past or present violations of most CAA requirements. In addition, the administrative penalty regime was made more powerful by the standard of review for penalty assessments prescribed by the Act. Consequently, during FY 2012, the Agency concluded 1780 civil administrative penalty orders and assessed more than $252 million in administrative penalties.[17]

Administrative Penalties and Procedures

Administrative penalties may be sought by the Agency in "matters where the total penalty sought does not exceed $200,000."[18] Moreover, the action must be brought within one year of the "first alleged date of violation."[19] These limits may be extended and increased in cases where the Administrator and Attorney General agree that extending the covered period of violation or increasing the penalty is appropriate.[20] A decision to extend is not subject to judicial review.

Administrative penalties are assessed by an administrative order for: (1) violation of a state implementation plan ("SIP") during federally assumed enforcement[21] or 30 days after the Administrator has issued a section 113(a)(1) notice to a state and the alleged violator that a permit or SIP provision has been violated;[22] (2) violations of any requirement relating to attainment and maintenance of national ambient air quality standards, hazardous air pollutants, acid deposition, permits, or stratospheric ozone protection; and (3) actions taken to construct or modify a major stationary source where the Administrator has made a finding that "a State is not acting in compliance with any requirement or prohibition of the Act relating to the construction of new sources or the modification of existing sources."[23]

The amount of the penalty that EPA will seek in any individual case will be based on the factors stated in section 113(e) of the Act, described later in this chapter with respect to civil penalties.

When the Administrator commences an administrative penalty action, he must give written notice to the alleged violator, who then has 30 days to request a hearing.[24] The fine is then assessed by an order issued after an opportunity for an adjudicatory hearing in accordance with the Administrative Procedure Act.[25] The discovery rules and hearing procedures applicable to such hearings took effect on August 23, 1999.[26]

Field Citation Program

Under section 113(d)(3) of the Act, the Administrator may implement by regulation a field citation program for minor violations. This program allows Agency officials to issue on-the-spot environmental citations with fines not to exceed $5,000 per day of violation.[27] The recipient of a citation may request a hearing or may simply pay the fine.[28] The time within which a hearing must be requested is to be established by regulation, and such hearing "shall provide a reasonable opportunity to be heard and to present evidence."[29] Payment of a field citation penalty is not a defense to other enforcement actions if the violation continues.[30]

EPA issued proposed regulations to implement the field citation program in 1994.[31] In May 2002, however, EPA announced that the field citation rulemaking had been withdrawn on March 19, 2002, and that EPA planned no further action on the program.[32]

Appeals of Administrative Penalties

Under section 113(d)(4) of the Act, administrative penalties can be appealed to the district court in one of the following locations: the District of Columbia; the location where the violation allegedly occurred; the alleged violator's residence; or the alleged violator's principal place of business.[33]

Section 113(d)(4) is the exclusive means of review for administrative penalties. Appeals must be made within 30 days after an administrative penalty becomes final or a final decision is rendered following a field citation hearing.[34] On appeal, the penalty shall be set aside only if there "is not substantial evidence in the record, taken as a whole, to support the finding," or if the Administrator's "assessment [of the penalty] constitutes an abuse of discretion."[35]

Failure to Pay a Fine

In the event of failure to pay an administrative penalty after it has become final, or after a court has entered final judgment in favor of the Administrator under section 113(d)(4) of the Act, the Administrator may request the Attorney General to bring an action to recover unpaid fines.[36] The "validity, amount, and appropriateness" of the underlying fine may not be questioned in this action.[37] Furthermore, the defendant is liable for interest, the government's costs, attorneys' fees, and a nonpayment penalty of "10 percent of the aggregate amount of such person's outstanding penalties and nonpayment penalties accrued as of the beginning of such quarter."[38]

Civil Enforcement

Despite the existence of the new administrative penalty program, EPA has continued to use its civil judicial enforcement authority, particularly in cases where the Agency seeks penalties that are higher than $200,000. EPA reported that there were 179 referrals of civil judicial enforcement cases to the Department of Justice in FY 2012.[39] More than $200 million in civil (administrative and judicial) penalties were assessed in FY 2012, up from approximately $152 million over the previous year.[40]

Besides expanding the Administrator's general civil enforcement authority, the 1990 Amendments to the Act provided the Administrator with other civil enforcement tools, discussed below.

Civil Penalty Actions

Section 113(b)(2) allows the Administrator to commence a civil action whenever an owner or operator of a covered source has violated or is in violation of *any requirement or prohibition of* a SIP, Title I, section 303 of Title III, Title IV, Title V (including a Title V permit), or Title VI.[41] The 1990 Amendments made it easier for EPA to assess penalties for past, non-continuing violations, and where the length of the period of violation is not clear. Unlike the pre-1990 Act, under which the Administrator could not bring an action for violation of a SIP unless the violation persisted 30 days after notice of the violation was given to the violator, amended section 113(a)(1) allows the Administrator to take action even if the violation does not persist.[42] In the case of a SIP or permit violation, however, unless EPA has assumed federal enforcement in a state, EPA may not bring a civil action until 30 days following notification by EPA of the alleged violation.[43] The Act provides that a civil penalty of up to $25,000 per day may be imposed for each violation.[44]

Inspections, Monitoring, and Entry

Under the pre-1990 Act, the Administrator had the authority to order any owner or operator of an emission source (or those subject to other requirements of the Act) to establish and maintain records; to make reports; to install, use, and maintain monitoring equipment or methods; to sample emissions; and to provide other information. Under section 114 of the Act as amended, the Administrator now may also order: (1) environmental audit procedures; (2) source owners and operators to keep records on control equipment parameters when direct monitoring is impractical; and (3) the submission of "compliance certifications."[45] These section 114 orders may be issued not only against owners and operators of sources, but also against any manufacturer of emissions control equipment or process equipment or against any person that the Administrator believes has information "necessary for the purposes set forth in this subsection."[46]

Section 114(a)(3) authorizes the Administrator to require compliance certifications by individual sources.[47] Such certifications are to identify the method used for determining compliance and provide information on the source's compliance status.[48] This provision is also the basis for EPA's Compliance Assurance Monitoring rule, described in Chapter 4 of this Handbook.

Penalty Assessment Criteria

Section 113(e) of the Act lists various factors for EPA and the courts to consider when penalties are assessed. This list of factors is nonexclusive and includes: (1) "the size of the business"; (2) "the economic impact of the penalty on the business"; (3) "the violator's full compliance history and good faith efforts to comply"; (4) "the duration of the violation established by any credible evidence"; (5) "payment by the violator of penalties previously assessed for the same violation"; (6) "the economic benefit of noncompliance"; and (7) "the seriousness of the violation."[49]

The Agency takes the position that the statutory ceilings and penalty assessment criteria set forth in the Act leave it with substantial discretion in setting civil penalties. EPA has published internal guidance documents – called civil penalty policies – that it uses to calculate the penalties it will seek in administrative enforcement actions and that it would deem acceptable in settlements of administrative and judicial actions.[50] In 1997, the Environmental Appeals Board ("EAB") ruled that the Agency's penalty policies may be used to guide penalty decisions even though the policies were established informally and not through notice and comment rulemakings.[51] At the same time, however, the EAB reaffirmed that administrative law judges are not bound by agency penalty policies when calculating the amount of a penalty.[52]

EPA has said that its "policy is that any civil penalty should at least recapture the economic benefit the violator has obtained through its unlawful actions."[53] EPA uses computer software called the BEN (short for "benefit") model to estimate how much money a violator saved through noncompliance with environmental regulations. In August 2005, EPA issued a "notice of final action" on how it will calculate the appropriate penalty based upon the BEN model.[54] The notice made changes to the existing model that EPA claimed will improve its "precision and function."[55] Two of the more significant changes involved "tailoring the discount/compound rate to the case and using a more precise inflation adjustment."[56] Although the BEN model may be used to estimate delayed or avoided compliance costs, it does not calculate the benefit gained from any illegal competitive advantage that a violator may have accrued.[57] The agency announced that it is committed to seeking to recover these costs and will do so on a case-by-case basis.[58]

Other Enforcement Authorities

Federally Assumed Enforcement

The Act allows the Administrator to take over the enforcement of a state plan or permit program if the state is not enforcing the plan or program effectively.[59] In addition, the Administrator has the power to assess administrative penalties while EPA is enforcing the SIP or the permit program.[60]

Compliance Orders

Under the pre-1990 Act, compliance orders issued by EPA had to specify a reasonable time for compliance. The amended Act requires compliance as expeditiously as possible, but in no case does it allow more than one year to attain compliance.[61] The amended Act also makes compliance orders nonrenewable, and it provides that the issuance of a compliance order does *not* affect either the right of the enforcement authority to assess penalties or the obligation of the violator to comply with the Act.[62]

In 2003, the compliance order regime was declared unconstitutional by the U.S. Court of Appeals for the Eleventh Circuit.[63] This case arose out of an administrative compliance order issued to the Tennessee Valley Authority ("TVA"), claiming that TVA had undertaken construction activities that triggered the new source review program without obtaining permits, and ordering TVA to obtain such permits subject to the threat of civil or criminal penalty. The court found that because the CAA regime allowed EPA to determine liability and impose penalties without a meaningful opportunity for the company to be heard, it violated the due process protections of the U.S. Constitution.[64]

Preventing New Source Construction

Section 113(a)(5) of the pre-1990 Act authorized the Administrator, in certain circumstances, to issue an administrative order or file a civil suit to prevent construction of new sources in *nonattainment* areas. In areas that have *attained* the ambient standards, sources are subject to review under the prevention of significant deterioration ("PSD") program under section 167, rather than section 113(a)(5).[65] Section 113(a)(5) now provides that the Administrator may issue an enforcement order or file a civil suit whenever he finds that "a State is not acting in compliance with any requirement or prohibition of [the Act] relating to the construction of new sources or the modification of existing sources . . . ."[66] This provision applies in both nonattainment and attainment areas.

Emergency Powers

The pre-1990 Act allowed emergency orders to be issued only when there was imminent and substantial endangerment to the health of persons, and the orders were effective for 24 hours. The amended Act allows emergency orders when there is "imminent and substantial endangerment to public health *or welfare, or the environment* . . . ."[67] The amended Act also removes the prohibition on EPA action where state or local authorities are already taking action.[68] The requirement that EPA consult with those authorities remains, however. Emergency orders are effective for 60 days and may be extended by the courts.[69]

Administrative Enforcement Subpoenas

The Administrator has authority to issue administrative enforcement subpoenas for obtaining information with respect to "any investigation, monitoring, reporting requirement, entry, compliance inspection, or administrative enforcement proceeding."[70] Penalties shall not be assessed for noncompliance with administrative subpoenas where the violator had "sufficient cause" to violate or to refuse to comply with the subpoena.[71]

Supplemental Environmental Projects Policy

In a 1995 policy statement, EPA indicated that supplemental environmental projects ("SEPs"), which are environmentally beneficial projects that a violator voluntarily agrees to perform, may be considered in settlement negotiations over civil penalties.[72] The "policy sets forth the types of projects that are permissible as SEPs, the penalty mitigation appropriate for a particular SEP, and the terms and conditions under which they may become part of a settlement."[73] In 2002, EPA updated and reaffirmed the policy stating that its continued use "provides the Agency with a useful tool for achieving environmental benefits beyond those gained by compliance with Federal and state laws."[74]

According to the Agency, there were 124 cases involving SEPs in FY 2012, and the total value of those SEPs was more than $44 million, up from 103 cases and $25 million in FY 2011, and a five-year high.[75]

Criminal Enforcement

In addition to being able to use an administrative penalty program and civil judicial mechanisms to enforce the Act, EPA has authority under section 113(c) of the Act to seek criminal sanctions against "any person" who knowingly violates almost any of the statute's prohibitions or requirements.[76] The term "person" includes both individuals and corporations, partnerships, and other business organizations.[77]

Although organizations are generally subject to larger fines for any given offense than are individuals, individuals are also subject to imprisonment.[78] Moreover, criminal sanctions apply to individuals that are non-senior corporate officials.[79] That is, other enforcement provisions of the Act apply only to "senior management personnel or a corporate officer," and not to a person who is "carrying out his normal activities and who is acting under orders from the employer" or who is "a stationary engineer or technician responsible for the operation, maintenance, repair, or monitoring of equipment and facilities and who often has supervisory and training duties but who is not senior management personnel or a corporate officer."[80] These exemptions for non-senior personnel, however, do *not* apply in the case of knowing and willful violations covered by section 113(c) of the Act.[81]

The 1990 Amendments to the Act increased most of the penalties associated with violations of the Act from misdemeanors to felonies, with corresponding increases in the maximum fines and jail terms. Criminal penalties under the 1990 Act are doubled for second and subsequent convictions.[82] The length of prison sentences for individuals and the amount of fines for individuals and organizations are determined with reference to the Federal Sentencing Guidelines.[83] These aspects of the criminal enforcement provisions are discussed further below.

Prohibited Conduct and Statutory Penalties

Violation of Emission Restrictions

Section 113(c) of the 1990 Act provides that any person who knowingly violates any requirement or prohibition of a SIP, or of virtually any substantive provision of the Act,[84] or of any rule, order, waiver, or permit promulgated or approved under such provisions, is subject to a fine of up to $250,000 or a prison term of up to 5 years, or both, in the case of an individual defendant.[85] An organizational defendant is subject to a fine of up to $500,000.[86]

False Statements

Section 113(c)(2) provides that any person who knowingly makes any false material statement in or omission from any document or fails to file or maintain any document required under the Act, or any person who knowingly tampers with monitoring equipment, is subject to a fine of up to $250,000 or a prison term of up to 2 years, or both, in the case of an individual defendant. An organizational defendant is subject to a fine of up to $500,000.[87]

Failure to Pay Fees

A knowing failure to pay any fee owed to the United States under Titles I, III, IV-A, V, or VI is punishable by a fine of up to $100,000 or a prison term of up to 1 year, or both, in the case of an individual defendant. An organizational defendant is subject to a fine of up to $500,000.[88]

Knowing Endangerment

Section 113(c)(5)(A), a criminal provision added to the Act in 1990, imposes a fine of up to $250,000 or a prison term of up to fifteen years, or both, on any person who knowingly releases any hazardous air pollutant, or any "extremely hazardous substance" listed in EPA rules, knowing that doing so places another person in "imminent danger of death or serious bodily injury."[89] An organization convicted under this provision is subject to a fine of up to $1 million per violation.[90]

While punishment under this provision can apply only to persons with *actual* knowledge, circumstantial evidence can be used in proving a defendant's possession of actual knowledge.[91] In determining whether a defendant had actual knowledge that his action "placed another person in imminent danger of death or serious bodily injury . . . the defendant is responsible only for actual awareness or actual belief possessed; and . . . knowledge possessed by a person other than the defendant, but not by the defendant, may not be attributed to the defendant."[92]

The Act recognizes "assumption of the risk" defenses where the defendant proves by a preponderance of the evidence that the conduct charged was freely consented to and a reasonably foreseeable hazard of an occupation, business, profession, or medical treatment or medical or scientific experimentation.[93] Responsible corporate officers are specifically included as potentially liable parties under this subsection.[94] Finally, a release allowed under a permit is not subject to an action brought under this subsection.[95]

Negligent Endangerment

Section 113(c)(4), the only misdemeanor provision added by the 1990 Amendments, imposes a fine of up to $100,000 or a prison term of up to one year, or both, on any person who *negligently* releases any hazardous air pollutant, or any "extremely hazardous substance" listed in EPA rules, and thereby negligently places another person in "imminent danger of death or serious bodily injury." For an organizational defendant, the maximum fine is $200,000.[96]

Fines Under the Criminal Fine Enforcement Act and the 2012 Federal Sentencing Guidelines

When an individual or a corporation is convicted under the criminal provisions of the CAA, the Criminal Fine Enforcement Act ("CFEA"), 18 U.S.C. §§ 3571 *et seq.*, and the 2012 Federal Sentencing Guidelines are used to help a court set the fines applicable to the individual or corporation.[97] The Guidelines also help determine the length of any prison term to be imposed. In 2005, the United States Supreme Court held that, in order to pass constitutional muster, the Guidelines must be considered advisory only.[98]

The CFEA provides a maximum penalty that can be assessed against an individual or corporation for each offense for which the defendant is convicted. That act provides that the maximum fine that an individual may pay for each felony will be $250,000.[99] The maximum fines for misdemeanors range from $5,000 to $100,000 per violation.[100] The fines for organizations can be as much as $500,000 for a felony and as much as $10,000 to $100,000 for misdemeanors.[101] These penalties are high, but since each day of a CAA violation may be considered a separate offense, the total amount of the penalty can climb even more steeply.

In cases where the penalty can be as much as $250,000 to $500,000 per day of violation, the courts do not simply set the fine at some random place between zero and $500,000. Instead, they must follow the 2012 Federal Sentencing Guidelines.[102] The following is a summary of what the 2012 Federal Sentencing Guidelines provide regarding fines and prison terms.

Individual Defendants

Fines. Under section 5E1.2 of the 2012 Federal Sentencing Guidelines, fines for individual defendants are based on the ability of the defendant to pay, the gross pecuniary loss or gain caused by the offense, and certain other equitable considerations.[103] To illustrate how a fine against an individual might be determined, consider the case of an individual defendant convicted of emitting a non-hazardous regulated air pollutant in violation of limitations imposed by a SIP. Assume that the defendant is convicted of a repeated or ongoing violation and that the offense is not only a violation of the state plan but also a violation of a CAA operating permit.

According to the 2012 Federal Sentencing Guidelines, the mishandling of environmental pollutants would be assigned a "Base Offense Level" of 6. This Base Level would increase by 6 levels (up to an Offense Level of 12) because the offense is ongoing or repetitive. Because the offense involves a discharge in violation of a permit, the Offense Level would increase by another 4 levels, up to 16.[104]

Having determined the Offense Level (16 in this case), one then goes to the Fine Table set out in section 5E1.2(c)(3) of the Guidelines.[105] That Table provides that for an Offense Level of 16, the fine for the individual defendant should be between $5,000 and $50,000.[106] The Commission notes in commentary, however, that where the maximum amount indicated in the Fine Table does not equal at least twice the amount of gain to the defendant or the loss resulting from the offense, then "an upward departure from the fine guideline may be warranted."[107]

The court then has some discretion to adjust the fine reached through the foregoing process. Specifically, in setting the final amount of the fine, the court must consider other factors, including: (1) the need for the combined sentence to reflect the seriousness of the offense; (2) any evidence presented as to the defendant's ability to pay the fine; (3) the burden that the fine might place on the defendant and his or her dependents; (4) any restitution or reparation that the defendant has made or is obligated to make; and (5) whether the defendant has previously been fined for a similar offense.[108] If the court imposes a lesser fine or waives the fine if it finds that the defendant cannot pay the fine or that paying the fine would unduly burden the defendant's dependents, the court must still impose a sanction that is punitive.[109] Community service is an alternative in such cases.[110]

Imprisonment. How the 2012 Federal Sentencing Guidelines affect the calculation of a prison term can be understood in the context of the above example, where the individual defendant is convicted of repeatedly discharging a non-hazardous pollutant in violation of both the SIP and an operating permit. As noted above, the Offense Level for this crime under the 2012 Federal Sentencing Guidelines is 16.

To determine the length of a prison term for someone convicted of a level 16 offense, one refers to the Sentencing Table in Part A of Chapter 5 of the 2012 Federal Sentencing Guidelines. Assuming that the defendant has not previously been convicted of a crime, that Table specifies that the judge in such a case *must* impose a sentence of between 21 and 27 months.[111] If the defendant has previously been convicted of a crime, the sentence may increase dramatically.

The judge may depart from the range specified in the Sentencing Table only under limited circumstances. In *Koon v. United States*, the U.S. Supreme Court explained the rigorous analysis that a federal court must apply before it may determine that a case is outside of the "heartland of typical cases" to which the 2012 Federal Sentencing Guidelines are intended to apply.[112] Although the Court also admonished sentencing courts that it was not the purpose of Congress in adopting the Guidelines to withdraw all sentencing discretion from district court judges,[113] departures, especially downward departures, generally are subject to close scrutiny by the appellate courts.[114]

Organizational Defendants

Fines. A fine structure for organizational defendants is set out in Chapter 8 of the 2012 Federal Sentencing Guidelines. Although these Organizational Sentencing guidelines do *not* specify fines for environmental offenses *per se*, many courts have looked to the Guidelines for general guidance in calculating appropriate sentences for environmental offenses.

Under the Guidelines, fines for organizational defendants are generally based on the greater of the gain to the defendant, the loss to the victim, or an amount determined by a table of fines that is graduated to reflect the seriousness of the crime.[115] In addition to paying a fine, an organizational defendant will, whenever practicable, also be ordered by the sentencing judge to remedy any harm caused by its offense.[116]

Other Factors Affecting Organizational Defendants. Most corporations understand the financial impact of paying what are likely to be substantial fines if they are convicted of CAA violations. Paying fines may be far less disruptive, however, than other impacts associated with a major criminal investigation.

The government has broad authority to investigate for evidence of a crime or evidence that no crime occurred. Upon a mere recitation of probable cause, government investigators can obtain search warrants from a court authorizing them to come onto corporate property – the plant site and corporate offices – and to seize documents within the scope of the warrant. They can compel people to appear and to testify before grand juries, causing distress and expense to subpoenaed employees. They can use coercive tactics and threats of prosecution to convince employees to provide evidence against the corporation or the most senior officers and employees in the corporation. The government can, in short, make the corporation's daily life extremely difficult while an investigation is underway. Careful compliance planning is important in light of these potential impacts, quite apart from the desire to avoid exposure to fines and penalties.

Enforcement and The "Credible Evidence" Rule

In February 1997, EPA promulgated regulations implementing three major CAA regulatory programs that significantly expand the kind of information the government and citizen suit plaintiffs can use to bring enforcement actions. Collectively known as the "credible evidence" ("CE") rule, these regulations govern the methods and procedures for determining compliance with numerical emission limits under SIPs, new source performance standards, and section 112.[117] Prior to the CE rule, if a regulation or permit issued under one of these programs specified a compliance determination procedure for a numerical emission standard, only that procedure could be used to determine compliance with that standard.[118] Under the CE rule, a violation of a numerical standard or emission limit could be established by any "credible evidence" that a violation would have been found had the applicable compliance test or procedure been performed.[119]

EPA promulgated the CE rule in response to the 1990 Amendments to section 113 allowing the use of "credible evidence (including evidence other than the applicable test method)" to show the duration of a violation for purposes of determining the amount of civil penalties.[120] The CE rule, however, does not limit the use of "credible evidence" to establishing the duration of a violation.[121] Rather, the rule applies to compliance certifications as well as to establishing whether a person has violated or is in violation of any emission standard or limit.[122] As the rule provides, "nothing . . . shall preclude the use, including the exclusive use, of any credible evidence or information" relevant to whether a source would have been in compliance with the applicable standard if the prescribed performance test or procedure had been performed.[123] EPA takes the position that because the CE rule merely clarifies pre-existing evidentiary rules, it applies to any alleged violation whether occurring before or after the effective date of the revisions.[124] In 2005, however, the U.S. Court of Appeals for the Eleventh Circuit held that data from a plant's continuous opacity monitoring system could not be used to prove violations before the date that the jurisdictional state adopted its own CE rule.[125]

Although the CE rule does not define the term "credible evidence," EPA states in the preamble to the rule that it expects that "most if not all of the data that EPA would consider as potentially credible evidence of an emission violation at a unit subject to monitoring under the agency's proposed [Compliance Assurance Monitoring] rule would be generated through means of appropriate, well-designed parametric or emission monitoring submitted by the source itself and approved by the permitting authority, or through other requirements in the source's permit."[126] Clearly, "credible evidence" will include any continuous monitoring, even if such monitoring was intended for purposes other than compliance with numerical emission limits.

Since its promulgation, there has been considerable debate concerning the practical effect of the CE rule on existing emission standards. That is, the stringency of an emission standard depends not only on the numerical limit but also on the protocol by which compliance with the numerical standard is determined. A change in the compliance protocol can affect the stringency of a standard as much as a change in the level of the numerical standard itself. The compliance protocols for an emission standard are typically developed in rulemaking proceedings (generally the same proceedings in which the standard was developed) that explore complex technical issues regarding sampling procedures, accuracy of measurement, and other matters that ensure that the data generated by the compliance method is consistent with the data used to establish the emission standard. On this basis, many emission standards specify periodic "stack tests" as the compliance protocol, although the standards may also be accompanied by rules that require collection of continuous data for purposes other than determining compliance with the numerical emissions standard, for example, to determine compliance with any applicable "general duty" requirement,[127] or to determine whether to require performance of the applicable compliance test. As a result, there may be substantial questions whether an existing numerical standard would have been adopted if the compliance protocol involved continuous monitoring.

As a result of these concerns, the 1997 CE rule was challenged in the U.S. Court of Appeals for the D.C. Circuit by numerous industry groups on the grounds that the rule could result in tightening numerical emission standards without compliance with required statutory criteria or administrative procedures.[128] The D.C. Circuit dismissed the petitions as unripe, holding that pre-enforcement review was not available due to the factual questions raised and lack of hardship pending review.[129] The court indicated, however, that the CE rule could become ripe for review if EPA took an enforcement action based on CE.[130] Although EPA and states have largely ignored the CE rule as an enforcement tool, environmental groups have used it to file citizen suits against industrial facilities in federal district courts alleging violation of opacity standards based on data recorded by continuous opacity monitoring data.[131]

Compliance Audits

In 1991, the Department of Justice released guidelines on the factors that prosecutors should consider in making criminal enforcement decisions under federal environmental statutes.[132] The guidelines encourage self-auditing and voluntary disclosure of environmental violations by the regulated community and list several factors that will weigh against criminal enforcement action, including: (1)

regular, comprehensive environmental audits; (2) timely voluntary disclosure of violations; (3) good faith efforts to remedy noncompliance; (4) an effective internal disciplinary system; and (5) prompt, good faith efforts to reach compliance agreements with federal and state authorities.[133]

After a formal review of its own environmental auditing guidelines, EPA in 1995 issued its own audit policy.[134] The policy sets forth the conditions under which EPA will reduce penalties assessed against regulated entities when they manage their own compliance responsibilities and disclose their own violations of environmental laws.[135]

Pursuant to the audit policy, entities that meet certain conditions are generally eligible for lower civil penalties (by eliminating the gravity-based penalties that would otherwise be assessed).[136] EPA issued minor revisions to the 1995 audit policy in 2000.[137] The 2000 revisions maintain the policy's basic structure and terms but broaden its availability. In the 1995 and 2000 renditions of the audit policy, EPA would generally not pursue criminal enforcement where a company discovered, voluntarily reported, and promptly corrected violations pursuant to a properly designed and implemented environmental audit program.[138] EPA reported that in FY 2010, 561 companies used the audit policy to resolve violations of 1967 facilities.[139]

The audit policy specifically does not establish a legal privilege for environmental audits. Numerous states have adopted their own audit privilege or immunity legislation. Such action has created conflict between state law voluntary disclosure, immunity, and environmental audit objectives, and EPA's desire for increased enforcement based on state Title V operating permit programs. In this regard, interest groups have threatened to sue the Agency if it approves Title V permit programs in states that have statutes creating environmental audit privileges or voluntary disclosure immunities, and have filed petitions to revoke delegated or approved programs in some states. These groups have argued that such delegation or approval would interfere with a primary purpose of the Title V permit program to ease citizen enforcement by "clarify[ing] and mak[ing] more readily enforceable a source's pollution control requirements."[140]

EPA has generally opposed state privilege and immunity legislation and has issued guidance describing circumstances in which such legislation will render a state's Title V program inadequate (based on the concern that such legislation could interfere with state enforcement of Title V permits).[141] Generally, the guidance provides that a state must demonstrate that it has "adequate" enforcement authority to secure delegation.[142] In addition, a state must preserve its ability to obtain immediate and complete injunctive relief, to obtain significant penalties, and to obtain criminal fines and sanctions.[143] The guidance encourages states to use audit "policies," not statutes.[144]

EPA has concluded that, since implementation of the audit policy began in 1995, "internal reviews of compliance have become more widely adopted by the regulated community, as part of good management."[145] In addition, EPA has found that "most violations disclosed under the Policy are not in the highest priority enforcement areas for protecting human health and the environment" and that the Agency "can reduce investment in the program to a limited national presence without undermining the incentives for regulated entities to do internal compliance reviews to find and correct violations."[146] As it contemplates reducing investment in the audit program, EPA is considering several options, including a modified Audit Policy program that is self-implementing.

Citizen Enforcement Authority

Citizen Suits

Congress included citizen suit provisions in the 1970 Amendments to the Act and broadened the ability of citizens to act as "private attorneys general" under the 1990 Amendments. The following paragraphs discuss the citizen suit provisions.

Civil Penalty Awards

Section 304 of the Act gives citizens authority to file suit against EPA for its failure to perform a nondiscretionary duty, or against individual sources or states alleged to be in violation of statutory requirements.[147] Before 1990, the Act gave federal district courts the authority to issue injunctive relief (that is, to order EPA to take certain actions or to order an individual source to cease violating the Act). The 1990 Amendments added another remedy in such cases: the district courts now have the explicit power to award civil penalties against defendants other than EPA.[148]

The penalties collected in citizen suits are held in a penalty fund to be used by the Administrator "to finance air compliance and enforcement activities."[149] The 1990 Amendments also provided that instead of ordering payment to the fund, district courts may order that civil penalties up to $100,000 be used in "beneficial mitigation projects which are consistent with this [Act] and enhance the public health or the environment."[150]

Past Violations

The 1990 Amendments allowed citizens to sue for past violations "if there is evidence that the alleged violation has been *repeated*."[151]

Effect of Citizen Suits on the United States

Suits in which the United States is not a party have no binding effect on the United States. No consent judgment can be entered prior to 45 days following receipt of the proposed consent judgment by the Administrator and the Attorney General. The United States can intervene in a citizen suit as of right at any time.[152]

Which District Courts Have Jurisdiction

The pre-1990 Act gave any federal district court the power to order the Administrator to perform any nondiscretionary duty. Under the amended Act, citizens may still sue in federal district court to compel performance of a non-discretionary duty, including a failure to act that constitutes unreasonable delay. In some cases, though, the choice of district court is not an open one. Specifically, in unreasonable delay suits involving final agency action referred to in section 307(b) (*e.g.*, many of the national rulemakings required by the Act), citizen suit plaintiffs may file only in a district court within the circuit in which such action would be reviewable under section 307(b).[153] Because many actions reviewable under section 307(b) must be brought in the D.C. Circuit,[154] such unreasonable delay cases will often have to be brought in the District Court for the District of Columbia.

At least 180 days before a citizen suit can be commenced for "unreasonable delay," the filing party must give notice to the Administrator, the state, and any alleged violator.[155]

Public Involvement in Settlements

The amended Act requires that 30 days before the filing of a consent order or settlement to which the United States is a party, such orders or settlements must be open to public comment by notice in the *Federal Register*.[156] This requirement applies to all consent orders or settlement agreements to which the United States is a party, except enforcement actions under sections 113 or 120 (a little-used section that authorizes noncompliance penalties) or Title II. Because of this provision, the United States must seek comment on the agreements that the government reaches with environmental groups and others suing EPA for not meeting statutory deadlines.

Bounty System

The Act allows the Administrator to award up to $10,000 to private citizens for information leading to penalties or convictions.[157] The payment is subject to "available appropriations for such purposes as provided in annual appropriation Acts." The Administrator may by regulation prescribe eligibility requirements.

On May 3, 1994, the Agency proposed rules setting forth the criteria and procedures for granting citizen awards.[158] The proposed rules described the criteria that the Agency would use in assessing the value of information and services and what is needed to adequately petition the Administrator for consideration of payment. The proposal also addressed confidentiality matters (because some citizens provide information or services on a confidential basis), and directions for providing information to the Agency.[159] As of mid-2013, EPA had not published final rules.

The Agency has taken the position, however, that section 113(f) is self-implementing and that awards may be granted pending final promulgation of the rules. On February 7, 1997, the Agency approved $37,000 in monetary awards under section 113(f) to 20 citizens who helped the Agency take successful enforcement actions under the Act.[160] Those were the first monetary awards given under that section of the Act.

Judicial Review of Final Agency Action

Under section 307(b) of the CAA, a judicial challenge to final Agency action must be brought in the appropriate United States Court of Appeals within 60 days after notice of that action is published in the *Federal Register*.[161] If the action is nationally applicable, or is of nationwide scope or effect and the Administrator publishes a determination to this effect, the petition for review must be filed in the U.S. Court of Appeals for the D.C. Circuit.[162] If the action is of local or regional effect, the petition must be filed in the appropriate regional U.S. Court of Appeals.[163]

Once an Agency action becomes final and the period for judicial review has expired, one is precluded from challenging issues resolved in that action in subsequent enforcement or review proceedings.[164] To the extent that new grounds arise affecting the validity of the Agency's action after the period for judicial review has expired (*e.g.*, the Agency issues an interpretation of the rule at odds with the basis for the rule described when it was promulgated), however, one may challenge the action within 60 days after the new grounds arise, based solely on those new grounds.[165]

The Act authorizes administrative petitions to reconsider rules based on grounds that arise after the close of the formal comment period but before the close of the period for judicial review.[166] A petition for reconsideration must show that the matter at issue could not have been raised during the public comment period and that it is of "central relevance" to the final rule.[167] The filing of an administrative petition for reconsideration is not a prerequisite to judicial review and does not extend the time for filing a petition for judicial review.[168]

Under the pre-1990 Act, an Agency decision to defer statutorily required action could give rise to confusion over whether jurisdiction to a challenge to the decision to defer would lie in the federal district court or the U.S. Court of Appeals. Under section 307(b)(2) of the 1990 Amendments, it is now clear that the Court of Appeals has exclusive jurisdiction where EPA has made a final decision to defer performance of a nondiscretionary statutory action.[169]

Notes

1. *See* EPA, Enforcement Annual Results for Fiscal Year 2012, *available at*

2. The number of EPA special agents and criminal investigators rose from about 50 in 1990 to more than 200 in 1998. In late 2007, there were only 168 investigators but the number increased steadily to 183 in FY 2008, 186 in FY 2009, and 206 in FY 2010, but then declined to 202 in FY 2011. *See* Robert Esworthy, Congressional Research Service, Federal Pollution Control Laws: How Are They Enforced?, CRS Report for Congress at 24 (July 7, 2012) ("Esworthy Report"), *available at* http://www.fas.org/sgp/crs/misc/RL34384.pdf.

3. EPA Enforcement Annual Results for FY 2012 at 13.

4. *Id.* EPA explained the decrease in new criminal cases opened and the number of defendants charged by the decline in case-carrying agents in its Office of Criminal Enforcement, Forensics and Training. *Id.*

5. *Id.* at 14. EPA further explains that "[t]he increased focus on tier 1 and 2 cases, which are generally more complex and more resource intensive, could also have contributed to fewer – but more significant – cases." *Id.* at 13.

6. *Id.* at 10. Although the total number of civil enforcement case conclusions decreased from 3705 in FY 2009 and 3666 in FY 2008, EPA explained that this is because "EPA continues to pursue larger more complex, risk-based enforcement cases leading to fewer initiations and conclusions in FY 11 and FY 12." *Id.*

7. *Id.* at 4.

8. EPA, EPA 300-R-95-004, Enforcement and Compliance Assurance Accomplishments Report: FY 1994 at 1-1 (May 1995), *available at* http://nepis.epa.gov/Exe/ZyPURL.cgi?Dockey=500006TW.txt.

9. EPA, FY08 – FY10 Compliance and Enforcement National Priority: Clean Air Act, New Source Review/Prevention of Significant Deterioration (Oct. 2007).

10. EPA, National Enforcement Initiatives for Fiscal Years 2008-2010; Clean Air Act: New Source Review/Prevention of Significant Deterioration, *available at* http://www.epa.gov/compliance/data/planning/initiatives/index.html.

11. All section references in this chapter are to the CAA unless otherwise indicated.

12. CAA § 113, 42 U.S.C. § 7413.

13. *Id.* § 113(d)(1), 42 U.S.C. § 7413(d)(1).

14. EPA, Civil Monetary Penalty Inflation Adjustment Rule: Final Rule, 61 Fed. Reg. 69,360, 69,360 (Dec. 31, 1996).

15. EPA, Civil Monetary Penalty Inflation Adjustment Rule: Final Rule, 69 Fed. Reg. 7121, 7126 Table 1 (Feb. 13, 2004).

16. EPA, Civil Monetary Penalty Inflation Adjustment Rule: Final Rule, 73 Fed. Reg. 75,340, 75,346 Table 1 (Dec. 11, 2008).

17. EPA Enforcement Annual Results for FY 2012 at 10.

18. CAA § 113(d)(1), 42 U.S.C. § 7413(d)(1). As noted above, every four years EPA raises the ceilings on penalties under its Civil Penalty Inflation Adjustment rule. For ease of discussion in this Handbook, however, the unadjusted penalty figures included in the Act will be used.

19. *Id.*

20. *Id.*

21. Federally assumed enforcement occurs when the Administrator finds that "violations of an applicable implementation plan or an approved permit program under [Title V] . . . are so widespread that such violations appear to result from a failure of the State . . . to enforce the plan or permit program . . . ." *Id.* § 113(a)(2), 42 U.S.C. § 7413(a)(2).

22. *Id.*

23. *Id.* § 113(d)(1), (a)(5), 42 U.S.C. § 7413(d)(1), (a)(5).

24. *Id.* § 113(d)(2), 42 U.S.C. § 7413(d)(2).

25. *See id.*; *see also* 5 U.S.C. §§ 554, 556.

26. *See* EPA, Consolidated Rules of Practice Governing the Administrative Assessment of Civil Penalties, Issuance of Compliance or Corrective Action Orders, and the Revocation, Termination or Suspension of Permits: Final Rule, 64 Fed. Reg. 40,138 (July 23, 1999) (codified at 40 C.F.R. pt. 22.

27. CAA § 113(d)(3), 42 U.S.C. § 7413(d)(3).

28. *Id.*

29. *Id.*

30. *Id.*

31. EPA, Field Citation Program: Notice of Proposed Rulemaking, 59 Fed. Reg. 22,776 (May 3, 1994).

32. EPA, Spring 2002 Regulatory Agenda; Semiannual Regulatory Agenda, 67 Fed. Reg. 33,724, 33,734 (May 13, 2002).

33. CAA § 113(d)(4), 42 U.S.C. § 7413(d)(4).

34. *Id.*

35. *Id.*

36. *Id.* § 113(d)(5), 42 U.S.C. § 7413(d)(5).

37. *Id.*

38. *Id.*

39. *See* EPA, Enforcement Annual Results for Fiscal Year 2012, *available at* http://www.epa.gov/enforcement/data/eoy2012/eoy-data.html (listing key results of compliance and enforcement activities under Accomplishments tab therein).

40. *Id.* at 6; EPA, Fiscal Year 2011: EPA Enforcement & Compliance Annual Results at 8 (Dec. 8, 2011), *available at* http://www.epa.gov/oecaerth/resources/reports/endofyear/eoy2011/resultscharts-fy2011.pdf (hereinafter "EPA Enforcement Annual Results for Fiscal Year 2011").

41. CAA § 113(b)(2), 42 U.S.C. § 7413(b)(2). In section 113(h), the term "operator" is defined to "include any person who is senior management personnel or a corporate officer. Except in the case of knowing and willful violations, such term shall not include any person who is a stationary engineer or technician responsible for the operation, maintenance, repair, or monitoring of equipment and facilities and who often has supervisory and training duties but who is not senior management personnel or a corporate officer." *Id.* § 113(h), 42 U.S.C. § 7413(h).

42. *Id.* § 113(a)(1), 42 U.S.C. § 7413(a)(1).

43. *Id.* § 113(a)(1)-(2), (b), 42 U.S.C. § 7413(a)(1)-(2), (b).

44. *Id.* § 113(b), 42 U.S.C. § 7413(b).

45. *Id.* § 114(a)(1)(C), (E), (F), 42 U.S.C. § 7414(a)(1)(C), (E), (F).

46. *Id.* § 114(a)(1), 42 U.S.C. § 7414(a)(1). Extensive information requests under section 114 of the Act are often EPA's first step in the enforcement process. More than 25 companies received "CAA Section 114" letters from the EPA in 2000, covering approximately 140 power plants. *See* "EPA Targets More Coal Plants," *Coal Outlook* (Oct. 30, 2000).

47. CAA § 114(a)(3), 42 U.S.C. § 7414(a)(3).

48. *Id.* § 114(a)(3)(B), (C), 42 U.S.C. § 7414(a)(3)(B), (C).

49. *Id.* § 113(e), 42 U.S.C. § 7413(e).

50. *See, e.g.*, Memorandum from William G. Rosenberg, Assistant Adm'r for Air & Radiation, EPA, and Edward E. Reich, Acting Assistant Adm'r for Enforcement, to EPA Reg'l Adm'rs, Regions I-X, et al., regarding Clean Air Act Stationary Source Civil Penalty Policy (Oct. 25, 1991), *available at* http://www.epa.gov/enforcement/air/documents/policies/stationary/penpol.pdf. In 1995, the Agency issued guidance on how penalty amounts should be pled and argued in administrative litigation. Memorandum from Robert Van Heuvelen, Director, Office of Regulatory Enforcement, EPA, to EPA Reg'l Counsel, Regions I-X, et al., regarding Guidance on Use of Penalty Policies in Administrative Litigation (Dec. 15, 1995), *available at* http://www.epa.gov/enforcement/waste/ documents/policies/gpoladminlitig-mem.pdf.

51. Order Affirming Initial Decision in Part and Vacating and Remanding in Part, *In the Matter of Employers Insurance Company of Wausau*, TSCA Appeal No. 95-6, 6 E.A.D. 735, 758 (EAB Feb. 11, 1997), *available at* http://www.epa.gov/eab/disk11/wausau.pdf. The EAB explained in its ruling that admin-

istrative law judges are free to ask EPA attorneys to explain how penalties are calculated and how they are consistent with the underlying statutes, but they must give the attorneys an opportunity to respond to any concerns they may have. *Id.* at 754 & n.20, 755-59.

52. *See also In re Allegheny Power Serv. Corp.*, CAA Appeal No. 99-4, 9 E.A.D. 636, 655 (EAB Feb. 15, 2001), *available at* http://www.epa.gov/eab/disk11/allegheny.pdf, *aff'd*, No. 6-01-cv-241 (S.D. W. Va. Apr. 5, 2002) (EPA's civil penalty policies "provide a framework that allows a presiding officer to apply his or her discretion to statutory penalty factors, thereby facilitating a uniform application of the factors.").

53. EPA, Calculation of the Economic Benefit of Noncompliance in EPA's Civil Penalty Enforcement Cases; Notice of Final Action and Response to Comment, 70 Fed. Reg. 50,326, 50,326 (Aug. 26, 2005).

54. *Id.*

55. *Id.* at 50,327.

56. *Id.*

57. *Id.* at 50,328.

58. *Id.* at 50,331.

59. CAA § 113(a)(2), 42 U.S.C. § 7413(a)(2).

60. *Id.* § 113(d)(1), 42 U.S.C. § 7413(d)(1).

61. *Id.* § 113(a)(4), 42 U.S.C. § 7413(a)(4).

62. *Id.*

63. *Tennessee Valley Auth. v. Whitman,* 336 F.3d 1236, 1239-40, 1248-49, 1256-60 (11th Cir. 2003).

64. *Id.* at 1258-59, 1267.

65. CAA § 113(a)(5), 42 U.S.C. § 7413(a)(5) (1988); *see also id.* § 167, 42 U.S.C. § 7477 (2011). In the pre-1990 Act, section 167 authorized the Administrator and states to "take such measures, including issuance of an order, or seeking injunctive relief, as necessary to prevent the construction" of major emitting facilities that failed first to get PSD permits. *Id.* § 167, 42 U.S.C. § 7477 (1988). The 1990 Amendments extended the Administrator's power under section 167 to stop both the construction and *modification* of major emitting facilities that do not conform to PSD requirements. *Id.* § 167, 42 U.S.C. § 7477 (2011).

66. *Id.* § 113(a)(5), 42 U.S.C. § 7413(a)(5) (2011).

67. *Id.* § 303, 42 U.S.C. § 7603 (emphasis added).

68. *Id.*

69. *Id.*

70. *Id.* § 307(a), 42 U.S.C. § 7607(a).

71. *Id.* § 113(e)(1), 42 U.S.C. § 7413(e)(1).

72. EPA, Interim Revised EPA Supplemental Environmental Projects Policy Issued; Notice, 60 Fed. Reg. 24,856, 24,856 (May 10, 1995), *superseded by* EPA, Final EPA Supplemental Environmental Projects Policy Issued; Notice, 63 Fed. Reg. 24,796, 24,796 (May 5, 1998).

73. 63 Fed. Reg. at 24,796.

74. Memorandum from Sylvia K. Lowrance, Acting Assistant Adm'r, EPA, to Reg'l Adm'rs, EPA Regions I-X, and Reg'l Counsel, EPA Regions I-X, regarding Supplemental Environmental Projects (SEP) Policy (Mar. 22, 2002), *available at* http://www.epa.gov/enforcement/documents/policies/sep/sepguide-mem.pdf.

75. EPA Enforcement Annual Results for FY 2012 at 7; EPA Enforcement Annual Results for Fiscal Year 2011 at 7. The total values of SEPs in fiscal years 2006, 2007, 2008, 2009, and 2010 were approximately $77, $30, $39, $41, and $23 million, respectively. *See* Esworthy Report at 48 Table B-4.

76. CAA § 113(c), 42 U.S.C. § 7413(c).

77. *Id.* § 302(e), 42 U.S.C. § 7602(e).

78. *Id.* § 113(c), (d)(1), 42 U.S.C. § 7413(c), (d)(1).

79. *See id.* § 113(h), 42 U.S.C. § 7413(h).

80. *Id.*

81. *Id.*

82. *Id.* § 113(c), 42 U.S.C. § 7413(c).

83. *See* U.S. Sentencing Comm'n, Guidelines Manual (Nov. 1, 2012), *available at* http://www.ussc.gov/Guidelines/2012_Guidelines/index.cfm (herein-after "2012 Federal Sentencing Guidelines").

84. The specific provisions for which criminal penalties may be sought are knowing violations of SIPs, section 113(a) orders, section 111(e) (new source performance standards), section 112 (hazardous air pollutants), section 129 (solid waste combustion), section 114 (inspections), sections 165(a) and 167 (PSD), section 303 (emergency orders), sections 502(a) and 503(c) (permits), or any provision relating to acid deposition control (Title IV) or stratospheric ozone control (Title VI).

85. CAA § 113(c)(1), 42 U.S.C. § 7413(c)(1).

86. *Id.*

87. *Id.* § 113(c)(2), 42 U.S.C. § 7413(c)(2).

88. *Id.* § 113(c)(3), 42 U.S.C. § 7413(c)(3).

89. *Id.* § 113(c)(5)(A), 42 U.S.C. § 7413(c)(5)(A).

90. *Id.*

91. *Id.* § 113(c)(5)(B), 42 U.S.C. § 7413(c)(5)(B).

92. *Id.*

93. CAA § 113(c)(5)(C), 42 U.S.C. § 7413(c)(5)(C).

94. *Id.* § 113(c)(6), 42 U.S.C. § 7413(c)(6).

95. *Id.* § 113(c)(5)(A), 42 U.S.C. § 7413(c)(5)(A).

96. *Id.* § 113(c)(4), 42 U.S.C. § 7413(c)(4).

97. Section 3571(e) of the CFEA states that its fine schedule applies unless the underlying law setting forth the offense (*e.g.,* the CAA) "specifies . . . a fine that is lower than the fine otherwise applicable under this section and such law, by specific reference, exempts the offense from the applicability of the fine otherwise applicable under this section . . . ." 18 U.S.C. § 3571(e). Because the CAA does not specifically provide that the CFEA is inapplicable, the CFEA's fine schedule will apply if it provides for a larger fine than would otherwise be imposed under the terms of the Act.

98. *See United States v. Booker*, 543 U.S. 220, 222, 245-46, 266 (2005). EPA Region V has indicated that the *Booker* decision is expected to impact the sentencing of individuals under the CAA. *See* EPA Region V, Office of Reg'l Counsel, Enforcement Action Summary FY 2005 January, *available at* http://web.archive.org/web/20081018053140/http://epa.gov/region5/orc/enfactions/enfactions2005/week-0105.htm (reporting that a federal district court judge re-sentenced a Clean Water Act defendant to a lesser sentence after the Supreme Court's ruling in *Booker*).

99. 18 U.S.C. § 3571(b)(3).

100. *Id.* § 3571(b)(4)-(6).

101. *Id.* § 3571(c).

102. Each spring, the U.S. Sentencing Commission ("USCC") proposes amendments to the sentencing guidelines. If they are not rejected by Congress, the amendments go into effect on November 1. In January 2013, the USCC published its first set of proposed amendments to the 2012 Federal Sentencing Guidelines. *See generally* U.S. Sentencing Comm'n, Proposed Amendments to the Sentencing Guidelines (Jan. 18, 2013), *available at* http://www.ussc.gov/ Legal/Amendments/Reader-Friendly/20130115_RFP_ Amendments.pdf.

103. 2012 Federal Sentencing Guidelines § 5E1.2.

104. *Id.* § 2Q1.3(a), (b)(1).

105. *Id.* § 5E1.2(c)(3).

106. *Id.* Section 5E1.2(c)(4) of the Guidelines provides that the maximum fine provided above does not apply "if the defendant is convicted under a statute authorizing (A) a maximum fine greater than $250,000, or (B) a fine for each day of violation. In such cases, the court may impose a fine up to the maximum authorized by the statute." *Id.* § 5E1.2(c)(4).

107. *Id.* § 5E1.2 cmt. 4.

108. *Id.* § 5E1.2(d)(1)-(4), (6).

109. *Id.* § 5E1.2(e).

110. *Id.*

111. *Id.*, Sentencing Table.

112. *Koon v. United States*, 518 U.S. 81, 94 (1996).

113. *Id.* at 92, 97-98, 113.

114. *See, e.g., United States v. Rybicki*, 96 F.3d 754, 757-59 (4th Cir. 1996).

115. 2012 Federal Sentencing Guidelines § 8C2.4.

116. *Id.* § 8B.1.2.

117. EPA, Credible Evidence Revisions: Final Rule, 62 Fed. Reg. 8314, 8323, 8328 (Feb. 24, 1997).

118. The only exceptions to this constraint were (i) the approval of an alternative method by the Administrator under carefully defined criteria, and (ii) the consent of the source owner or operator in the case of certain alternative methods specified in the regulations. *Id.* at 8326.

119. *Id.* at 8316.

120. *Id.* at 8321.

121. *Id.*

122. *Id.* at 8328.

123. *Id.*

124. *See* Steven A. Herman, Assistant Adm'r, EPA, to Reg'l Adm'rs, EPA Regions I-X, regarding Interim Policy and Guidance on the Use of 'Credible Evidence' in Air Enforcement Activities at 2 (Apr. 29, 1997), *available at* http://www.epa.gov/enforcement/air/documents/policies/stationary/credevinterim.pdf.

125. *Sierra Club v. Tennessee Valley Auth.*, 430 F.3d 1337, 1339-40 (11th Cir. 2005).

126. 62 Fed. Reg. at 8318. Compliance Assurance Monitoring is discussed in Chapter 4 of this Handbook.

127. For instance, source owners and operators have a general duty under 40 C.F.R. § 60.11(d) to operate facilities subject to new source performance standards in a manner "consistent with good air pollution control practice for minimizing emissions."

128. *Clean Air Implementation Project v. EPA*, 150 F.3d 1200, 1201, 1203-04 (D.C. Cir. 1998).

129. *Id.* at 1205.

130. *Id.* at 1204.

131. *See, e.g., Sierra Club v. Pub. Serv. Co. of Colorado, Inc.*, 894 F. Supp. 1455, 1456, 1458-60 (D. Colo. 1995).

132. *See, e.g.,* U.S. Sentencing Comm'n, Guidelines Manual, Part Q (Nov. 1, 1999), *available at* http://www.ussc.gov/Guidelines/1991_guidelines/1991_ manual.cfm (hereinafter "1991 Federal Sentencing Guidelines").

133. *Id.* § 8B.1.2 cmt.

134. EPA, Incentives for Self-Policing: Discovery, Disclosure, Correction and Prevention of Violations; Final Policy Statement, 60 Fed. Reg. 66,706 (Dec. 22, 1995).

135. *Id.* at 66,711-12.

136. *Id.* at 66,707-08. Specifically, the policy sets out nine conditions that a regulated entity must meet in order for EPA to decline to seek, or to reduce, gravity-based penalties: (1) systematic discovery; (2) voluntary disclosure; (3) prompt disclosure; (4) discovery or disclosure independent of government or third party plaintiff; (5) correction and remediation; (6) prevent recurrence; (7) no repeat violations; (8) certain violations excluded; and (9) cooperation. *See id.* at 66,711-12.

137. *See* EPA, Incentives for Self-Policing: Discovery, Disclosure, Correction, and Prevention of Violations; Final Policy Statement, 65 Fed. Reg. 19,618 (Apr. 11, 2000). In 2008, EPA published its interim approach for application of the audit policy to new owners, which became effective upon publication, stating that the Agency's intent to tailor Audit Policy incentives was that new owners that want to make a "clean start" at their recently acquired facilities can do so by addressing environmental noncompliance that began prior to acquisition of such facilities. EPA, Interim Approach to Applying the Audit Policy to New Owners; Notice; Request for Comment, 73 Fed. Reg. 44,991, 44,991 (Aug. 1, 2008).

138. 60 Fed. Reg. at 66,707; 65 Fed. Reg. at 19,620. EPA has stated that "systematic discovery" is not a requirement for eligibility for this incentive, although the entity

must be acting in good faith and adopt a systematic approach to preventing recurring violations. 60 Fed. Reg. at 66,709; 65 Fed. Reg. at 19,618-19, 19,620-21.

139. EPA, National Enforcement Trends (NETs), Fiscal Year 2010 Enforcement and Compliance Assurance Numbers at a Glance at A-1b (Oct. 2010), *available at* http://www.epa.gov/compliance/resources/report/nets/ numbers/nets10-numbersataglance-a.pdf.

140. S. Rep. No. 101-228 at 347 (1989), *reprinted in* 1990 U.S.C.C.A.N. 3385, 3730.

141. Memorandum from Steven A. Herman, Assistant Adm'r, EPA, to Reg'l Adm'rs, EPA, regarding Statement of Principles, Effect of State Audit Immunity/Privilege Laws on Enforcement Authority for Federal Programs (Feb. 14, 1997), *available at* http://www.epa.gov/wastes/laws-regs/state/policy/ audit.pdf.

142. *Id.* at 1-2.

143. *Id.* at 2.

144. *Id.*

145. EPA, FY 2013, Office of Enforcement and Compliance Assurance (OECA) National Program Manager (NPM) Guidance at 15 (Apr. 30, 2012), *available at* http://nepis.epa.gov/Exe/ZyPDF.cgi?Dockey=P100F6FG.PDF.

146. *Id.*

147. CAA § 304, 42 U.S.C. § 7604.

148. *Id.* § 304(a), 42 U.S.C. § 7604(a).

149. *Id.* § 304(g)(1), 42 U.S.C. § 7604(g)(1).

150. *Id.* § 304(g)(2), 42 U.S.C. § 7604(g)(2).

151. *Id.* § 304(a)(3), 42 U.S.C. § 7604(a)(3) (emphasis added).

152. *Id.* § 304(c)(3), 42 U.S.C. § 7604(c)(3).

153. *Id.* § 304(a), 42 U.S.C. § 7604(a).

154. *Id.* § 307(b), 42 U.S.C. § 7607(b).

155. *Id.* § 304(a), 42 U.S.C. § 7604(a).

156. *Id.* § 113(g), 42 U.S.C. § 7413(g).

157. *Id.* § 113(f), 42 U.S.C. § 7413(f).

158. EPA, Regulations Governing Awards Under Section 113(f) of the Clean Air Act: Notice of Proposed Rule, 59 Fed. Reg. 22,795 (May 3, 1994).

159. *Id.* at 22,795-96.

160. According to the Agency, one of the 20 awards was for the maximum amount while the others were for less. The Agency indicated that it assessed a total of more than $1.5 million in civil and administrative penalties in the cases involved. Press Release, EPA, First Monetary Awards Approved for Citizens Assistance in Enforcement Cases Under the Clean Air Act (Feb. 18, 1997).

161. CAA § 307(b), 42 U.S.C. § 7607(b).

162. *Id.*

163. *Id.*

164. *Id.* § 307(b)(2), 42 U.S.C. § 7607(b)(2).

165. *Id.* § 307(b)(1), 42 U.S.C. § 7607(b)(1).

166. *Id.* § 307(d)(7)(B), 42 U.S.C. § 7607(d)(7)(B).

167. *Id.*
168. *Id.* § 307(b)(1), 42 U.S.C. § 7607(b)(1).
169. *Id.* § 307(b)(2), 42 U.S.C. § 7607(b)(2).

Chapter 12

TRENDS IN CLEAN AIR ACT REGULATION AND LEGISLATION

The Clean Air Act ("CAA") is not self-implementing; EPA must implement the Act through rulemaking. To ensure prompt action, Congress set numerous deadlines for Agency action. Since the Act was amended in 1990, many regulatory proceedings have been completed. Many others, however, are still underway, and the Act requires periodic review and updating of many of its other programs. In planning for compliance, it is important to review periodically the status of EPA's implementation activities and anticipated agendas for regulatory and legislative action.

EPA's Regulatory Agenda

The 1990s witnessed a flood of new CAA rules, including air toxics technology-based standards, new source performance standards, revised national ambient air quality standards, rules regarding mobile source emissions standards and fuel composition, and stratospheric ozone protection rules. These implementation proceedings have continued into the new millennium, often in response to statutory requirements that EPA review periodically the adequacy of existing standards. Moreover, the new millennium has brought forth an entirely new set of regulations designed to address climate change. EPA publishes its regulatory agenda once a year, and it can be accessed from EPA's website at http://www2.epa.gov/laws-regulations/regulatory-agendas-and-regulatory-plans.

In many cases, regulatory proceedings are subject to statutory deadlines that have been missed, resulting in litigation or consent agreements to establish new, judicially enforceable deadlines. There are a variety of reasons for EPA's delay in issuing important CAA regulations. In many cases, EPA simply does not have the staff or resources to conduct proceedings in a timely fashion. In other cases, EPA has used advisory committees or regulatory negotiation in an attempt to encourage compromise on complex issues, and this approach may take longer than traditional rulemaking.

When EPA misses statutory deadlines, interest groups often file suit in district court against the Agency to establish deadlines for Agency action. Regulatory schedules imposed by district courts as a result of citizen suits have been a driving force behind promulgation of many of the new regulatory programs established since 1990, including the revised national ambient air quality standards for ozone and particulate matter, new source performance standards, and air toxics standards. The citizen suit-based schedules for regulatory action can influence the scope of public input and inter-agency review, as well as the adequacy of the final rule itself. The problems created by statutory deadlines merit careful consideration by Congress in any new CAA-related legislation.

EPA's heavy regulatory agenda has also led the Agency to explore new ways to implement the Act. For example, soon after enactment of the 1990 Amendments, EPA announced a "consensus building" approach to regulation. This approach involved increased reliance on advisory committees and regulatory negotiation in an attempt to speed the regulatory process by giving interested parties an opportunity for early input. Unfortunately, this approach did not always result in quicker implementation of the Act, but often in time-consuming "negotiation" that ultimately gave way to traditional rulemaking.

Another product of the Agency's heavy regulatory agenda is an increased reliance on guidance and policy statements to give content to regulatory requirements. While the D.C. Circuit has cautioned EPA on substituting guidance for rulemaking,[1] this practice has accelerated in recent years. Subjects for Agency guidance include Title V permit implementation,[2] new source permitting,[3] and emissions monitoring and compliance requirements.[4]

Finally, the Agency engages in policy development through enforcement proceedings. Perhaps the most striking example of this is the Agency's new source enforcement initiative (discussed in Chapter 11), which the Agency itself has characterized as a new approach to regulating existing facilities.[5] Developing policy through enforcement, of course, raises due process concerns, as the courts have recognized.[6]

Formulating compliance strategies in response to the regulatory uncertainties created by constantly evolving regulatory obligations remains a challenge. In some cases, drafts of proposed EPA rules have been used to inform compliance planning. In other cases, states have assumed a more important role in interpreting and implementing the Act, providing some protection for good faith compliance efforts. In still other cases, historical EPA guidance has been used in an attempt to predict how EPA might act under programs that have their roots in the pre-1990 Act. Needless to say, acting on tentative or partial information entails risks, which is only emphasized by EPA's recent enforcement actions.

Clean Air Act Legislation

Several years after the CAA Amendments of 1990 were signed into law, Congress started to debate issues raised by EPA's implementation of that legislation. That debate has been going on almost continuously since that time, with the most prominent areas of discussion being interstate and international air pollution and climate change.

In February 2002, in response to legislative initiatives calling for new requirements to reduce power plant air pollutant emissions, the Bush Administration proposed comprehensive legislation – known as "the Clear Skies Initiative" – to establish additional mandatory reductions in emissions of sulfur dioxide ("SO_2"), nitrogen oxides ("NOx"), and mercury from the electric utility sector.[7] The legislation would have established phased reductions of the three pollutants, achieving a cumulative 70 percent reduction from 2002 levels by 2018. The legislation also would have addressed other power plant CAA obligations, such as new source review and regional haze regulations, in order to conform those rules to a new timetable and provide increased regulatory certainty.

In January 2004, in the absence of action on the President's Clear Skies Initiative, EPA proposed a similar (but geographically more limited) regulatory alternative – the "Clean Air Interstate Rule" ("CAIR"). EPA finalized the rule in 2005.[8] According to EPA, when fully implemented, CAIR (discussed above in Chapter 2) would reduce SO_2 emissions from power plants in 28 eastern states and the District of Columbia by more than 70 percent and NOx emissions by more than 60 percent from 2003 levels. As discussed in Chapter 2, CAIR was ultimately remanded to the D.C. Circuit as inconsistent with law, but left in place pending remand rulemaking.[9] The replacement rule developed on remand – called the Cross-State Air Pollution Rule – was also vacated by the D.C. Circuit as contrary to law.[10] As a result, CAIR continues in place as the operative interstate air pollution rule, despite having been overturned by the court several years ago. This is but one of a number of examples of the importance of and need for periodic legislation to update the CAA to address new pollution issues that do not fit easily within the existing CAA structure.

In sum, implementation of the CAA will continue to present significant challenges for both EPA and industry – challenges that will expand in scope and complexity as interstate and international air pollution issues, including regulation of greenhouse gas emissions, increasingly become the focus of the legislative debate.

Notes

1. *See Appalachian Power Co. v. EPA*, 208 F.3d 1015, 1028 (D.C. Cir. 2000).

2. *See* EPA, White Paper for Streamlined Development of Part 70 Permit Applications (July 10, 1995), *available at* www.epa.gov/region7/air/title5/t5memos/fnlwtppr.pdf; EPA, White Paper Number 2 for Improved Implementation of the Part 70 Operating Permits Program (Mar. 5, 1996), *available at* www.epa.gov/ttn/oarpg/t5/memoranda/wtppr-2.pdf.

3. *See, e.g.*, Letter from Stephen D. Page, Dir., Office of Air Quality Planning & Standards, EPA, to Paul Plath, Senior Partner, E3 Consulting, LLC (Dec. 13, 2005), *available at* http://www.epa.gov/region07/air/nsr/nsrmemos/ igccbact.pdf (stating that EPA believes permit writers do not have to consider the use of integrated gasification combined cycle as best available control technology in writing Clean Air Act permits for new coal-fired power plants). Several environmental groups challenged EPA's letter by claiming it was equivalent to a final agency action and that EPA violated federal law by not taking comment on its decision. *See* Intervenor Pacificorp's Brief, *Utah Chapter of the Sierra Club v. Utah Air Quality Bd.*, No. 20080113-SC, 2008 WL 8973170, at *35 nn.20-21 (Utah July 3, 2008).

4. For example, several states have included limits in Title V permits that transform monitoring parameters into "never-to-be-exceeded" limits. Ohio facilities have successfully appealed their Title V permits to the state's Environmental Review Appeals Commission ("ERAC") on the ground that such operational restrictions are not authorized. *General Electric Lighting v. Jones*, Case No. ERAC 185017, 2005 WL 3778691 (ERAC Mar. 1, 2005); *see also General Electric Lighting v. Jones*, Case No. ERAC 185017 (ERAC Aug. 21, 2003). The ERAC found that "the inclusion of any operational restriction which can[not] be *demonstrated to directly relate to the enforceability of an existing applicable requirement* and . . . not [to] alter that underlying requirement" is not lawful. *General Electric Lighting*, 2005 WL 3778691 at *9 (emphasis in original).

5. Jim Jackson & Chris Oh, Office of Enforcement and Compliance Assurance, EPA, Internal Enforcement Memorandum, *Coal-Fired Power Plants* (undated, *ca.* 1998).

6. *See, e.g., Tenn. Valley Auth. v. Whitman*, 336 F.3d 1236, 1244-45, 1258-59 (11th Cir. 2003).

7. The official title of the legislation as introduced is "a bill to amend the Clean Air Act to reduce air pollution through expansion of cap-and-trade programs, to provide an alternative regulatory classification for units subject to the cap and trade program, and for other purposes." *See* Clear Skies Act, S. 485, 108th Cong. (2003); Clear Skies Act, H.R. 999, 108th Cong. (2003). Both the Senate and House of Representatives versions of this legislation were introduced on February 27, 2003.

8. *See* EPA, Rule To Reduce Interstate Transport of Fine Particulate Matter and Ozone (Clean Air Interstate Rule); Revisions to Acid Rain Program; Revisions to the NOx SIP Call: Final Rule, 70 Fed. Reg. 25,162 (May 12, 2005). The final version of CAIR covers a slightly different set of states than the proposed version and includes both seasonal and annual cap-and-trade programs for NOx. Following its publication, EPA received twelve separate petitions for reconsideration of CAIR. In response, EPA determined that its decisions in the final CAIR rule were reasonable and should not be changed. *See* EPA, Rule To Reduce Interstate Transport of Fine Particulate Matter and Ozone (Clean Air Interstate Rule): Reconsideration: Final Notice of Reconsideration, 71 Fed. Reg. 25,304 (Apr. 28, 2006).

9. *North Carolina v. EPA*, 531 F.3d 896, *on reh'g* 550 F.3d 1176, 1178 (D.C. Cir. 2008).

10. *EME Homer City Generation, L.P. v. EPA*, 696 F.3d 7 (D.C. Cir. 2012), *cert. granted* 2013 WL 1283840 (U.S. June 24, 2013).

Appendix 1

ACRONYMS

μg/m3	Micrograms per cubic met
AOS	Alternative operating scenario(s)
AQA	Air Quality Act
AQRV(s)	Air quality-related value(s)
BACM	Best available control measures
BACT	Best available control technology
BART	Best available retrofit technology
BSER	Best system of emission reduction
CAA	Clean Air Act
CAAAC	Clean Air Act Advisory Committee
CAFE	Corporate average fuel economy
CAIR	Clean Air Interstate Rule
CAM	Compliance assurance monitoring
CAMR	Clean Air Mercury Rule
CARB	California Air Resources Board
CASAC	Clean Air Scientific Advisory Committee
CCS	Carbon capture and storage (or carbon capture and sequestration)
CCT	Clean coal technology
CE	Credible evidence
CEMS	Continuous emission monitoring system
CENRAP	Central Regional Air Planning Association
CERCLA	Comprehensive Environmental Response, Compensation, and Liability Act
CF	Clean fuels
CFC(s)	Chlorofluorocarbon(s)
CFEA	Criminal Fine Enforcement Act
CH4	Methane
CISWI	Commercial and industrial solid waste incineration units
CO	Carbon monoxide
CO2	Carbon dioxide
CO2e	Carbon dioxide equivalent
CSAPR	Cross-State Air Pollution Rule
CSB	Chemical Safety and Hazard Investigation Board
CTG(s)	Control technique guideline(s)

DCIA	Debt Collection and Improvement Act
EAB	Environmental Appeals Board
EGU(s)	Electric generating unit(s)
EHS	Extremely hazardous substance(s)
EISA	Energy Independence and Security Act
EPA	United States Environmental Protection Agency
EPCRA	Emergency Planning and Community Right-To-Know Act
FCPP	Four Corners Power Plant
FIP(s)	Federal implementation plan(s)
FLAG	Federal Land Managers' Air Quality Related Values Work Group
FLM	Federal land manager
FY	Fiscal year
g/mi	Grams per mile
GACT	Generally available control technology
GHG(s)	Greenhouse gas(es)
GVWR	Gross vehicle weight rating
HAP(s)	Hazardous air pollutant(s)
HBFC(s)	Hydrobromofluorocarbon(s)
HCFC(s)	Hydrochlorofluorocarbon(s)
HFC(s)	Hydrofluorocarbon(s)
HEW	Health, Education, and Welfare
I/M	Inspection and maintenance
ICTA	International Center for Technology Assessment
IGCC	Integrated gasification combined cycle
ISA	Integrated science assessment
IUVP	In-use verification program
kg/hr	Kilograms per hour
LAER	Lowest achievable emission rate
lbs CO2/MWh	Pounds of carbon dioxide per megawatt hour
lb/mmBtu	Pounds per million British thermal units
LEV(s)	Low emission vehicle(s)
MACT	Maximum available control technology
MANE-VU	Mid-Atlantic/Northeast Visibility Union
mmBtu/hour	Million British thermal units per hour
mpg	Miles per gallon
MRPO	Midwest Regional Planning Organization
MTBE	Methyl tertiary butyl ether
MW	Megawatts
N2O	Nitrous oxide
NAAQS	National ambient air quality standards
NESHAPs	National emission standards for hazardous air pollutants
NGS	Navajo Generating Station

NHTSA	National Highway Traffic Safety Administration
NNSR	Nonattainment new source review
NO2	Nitrogen dioxide
NOx	Nitrogen oxides
NSPS	New source performance standard(s)
NSR	New source review
OAQPS	Office of Air Quality Planning and Standards
OSHA	Office of Health and Safety Administration
PAL(s)	Plantwide applicability limit(s)
PFC(s)	Perfluorocarbon(s)
PM	Particulate matter
PM2.5	Fine particulate matter
PM10	Coarse particulate matter
POTW(s)	Publicly owned treatment work(s)
ppb	Parts per billion
ppm	Parts per million
PSD	Prevention of significant deterioration
PSM	Process safety management
RACM	Reasonably available control measures
RACT	Reasonably available control technology
RCRA	Resource Conservation and Recovery Act
RFG	Reformulated gasoline
RFP	Reasonable further progress
RFS	Renewable fuel standard
RMP	Risk management plan
RMRR	Routine maintenance, repair, and replacement
RPO(s)	Regional planning organization(s)
RTA	Regional transport area
RTR	Risk and technology review
SCR	Selective catalytic reduction
SEP(s)	Supplement environmental project(s)
SF6	Sulfur hexafluoride
SIC	Standard industrial classification
SIP(s)	State implementation plan(s)
SJGS	San Juan Generating Station
SNAP	Significant new alternatives policy
SNCR	Selective noncatalytic reduction
SO2	Sulfur dioxide
SOx	Sulfur oxides
SSM	Startup, shutdown, and malfunction
TAR	Tribal Authority Rule
TCM(s)	Transportation control measure(s)
tpy	Tons per year

TVA	Tennessee Valley Authority
USCC	United States Sentencing Commission
VISTAS	Visibility Improvement State and Tribal Association of the Southeast
VMT	Vehicle miles traveled
VOC(s)	Volatile organic compound(s)
WRAP	Western Regional Air Partnership
ZEV(s)	Zero-emission vehicle(s)

Appendix 2

SOURCE CATEGORIES SUBJECT TO CLEAN AIR ACT PROGRAMS

NSPS Source Categories for New, Modified, and Reconstructed Sources

- (40 C.F.R. Part 60)
- Fossil-Fuel Fired Steam Generators (construction or modification commenced after Aug. 17, 1971) (Subpart D)
- Electric Utility Steam Generating Units (construction, modification or reconstruction commenced after Sept. 18, 1978) (Subpart Da)
- Industrial-Commercial-Institutional Steam Generating Units (construction, modification or reconstruction commenced after June 19, 1984) (Subpart Db)
- Small Industrial-Commercial-Institutional Steam Generating Units (construction, modification or reconstruction commenced after June 9, 1989) (Subpart Dc)
- Incinerators (construction or modification commenced after Aug. 17, 1971) (Subpart E)
- Municipal Waste Combustors (construction commenced between Dec. 20, 1989, and Sept. 20, 1994; modification or reconstruction commenced between Dec. 20, 1989, and June 19, 1996) (Subpart Ea)
- Large Municipal Waste Combustors (construction commenced after Sept. 20, 1994; modification or reconstruction commenced after June 19, 1996) (Subpart Eb)
- Hospital/Medical/Infectious Waste Incinerators (construction commenced after June 20, 1996; modification commenced after Mar. 16, 1998) (Subpart Ec) Portland Cement Plants (construction or modification commenced after Aug. 17, 1971) (Subpart F)
- Nitric Acid Plants (construction or modification commenced between Aug. 17, 1971, and Oct. 14, 2011) (Subpart G)
- Nitric Acid Plants (construction, modification or reconstruction commenced after Oct. 14, 2011) (Subpart Ga)

- Sulfuric Acid Plants (construction or modification commenced after Aug. 17, 1971) (Subpart H)
- Hot Mix Asphalt Facilities (construction or modification commenced after June 11, 1973) (Subpart I)
- Petroleum Refineries (for fluid catalytic cracking unit catalyst regenerators or fuel gas combustion devices, construction, modification or reconstruction commenced between June 11, 1973, and May 14, 2007 (non-flare), or June 24, 2008 (flare); for Claus sulfur recovery plants, between Oct. 4, 1976, and May 14, 2007) (Subpart J)
- Petroleum Refineries (except for flares and delayed coking units, construction, modification or reconstruction commenced after May 14, 2007; for flares, after June 24, 2008; for delayed coking units, various dates) (Subpart Ja)
- Storage Vessels for Petroleum Liquids (construction, modification or reconstruction commenced between June 11, 1973 (vessels 40,000-65,000 gal), or Mar. 8, 1974 (vessels over 65,000 gal), and May 19, 1978) (Subpart K)
- Storage Vessels for Petroleum Liquids (construction, modification or reconstruction commenced between May 19, 1978, and July 23, 1984) (Subpart Ka)
- Volatile Organic Liquid Storage Vessels, Including Petroleum Liquid Storage Vessels (construction, modification or reconstruction commenced after July 23, 1984) (Subpart Kb)
- Secondary Lead Smelters (construction or modification commenced after June 11, 1973) (Subpart L)
- Secondary Brass and Bronze Production Plants (construction or modification commenced after June 11, 1973) (Subpart M)
- Primary Emissions from Basic Oxygen Process Furnaces (construction or modification commenced after June 11, 1973) (Subpart N)
- Secondary Emissions from Basic Oxygen Process Steelmaking Facilities (construction, modification or reconstruction commenced after Jan. 20, 1983) (Subpart Na)
- Sewage Treatment Plants (construction or modification commenced after June 11, 1973) (Subpart O)
- Primary Copper Smelters (construction or modification commenced after Oct. 16, 1974) (Subpart P)
- Primary Zinc Smelters (construction or modification commenced after Oct. 16, 1974) (Subpart Q)
- Primary Lead Smelters (construction or modification commenced after Oct. 16, 1974) (Subpart R) Primary Aluminum Reduction Plants (construction or modification commenced after Oct. 23, 1974) (Subpart S)
- Phosphate Fertilizer Industry: Wet-Process Phosphoric Acid Plants (construction or modification commenced after Oct. 22, 1974) (Subpart T)

- Phosphate Fertilizer Industry: Superphosphoric Acid Plants (construction or modification commenced after Oct. 22, 1974) (Subpart U)
- Phosphate Fertilizer Industry: Diammonium Phosphate Plants (construction or modification commenced after Oct. 22, 1974) (Subpart V)
- Phosphate Fertilizer Industry: Triple Superphosphate Plants (construction or modification commenced after Oct. 22, 1974) (Subpart W)
- Phosphate Fertilizer Industry: Granular Triple Superphosphate Storage Facilities (construction or modification commenced after Oct. 22, 1974) (Subpart X)
- Coal Preparation and Processing Plants (construction, modification or reconstruction commenced after Oct. 27, 1974) (Subpart Y)
- Ferroalloy Production Facilities (construction or modification commenced after Oct. 21, 1974) (Subpart Z)
- Steel Plants: Electric Arc Furnaces (construction, modification or reconstruction commenced between Oct. 21, 1974, and Aug. 17, 1983) (Subpart AA)
- Steel Plants: Electric Arc Furnaces and Argon-Oxygen Decarburization Vessels (construction, modification or reconstruction commenced after Aug. 17, 1983) (Subpart AAa)
- Kraft Pulp Mills (construction or modification commenced after Sept. 24, 1976) (Subpart BB)
- Glass Manufacturing Plants (construction or modification commenced after June 15, 1979) (Subpart CC)
- Grain Elevators (construction, modification or reconstruction commenced after Aug. 3, 1978) (Subpart DD)
- Surface Coating of Metal Furniture (construction, modification or reconstruction commenced after Nov. 28, 1980) (Subpart EE)
- Stationary Gas Turbines (construction, modification or reconstruction commenced after Oct. 3, 1977) (Subpart GG)
- Lime Manufacturing Plants (construction or modification commenced after May 3, 1977) (Subpart HH)
- Lead-Acid Battery Manufacturing Plants (construction or modification commenced after Jan. 14, 1980) (Subpart KK)
- Metallic Mineral Processing Plants (construction or modification commenced after Aug. 24, 1982) (Subpart LL)
- Automobile and Light Duty Truck Surface Coating Operations (construction, modification or reconstruction commenced after Oct. 5, 1979) (Subpart MM)
- Phosphate Rock Plants (construction, modification or reconstruction commenced after Sept. 21, 1979) (Subpart NN)
- Ammonium Sulfate Manufacture (construction or modification commenced after Feb. 4, 1980) (Subpart PP)

- Graphic Arts Industry: Publication Rotogravure Printing (construction, modification or reconstruction commenced after Oct. 28, 1980) (Subpart QQ)
- Pressure Sensitive Tape and Label Surface Coating Operations (construction, modification or reconstruction commenced after Dec. 30, 1980) (Subpart RR)
- Industrial Surface Coating: Large Appliances (construction, modification or reconstruction commenced after Dec. 24, 1980) (Subpart SS)
- Metal Coil Surface Coating (construction, modification or reconstruction commenced after Jan. 5, 1981) (Subpart TT)
- Asphalt Processing and Asphalt Roofing Manufacture (construction or modification commenced after May 26, 1981 (storage tanks or blowing stills for nonroofing asphalt only), or Nov. 18, 1980 (other facilities)) (Subpart UU)
- Equipment Leaks of VOC in the Synthetic Organic Chemicals Manufacturing Industry (construction, modification or reconstruction commenced between Jan. 5, 1981, and Nov. 7, 2006) (Subpart VV)
- Equipment Leaks of VOC in the Synthetic Organic Chemicals Manufacturing Industry (construction, modification or reconstruction commenced after Nov. 7, 2006) (Subpart VVa)
- Beverage Can Surface Coating Industry (construction, modification or reconstruction commenced after Nov. 26, 1980) (Subpart WW)
- Bulk Gasoline Terminals (construction or modification commenced after Dec. 17, 1980) (Subpart XX)
- New Residential Wood Heaters (manufactured after July 1, 1988, or sold at retail after July 1, 1990) (Subpart AAA)
- Rubber Tire Manufacturing Industry (construction, modification or reconstruction commenced after Jan. 20, 1983) (Subpart BBB)
- VOC Emissions from the Polymer Manufacturing Industry (construction, modification or reconstruction commenced after Sept. 30, 1987 (certain polypropylene and polyethylene facilities), or Jan. 10, 1989 (other facilities)) (Subpart DDD)
- Flexible Vinyl and Urethane Coating and Printing (construction, modification or reconstruction commenced after Jan. 8, 1983) (Subpart FFF)
- Equipment Leaks of VOC in Petroleum Refineries (construction, modification or reconstruction commenced between Jan. 4, 1983, and Nov. 7, 2006) (Subpart GGG)
- Equipment Leaks of VOC in Petroleum Refineries (construction, modification or reconstruction commenced after Nov. 7, 2006) (Subpart GGGa)
- Synthetic Fiber Production Facilities (construction or reconstruction commenced after Nov. 23, 1982) (Subpart HHH)

- VOC Emissions from the Synthetic Organic Chemical Manufacturing Industry Air Oxidation Unit Processes (construction, modification or reconstruction commenced after Oct. 21, 1983) (Subpart III)
- Petroleum Dry Cleaners (construction or modification commenced after Dec. 14, 1982) (Subpart JJJ)
- Equipment Leaks of VOC from Onshore Natural Gas Processing Plants (construction, modification or reconstruction commenced between Jan. 20, 1984, and Aug. 23, 2011) (Subpart KKK)
- SO$_2$ Emissions from Onshore Natural Gas Processing (construction, modification or reconstruction commenced between Jan. 20, 1984, and Aug. 23, 2011) (Subpart LLL)
- VOC Emissions from Synthetic Organic Chemical Manufacturing Industry Distillation Operations (construction, modification or reconstruction commenced after Dec. 30, 1983) (Subpart NNN)
- Nonmetallic Mineral Processing Plants (construction, modification or reconstruction commenced after Aug. 31, 1983) (Subpart OOO)
- Wool Fiberglass Insulation Manufacturing Plants (construction, modification or reconstruction commenced after Feb. 7, 1984) (Subpart PPP)
- VOC Emissions from Petroleum Refinery Wastewater Systems (construction, modification or reconstruction commenced after May 4, 1987) (Subpart QQQ)
- VOC Emissions from Synthetic Organic Chemical Manufacturing Industry Reactor Processes (construction, modification or reconstruction commenced after June 29, 1990) (Subpart RRR)
- Magnetic Tape Coating Facilities (construction, modification or reconstruction commenced after Jan. 22, 1986) (Subpart SSS)
- Industrial Surface Coating: Surface Coating of Plastic Parts for Business Machines (construction, modification or reconstruction commenced after Jan. 8, 1986) (Subpart TTT)
- Calciners and Dryers in Mineral Industries (construction, modification or reconstruction commenced after Apr. 23, 1986) (Subpart UUU)
- Polymeric Coating of Supporting Substrates Facilities (construction, modification or reconstruction commenced after Apr. 30, 1987) (Subpart VVV)
- Municipal Solid Waste Landfills (construction, modification or reconstruction commenced after May 30, 1991) (Subpart WWW)
- Small Municipal Waste Combustion Units (construction commenced after Aug. 30, 1999; modification or reconstruction commenced after June 6, 2001) (Subpart AAAA)
- Commercial and Industrial Solid Waste Incineration Units (construction commenced after Nov. 30, 1999; modification or reconstruction commenced after June 1, 2001) (Subpart CCCC)

- Other Solid Waste Incineration Units (construction commenced after Dec. 9, 2004; modification or reconstruction commenced after June 16, 2006) (Subpart EEEE)
- Stationary Compression Ignition Internal Combustion Engines (construction, modification or reconstruction commenced after July 11, 2005) (Subpart IIII)
- Stationary Spark Ignition Internal Combustion Engines (for owners and operators, construction, modification or reconstruction commenced after June 12, 2006; for manufacturers, various dates) (Subpart JJJJ)
- Stationary Combustion Turbines (construction, modification or reconstruction commenced after Feb. 18, 2005) (Subpart KKKK)
- New Sewage Sludge Incineration Units (construction commenced after Oct. 14, 2010; modification commenced after Sept. 21, 2011) (Subpart LLLL)
- Crude Oil and Natural Gas Production, Transmission and Distribution (construction, modification or reconstruction commenced after Aug. 23, 2011) (Subpart OOOO)

Existing Sources Subject to Emissions Guidelines Under Section 111(d)

- (40 C.F.R. Part 60) Large Municipal Waste Combustors (construction commenced on or before Sept. 20, 1994) (Subpart Cb)
- Municipal Solid Waste Landfills (construction, reconstruction or modification commenced before May 30, 1991) (Subpart Cc)
- Sulfuric Acid Production Units (Subpart Cd)
- Hospital/Medical/Infectious Waste Incinerators (construction commenced on or before Dec. 1, 2008; modification commenced on or before Apr. 6, 2010) (Subpart Ce)
- Small Municipal Waste Combustion Units (construction commenced on or before Aug. 30, 1999) (Subpart BBBB)
- Commercial and Industrial Solid Waste Incineration Units (construction commenced on or before Nov. 30, 1999) (Subpart DDDD)
- Other Solid Waste Incineration Units (construction commenced on or before Dec. 9, 2004) (Subpart FFFF)
- Existing Sewage Sludge Incineration Units (construction commenced on or before Oct. 14, 2010) (Subpart MMMM)

PSD Source Categories

(40 C.F.R. § 52.21(b)(1))

The following source categories are subject to the 100 ton per year (tpy) definition of "major stationary source" under the PSD rules, *i.e.*, if they emit or have the potential to emit at least 100 tpy of any pollutant subject to CAA regulation, other than hazardous air pollutants listed under Section 112. Other stationary sources are subject to PSD rules if they emit or have the potential to emit at least 250 tpy of such a pollutant. A stationary source is subject to PSD regulations for greenhouse gases if it is a major stationary source for another pollutant and emits or has the potential to emit 75,000 tpy of carbon dioxide equivalent emissions (tpy CO_2e) or if it otherwise emits or has the potential to emit 100,000 tpy CO_2e. 40 C.F.R. § 52.21(b)(49) (2012).

- Fossil Fuel-Fired Steam Electric Plants of more than 250 million Btu/hr heat input
- Coal Cleaning Plants (with thermal dryers)
- Kraft Pulp Mills
- Portland Cement Plants
- Primary Zinc Smelters
- Iron and Steel Mill Plants
- Primary Aluminum Ore Reduction Plants (with thermal dryers)
- Primary Copper Smelters
- Municipal Incinerators capable of charging more than 250 tons of refuse per day
- Hydrofluoric Acid Plants
- Sulfuric Acid Plants
- Nitric Acid Plants
- Petroleum Refineries
- Lime Plants
- Phosphate Rock Processing Plants
- Coke Oven Batteries
- Sulfur Recovery Plants
- Carbon Black Plants (furnace process)
- Primary Lead Smelters
- Fuel Conversion Plants
- Sintering Plants
- Secondary Metal Production Plants
- Chemical Process Plants (not including ethanol production facilities producing ethanol by natural fermentation included in NAICS codes 325193 or 312140)
  - Fossil-Fuel Boilers (or combinations thereof) totaling more than 250 million Btu/Hr heat input

- Petroleum Storage and Transfer Units with a total storage capacity exceeding 300,000 barrels
- Taconite Ore Processing Plants
- Glass Fiber Processing Plants
- Charcoal Production Plants

Section 112 Maximum Achievable Control Technology (MACT) Source Categories: Major Sources

INDUSTRY GROUP Source Category[1]	Standard First Promulgated in Federal Register at	Codified at 40 C.F.R. Part 63 Subpart
FUEL COMBUSTION		
Coal- and Oil-fired Electric Utility Steam Generating Units[2]	77 Fed. Reg. 9304 (Feb. 16, 2012)	UUUUU
Combustion Turbines	69 Fed. Reg. 10,512 (Mar. 5, 2004)	YYYY
Engine Test Cells/Stands	68 Fed. Reg. 28,774 (May 27, 2003)	PPPPP
Industrial Boilers	69 Fed. Reg. 55,218 (Sept. 13, 2004)	DDDDD
Institutional/Commercial Boilers	69 Fed. Reg. 55,218 (Sept. 13, 2004)	DDDDD
Process Heaters	69 Fed. Reg. 55,218 (Sept. 13, 2004)	DDDDD
Reciprocating Internal Combustion Engines	69 Fed. Reg. 33,474 (June 15, 2004)	ZZZZ
NON-FERROUS METALS PROCESSING		
Primary Aluminum Production	62 Fed. Reg. 52,384 (Oct. 7, 1997)	LL
Primary Copper Smelting	67 Fed. Reg. 40,478 (June 12, 2002)	QQQ
Primary Lead Smelting	64 Fed. Reg. 30,194 (June 4, 1999)	TTT
Primary Magnesium Refining	68 Fed. Reg. 58,615 (Oct. 10, 2003)	TTTTT
Secondary Aluminum Production	65 Fed. Reg. 15,689 (Mar. 23, 2000)	RRR
Secondary Lead Smelting	60 Fed. Reg. 32,587 (June 23, 1995)	X
FERROUS METALS PROCESSING		
Coke Ovens: Charging, Top Side, and Door Leaks	58 Fed. Reg. 57,898 (Oct. 27, 1993)	L
Coke Ovens: Pushing, Quenching, and Battery Stacks	68 Fed. Reg. 18,008 (Apr. 14, 2003)	CCCCC
Ferroalloys Production: Ferromanganese and Silicomanganese	64 Fed. Reg. 27,450 (May 20, 1999)	XXX
Integrated Iron and Steel Manufacturing	68 Fed. Reg. 27,646 (May 20, 2003)	FFFFF
Iron Foundries	69 Fed. Reg. 21,906 (Apr. 22, 2004)	EEEEE
Steel Foundries	69 Fed. Reg. 21,906 (Apr. 22, 2004)	EEEEE
Steel Pickling—HCl Process Facilities and Hydrochloric Acid Regeneration Plants	64 Fed. Reg. 33,202 (June 22, 1999)	CCC
MINERAL PRODUCTS PROCESSING		
Asphalt Processing	68 Fed. Reg. 24,562 (May 7, 2003)	LLLLL
Asphalt Roofing Manufacturing	68 Fed. Reg. 24,562 (May 7, 2003)	LLLLL
Asphalt/Coal Tar Application—Metal Pipes	69 Fed. Reg. 130 (Jan. 2, 2004)	MMMM
Brick and Structural Clay Products Manufacturing[3]	68 Fed. Reg. 26,690 (May 16, 2003)	JJJJJ
Clay Ceramics Manufacturing[4]	68 Fed. Reg. 26,690 (May 16, 2003)	KKKKK
Lime Manufacturing	69 Fed. Reg. 394 (Jan. 5, 2004)	AAAAA
Mineral Wool Production	64 Fed. Reg. 29,490 (June 1, 1999)	DDD

[1] Unless otherwise noted, these source categories are listed at 67 Fed. Reg. 6521 (Feb. 12, 2002). Section 112 requires EPA to publish a list of all categories and subcategories of sources of listed hazardous air pollutants and to revise the list to reflect newly added categories at least every 8 years. CAA § 112(c)(1), 42 U.S.C. § 7412(c)(1). The most recent list was published in 2002.

[2] EPA added this source category to the list in 2000 after finding that it was appropriate and necessary to regulate such units under CAA section 112. 65 Fed. Reg. 79,825 (Dec. 20, 2000). In 2005, EPA revoked its finding and delisted the category. 70 Fed. Reg. 15,994 (Mar. 29, 2005). The D.C. Circuit vacated the 2005 delisting rule in 2008, restoring this category to the list. *New Jersey v. EPA*, 517 F.3d 574 (D.C. Cir. 2008).

[3] Added to source category list by 67 Fed. Reg. 47,894 (July 22, 2002).

[4] Added to source category list by 67 Fed. Reg. 47,894 (July 22, 2002).

MACT Source Categories: Major Sources (Cont'd)

INDUSTRY GROUP Source Category	Standard Promulgated in Federal Register at	Codified at 40 C.F.R. Part 63 Subpart
Portland Cement Manufacturing	64 Fed. Reg. 31,898 (June 14, 1999)	LLL
Refractory Products Manufacturing	68 Fed. Reg. 18,730 (Apr. 16, 2003)	SSSSS
Taconite Iron Ore Processing	68 Fed. Reg. 61,868 (Oct. 30, 2003)	RRRRR
Wool Fiberglass Manufacturing	64 Fed. Reg. 31,695 (June 14, 1999)	NNN
PETROLEUM AND NATURAL GAS PRODUCTION AND REFINING		
Oil and Natural Gas Production	64 Fed. Reg. 32,610 (June 17, 1999)	HH
Natural Gas Transmission and Storage	64 Fed. Reg. 32,610 (June 17, 1999)	HHH
Petroleum Refineries—Catalytic Cracking Units, Catalytic Reforming Units, and Sulfur Recovery Units	67 Fed. Reg. 17,762 (Apr. 11, 2002)	UUU
Petroleum Refineries—Other Sources Not Distinctly Listed	60 Fed. Reg. 43,244 (Aug. 18, 1995)	CC
LIQUIDS DISTRIBUTION		
Gasoline Distribution (Stage 1)	59 Fed. Reg. 64,303 (Dec. 14, 1994)	R
Marine Tank Vessel Loading Operations	60 Fed. Reg. 48,388 (Sept. 19, 1995)	Y
Organic Liquids Distribution (Non-Gasoline)	69 Fed. Reg. 5038 (Feb. 3, 2004)	EEEE
SURFACE COATING PROCESSES		
Aerospace Industries	60 Fed. Reg. 45,948 (Sept. 1, 1995)	GG
Automobile and Light Duty Truck (Surface Coating)	69 Fed. Reg. 22,602 (Apr. 26, 2004)	IIII
Large Appliance (Surface Coating)	67 Fed. Reg. 48,254 (July 23, 2002)	NNNN
Magnetic Tape Manufacturing Operations	59 Fed. Reg. 64,596 (Dec. 15, 1994)	EE
Manufacture of Paints, Coatings, and Adhesives	68 Fed. Reg. 63,852 (Nov. 10, 2003)	FFFF
Metal Can (Surface Coating)	68 Fed. Reg. 64,432 (Nov. 13, 2003)	KKKK
Metal Coil (Surface Coating)	67 Fed. Reg. 39,794 (June 10, 2002)	SSSS
Metal Furniture (Surface Coating)	68 Fed. Reg. 28,606 (May 23, 2003)	RRRR
Miscellaneous Metal Parts and Products (Surface Coating)	69 Fed. Reg. 130 (Jan. 2. 2004)	MMMM
Paper and Other Web Coating (Surface Coating)	67 Fed. Reg. 72,330 (Dec. 4, 2002)	JJJJ
Plastic Parts and Products (Surface Coating)	69 Fed. Reg. 20,968 (Apr. 19, 2004)	PPPP
Printing, Coating, and Dyeing of Fabrics	68 Fed. Reg. 32,172 (May 29, 2003)	OOOO
Printing/Publishing	61 Fed. Reg. 27,132 (May 30, 1996)	KK
Shipbuilding and Ship Repair (Surface Coating)	60 Fed. Reg. 64,330 (Dec. 15, 1995)	II
Wood Building Products (Surface Coating)	68 Fed. Reg. 31,746 (May 28, 2003)	QQQQ
Wood Furniture Manufacturing Operations	60 Fed. Reg. 62,930 (Dec. 7, 1995)	JJ
WASTE TREATMENT AND DISPOSAL		
Hazardous Waste Combustors	64 Fed. Reg. 52,828 (Sept. 30, 1999)	EEE
Municipal Solid Waste Landfills	66 Fed. Reg. 2227 (Jan. 16, 2003)	AAAA
Off-Site Waste and Recovery Operations	61 Fed. Reg. 34,140 (July 1, 1996)	DD
Publicly Owned Treatment Works (POTW)	64 Fed. Reg. 57,572 (Oct. 26, 1999)	VVV
Site Remediation	68 Fed. Reg. 58,172 (Oct. 8, 2003)	GGGGG

MACT Source Categories: Major Sources (Cont'd)

INDUSTRY GROUP Source Category	Standard Promulgated in Federal Register at	Codified at 40 C.F.R. Part 63 Subpart
AGRICULTURAL CHEMICALS PRODUCTION		
Pesticide Active Ingredient Production	64 Fed. Reg. 33,549 (June 23, 1999)	MMM
FIBERS PRODUCTION PROCESSES		
Acrylic Fibers/Modacrylic Fibers Production	64 Fed. Reg. 34,854 (June 29, 1999)	YY
Spandex Production	67 Fed. Reg. 46,258 (July 12, 2002)	YY
FOOD AND AGRICULTURE PROCESSES		
Manufacturing of Nutritional Yeast	66 Fed. Reg. 27,876 (May 21, 2001)	CCCC
Solvent Extraction for Vegetable Oil Production	66 Fed. Reg. 19,006 (Apr. 12, 2001)	GGGG
PHARMACEUTICAL PRODUCTION PROCESSES		
Pharmaceuticals Production	63 Fed. Reg. 50,280 (Sept. 21, 1998)	GGG
POLYMERS AND RESINS PRODUCTION		
Acetal Resins Production	64 Fed. Reg. 34,854 (June 29, 1999)	YY
Acrylonitrile-Butadiene-Styrene Production	61 Fed. Reg. 48,208 (Sept. 12, 1996)	JJJ
Alkyd Resins Production	68 Fed. Reg. 63,852 (Nov. 10, 2003)	FFFF
Amino Resins Production	65 Fed. Reg. 3276 (Jan. 20, 2000)	OOO
Boat Manufacturing	66 Fed. Reg. 44,218 (Aug. 22, 2001)	VVVV
Butyl Rubber Production	61 Fed. Reg. 46,906 (Sept. 5, 1996)	U
Cellulose Ethers Production	67 Fed. Reg. 40,044 (June 11, 2002)	UUUU
Epichlorohydrin Elastomers Production	61 Fed. Reg. 46,906 (Sept. 5, 1996)	U
Epoxy Resins Production	60 Fed. Reg. 12,670 (Mar. 3, 1995)	W
Ethylene-Propylene Rubber Production	61 Fed. Reg. 46,906 (Sept. 5, 1996)	U
Flexible Polyurethane Foam Production	63 Fed. Reg. 53,980 (Oct. 7, 1998)	III
Hypalon (tm) Production	61 Fed. Reg. 46,906 (Sept. 5, 1996)	U
Maleic Anhydride Copolymers Production	68 Fed. Reg. 63,852 (Nov. 10, 2003)	FFFF
Methyl Methacrylate-Acrylonitrile-Butadiene-Styrene Production	61 Fed. Reg. 48,208 (Sept. 12, 1996)	JJJ
Methyl Methacrylate-Butadiene-Styrene Terpolymers Production	61 Fed. Reg. 48,208 (Sept. 12, 1996)	JJJ
Neoprene Production	61 Fed. Reg. 46,906 (Sept. 5, 1996)	U
Nitrile Butadiene Rubber Production	61 Fed. Reg. 46,906 (Sept. 5, 1996)	U
Nitrile Resins Production	61 Fed. Reg. 48,208 (Sept. 12, 1996)	JJJ
Non-Nylon Polyamides Production	60 Fed. Reg. 12,670 (Mar. 3, 1995)	W
Phenolic Resins Production	65 Fed. Reg. 3276 (Jan. 20, 2000)	OOO
Polybutadiene Rubber Production	61 Fed. Reg. 46,906 (Sept. 5, 1996)	U
Polycarbonates Production	64 Fed. Reg. 34,854 (June 29, 1999)	YY
Polyester Resins Production	68 Fed. Reg. 63,852 (Nov. 10, 2003)	FFFF
Polyether Polyols Production	64 Fed. Reg. 29,420 (June 1, 1999)	PPP
Polyethylene Terephthalate Production	61 Fed. Reg. 48,208 (Sept. 12, 1996)	JJJ
Polymerized Vinylidene Chloride Production	68 Fed. Reg. 63,852 (Nov. 10, 2003)	FFFF
Polymethyl Methacrylate Resins Production	68 Fed. Reg. 63,852 (Nov. 10, 2003)	FFFF
Polystyrene Production	61 Fed. Reg. 48,208 (Sept. 12, 1996)	JJJ
Polysulfide Rubber Production	61 Fed. Reg. 46,906 (Sept. 5, 1996)	U
Polyvinyl Acetate Emulsions Production	68 Fed. Reg. 63,852 (Nov. 10, 2003)	FFFF
Polyvinyl Alcohol Production	68 Fed. Reg. 63,852 (Nov. 10, 2003)	FFFF
Polyvinyl Butyral Production	68 Fed. Reg. 63,852 (Nov. 10, 2003)	FFFF

MACT Source Categories: Major Sources (Cont'd)

INDUSTRY GROUP Source Category	Standard Promulgated in Federal Register at	Codified at 40 C.F.R. Part 63 Subpart
Polyvinyl Chloride and Copolymers Production	77 Fed. Reg. 22,848 (Apr. 17, 2012)[5]	J, HHHHHHH
Reinforced Plastic Composites Production	68 Fed. Reg. 19,375 (Apr. 21, 2003)	WWWW
Styrene Acrylonitrile Production	61 Fed. Reg. 48,208 (Sept. 12, 1996)	JJJ
Styrene-Butadiene Rubber and Latex Production	61 Fed. Reg. 46,906 (Sept. 5, 1996)	U
PRODUCTION OF INORGANIC CHEMICALS		
Ammonium Sulfate Production— Caprolactam By-Product Plants	68 Fed. Reg. 63,852 (Nov. 10, 2003)	FFFF
Carbon Black Production	67 Fed. Reg. 46,258 (July 12, 2002)	YY
Chlorine Production: Mercury Cell Chlor-Alkali Plants[6]	68 Fed. Reg. 70,904 (Dec. 19, 2003)	IIIII
Cyanide Chemicals Manufacturing	67 Fed. Reg. 46,258 (July 12, 2002)	YY
Hydrochloric Acid Production	68 Fed. Reg. 19,076 (Apr. 17, 2003)	NNNNN
Hydrogen Fluoride Production	64 Fed. Reg. 34,854 (June 29, 1999)	YY
Phosphate Fertilizers Production	64 Fed. Reg. 31,358 (June 10, 1999)	BB
Phosphoric Acid Manufacturing	64 Fed. Reg. 31,358 (June 10, 1999)	AA
PRODUCTION OF ORGANIC CHEMICALS		
Ethylene Processes	67 Fed. Reg. 46,258 (July 12, 2002)	YY
Quaternary Ammonium Compounds Production	68 Fed. Reg. 63,852 (Nov. 10, 2003)	FFFF
Synthetic Organic Chemical Manufacturing	59 Fed. Reg. 19,402 (Apr. 22, 1994)	F, G, H, I
MISCELLANEOUS PROCESSES		
Benzyltrimethylammonium Chloride Production	68 Fed. Reg. 63,852 (Nov. 10, 2003)	FFFF
Carbonyl Sulfide Production	68 Fed. Reg. 63,852 (Nov. 10, 2003)	FFFF
Chelating Agents Production	68 Fed. Reg. 63,852 (Nov. 10, 2003)	FFFF
Chlorinated Paraffins Production	68 Fed. Reg. 63,852 (Nov. 10, 2003)	FFFF
Chromic Acid Anodizing	60 Fed. Reg. 4948 (Jan. 25, 1995)	N
Commercial Dry Cleaning (Perchloroethylene)—Transfer Machines	58 Fed. Reg. 49,376 (Sept. 22, 1993)	M
Commercial Sterilization Facilities	59 Fed. Reg. 62,585 (Dec. 6, 1994)	O
Decorative Chromium Electroplating	60 Fed. Reg. 4948 (Jan. 25, 1995)	N
Ethylidene Norbornene Production	68 Fed. Reg. 63,852 (Nov. 10, 2003)	FFFF
Explosives Production	68 Fed. Reg. 63,852 (Nov. 10, 2003)	FFFF
Flexible Polyurethane Foam Fabrication Operations	68 Fed. Reg. 18,062 (Apr. 14, 2003)	MMMMM
Friction Materials Manufacturing	67 Fed. Reg. 64,498 (Oct. 18, 2002)	QQQQQ
Halogenated Solvent Cleaners	59 Fed. Reg. 61,801 (Dec. 2, 1994)	T
Hard Chromium Electroplating	60 Fed. Reg. 4948 (Jan. 25, 1995)	N
Hydrazine Production	68 Fed. Reg. 63,852 (Nov. 10, 2003)	FFFF
Industrial Dry Cleaning (Perchloroethylene)—Dry-to-dry Machines	58 Fed. Reg. 49,376 (Sept. 22, 1993)	M
Industrial Dry Cleaning (Perchloroethylene)—Transfer Machines	58 Fed. Reg. 49,376 (Sept. 22, 1993)	M

---

[5] EPA's original NESHAP for this category, at 67 Fed. Reg. 45,886 (July 10, 2002), was vacated by the D.C. Circuit. *See Mossville Envt'l Action Now v. EPA*, 370 F.3d 1232 (D.C. Cir. 2004).

[6] Added to source category list by 68 Fed. Reg. 70,948 (Dec. 19, 2003).

MACT Source Categories: Major Sources

INDUSTRY GROUP Source Category	Standard Promulgated in Federal Register at	Codified at 40 C.F.R. Part 63 Subpart
Industrial Process Cooling Towers	59 Fed. Reg. 46,339 (Sept. 8, 1994)	Q
Leather Finishing Operations	67 Fed. Reg. 9156 (Feb. 27, 2002)	TTTT
Miscellaneous Viscose Processes	67 Fed. Reg. 40,044 (June 11, 2002)	UUUU
OBPA/1,3-Diisocyanate Production	68 Fed. Reg. 63,852 (Nov. 10, 2003)	FFFF
Paint Stripping Operations[7]	---	---
Photographic Chemicals Production	68 Fed. Reg. 63,852 (Nov. 10, 2003)	FFFF
Phthalate Plasticizers Production	68 Fed. Reg. 63,852 (Nov. 10, 2003)	FFFF
Plywood and Composite Wood Products	69 Fed. Reg. 45,944 (July 30, 2004)	DDDD
Pulp and Paper Production	63 Fed. Reg. 18,504 (Apr. 15, 1998) 66 Fed. Reg. 3180 (Jan. 12, 2001)	S MM
Rubber Chemicals Manufacturing	68 Fed. Reg. 63,852 (Nov. 10, 2003)	FFFF
Rubber Tire Manufacturing	67 Fed. Reg. 45,588 (July 9, 2002)	XXXX
Semiconductor Manufacturing	68 Fed. Reg. 27,913 (May 22, 2003)	BBBBB
Symmetrical Tetrachloropyridine Production	68 Fed. Reg. 63,852 (Nov. 10, 2003)	FFFF
Wet-Formed Fiberglass Mat Production	67 Fed. Reg. 17,824 (Apr. 11, 2002)	HHHH

---

[7] EPA has not promulgated standards for the Paint Stripping Operations category. EPA determined that no major source paint stripping operations were conducted independent of surface coating, and therefore those major sources were already controlled under the applicable surface coating standards. *See* 72 Fed. Reg. 52,958, 52,965 (Sept. 17, 2007).

Section 112 MACT Source Categories: Area Sources

Source (unless otherwise noted): 67 Fed. Reg. 70,427 (Nov. 22, 2002)

Source Category[8]	Standard Promulgated in Federal Register at	Codified at 40 C.F.R. Part 63 Subpart
Acrylic/Modacrylic Fibers Production	72 Fed. Reg. 38,864 (July 16, 2007)	LLLLLL
Agricultural Chemicals and Pesticides Manufacturing	74 Fed. Reg. 56,008 (Oct. 29, 2009)	VVVVVV
Aluminum Foundries	74 Fed. Reg. 30,366 (June 25, 2009)	ZZZZZZ
Asphalt Processing and Asphalt Roofing Manufacturing	74 Fed. Reg. 63,236 (Dec. 2, 2010)	AAAAAAA
Brick and Structural Clay Products Manufacturing	---	---
Carbon Black Production	72 Fed. Reg. 38,864 (July 16, 2007)	MMMMMM
Chemical Manufacturing: Chromium Compounds	72 Fed. Reg. 38,864 (July 16, 2007)	NNNNNN
Chemical Preparations	74 Fed. Reg. 69,194 (Dec. 30, 2010)	BBBBBBB
Chromic Acid Anodizing	60 Fed. Reg. 4948 (Jan. 25, 1995)	N
Clay Ceramics Manufacturing	72 Fed. Reg. 73,180 (Dec. 26, 2007)	RRRRRR
Commercial Sterilization Facilities	69 Fed. Reg. 62,585 (Dec. 6, 1994)	O
Copper Foundries	74 Fed. Reg. 30,366 (June 25, 2009)	ZZZZZZ
Cyclic Crude and Intermediate Production	74 Fed. Reg. 56,008 (Oct. 29, 2009)	VVVVVV
Decorative Chromium Electroplating	60 Fed. Reg. 4948 (Jan. 25, 1995)	N
Dry Cleaning Facilities	58 Fed. Reg. 49,354 (Sept. 22, 1993)	M
Electric Arc Furnace Steelmaking Facilities	72 Fed. Reg. 74,088 (Dec. 28, 2007)	YYYYY
Ferroalloys Production	73 Fed. Reg. 78,637 (Dec. 23, 2008)	YYYYYY
Flexible Polyurethane Foam Fabrication	72 Fed. Reg. 38,864 (July 16, 2007)	OOOOOO
Flexible Polyurethane Foam Production	72 Fed. Reg. 38,864 (July 16, 2007)	OOOOOO
Gasoline Distribution (Stage 1)	73 Fed. Reg. 1916 (Jan. 10, 2008)	BBBBBB, CCCCCC
Gold Mine Ore Processing and Production[9]	76 Fed. Reg. 9450 (Feb. 17, 2011)	EEEEEE
Halogenated Solvent Cleaners	59 Fed. Reg. 61,801 (Dec. 2, 1994)	T
Hard Chromium Electroplating	60 Fed. Reg. 4948 (Jan. 25, 1995)	N
Hazardous Waste Combustors	64 Fed. Reg. 52,827 (Sept. 30, 1999)	EEE
Hospital Sterilizers	72 Fed. Reg. 73,611 (Dec. 28, 2007)	WWWWW
Industrial Boilers	76 Fed. Reg. 15,554 (Mar. 21, 2011)	JJJJJJ
Industrial Inorganic Chemical Manufacturing	74 Fed. Reg. 56,008 (Oct. 29, 2009)	VVVVVV
Industrial Organic Chemical Manufacturing	74 Fed. Reg. 56,008 (Oct. 29, 2009)	VVVVVV
Inorganic Pigments Manufacturing	74 Fed. Reg. 56,008 (Oct. 29, 2009)	VVVVVV
Institutional/Commercial Boilers	76 Fed. Reg. 15,554 (Mar. 21, 2011)	JJJJJJ
Iron Foundries	73 Fed. Reg. 226 (Jan. 2, 2008)	ZZZZZ
Lead Acid Battery Manufacturing	72 Fed. Reg. 38,864 (July 16, 2007)	PPPPPP
Medical Waste Incinerators	---	---
Mercury Cell Chlor-Alkali Plants	68 Fed. Reg. 70,904 (Dec. 19, 2003)	IIIII
Metal Fabrication and Finishing: Electrical and Electronic Equipment Finishing Operations	73 Fed. Reg. 42,978 (July 23, 2008)	XXXXXX

---

[8] Unless otherwise noted, these source categories are listed at 67 Fed. Reg. 70,427 (Nov. 22, 2002). Section 112 requires EPA to publish a list of all categories and subcategories of sources of listed hazardous air pollutants and to revise the list to reflect newly added categories at least every 8 years. CAA § 112(c)(1), 42 U.S.C. § 7412(c)(1). The most recent list was published in 2002.

[9] Added to source category list by 76 Fed. Reg. 9450 (Feb. 17, 2011).

MACT Source Categories: Area Sources (Cont'd)

Source Category	NESHAP Promulgated in Federal Register at	Codified at 40 C.F.R. Part 63 Subpart
Metal Fabrication and Finishing: Fabricated Metal Products Manufacturing, not elsewhere classified	73 Fed. Reg. 42,978 (July 23, 2008)	XXXXXX
Metal Fabrication and Finishing: Fabricated Plate Work (Boiler Shops)	73 Fed. Reg. 42,978 (July 23, 2008)	XXXXXX
Metal Fabrication and Finishing: Fabricated Structural Metal Manufacturing	73 Fed. Reg. 42,978 (July 23, 2008)	XXXXXX
Metal Fabrication and Finishing: Heating Equipment Manufacturing, Except Electric	73 Fed. Reg. 42,978 (July 23, 2008)	XXXXXX
Metal Fabrication and Finishing: Industrial Machinery and Equipment Finishing Operations	73 Fed. Reg. 42,978 (July 23, 2008)	XXXXXX
Metal Fabrication and Finishing: Iron and Steel Forging	73 Fed. Reg. 42,978 (July 23, 2008)	XXXXXX
Metal Fabrication and Finishing: Primary Metals Products Manufacturing	73 Fed. Reg. 42,978 (July 23, 2008)	XXXXXX
Metal Fabrication and Finishing: Valves and Pipe Fittings Manufacturing	73 Fed. Reg. 42,978 (July 23, 2008)	XXXXXX
Miscellaneous Organic Chemical Manufacturing	74 Fed. Reg. 56,008 (Oct. 29, 2009)	VVVVVV
Miscellaneous Surface Coating	73 Fed. Reg. 1738 (Jan. 9, 2008)	HHHHHH
Motor Vehicle and Mobile Equipment Surface Coating	73 Fed. Reg. 1738 (Jan. 9, 2008)	HHHHHH
Municipal Solid Waste Landfills	68 Fed. Reg. 2227 (Jan. 16, 2003)	AAAA
Municipal Waste Combustors	---	---
Oil and Natural Gas Production	72 Fed. Reg. 26 (Jan. 3, 2007)	HH
Other Nonferrous Foundries	74 Fed. Reg. 30,366 (June 25, 2009)	ZZZZZZ
Other Solid Waste Incinerators (Human/Animal Cremation)	---	---
Paint Stripping Operations	73 Fed. Reg. 1738 (Jan. 9, 2008)	HHHHHH
Paints and Allied Products Manufacturing	74 Fed. Reg. 64,504 (Dec. 3, 2009)	CCCCCCC
Pharmaceutical Production	74 Fed. Reg. 56,008 (Oct. 29, 2009)	VVVVVV
Plastic Materials and Resins Manufacturing	74 Fed. Reg. 56,008 (Oct. 29, 2009)	VVVVVV
Plating and Polishing	73 Fed. Reg. 37,728 (July 1, 2008)	WWWWWW
Polyvinyl Chloride and Copolymers Production	72 Fed. Reg. 2930 (Jan. 23, 2007)	DDDDDD
Portland Cement	71 Fed. Reg. 76,517 (Dec. 20, 2006)	LLL
Prepared Feeds Manufacturing	75 Fed. Reg. 522 (Jan. 5, 2010)	DDDDDDD
Pressed and Blown Glass & Glassware Manufacturing	72 Fed. Reg. 73,180 (Dec. 26, 2007)	SSSSS
Primary Copper Smelters	72 Fed. Reg. 2930 (Jan. 23, 2007)	EEEEE
Primary Nonferrous Metals—Zinc, Cadmium, and Beryllium	72 Fed. Reg. 2930 (Jan. 23, 2007)	GGGGGG
Publicly Owned Treatment Works	64 Fed. Reg. 57,572 (Oct. 26, 1999)	VVV
Secondary Copper Smelting	72 Fed. Reg. 2930 (Jan. 23, 2007)	FFFFFF
Secondary Lead Smelting	60 Fed. Reg. 32,587 (June 23, 1995)	X
Secondary Nonferrous Metals	72 Fed. Reg. 73,180 (Dec. 26, 2007)	TTTTTT

MACT Source Categories: Area Sources (Cont'd)

Source Category	NESHAP Promulgated in Federal Register at	Codified at 40 C.F.R. Part 63 Subpart
Sewage Sludge Incineration	---	---
Stationary Reciprocating Internal Combustion Engines	69 Fed. Reg. 33,474 (June 15, 2004)	ZZZZ
Steel Foundries	73 Fed. Reg. 226 (Jan. 2, 2008)	ZZZZZ
Synthetic Rubber Manufacturing	74 Fed. Reg. 56,008 (Oct. 29, 2009)	VVVVVV
Wood Preserving	72 Fed. Reg. 38,864 (July 16, 2007)	QQQQQQ

Appendix 3

POLLUTANTS SUBJECT TO CLEAN AIR ACT PROGRAMS

NAAQS Criteria Pollutants

(40 C.F.R. Part 50)
Sulfur Dioxide (SO_2)
Particulate Matter (PM_{10} and $PM_{2.5}$)
Carbon Monoxide (CO)
Ozone (O_3)
Nitrogen Dioxide (NO_2)
Lead (Pb)

NSPS Pollutants

(40 C.F.R. Part 60)
Acid Mist
Carbon Monoxide
Particulate Matter
Fluorides
Fugitive Ash
Fugitive Coal Dust
Hydrogen Sulfide
Municipal Waste Combustor Acid Gases (hydrogen chloride, nitrogen oxides, sulfur dioxide)
Municipal Waste Combustor Organics (dioxins, furans)
Municipal Waste Combustor Metals (cadmium, lead, mercury)
Nitrogen Oxides
Non-Methane Hydrocarbons
Opacity/Visible Emissions
Sulfur Dioxide
Sulfur Oxides
Total Reduced Sulfur
Volatile Organic Compounds

PSD Pollutants and Significance Levels

(40 C.F.R. § 52.21(b)(23)(i))

For pollutants not listed below, "any emissions rate" is deemed significant. 40 C.F.R. § 51.21(b)(23)(ii) (2012). The provisions of the PSD program do not apply to hazardous air pollutants listed under Section 112 of the Act. CAA § 112(b)(6), 42 U.S.C. § 7412(b)(6); 40 C.F.R. § 51.21(b)(50)(v). In addition, any emissions rate or any net emissions increase associated with a major stationary source or major modification that would construct within 10 kilometers of a Class I area and have an impact on that area equal to or greater than 1 $\mu g/m^3$ (24-hour average) is considered significant. Id. § 51.21(b)(23)(iii). For greenhouse gases, "significant" is defined as 75,000 tons per year of carbon dioxide equivalent emissions (tpy CO_2e). Id. § 51.21(b)(49)(iii).

Carbon Monoxide (100 tpy)
Nitrogen Oxides (NOx) (40 tpy)
Sulfur Dioxide (40 tpy)
Particulate Matter:
- Total PM (25 tpy)
- PM_{10} (15 tpy)
- $PM_{2.5}$ (10 tpy of direct $PM_{2.5}$; 40 tpy of SO_2; 40 tpy of NOx unless demonstrated not to be a $PM_{2.5}$ precursor)
Ozone (40 tpy of VOCs or NOx)
Lead (0.6 tpy)
Fluorides (3 tpy)
Sulfuric Acid Mist (7 tpy)
Hydrogen Sulfide (H_2S) (10 tpy)
Total Reduced Sulfur, including H_2S (10 tpy)
Reduced Sulfur Compounds, including H_2S (10 tpy)
Municipal Waste Combustor Organics (3.2×10^{-6} megagrams per year)
Municipal Waste Combustor Metals (14 megagrams per year)
Municipal Waste Combustor Acid Gases (36 megagrams per year)
Municipal Solid Waste Landfills Emissions, measured as non-methane organic compounds (45 megagrams per year)
Greenhouse Gases: Carbon dioxide, nitrous oxide, methane, hydrofluorocarbons, perfluorocarbons, and sulfur hexafluoride (75,000 tpy CO_2e)

Nonattainment Pollutants and Significance Levels

(40 C.F.R. Part 51, Appendix S, II.A.10)

Carbon Monoxide (100 tpy; 50 tpy in serious CO nonattainment area if stationary sources contribute significantly)

Nitrogen Oxides (40 tpy)

Particulate Matter:

- Total PM (25 tpy)
- PM_{10} (15 tpy)
- $PM_{2.5}$ (10 tpy direct $PM_{2.5}$; 40 tpy SO_2)

Ozone (40 tpy of VOCs or NOx; 25 tpy of VOCs or NOx in serious or severe ozone nonattainment area; any increase of VOCs or NOx in extreme ozone nonattainment area)

Lead (0.6 tpy)

Sulfur Dioxide (40 tpy)

Section 112 Hazardous Air Pollutants

(CAA § 112(b)(1), 42 U.S.C. § 7412(b)(1); 40 C.F.R. Part 63, Subpart C)

CAS number	Chemical name
57147	1,1-Dimethyl hydrazine
79005	1,1,2-Trichloroethane
79345	1,1,2,2-Tetrachloroethane
96128	1,2-Dibromo-3-chloropropane
122667	1,2-Diphenylhydrazine
106887	1,2-Epoxybutane
75558	1,2-Propylenimine (2-Methyl aziridine)
120821	1,2,4-Trichlorobenzene
106990	1,3-Butadiene
542756	1,3-Dichloropropene
1120714	1,3-Propane sultone
106467	1,4-Dichlorobenzene(p)
123911	1,4-Dioxane (1,4-Diethyleneoxide)
53963	2-Acetylaminofluorene
532274	2-Chloroacetophenone
79469	2-Nitropropane
540841	2,2,4-Trimethylpentane

1746016	2,3,7,8-Tetrachlorodibenzo-p-dioxin
94757	2,4-D, salts and esters
51285	2,4-Dinitrophenol
121142	2,4-Dinitrotoluene
95807	2,4-Toluene diamine
584849	2,4-Toluene diisocyanate
95954	2,4,5-Trichlorophenol
88062	2,4,6-Trichlorophenol
91941	3,3-Dichlorobenzidene
119904	3,3-Dimethoxybenzidine
119937	3,3'-Dimethyl benzidine
92671	4-Aminobiphenyl
92933	4-Nitrobiphenyl
100027	4-Nitrophenol
101144	4,4-Methylene bis(2-chloroaniline)
101779	4,4'-Methylenedianiline
534521	4,6-Dinitro-o-cresol, and salts
75070	Acetaldehyde
60355	Acetamide
75058	Acetonitrile
98862	Acetophenone
107028	Acrolein
79061	Acrylamide
79107	Acrylic acid
107131	Acrylonitrile
107051	Allyl chloride
62533	Aniline
1332214	Asbestos
71432	Benzene (including benzene from gasoline)
92875	Benzidine
98077	Benzotrichloride
100447	Benzyl chloride
57578	beta-Propiolactone
92524	Biphenyl

117817	Bis(2-ethylhexyl)phthalate (DEHP)
542881	Bis(chloromethyl)ether
75252	Bromoform
156627	Calcium cyanamide
133062	Captan
63252	Carbaryl
75150	Carbon disulfide
56235	Carbon tetrachloride
463581	Carbonyl sulfide
120809	Catechol
133904	Chloramben
57749	Chlordane
7782505	Chlorine
79118	Chloroacetic acid
108907	Chlorobenzene
510156	Chlorobenzilate
67663	Chloroform
107302	Chloromethyl methyl ether
126998	Chloroprene
1319773	Cresols/Cresylic acid (isomers and mixture)
98828	Cumene
3547044	DDE
334883	Diazomethane
132649	Dibenzofurans
84742	Dibutylphthalate
111444	Dichloroethyl ether (Bis(2-chloroethyl)ether)
62737	Dichlorvos
111422	Diethanolamine
64675	Diethyl sulfate
60117	Dimethyl aminoazobenzene
79447	Dimethyl carbamoyl chloride
68122	Dimethyl formamide
131113	Dimethyl phthalate
77781	Dimethyl sulfate

106898	Epichlorohydrin (1-Chloro-2,3-epoxypropane)
140885	Ethyl acrylate
100414	Ethyl benzene
51796	Ethyl carbamate (Urethane)
75003	Ethyl chloride (Chloroethane)
106934	Ethylene dibromide (Dibromoethane)
107062	Ethylene dichloride (1,2-Dichloroethane)
107211	Ethylene glycol
151564	Ethylene imine (Aziridine)
75218	Ethylene oxide
96457	Ethylene thiourea
75343	Ethylidene dichloride (1,1-Dichloroethane)
50000	Formaldehyde
76448	Heptachlor
118741	Hexachlorobenzene
87683	Hexachlorobutadiene
77474	Hexachlorocyclopentadiene
67721	Hexachloroethane
822060	Hexamethylene-1,6-diisocyanate
680319	Hexamethylphosphoramide
110543	Hexane
302012	Hydrazine
7647010	Hydrochloric acid
7664393	Hydrogen fluoride (Hydrofluoric acid)
123319	Hydroquinone
78591	Isophorone
58899	Lindane (all isomers)
108394	m-Cresol
108383	m-Xylenes
108316	Maleic anhydride
67561	Methanol
72435	Methoxychlor
74839	Methyl bromide (Bromomethane)

74873	Methyl chloride (Chloromethane)
71556	Methyl chloroform (1,1,1-Trichloroethane)
60344	Methyl hydrazine
74884	Methyl iodide (Iodomethane)
108101	Methyl isobutyl ketone (Hexone)
624839	Methyl isocyanate
80626	Methyl methacrylate
1634044	Methyl tert butyl ether
75092	Methylene chloride (Dichloromethane)
101688	Methylene diphenyl diisocyanate (MDI)
684935	N-Nitroso-N-methylurea
62759	N-Nitrosodimethylamine
59892	N-Nitrosomorpholine
121697	N,N-Diethyl aniline (N,N-Dimethylaniline)
91203	Naphthalene
98953	Nitrobenzene
90040	o-Anisidine
95487	o-Cresol
95534	o-Toluidine
95476	o-Xylenes
106445	p-Cresol
106503	p-Phenylenediamine
106423	p-Xylenes
56382	Parathion
82688	Pentachloronitrobenzene (Quintobenzene)
87865	Pentachlorophenol
108952	Phenol
75445	Phosgene
7803512	Phosphine
7723140	Phosphorus
85449	Phthalic anhydride
1336363	Polychlorinated biphenyls (Aroclors)
123386	Propionaldehyde
114261	Propoxur (Baygon)

78875	Propylene dichloride (1,2-Dichloropropane)
75569	Propylene oxide
91225	Quinoline
106514	Quinone
100425	Styrene
96093	Styrene oxide
127184	Tetrachloroethylene (Perchloroethylene)
7550450	Titanium tetrachloride
108883	Toluene
8001352	Toxaphene (chlorinated camphene)
79016	Trichloroethylene
121448	Triethylamine
1582098	Trifluralin
108054	Vinyl acetate
593602	Vinyl bromide
75014	Vinyl chloride
75354	Vinylidene chloride (1,1-Dichloroethylene)
1330207	Xylenes (isomers and mixture)
()	Beryllium Compounds
()	Cadmium Compounds
()	Chromium Compounds
()	Cobalt Compounds
()	Coke Oven Emissions
()	Cyanide Compounds1
()	Glycol ethers2
()	Lead Compounds
()	Antimony Compounds
()	Arsenic Compounds (inorganicincluding arsine)
()	Manganese Compounds
()	Mercury Compounds
()	Fine mineral fibers3
()	Nickel Compounds
()	Polycylic Organic Matter4

()   Radionuclides (including radon)5

()   Selenium Compounds

NOTE: For all listings above that contain the word "compounds" and for glycol ethers, the following applies: Unless otherwise specified, these listings are defined as including any unique chemical substance that contains the named chemical (i.e., antimony, arsenic, etc.) as part of that chemical's infrastructure.

[1] $X'CN$ where $X = H'$ or any other group where a formal dissociation may occur. For example KCN or $CA(CN)_2$.

[2] Glycol ethers include mono- and di-ethers of ethylene glycol, diethylene glycol and triethylene glycol $R\text{-}(OCH_2CH_2)_n\text{-}OR'$ where
     $n = 1, 2,$ or 3;
     R = alkyl C7 or less; or
     R = phenyl or alkyl substituted phenyl;
     R' = H or alkyl C7 or less; or
     OR' consisting of carboxylic acid ester, sulfate, phosphate, nitrate, or sulfonate.

[In addition, the substance ethylene glycol monobutyl ether (EGBE,2-Butoxyethanol) (CAS Number 111-76-2) is deleted from the list of hazardous air pollutants. 40 C.F.R. § 63.62.]

[3] Includes mineral fiber emissions from facilities manufacturing or processing glass, rock, or slag fibers (or other mineral derived fibers) of average diameter 1 micrometer or less.

[4] Includes organic compounds with more than one benzene ring, and which have a boiling point greater than or equal to 100°C.

[5] A type of atom that spontaneously undergoes radioactive decay.

Accidental Release Prevention

(40 C.F.R. § 68.130)

LIST OF REGULATED TOXIC SUBSTANCES AND THRESHOLD
QUANTITIES

(Alphabetical Order – 77 Substances)			
Chemical name	CAS No.	Threshold quantity (lbs)	Basis for listing
Acrolein [2-Propenal]	107-02-8	5,000	b
Acrylonitrile [2-Propenenitrile]	107-13-1	20,000	b
Acrylyl chloride [2-Propenoyl chloride]	814-68-6	5,000	b
Allyl alcohol [2-Propen-l-ol]	107-18-61	15,000	b
Allylamine [2-Propen-l-amine]	107-11-9	10,000	b
Ammonia (anhydrous)	7664-41-7	10,000	a, b
Ammonia (conc 20% or greater)	7664-41-7	20,000	a, b
Arsenous trichloride	7784-34-1	15,000	b
Arsine	7784-42-1	1,000	b
Boron trichloride [Borane, trichloro-]	10294-34-5	5,000	b
Boron trifluoride [Borane, trifluoro-]	7637-07-2	5,000	b
Boron trifluoride compound with methyl ether (1:1) [Boron, trifluoro[oxybis[metane]]-, T-4-	353-42-4	15,000	b
Bromine	7726-95-6	10,000	a, b
Carbon disulfide	75-15-0	20,000	b
Chlorine	7782-50-5	2,500	a, b
Chlorine dioxide [Chlorine oxide (ClO_2)]	10049-04-4	1,000	c
Chloroform [Methane, trichloro-]	67-66-3	20,000	b
Chloromethyl ether [Methane, ox-ybis[chloro-]	542-88-1	1,000	b
Chloromethyl methyl ether [Methane, chloromethoxy-]	107-30-2	5,000	b
Crotonaldehyde [2-Butenal]	4170-30-3	20,000	b
Crotonaldehyde, (E)- [2-Butenal, (E)-]	123-73-9	20,000	b
Cyanogen chloride	506-77-4	10,000	c
Cyclohexylamine [Cyclohexanamine]	108-91-8	15,000	b
Diborane	19287-45-7	2,500	b
Dimethyldichlorosilane [Silane, dichloromethyl-]	75-78-5	5,000	b

Accidental Release Prevention (Cont'd)

TOXIC SUBSTANCES (Cont'd)

(Alphabetical Order – 77 Substances)			
Chemical name	CAS No.	Threshold quantity (lbs)	Basis for listing
1,1-Dimethylhydrazine [Hydrazine, 1,1-dimethyl-]	57-14-7	15,000	b
Epichlorohydrin [Oxirane, (chloromethyl)-]	106-89-8	20,000	b
Ethylenediamine [1,2-Ethanediamine]	107-15-3	20,000	b
Ethyleneimine [Aziridine]	151-56-4	10,000	b
Ethylene oxide [Oxirane]	75-21-8	10,000	a, b
Fluorine	7782-41-4	1,000	b
Formaldehyde (solution)	50-00-0	15,000	b
Furan	110-00-9	5,000	b
Hydrazine	302-01-2	15,000	b
Hydrochloric acid (conc 37% or greater)	7647-01-0	15,000	d
Hydrocyanic acid	74-90-8	2,500	a, b
Hydrogen chloride (anhydrous) [Hydrochloric acid]	7647-01-0	5,000	a
Hydrogen fluoride/Hydrofluoric acid (conc 50% or greater) [Hydrofluoric acid]	7664-39-3	1,000	a, b
Hydrogen selenide	7783-07-5	500	b
Hydrogen sulfide	7783-06-4	10,000	a, b
Iron, pentacarbonyl- [Iron carbonyl (FE(CO)$_5$), (TB-5-11)-]	13463-40-6	2,500	b
Isobutyronitrile [Propanenitrile, 2-methyl-]	78-82-0	20,000	b
Isopropyl chloroformate [Carbonochloridic acid, 1-methylethyl ester]	108-23-6	15,000	b
Methacrylonitrile [2-Propenenitrile, 2-methyl-]	126-98-7	10,000	b
Methyl chloride [Methane, chloro-]	74-87-3	10,000	a
Methyl chloroformate [Carbonochloridic acid, methylester]	79-22-1	5,000	b
Methyl hydrazine [Hydrazine, methyl-]	60-34-4	15,000	b
Methyl isocyanate [Methane, isocyanato-]	624-83-9	10,000	a, b
Methyl mercaptan [Methanethiol]	74-92-1	10,000	b

Accidental Release Prevention (Cont'd)

TOXIC SUBSTANCES (Cont'd)

(Alphabetical Order – 77 Substances)

Chemical name	CAS No.	Threshold quantity (lbs)	Basis for listing
Methyl thiocyanate [Thiocyanic acid, methyl ester]	556-64-9	20,000	b
Methyltrichlorosilane [Silane, trichloromethyl-]	75-79-6	5,000	b
Nickel carbonyl	13463-39-3	1,000	b
Nitric acid (conc. 80% or greater)	7697-37-2	15,000	b
Nitric oxide [Nitrogen oxide (NO)]	10102-43-9	10,000	b
Oleum (Fuming Sulfuric acid) [Sulfuric acid, mixture with sulfur trioxide] [1]	8014-95-7	10,000	e
Peracetic acid [Ethaneperoxoic acid]	79-21-0	10,000	b
Perchloromethylmercaptan [Methanesulfenyl chloride, trichloro-]	594-42-3	10,000	b
Phosgene [Carbonic dichloride]	75-44-5	500	a, b
Phosphine	7803-51-2	5,000	b
Phosphorus oxychloride [Phosphoryl chloride]	10025-87-3	5,000	b
Phosphorus trichloride [Phosphorous trichloride]	7719-12-2	15,000	b
Piperidine	110-89-4	15,000	b
Propionitrile [Propanenitrile]	107-12-0	10,000	b
Propyl chloroformate [Carbonochloridic acid, propylester]	109-61-5	15,000	b
Propyleneimine [Aziridine, 2-methyl-]	75-55-8	10,000	b
Propylene oxide [Oxirane, methyl-]	75-56-9	10,000	b
Sulfur dioxide (anhydrous)	7446-09-5	5,000	a, b
Sulfur tetrafluoride [Sulfur fluoride (SF_4), (T-4)-]	7783-60-0	2,500	b
Sulfur trioxide	7446-11-9	10,000	a, b
Tetramethyllead [Plumbane, tetramethyl-]	75-74-1	10,000	b
Tetranitromethane [Methane, tetranitro-]	509-14-8	10,000	b
Titanium tetrachloride [Titanium chloride ($TiCl_4$) (T-4)-]	7550-45-0	2,500	b

Accidental Release Prevention (Cont'd)

TOXIC SUBSTANCES (Cont'd)

(Alphabetical Order – 77 Substances)			
Chemical name	CAS No.	Threshold quantity (lbs)	Basis for listing
Toluene 2,4-diisocyanate [Benzene, 2,4-diisocyanato-1-methyl-][1]	584-84-9	10,000	a
Toluene 2,6-diisocyanate [Benzene, 1,3-diisocyanato-2-methyl-][1]	91-08-7	10,000	a
Toluene diisocyanate (unspecified isomer) [Benzene, 1,3-diisocyanatomethyl-][1]	26471-62-5	10,000	a
Trimethylchlorosilane [Silane, chlorotrimethyl-]	75-77-4	10,000	b
Vinyl acetate monomer [Acetic acid ethenyl ester]	108-05-4	15,000	b

[1] The mixture exemption in 40 C.F.R. § 68.115(b)(1) does not apply to the substance.

Note: Basis for Listing:
a   Mandated for listing by Congress.
b   On EHS list, vapor pressure 10 mmHg or greater.
c   Toxic gas.
d   Toxicity of hydrogen chloride, potential to release hydrogen chloride, and history of accidents.
e   Toxicity of sulfur trioxide and sulfuric acid, potential to release sulfur trioxide, and history of accidents.

Accidental Release Prevention (Cont'd)

LIST OF REGULATED FLAMMABLE SUBSTANCES[1] AND THRESHOLD
QUANTITIES

(Alphabetical Order – 63 Substances)			
Chemical name	CAS No.	Threshold quantity (lbs)	Basis for listing
Acetaldehyde	75-07-0	10,000	g
Acetylene [Ethyne]	74-86-2	10,000	f
Bromotrifluorethylene [Ethene, bromotrifuloro-]	598-73-2	10,000	f
1,3-Butadiene	106-99-0	10,000	f
Butane	106-97-8	10,000	f
1-Butene	106-98-9	10,000	f
2-Butene	107-01-7	10,000	f
Butene	25167-67-3	10,000	f
2-Butene-cis	590-18-1	10,000	f
2-Butene-trans [2-Butene, (E)]	624-64-6	10,000	f
Carbon oxysulfide [Carbon oxide sulfide (COS)]	463-58-1	10,000	f
Chlorine monoxide [Chlorine oxide]	7791-21-1	10,000	f
2-Chloropropylene [1-Propene, 2-chloro-]	557-98-2	10,000	g
1-Chloropropylene [1-Propene, 1-chloro-]	590-21-6	10,000	g
Cyanogen [Ethanedinitrile]	460-19-5	10,000	f
Cyclopropane	75-19-4	10,000	f
Dichlorosilane [Silane, dichloro-]	4109-96-0	10,000	f
Difluoroethane [Ethane, 1,1-difluoro-]	75-37-6	10,000	f
Dimethylamine [Methanamine, N-methyl-]	124-40-3	10,000	f
2,2-Dimethylpropane [Propane, 2,2-dimethyl]	463-82-1	10,000	f
Ethane	74-84-0	10,000	f
Ethyl acetylene [1-Butyne]	107-00-6	10,000	f
Ethylamine [Ethanamine]	75-04-7	10,000	f
Ethyl chloride [Ethane, chloro-]	75-00-3	10,000	f
Ethylene [Ethene]	74-85-1	10,000	f
Ethyl ether [Ethane, 1,1'-oxybis-]	60-29-7	10,000	g
Ethyl mercaptan [Ethanethiol]	75-08-1	10,000	g

Accidental Release Prevention (Cont'd)

FLAMMABLE SUBSTANCES[1] (Cont'd)

(Alphabetical Order – 63 Substances)			
Chemical name	CAS No.	Threshold quantity (lbs)	Basis for listing
Ethyl nitrite [Nitrous acid, ethyl ester]	109-95-5	10,000	f
Hydrogen	1333-74-0	10,000	f
Isobutane [Propane, 2-methyl]	75-28-5	10,000	f
Isopentane [Butane, 2-methyl-]	78-78-4	10,000	g
Isoprene [1,3-Butadinene, 2-methyl-]	78-79-5	10,000	g
Isopropylamine [2-Propanamine]	75-31-0	10,000	g
Isopropyl chloride [Propane, 2-chloro-]	75-29-6	10,000	g
Methane	74-82-8	10,000	f
Methylamine [Methanamine]	74-89-5	10,000	f
3-Methyl-1-butene	563-45-1	10,000	f
2-Methyl-1-butene	563-46-2	10,000	g
Methyl ether [Methane, oxybis-]	115-10-6	10,000	f
Methyl formate [Formic acid, methyl ester]	107-31-3	10,000	g
2-Methylpropene [1-Propene, 2-methyl-]	115-11-7	10,000	f
1,3-Pentadiene	504-60-9	10,000	f
Pentane	109-66-0	10,000	g
1-Pentene	109-67-1	10,000	g
2-Pentene, (E)-	646-04-8	10,000	g
2-Pentene, (Z)-	627-20-3	10,000	g
Propadiene [1,2-Propadiene]	463-49-0	10,000	f
Propane	74-98-6	10,000	f
Propylene [1-Propene]	115-07-1	10,000	f
Propyne [1-Propyne]	74-99-7	10,000	f
Silane	7803-62-5	10,000	f
Tetrafluoroethylene [Ethene, tetrafluoro-]	116-14-3	10,000	f
Tetramethylsilane [Silane, tetramethyl-]	75-76-3	10,000	g
Trichlorosilane [Silane, trichloro-]	10025-78-2	10,000	g
Trifluorochloroethylene [Ethene, chlorotrifluoro-]	79-38-9	10,000	f
Trimethylamine [Methanamine, N,N-dimethyl-]	75-50-3	10,000	f
Vinyl acetylene [1-Buten-3-yne]	689-97-4	10,000	f

Accidental Release Prevention (Cont'd)

FLAMMABLE SUBSTANCES[1] (Cont'd)

(Alphabetical Order – 63 Substances)			
Chemical name	CAS No.	Threshold quantity (lbs)	Basis for listing
Vinyl chloride [Ethene, chloro-]	75-01-4	10,000	a, f
Vinyl ethyl ether [Ethene, ethoxy-]	109-92-2	10,000	g
Vinyl fluoride [Ethene, fluoro-]	75-02-5	10,000	f
Vinylidene chloride [Ethene, 1,1-dichloro-]	75-35-4	10,000	g
Vinylidene fluoride [Ethene, 1,1-difluoro-]	75-38-7	10,000	f
Vinyl methyl ether [Ethene, methoxy-]	107-25-5	10,000	f

[1] A flammable substance when used as a fuel or held for sale as a fuel at a retail facility is excluded from all provisions of this part (*see* 40 C.F.R. § 68.126).

Note: Basis for Listing:
a   Mandated for listing by Congress.
f   Flammable gas.
g   Volatile flammable liquid.

ABOUT THE AUTHORS

The principal author of the fourth edition of the Clean Air Handbook is **F. William Brownell**. He is a graduate of the Georgetown University Law Center and is the chair of the Executive Committee for Hunton & Williams LLP. Before ascending to overall leadership of the firm, he was the head the Hunton & Williams' environmental team for many years. His practice covers a broad range of environmental issues in proceedings before federal and state agencies, federal and state courts, and Congress. He has represented clients in most of the major rulemakings and judicial review proceedings under the Clean Air Act since the Act was amended in 1977, as well as in citizen suits and enforcement actions. Besides Clean Air Act issues, Mr. Brownell's practice extends to issues arising under many other U.S. environmental statutes. He is a member of the Bars of the District of Columbia, the Supreme Court of the United States, and most of the U.S. Circuit Courts of Appeals. He speaks and writes frequently on environmental and administrative law issues, and he has been recognized as a top environmental lawyer by many ranking services, including being named as one of the five most admired environmental lawyers by *Law360* and as a Band 1 lawyer by *Chambers USA*.

This edition of the Clean Air Handbook also reflects the contributions of other members of the Hunton & Williams Environmental Team. Other significant contributors include **Allison D. Wood** and **Lucinda Minton Langworthy** with respect to the Title I air quality standards and nonattainment program; **Craig S. Harrison** with respect to control technology regulation; **Lauren E. Freeman** with respect to the Title IV acid deposition program and Title V operating permit program; **Lee B. Zeugin** and **Elizabeth L. Horner** with respect to the hazardous air pollutants program; **Aaron M. Flynn** with respect to visibility protection; **Allison D. Wood** and **Tauna M. Szymanski** with respect to climate change; **Andrew D. Knudsen** with respect to the Title II mobile sources and fuels program; and **David S. Harlow** with respect to the Title VI stratospheric ozone protection program. **Allison D. Wood** and **Tauna M. Szymanski** were also responsible for final editing and formatting of the handbook, with support from **Sherry L. Fisher**, environmental policy advisor, and paralegal **Radoslawa Boczkaj-Gonzalez**.

Hunton & Williams has been named a "Top Environmental Firm" by *Law360* for three consecutive years (2011-2013) and was named "Best Law Firm: Environmental Law" in the 2013 edition of *U.S. News – Best Lawyers*.

Hunton & Williams has provided domestic and international clients with a full range of environmental services for more than 30 years. The firm more than 60 experienced environmental lawyers in the United States, Brussels, and Bangkok. They are supported by numerous other experienced environmental litigators, government relations professionals, and others. These services include developing the sophisticated legal and technical arguments needed to participate meaningfully in administrative proceedings before federal and state agencies; counseling clients on environmental permitting and enforcement issues that arise when they plan, build, and operate their facilities; providing clients with prompt and informed assessments of the environmental risks that arise in business and real estate transactions; representing clients in the development of national and state legislation; and providing clients with experienced representation in trial and appellate court proceedings on environmental issues.

Hunton & Williams' environmental experience extends to all of the major U.S. environmental statutes, including the Clean Air Act; the Clean Water Act; the Safe Drinking Water Act; the Resource Conservation and Recovery Act (RCRA); the Comprehensive Environmental Response, Compensation, and Liability Act (CERCLA or Superfund); the Emergency Planning and Community Right-to-Know Act (EPCRA); the Oil Pollution Act (OPA); the Toxic Substances Control Act (TSCA); the National Environmental Policy Act (NEPA); and to all of the major environmental initiatives undertaken by the European Community. Since the firm's team represents companies throughout the United States and abroad, its members are also familiar with many state and non-U.S. environmental statutes and regulations. The clients that Hunton & Williams represents on these environmental issues include a range of industrial and governmental organizations, including chemical and petrochemical companies, automobile manufacturers, pulp and paper companies, petroleum companies, coal companies, electric utilities, waste incinerators, water disposal facilities, breweries, telecommunications companies, urban transportation systems, flexible packagers, fiber and textile manufacturers, waste disposal companies, metal finishers, and many others.

Because environmental issues frequently affect other disciplines, Hunton & Williams has developed interdisciplinary practice groups as needed to respond to clients' needs. These groups include lawyers focusing on corporate and financial transactions, real estate law, and lobbying. Hunton & Williams has also developed working relationships with numerous technical and economic consultants and public relations firms. These interdisciplinary practice groups allow Hunton & Williams to address comprehensively the full range of complex issues related to the environment.